€ 9,-

Eine Ausstellung des Griechischen Kulturministeriums
in Zusammenarbeit mit dem
Niederrheinischen Museum der Stadt Duisburg

CRETE
The cradle of Europe

CRÈTE
Le réveil de l'Europe

Die Ausstellung wurde durch großzügige finanzielle Unterstützung der ▲ Stadtsparkasse Duisburg ermöglicht.

Die Kommission der Europäischen Gemeinschaften, Brüssel, förderte die dreisprachige Herausgabe
des Begleitbandes auf großzügige Weise.

14. DUISBURGER AKZENTE 1990
„Unser Haus Europa"

KRETA

Das Erwachen Europas

Begleitband zur Ausstellung
im Niederrheinischen Museum der Stadt Duisburg
22. April bis 29. Juli 1990

Stadt Duisburg

Titelbild:
Siegelabdruck mit der Darstellung einer minoischen Palaststadt.
Wahrscheinlich ist Ku-tu-na-ju, das griechische Kydonia und heutige Chaniá, dargestellt.
Vgl. Kat.-Nr. 1

Die Ausstellung steht unter der Schirmherrschaft von
S.E. Leonidas A. Evangelidis, Botschafter der Griechischen Republik

Herausgeber:
Niederrheinisches Museum der Stadt Duisburg
Friedrich-Wilhelm-Straße 64
4100 Duisburg 1

Öffnungszeiten:
Mo geschlossen
Di, Do – Sa 10 – 17 Uhr
Mi 10 – 16 Uhr
So 11 – 17 Uhr

Redaktion:
Dr. Tilmann Bechert und Werner Pöhling

Übersetzungen:
Catrin Leclerc, Ingrid Liwieratou-Uffhausen, William Phelps, Birgit Streich und Mireille Teissedre

Photovorlagen:
Stephanos Alexandrou (Athen). – Tilmann Bechert (Duisburg). – Hirmer-Verlag München. – Bernd Kirtz (Duisburg). – Wolf-Dietrich Niemeier (Freiburg i. Br.). – Peter Niesporek (Duisburg), – Wolfgang Schiering (Mannheim). – Gernot Tromnau (Duisburg). – Yannis Tzédakis (Athen). – CMS (Marburg/Lahn).

Ausstellungskonzeption und Design:
Dr. Yannis Tzédakis und Vassiliki Drouga

Organisation und Ausführung:
Dr. Gernot Tromnau, Dr. Tilmann Bechert, Erwin Kiel, Michael in het Panhuis, Werner Pöhling, Rudolf Szymczak

Gesamtherstellung:
Graphischer Betrieb Karl Plitt, Oberhausen

© Griechisches Kulturministerium Athen
   Niederrheinisches Museum der Stadt Duisburg
   sowie die Autoren und Photographen 1990

Alle Rechte vorbehalten. Da es sich bei den Exponaten um bisher unveröffentlichtes Fundmaterial aus archäologischen Grabungen handelt, ist es ohne ausdrückliche Genehmigung des Griechischen Kulturministeriums nicht gestattet, diesen Begleitband oder Teile daraus auf irgendeine Weise zu reproduzieren oder zu vervielfältigen.

ISBN 3-923576-67-6

Inhalt:

Vorwort (Gernot Tromnau)   7

Allgemeiner Teil   9
Leonhard Schumacher
Europa: Vom Mythos zur geographischen Vorstellung   11
(englisch S. 24 ff., französisch S. 29 ff.)

Archäologischer Teil   35
Wolfgang Schiering
Kreta. Das Erwachen Europas – aus archäologischer Sicht   37
(englisch S. 63 ff., französisch S. 73 ff.)

Wolf-Dietrich Niemeier
Die minoische Kultur Kretas: Versuch eines historischen Abrisses   47
(englisch S. 66 ff., französisch S. 77 ff.)

Yannis Tzédakis
Minoische Archäologie in Westkreta   57
(englisch S. 70 ff., französisch S. 82 ff.)

Katalog (Eleni Papadopoulou)   85
(englisch S. 137 ff., französisch S. 153 ff.)
Die Paläste   (Nr. 1 – 16)
Die minoische Gesellschaft   (Nr. 17 – 120)
Religion und Kult   (Nr. 121 – 145)
Grab und Tod   (Nr. 146 – 180)

Kreta-Karte mit eingetragenem Labyrinthzeichen und dem Namen „Laberinto" aus dem Mercator-Atlas von 1606.

Vorwort

Vermutlich werden nur wenige Besucher der Ausstellung „Kreta – Das Erwachen Europas" ahnen, daß bereits Mitte des 16. Jahrhunderts in Duisburg ein für ganz Europa und darüber hinaus bedeutungsvolles Werk entstanden ist: die aus 15 Blättern bestehende 159 x 132 cm große Europakarte von Gerhard Mercator aus dem Jahre 1554. Mit dem Erscheinen dieser Karte wurden die längst überholten Vorstellungen des Ptolemäus weitgehend korrigiert und die Lage der Länder Europas zueinander erstmals richtig wiedergegeben. Etwa 150 Jahre lang sollte diese Europakarte Vorbild für die nachfolgenden Kartographen bleiben und somit entscheidend den Ruhm Mercators als besten Kartenstecher seiner Zeit festliegen.

Mercator hatte für die Erstellung aller seiner Karten das gesamte ihm damals zugängliche Quellenmaterial sorgfältig und äußerst kritisch durchgearbeitet. Als ein Jahr nach seinem Tode eine Kartensammlung unter dem Titel „Atlas sive Cosmographicae meditationes de fabrica mundi et fabricati figura" herausgegeben wird, enthält dieser erste sogenannte „Atlas" des Jahres 1595 auch eine Karte, die die Mittelmeerinsel Candia (Kreta) zeigt. Etwa in ihrer Mitte ist das „Laberinto" eingezeichnet und auch als solches benannt. Mercator kannte sich natürlich in der griechischen Mythologie aus und brachte, wie damals allgemein angenommen wurde, eine Höhle mit verwundenen Gängen am Fuß des Ida-Gebirges in Mittelkreta mit dem sagenhaften Labyrinth des Königs Minos von Knossos in einen Zusammenhang. Als Sir Arthur John Evans an der Nordküste Kretas ab 1899 ein Gewirr von miteinander verbundenen Räumen freilegte und dieses Gebäude als den Palast von Knossos erkannte, wurden dabei auch zahlreiche in die Gemäuer gravierte Doppelaxtsymbole entdeckt. Da „Labyrinth" in Anlehnung an den vorgriechischen Wortstamm auch als „Haus der Doppeläxte" gedeutet werden kann, verbindet man im allgemeinen heute mit dem Palast von Knossos eine zweifache Deutung: das Labyrinth als irreführendes Wegesystem und das sakrale Symbol der Doppelaxt mit zwei gegenüberliegenden Schneiden und einem mittelständigen Schaft.

Besonders während der Bronzezeit war die Doppelaxt im ägäischen Gebiet und darüber hinaus ein weitverbreitetes kultisches Symbol, das, in Bronze gegossen, seiner Machart nach nicht als Gebrauchsgerät benutzt werden konnte. Solche bronzenen Doppeläxte wurden u. a. auch im Mittelrheingebiet z. B. bei Mainz und sogar in Skandinavien gefunden. Sie sind dort eindeutige Fremdkörper im archäologischen Fundgut und weisen auf Beziehung zum Mittelmeerraum hin. Importfunden, die über Kreta das Festland Europas mit gesicherten Daten verschiedener Dynastien des alten Ägyptens verbanden, verdankt die Altertumsforschung erste Anhaltspunkte für eine absolute Datierung auch der hiesigen Bronzezeit, die somit aus dem Dunkel der urgeschichtlichen Zeit heraustritt und die Frühgeschichte in Europa einleitet.

Das Niederrheinische Museum ist den Autoren der Beiträge zum vorliegendem Begleitband, den Leihgebern und allen anderen an der Realisierung der Ausstellung beteiligten Institutionen und Personen, besonders dem Direktor der Antikenverwaltung im Kulturministerium Griechenlands, Herrn Dr. Yannis Tzédakis, in dessen Händen der größte Teil der konzeptionellen und organisatorischen Arbeiten lag, zu aufrichtigem Dank verpflichtet.

Ritzung des Symbols einer Doppelaxt im Großen Palast von Knossos.

Wir empfinden es als eine Ehre und einen großen Vertrauensbeweis, daß diese Ausstellung mit zum Teil erstmalig in der Öffentlichkeit gezeigten kostbaren Fundstücken der minoischen Kultur drei Monate lang in Duisburg zu sehen ist und den Besuchern vielfältige Einblicke in die älteste Hochkultur Europas bietet. Aus gutem Grund wird die Ausstellung als Auftakt zu den 14. Duisburger Akzenten eröffnet, die unter dem Thema „Unser Haus Europa" stehen.

Gernot Tromnau
Direktor des Niederrheinischen Museums
der Stadt Duisburg

Allgemeiner Teil

Europa: Vom Mythos zur geographischen Vorstellung*

Leonhard Schumacher

Geschichtswissenschaft und Gesellschaftswissenschaften allgemein sehen sich oft – zuweilen mit Recht – dem Vorwurf des eurozentrischen Weltbildes und eurozentrischer Fragestellungen ausgesetzt.[1] Das Rahmenthema 'Unser Haus Europa' der diesjährigen Duisburger Akzente könnte diesem Vorurteil Vorschub leisten. Natürlich bildet der Gemeinsame Markt im Blick auf 1992 unter politischen, wirtschaftlichen und sozialen Aspekten ein wesentliches Element unserer Problematik, doch wird unter historischen Gesichtspunkten ebenso deutlich, daß Europa die Welt nicht nur beeinflußt und verändert hat, sondern auch selbst in erheblichem Maße durch außereuropäische Einflüsse geprägt worden ist. Von der antiken Seidenstraße über Marco Polo könnten wir den Bogen bis zum Grundnahrungsmittel 'Kartoffel', religiösen Sekten und fundamentalistischen Strömungen innerhalb der Kirchengemeinschaften schlagen. Zugleich werden aber allenthalben auch Unterschiede in politischen und sozialen Strukturen, im kulturellen und mentalen Bereich deutlich, deren Eigentümlichkeit und Fremdartigkeit den Europäer als Weltbürger zuweilen überraschen, verunsichern oder abstoßen. Der kürzlich ins Deutsche übertragene Essay von Paul Westheim, „La cavalera – Der Tod in Mexiko" (Hanau 1989), bietet ein eindrucksvolles Beispiel unterschiedlicher Mentalität in der Bewertung menschlichen Lebens und Sterbens.

Fremdartig oder zumindest entfremdet erscheinen uns allerdings bei genauerer Betrachtung bereits die Wurzeln unserer eigenen 'europäischen' Kultur: die politischen Mechanismen der sog. 'demokratischen' griechischen Polis ebenso wie ihre ökonomischen Bedingungen und ihre religiösen Vorstellungen, die in ganz eigentümlicher Weise vom Mythos geprägt und in Mythen zum Ausdruck gebracht worden sind.[2] Aus moderner Sicht mag man die zahllosen Liebschaften des Zeus belächeln, Feministinnen mögen sie als Manifestation männlicher Unterdrückungs- und Ausbeutungsmechanismen einer patriarchalischen Gesellschaft brandmarken. Für die archaischen Griechen personalisierten sich im

1 Schwarzfigurige Halsamphora des 'Edinburgh-Malers' (Anfang 5. Jh. v. Chr.). Boston, Museum of Fine Arts.

Mythos zunächst religiöse Vorstellungen, die als System Ausdruck der Weltdeutung waren und schließlich auch die Identität der Hellenen in ihrer geschichtlichen Dimension spiegelten. Als Beispiel für den letzteren Aspekt genügt einstweilen der Hinweis auf Heinrich Schliemann und die durch die Homerischen Mythen inspirierten Grabungen in Troja, Mykene und Knossos.

In der Regel erschwert die komplexe Genese eines bestimmten Mythos dem unbefangenen Leser das Verständnis. Die unterschiedlichen Aspekte – personalisierte religiöse Vorstellung, Weltdeutung und Spiegel geschichtlicher Ereignisse – lassen sich aufgrund ihrer Kontamination nicht immer eindeutig differenzieren, zumal verschiedene Zeitstufen zu berücksichtigen sind. Im Falle des Europa-Mythos können wir die Entwicklung noch einigermaßen deutlich nachvollziehen.

Erstmalig wird der Name literarisch im Okeaninenkatalog der Theogonie Hesiods (357 - 359) um 700 v. Chr. genannt[2a]: '(Tethys aber gebar dem Okeanos ... der Töchter heiliges Geschlecht:)

die anziehende Petraie, Menestho und Europe,
Metis, Eurynome und Telesto mit krokusfarbenem Gewand,
Chryseis, Asie, die Verlangen erweckende Kalypso' (usw.).

Von den Töchtern des Okeanos interessieren uns hier nur zwei: Europa und Asia. Da beide Namen durch viele andere gesperrt sind, ist von Hesiod offenbar keine Gegenüberstellung beabsichtigt, ein Bezug auf die gleichnamigen Kontinente daher unwahrscheinlich.

Über die Etymologie des Namens Europa[3] besteht bislang noch keine Einigung, doch wird durchweg eine Ableitung aus dem Semitischen – 'ereb' im Sinne von 'Dunkel' bzw. 'Land der untergehenden Sonne' – abgelehnt zugunsten eines (vor)griechischen Ursprungs: die weibliche Form des Adjektivs $εὐρωπός$ bedeutete demnach 'aussehend wie $εὐρώς$', wobei $εὐρώς$ allgemein als 'Feuchtigkeit' oder speziell als 'das Dunkle im Wasser' zu deuten sei. In Konsequenz bezeichne Europe bzw. Europa das 'dunkle / tiefe Wasser', personifiziere die Gottheit des 'Tiefen Wassers'. Entsprechend dürfte Asie/Asia – abgeleitet von $ἄσις$ (Schlamm) – die Göttin des 'stehenden, flachen (Brack)wassers' meinen. Passend zum Vater Okeanos dürfen wir für die erste Stufe der Entwicklung um 700 v. Chr. Europa und Asia als Nymphen fassen.

In diesem Sinne begegnet der Name Europa, auf die wir uns hier konzentrieren wollen, bzw. ihr maskulines Pendant Europos als Flußname hauptsächlich in Zentral- und Nordgriechenland: Böotien, Epirus, Thessalien und Makedonien[4]. In der Landschaft Perrhaibia fließt der Europos, der nördlich von Larissa in den Peneios mündet. Mit dem Beinamen Europe wurde Demeter als Gottheit des Wachstums im böotischen Lebadeia verehrt, der Kult einer

2 *Europa auf dem Stier. Metope vom Tempel Y in Selinunt (Mitte 6. Jh. v. Chr.). Palermo, Museo Archeologico.*

chthonischen (Erd)-Göttin namens Europa, die Zeus in einer Erdgrotte bewachte, ist für Teumessos in Böotien bezeugt.[5]

Diese Verbindung zu Zeus legte es nahe, die Brücke zu dem weitaus bekannteren Europa-Mythos der Ilias zu schlagen. Um seine Gemahlin Hera zu versöhnen, scheute der Göttervater nicht den Vergleich mit seinen zahlreichen Liebschaften. Seine Liebe zu ihr sei größer und verzehrender als zu Dia, der Gemahlin des Ixion, zu Danae, zu Semele, Alkmene, Demeter oder Leto, größer auch als zu Europe, 'des Phoinix Tochter ... / die Rhadamanthys gebar, den göttlichen Helden, und Minos' (Hom. Il. 14, 321f.). Dieselbe Version bzgl. der Abstammung Europas bieten auch die Hesiod zugeschriebenen 'Frauenkataloge',[6] ohne allerdings eine Verbindung zur böotischen Europa zu schlagen. Unter diesen Voraussetzungen dürfen wir davon ausgehen, daß die Gleichsetzung erst im 7. bzw. 6. Jh. v. Chr. erfolgte.

Der Mythos zählt zu den bekanntesten Themen der griechisch-römischen Antike und wurde in der darstellenden Kunst bis zur Gegenwart ungemein häufig variiert.[7] Den sicher bekannten Inhalt brauchen wir hier nur zu skizzieren: Der Göttervater Zeus wurde von Liebe zu der schönen Königstochter ergriffen und verwandelte sich in einen prachtvollen weißen Stier. In dieser Gestalt näherte er sich Europa, die mit ihren Freundinnen am Gestade des Meeres spielte. Das Mädchen faßte Zutrauen zu dem sanften Tier, streichelte es und schwang sich schließlich auf seinen Rücken, worauf der Stier mit ihr über das Meer entfloh. Später gab er sich als Zeus zu erkennen und zeugte mit Europa mehrere Söhne.[8]

Die bildlichen Darstellungen konzentrieren sich auf die Phasen der eigentlichen Entführung. Auf dem (rotfigurigen) Glockenkrater von Tarquinia (um 490 v. Chr.) faßt Europa den Stier mit pretiöser Geste am linken Horn,[9] während der Edinburgh-Maler auf einer (schwarzfigurigen) Halsamphora (Anfang des 5. Jhs.) das Mädchen bereits auf dem Stiere sitzend darstellt (Abb. 1).[10] Ebenso faßt eine Metope vom Fries des archaischen Tempels Y von Selinunt (Abb. 2)[11] die Szene um die Mitte des 6. Jhs. v. Chr. Am bekanntesten ist vielleicht das pompejanische Fresko aus der Casa di Iasone, das jetzt im Nationalmuseum Neapel zu bewundern ist (Abb. 3).[12] Nach einem frühhellenistischen Vorbild hat der Künstler in augusteischer Zeit (um 10 n. Chr.) die Entführung in zarten Pastelltönen dargestellt. Europa sitzt mit entblößtem Oberkörper bereits auf einem hellbraunen Stier, den eine ihrer Gespielinnen aufzuhalten versucht. Offenbar ist hier der Moment der Flucht erfaßt.

Neuzeitliche Versionen konzentrieren sich überwiegend auf die zentrale Szene des Mädchens auf dem Rücken des Stieres,[13] der etwa bei Tizian (1562) das Meer kraftvoll durch-

4 *Europa auf dem Stier. Darstellung auf dem Bronzeportal des Filarete, Ausschnitt (1445). Rom, Petersdom (Photo O. Hein/R. Mader).*

schwimmt.[14] Als Miniatur begegnet das Sujet bereits im Randfries der Bronzetür des Filarete vom Mittelportal des Petersdomes (1445) neben vielen anderen mythologischen Darstellungen (Abb. 4).[15] Fast zeitgleich entstand in Ferrara(?) ein Gobelin nach dem Entwurf des Ercole de' Roberti (?),[16] der den Europa-Mythos in zwei Phasen ins Bild setzte: links hat die Königstochter inmitten ihrer Gespielinnen den Stier bestiegen, der dann rechts mit seiner Beute über das Meer entflieht. Dieselbe Bildfolge bietet eine Cassone-Tafel von der Aussteuer-Truhe einer italienischen Adelstochter (um 1480),[17] wo sich Zeus der Europa schließlich als junger Mann offenbart (Abb. 5). Die

Doppelerscheinung des Zeus in Stier- und Menschengestalt akzentuierte Anne-Louis Girodet zu Beginn des 19. Jhs. in einer illustrierten Übersetzung des griechischen Lyrikers Anakreon (1825).[18]

Aus der Vielzahl der Darstellungen des Mythos in unserem Jahrhundert müssen wir uns ebenfalls auf wenige Beispiele beschränken. Die massive Fassung der an einen im Meer schwimmenden Stier geschmiegten Frau von Felix Vallotton (1908) hat nahezu kosmischen Charakter.[19] Bei Picasso (1946) thront eine dominante Europa auf dem Nacken des Stieres, den sie mit kraftvoller Hand am Horn lenkt.[20] Die Federzeichnung von Georges Braque (undatiert) zeichnet sich durch eine mehrdimensionale Perspektive aus und läßt die innige Beziehung zwischen Frau und Stier ahnen.[21] Der dahinstürmende Bulle der Lithographie von Gino von Finetti (1915)[22] trägt eine Dame der Halbwelt, die graziös und lasziv zugleich diesen Ritt genießt, wohin er sie auch führen mag. Europa als Allegorie morbider Lebenslust angesichts einer unwägbaren Zukunft ist hier im Kriegsjahr 1915 von dem Berliner Sezessionisten eindrucksvoll gestaltet (Abb. 6). Als jüngste der mir bekannten Fassungen des Motivs sei schließlich ein Aquarell des Berliner Malers Klaus Fußmann (1987) genannt, das besondere Beachtung schon aufgrund der eigenen Interpretation des Künstlers verdient.[23]

Schauplatz der Entführung im antiken Mythos ist durchweg Phönikien; darauf weist schon der sprechende Name Phoinix, den Homer als Vater der Europa benannte. In späterer Überlieferung wird das Mädchen auch als Tochter des Agenor bezeichnet, der als König in Tyros bzw. Sidon herrschte. Beide Varianten deuten demnach an, daß der Europa-Mythos aus Kontakten zwischen Phönikern im heutigen Libanon und Griechen entstanden ist bzw. diese voraussetzte. Folgen wir der jüngeren Version, so hatte Agenor neben seiner Tochter Europa mehrere Söhne, die alle

3 Die Entführung der Europa. Fresko aus Pompeji, IX 5, 18 (um 10 n. Chr.). Napoli, Museo Nazionale.

5 Die Entführung der Europa. Cassone-Tafel des Girolamo da Cremona (?) (um 1480). Paris, Musée du Louvre.

sprechende Namen tragen: Phoinix (Phönikien), Kilix (Kilikien), Kadmos, den Gründungsheros von Theben (Kadmeia), Thasos, den Heros der gleichnamigen Insel in der nördlichen Ägäis, und Phineus, den die Argonautensage als König in Thrakien nennt. Sie wurden im Mythos von ihrem Vater ausgesandt, um ihre Schwester zu suchen, kehrten indessen nicht mehr in ihre Heimat zurück.[24]

Insgesamt bietet die Mythologie hier einen Reflex der vielfältigen Beziehungen und des wechselseitigen Einflusses zwischen phönikischer und griechischer Welt vor allem in den sog. 'Dark Ages' (12.-8. Jh. v. Chr.).[25] Die Problematik kann hier nur an zwei repräsentativen Beispielen angerissen werden. Beide beziehen sich auf die Präsenz der Phöniker in der Ägäis und werden von Herodot überliefert. Im ersten Text geht es um den Kult des Herakles, der den Historiker interessierte.

'Um Genaueres (über Herakles) zu erfahren, fuhr ich sogar nach Tyros in Phoinikien, weil ich hörte, dort stehe ein Herakles-Tempel. Ich fand ihn auch, reich geschmückt mit vielen Weihgeschenken. ... In Tyros habe ich noch einen zweiten Tempel des Herakles besucht, der hier den Beinamen Thasios führte. So bin ich denn nach Thasos gefahren und fand dort einen Tempel, den Phoiniker erbaut haben. Auf der Suche nach Europa hatten sie Thasos gegründet' (Hdt. 2,44,1-4).

Trotz eines weiteren Hinweises bei Herodot auf die Entdeckung eines Bergwerks auf der Insel durch Phöniker und archäologischer Spuren phönikischer Aktivitäten in der nördlichen Ägäis[26] wird der historische Gehalt seines Berichts in der neueren Forschung eher skeptisch beurteilt,[27] doch wird man zumindest festhalten dürfen, daß die Überlieferung einen mythologischen Reflex der Beziehungen zwischen Phönikien und den griechischen Inseln bietet.

Ähnliches gilt für Herodots Vorstellung von der Entstehung der griechischen Schrift aus einer (adaptierten) Übernahme des phönikischen Alphabets:[28]

'Jene mit Kadmos (in Hellas) eingewanderten Phoiniker' ... – erzählt Herodot (5.58-59) – 'haben durch ihre Ansiedlung (in Böotien: Theben/Kadmeia) viele Wissenschaften und Künste zu den Hellenen gebracht, vor allem die Buchstabenschrift ... Anfangs benutzten (die Kadmeier) dieselben Schriftzeichen wie die übrigen Phoiniker. Später aber veränderte sich zusammen mit ihrer Sprache auch die Form ihrer Buchstaben. Der hellenische Stamm der Ionier, damals unmittelbar benachbart, übernahm durch Unterweisung die Schriftzeichen von den Phoinikern, bildete sie für sich auch etwas um und bezeichnete sie als 'phoinikische' (Buchstaben) $Φοινικ$-

6 Gino von Finetti, Europa. Lithographie von 1915, die Europa als Allegorie morbider Lebenslust zeigt.

ήια· *τὰ τῶν Φοινίκων γράμματα*. Dies war durchaus recht und billig, denn die Phoiniker hatten sie ja in Hellas eingeführt ... Buchstaben aus der Zeit des Kadmos habe ich selbst gesehen im Heiligtum des Apollo Ismenios im böotischen Theben ...'

Auf die Entstehung der griechischen Schrift brauchen wir im Detail nicht einzugehen,[29] doch stimmen die Buchstaben der archaischen Zeit formal mit den altsemitischen Schriftzeichen weitgehend überein, wobei allerdings einzelne Zeichen einen neuen Lautwert als Vokale erhielten: der im Semitischen als Konsonant empfundene Stimmabsatz aleph (Rind) wurde etwa zum griechischen im Lautwert a. Unsere Terminologie des Alphabets spiegelt diese Genese der Schrift, deren Kern Herodot im Bild des Kadmos-Mythos zutreffend überliefert. In der Presse wurde kürzlich die 'Entzifferung' des berühmten 'Diskos von Phaistos' durch eine Duisburger Lehrerin kolportiert.[30] Ob im Ergebnis zutreffend oder nicht, fügt sich die berichtete Methode einer Lesung anhand semitischer Schriftzeichen in diesen skizzierten Kontext.

Fundort der beidseitig mit Schrift- oder Bildzeichen bedeckten runden Tonscheibe war der minoische Palast von Phaistos in Südkreta. Bekanntlich war Kreta die Insel, wohin Zeus im Mythos Europa entführt hat – um den populären Titel von Hans-Georg Wunderlich zu gebrauchen: „Wohin der Stier Europa trug".[31] Dessen These von der Funktion minoischer Paläste als riesige Nekropolen - Stätten der Toten - dürfen wir getrost auf sich beruhen lassen. Die Kreta-Ausstellung im Niederrheinischen Museum wird Ihnen genügend Informationen bieten, daß die Paläste von Phaistos, Knossos, Malia, Hagia Triada, Zakros oder Archanes Mittelpunkte des sozialen, politischen, wirtschaftlichen und religiösen Lebens der minoischen Kultur waren.[32]

Im Schnittpunkt zwischen Ägypten, Phönikien und Griechenland gelegen gilt Kreta mit Recht als die Wiege der europäischen Kultur. Im Mythos wurde hier Zeus - *Κρηταγενής* - in einer Berggrotte im Ida- bzw. Dikte-Gebirge von der Ziege Amaltheia und den heiligen Bienen genährt. Die vielfältigen Funktionen dieses Himmels- und Wettergottes lassen ebenso wie seine Epiklesen auch orientalische Einflüsse (El, Hadad, Baalim) erkennen.[33] Die spätere Tradition seines Grabes auf Kreta, der die Kreter ihren Ruf als 'größte Lügner' verdankten,[34] dürfte aus einer synkretistischen Gleichung des griechischen Gottes mit dem ägyptischen Osiris als Gott des vegetativen Werdens und Vergehens resultieren.[35]

Die praktisch einhellige Tradition von der Entführung Europas nach Kreta, wo Zeus sich mit ihr am Ida-Gebirge bzw. bei Gortyn vereinigte, läßt eine Kombination des Mythos mit ursprünglichen Lokalkulten noch erkennen. In unserer durch die Zeugnisse der darstellenden Kunst geprägten Vorstellung verbinden wir den Europa-Mythos durchweg mit der Frau auf dem Stier. In der Antike ist das Motiv keineswegs so eindeutig gefaßt. Eine auf dem Stier sitzende weibliche Gestalt muß nicht unbedingt als Europa verstanden werden,[36] umgekehrt ist Europa auch ohne den Stier zu identifizieren.[37] Als Zentrum ihres kretischen Kultes dürfen wir Gortyn am Lernaios in der Mesara-Ebene fassen, wo sich die Königstochter unter einer Platane dem Göttervater hingegeben haben soll. Münzen der Stadt zeigen denn auch im 5. Jh. v. Chr. die bekannte Darstellung der Frau auf dem Stier;[38] ebenso ist dann aber im Verlauf des 4. Jhs. v. Chr. eine weibliche Gestalt, sitzend in einer Baumkrone (Weide), als Europa zu deuten.[39] Auf einem jüngeren Stater (um 300 v. Chr.) wird sie von Zeus in Gestalt eines Adlers mit geöffneten Schwingen begattet (Abb. 7).[40] Der Stier ist jeweils auf die Rückseite der Prägung gesetzt.

Die Darstellungen lassen einen älteren Kern des Mythos, wie er uns in Böotien und bei Hesiod schon begegnete, noch erahnen. Europa wird hier als (Baum)-Nymphe bzw. als Göttin des Wachstums verstanden. In Kombination mit dem Stier ist sie die *Πότνια ταυρῶν*, die Herrin der Stiere, oder allgemeiner als *Πότνια θηρῶν*, Herrin der Tiere, zu deuten.[41] Auch hier werden Verbindungslinien zu orientalischen Kulten der Astarte, Mâ Bellona, Mater Deum Magna Idaea deutlich.[42] Im minoischen Kult spielte der Stier bekanntlich eine zentrale Rolle. Die zahlreichen Darstellungen des 16./15. Jhs. im Palast von Knossos - etwa das bemalte Hochrelief vom Nordeingang oder das Steatitrhyton aus dem Kleinen Palast - belegen dies ebenso wie die kretischen Stierspiele, wie sie z. B. ein Fresko in den verschiedenen Phasen des Auf- und Abschwungs der Akrobaten/-innen veranschaulicht.[43] Zu erinnern ist in diesem Zusammenhang auch an den Mythos von Pasiphaë, die in der Vereinigung mit dem Stier aus dem Meere (*ἱερὸς γάμος*) den Minotauros zeugte.[44] Einzelheiten dieser vielschichtigen Kultentstehung können wir hier nicht behandeln, doch bleibt festzuhalten, daß der Europa-Mythos Elemente der orientalischen, minoischen und griechischen Religion kontaminiert hat und damit auch die wechselseitigen Einflüsse unterschiedlicher Kulturkreise spiegelt.

Den frühesten Hinweis auf Europa als geographische Bezeichnung bietet um 600 v. Chr. der homerische Hymnos an den pythischen Apollo von Delphi. Inhaltlich deckt sich die Vorstellung mit der skizzierten Verbreitung des archaischen Europa-Kultes in Mittel- und Nordgriechenland. Eben diese Gebiete werden hier als 'Europa' zusammengefaßt und von anderen Regionen - der Peloponnes und den griechischen Inseln - abgesetzt: Von überall sollten Griechen das Apollo-Heiligtum in Delphi besuchen und Orakel einholen,

> 'alle, die in der Peloponnes, der üppigen, leben, die Europa bewohnen und die ringsumflossenen Inseln' ([Hom.] hymn. Apoll. 290 f.)

Die Differenzierung dokumentiert mit aller Deutlichkeit, daß Europa hier noch nicht den Kontinent bezeichnet, sondern das griechische Festland ohne die Peloponnes. Erst gegen Ende des 6. Jhs. wurden die Akzente verschoben und im Zusammenhang mit den Perserkriegen dann popularisiert. Die Ursprünge dieser Entwicklung waren bereits für Herodot (4,45,4-5) nicht mehr nachvollziehbar:

> 'Von Europa weiß niemand, ob es vom Meer umflossen oder wonach es

benannt ist; auch nicht, wer ihm den Namen Europa gegeben hat, wenn wir nicht annehmen wollen, das Gebiet habe von der Tyrierin Europa seinen Namen erhalten... Aber diese Europa stammte offenbar aus Asien und ist nie in das Land gekommen, das heute von den Griechen als Europa bezeichnet wird – ἐς τὴν γῆν ταύτην, ἥτις νῦν ὑπὸ Ἑλλήνων Εὐρώπη καλέεται. Vielmehr ist sie von Phoinikien nach Kreta und von dort aus nach Lykien gelangt.'

Die erste Weltkarte wurde von Anaximander, dem Schüler des Thales, um die Mitte des 6. Jhs. gezeichnet und dann von Hekataios aus Milet um 500 v. Chr. im Detail ausgearbeitet.[45] Ausgehend von der rings vom Okeanos umspülten Erdscheibe bildet das Mittelmeer die Zentralachse, nach Osten verlängert durch das Schwarze und das Kaspische Meer. Diese Mittelachse scheidet Europa im Norden von Asien im Süden, wobei Libyen/Afrika als Teil Asiens aufgefaßt wurde. Die Bezeichnung des nördlichen Kontinents Europa resultierte vermutlich als pars pro toto aus einer Übertragung des Namens von Zentralgriechenland auf das gesamte angrenzende Gebiet im Norden und Westen. Asien bildete nach Herodot (1,4,4), der in der Folgezeit Libyen/Afrika als dritten Erdteil differenzierte,[46] den Machtbereich der Achaimeniden: 'Die Perser haben sich Asien mit den dort lebenden barbarischen Völkern zu eigen gemacht, Europa aber und das Land der Griechen betrachten sie als außerhalb ihres Herrschaftsgebietes.' Die natürliche Grenze bildete die Propontis (Marmara-Meer) mit dem Hellespont bzw. den Dardanellen im Süden und dem Bosporus im Norden.

Bemerkenswert erscheint in diesem Zusammenhang vor allem, daß Europa als geographische Bezeichnung von Herodot speziell auf die Region übertragen wurde, die dem persischen Hoheitsgebiet unmittelbar benachbart war, nämlich das Gebiet nördlich und westlich der Propontis. So läßt der Historiker (7,8,ß1) den Großkönig Xerxes im Kriegsrat die Offensive gegen Griechenland mit der Bemerkung erläutern: 'Ich will eine Brücke über den Hellespont schlagen und mein Heer durch Europa gegen Griechenland führen' – μέλλω ζεύξας τὸν Ἑλλήσποντον ἐλᾶν στρατὸν διὰ τῆς Εὐρώπης ἐπὶ τὴν Ἑλλάδα.[47] Diese nunmehr verengende Übertragung des Namens Europa auf das nördliche Griechenland – darauf werden wir noch zurückkommen – findet sich bei Herodot mehrfach, wenngleich nicht immer so deutlich: so ließ Dareios I. nach seinem gescheiterten Skythenfeldzug den Megabazos als Strategen in Europa – konkret: in Thrakien – zurück, der dann die Paionen ἐκ τῆς Εὐρώπης ἐς τὴν Ἀσίαν umsiedeln sollte.[48]

Europa im engeren Sinne faßt Herodot demnach als das Gebiet der Thraker, evtl. unter Einbeziehung von Teilen Makedoniens, erweitert dann den Begriff bei der Heerschau des Xerxes auf ganz Nordgriechenland einschließlich Thessaliens in deutlicher Abgrenzung zu Hellas.[49] Andererseits verwendet der Historiker dieselbe Bezeichnung aber auch für den gesamten Kontinent, wenn er etwa den General Mardonios im Kriegsrat des Xerxes von den Ioniern in Europa – Ἴωναι οἱ ἐν τῇ Εὐρώπῃ – reden läßt, gegen die der Großkönig seine gesamte Streitmacht aus Asien – πλῆθος τὸ ἐκ τῆς Ἀσίης – heranführen werde.[50] Im Zuge dieser Konflikte zwischen Perserreich und Griechentum wurde jedenfalls die Polarisierung von Asien und Europa als Auseinandersetzung zwischen Ost und West zum Allgemeingut. Die Siege von Marathon, Salamis und Plataiai stilisierten die Griechen zu Rettern Europas vor orientalischer Despotie. Am Rande sei bemerkt, daß die Griechen sich seit Beginn

7 Stater von Gortyn/Südkreta (um 300–280/270 v. Chr.). Auf der Vorderseite Europa im Baum mit Zeus als Adler.

des 7. Jhs. v. Chr. auch über kontinentale Grenzen hinweg als hellenische Gemeinschaft fühlten.[51] Mit gewissen Einschränkungen könnte man sogar von hellenischem 'Nationabewußtsein' sprechen, manifestiert in blutsmäßiger Verwandtschaft, gleicher Sprache, gemeinsamer Religion, vergleichbaren Sitten und Gebräuchen aller Griechen,[52] die sich politisch aber natürlich in eine Vielzahl von souveränen Poleis gliederten. Bei der aktuellen Diskussion um einen deutschen Zentralstaat erscheint mir dieser Aspekt durchaus von Interesse.

Für Herodot markierte im äußersten Osten der sagenhafte Araxes die Grenze zwischen Asien und Europa, überwiegend wurde die Grenze indessen durch den Tanais (Don) bzw. den kolchischen Phasis südlich des Kaukasus bestimmt.[53] Über die Ausdehnung des Kontinents Europa nach Westen und Norden konnte der Historiker keine Angaben machen. Erst die Fahrt des Pytheas von Marseille zum sagenhaften Thule vermittelte um 300 v. Chr. genauere Vorstellungen,[54] die Eratosthenes in seiner berühmten Weltkarte verarbeitet hat.[55] In römischer Zeit wurden diese Ergebnisse durch die Aufklärungsfahrt des Cn. Iulius Agricola zu den Orkney-Inseln dann partiell bestätigt.[56] Um die Mitte des 2. Jhs. n. Chr. faßte der Mathematiker, Astronom und Geograph Claudius Ptolemaeus den Kenntnisstand in seiner 'Einführung in die Geographie' - γεωγραφικὴ ὑπήγησις zusammen,[57] deren Weltbild, soweit bekannt, für das gesamte Mittelalter bis in die frühe Neuzeit verbindlich blieb. Die Entdeckung Amerikas auf der Suche nach einem westlichen Seeweg nach Indien resultiert aus den Berechnungen des Ptolemaeus. Erst Gerhard Mercator schuf mit seiner Projektions-

8 Giovanni Battista Tiepolo, Europa als Allegorie auf den gleichnamigen Erdteil. Würzburg, Residenz (vor 1753).

technik eine neue Grundlage der wissenschaftlichen Kartographie.[58] Die ungemein interessanten Entwicklungen können wir hier nicht einmal skizzieren.

Europa als Name des Kontinents hat sich bereits seit dem 5. Jh. v. Chr. durchgesetzt und bezeichnete das Gebiet vom Atlantik im Westen bis zum Don (Tanais) im Osten mit der südlichen Verlängerung über Bosporus und Dardanellen. Die Insel Kreta wurde allerdings erst nach Herodot als Teil Europas eingeschätzt.[59] Frühzeitig hat die geographische Abgrenzung auch typologisch die Vorstellung von den Bewohnern dieses Kontinents geprägt, durchweg in pointierter Antithese zum

Wesen der Asiaten. Bereits in der pseudo-hippokratischen Schrift 'Von der Umwelt' wird dieser Gegensatz nicht historisch, sondern anthropologisch begründet.[60] Infolge der klimatischen Bedingungen und der materiellen Voraussetzungen seien die Asiaten durchweg ausgeglichener, sanfter und friedfertiger als die Europäer, die als tatkräftig, rauh und kriegerisch charakterisiert werden:

'Die häufigen Wechsel der Jahreszeiten (Witterungen) erzeugen' - so Ps. Hippokrates (aër. 23, p. I 67 Kühlewein) - 'Wildheit und schwächen die sanfte und milde Gemütsart. Daher halte ich die Europäer auch für tapferer als die Asiaten. Denn im ewigen Einerlei (der klimatischen Bedingungen) entstehen Leichtfertigkeit und Arbeitsscheu, dagegen entwickelt sich in einem Lande heftiger und sich oft wiederholender Wechsel die Stärkung von Körper und Geist. Aus träger Ruhe und Gleichgültigkeit erwächst die Feigheit, aus Abhärtung und Ertragen von Mühsal hingegen Tapferkeit.'

Diese Typologie hat auch Konsequenzen für die körperliche Konstitution der Menschen, wobei die Schrift durchaus regionale Unterschiede innerhalb der Kontinente berücksichtigt. Im allgemeinen aber seien, von Ausnahmen abgesehen, die Europäer eher hochgewachsen und kräftig von Statur, die Asiaten feingliedrig und kleinwüchsig.

In bezug auf das Erscheinungsbild der Europa als Personifizierung des Erdteils vermag man diese Typologie noch einigermaßen nachzuvollziehen. Als wohl bekannteste Allegorie darf die Ausgestaltung des Treppenhauses in der Würzburger Residenz durch Giovanni Battista Tiepolo (1751/53) gelten.[61] Sein 'Weltbild' zeigt die nunmehr vier Kontinente als weibliche Gestalten auf einem jeweils signifikanten Tier gelagert: Amerika mit der Federkrone auf einem riesigen Alligator, Afrika auf dem Dromedar, Asia auf einem indischen Elephanten, auf dem bekannten Stier des Mythos schließlich Europa, die im Unterschied zur feingliedrigen Asia recht matronenhaft wirkt (Abb. 8). Anders als die beiden barbusigen Kontinente der 'Dritten Welt' tragen Europa und Asia hochgeschlossene Gewänder.

Typologisch interessant erscheint auch der Kupferstich von Philip Galle, der im 16. Jh. den Herrschaftsanspruch einer walkürenhaften Europa durch Krone und Szepter symbolisierte.[62] Ähnlich faßte Cesare Ripa in seiner Iconologia (1603) die Personifizierung der Europa

9 Cesare Ripa, Iconologia (Roma 1603) mit Europa als „Königin der Welt".

als 'regina di tutto il mondo' mit einer Krone. Der Stier ist hier durch das Pferd ersetzt, das die königliche Stellung des europäischen Kontinents unterstreichen soll (Abb. 9).[63] Ikonologisch spielte der Stier des Mythos bei frühen Personifizierungen des Erdteils Europa keine Rolle. Ein Dipinto auf gekalkter Leinwand (1040/80) zeigt zwar eine weibliche Gestalt auf dem Stier,[64] doch handelt es sich bei dieser Allegorie im Rahmen des dargestellten Weltgerichts nicht um Europa, sondern um das Festland im Gegensatz zum Meer, symbolisiert durch eine Nereide auf dem Seedrachen.

Aus der Antike ist nur ein Zeugnis in der Zuweisung auf den Kontinent gesichert. Das Relief vom Palazzo Chigi (1. Jh. v. Chr.) bietet eine Allegorie der Europa links und der Asia rechts, beide mit Mauerkrone und im Chiton, die einen Schild mit einer Schlachtdarstellung halten (Abb. 10).[65] Die Identifizierung ergibt sich aus den Inschriften, welche die Kampfszene als Auseinandersetzung zwischen Orient und Okzident charakterisieren: konkret handelt es sich um die Schlacht bei Gaugamela/Arbela, wo Alexander den Großkönig Darius (III.) besiegte.

Inhaltlich geht es also um den Konflikt zwischen Ost und West – Europa und Asien –, wie er seit den Perserkriegen in zahlreichen Variationen ideologisch akzentuiert wurde. Die geographischen Grenzen sind dabei zeitweise entsprechend der jeweiligen Situation durchaus als sekundär eingeschätzt worden. So lokalisierte etwa Appian das Schlachtfeld von Philippi,[66] wo Brutus und Cassius 42 v. Chr. den Tod fanden, nahe dem Hauptpaß zwischen Europa

10 Relief vom Palazzo Chigi in Rom (2. Jh. v. Chr.). Umzeichnung.

und Asien, acht Stadien (ca. 1,5 km) entfernt vom δίοδος ἐς τὴν Ἀσίαν τε καὶ Εὐρώπην. Ost und West stießen nach dieser Version also auf der Höhe von Kabálla in der heutigen Provinz Mazedonien aufeinander.

Werfen wir abschließend noch einen Blick auf die weitere Entwicklung der geographischen Terminologie, so erscheint bemerkenswert, daß im Zuge der diokletianischen Neuordnung der Name Europa eine der kleinsten Provinzen des Römischen Reiches bezeichnet,[67] das Gebiet im unmittelbaren Hinterland von Byzanz/Konstantinopel, welches dem Kontinent Asien direkt benachbart ist (Abb. 11).[68] Dieses Phänomen der territorialen Begrenzung bzw. Verengung des Europa-Namens begegnete uns bereits bei Herodot. Die spätantike Provinz Europa als Teil der Diözese Thrakia bezeichnet somit den exponierten Teil des Kontinents mit dem Namen des gesamten Erdteils; sprachwissenschaftlich könnte man den Befund als Form der Katachrese werten.

Mit geringfügigen Erweiterungen gehört das Territorium der spätantiken Provinz Europa heute bekanntlich zum Staatsgebiet der Türkei. Je nach politischem Standort könnte man dieses Ergebnis einer langen historischen Entwicklung als letztes Bollwerk Asiens in Europa einschätzen. Im Blick auf die Entwicklung der EG möchte ich den Befund eher als Indiz

11 Tabula Peutingeriana, Segm. VIII/IX, Ausschnitt. Mittelalterliche Kopie um 1200 eines spätantiken Originals.

für die Assoziations- bzw. Integrationsfähigkeit der Türkei in die Europäische Gemeinschaft werten. Im politischen Konzept des Imperium Romanum spielten die kontinentalen Grenzen Europas, Asiens und Afrikas aufgrund des universalen Herrschaftsanspruchs keine entscheidende Rolle. Unter Verzicht auf die ideologische Komponente bietet dieser Aspekt im Sinne von Kants 'Idee einer allgemeinen Geschichte in weltbürgerlicher Absicht' durchaus positive Perspektiven.[69]

* Vortrag im Rahmen der 14. Duisburger Akzente 'Unser Haus in Europa' (24. 4. 1990); für den Druck wurde das Manuskript um die Anmerkungen erweitert, Abbildungen konnten nur in begrenztem Umfang reproduziert werden.

1 Vgl. etwa Chr. Meier: Jenseits von Europa. Geschichtswissenschaft heute muß den Dialog mit anderen Kulturen wagen, ZEIT vom 24. 3. 1989, S. 54; J. Osterhammel: Galoppierende Welt-Fremdheit der deutschen Historiker. Die vielfältigen Beziehungen zwischen Europa und dem armen Rest der Welt werden von der Geschichtswissenschaft weiter vernachlässigt, Frankfurter Rundschau vom 24. 10. 1989, S. 9.

2 Vgl. K. Kerenyi (Hrsg.): Die Eröffnung des Zugangs zum Mythos (Darmstadt 1967); F. Graf: Griechische Mythologie. Eine Einführung (Zürich 1985); (München 1985); K. Hübner: Die Wahrheit des Mythos (München 1985); J.-P. Vernant: Myhte et société en Grèce ancienne (Paris 1974).

2a vgl. F. Fischer: Nereiden und Okeaniden in Hesiods Theogonie (Diss. Halle 1934) bes. 40-49.

3 Vgl. W. Aly: Lexikalische Streifzüge 4. Europe, Glotta 5 (1914) 63-74; L. Deroy: Le nom de l'Europe, son origine et son histoire, RIO 11 (1959) 1-22; B. W. Dombrowski: Der Name Europas auf seinem griechischen und altsyrischen Hintergrund. Ein Beitrag zur ostmediterranen Kultur- und Religionsgeschichte in frühgriechischer Zeit (Amsterdam 1984); C. Milani: Note etimologiche su Europe, in M. Sordi (Hrsg.): L'Europa nel mondo antico (Milano 1986) 3-11; F. Luciani: La presunta origine semitica del nome Europa, ebd. 12-26.

4 Vgl. etwa M. Ninck: Die Entdeckung von Europa durch die Griechen (Basel 1945) bes. 15-23; Belege auch bei H. Steuding: Europa, in W. H. Roscher: Ausführliches Lexikon der griechischen und römischen Mythologie I (Leipzig 1884-1886) 1409-1419.

5 Vgl. Strabo 9,5,20 (Europos); Paus. 9,39,4-5 (Lebadeia); Paus 9,19,1 (Teumessos); dazu auch Philostr. epist. 47 (Böotischer Zeus); insgesamt L. Prandi: Europa e i Cadmei: La 'versione beotica' del mito, in: M. Sordi (wie Anm. 3) 37-48.

6 [Hesiod] frg. 140/141 Merkelbach/West; vgl. M. L. West: The Hesiodic Catalogue of Women (Oxford 1985) bes. 82-84 und 144-154.

7 Vgl. E. Zahn: Europa und der Stier (Diss. Würzburg 1982, Würzburg 1983); M. Robertson: Europa, in: Lexicon Iconographicum Mythologiae Classicae [LIMC] IV (Zürich 1988) 76-82 s. v.; zur Rezeption vgl. unter Anm. 13.

8 Zur literarischen Überlieferung vgl. L. De Brauw: Europa en de Stier (Diss. Amsterdam 1940) bes. 11-51; W. Bühler: Die Europa des Moschos. Text, Übers., Komm. (Wiesbaden 1960); Ders.: Europa. Ein Überblick über die Zeugnisse des Mythos in der antiken Literatur und Kunst (München 1968) bes. 7-46; ergänzend R. Merkelbach: Roman und Mysterium in der Antike (München/Berlin 1962) 326-332: Die Europa des Moschos.

9 E. Zahn (wie Anm. 7) Nr. 27; M. Robertson (wie Anm. 7) Nr. 2; J. Boardman/M. Hirmer u. a.: Die griechische Kunst (München 1966) 134 mit Taf. XXIII.

10 E. Zahn (wie Anm. 7) Nr. 21; vgl. ebd. Nr. 20; M. Robertson (wie Anm. 7) Nr. 32 bzw. Nr. 31. Auf der erstgenannten Halsamphora wird Europa auf dem Stier flankiert von Hermes (rechts) und Aphrodite (?) (links).

11 L. Giuliani: Die archaischen Metopen von Selinunt (Mainz 1979) 43-50 mit Taf. 10; E. Zahn (wie Anm. 7) Nr. 5; M. Robertson (wie Anm. 7) Nr. 78.

12 E. Zahn (wie Anm. 7) Nr. 274; M. Robertson (wie Anm. 7) Nr. 125; vgl. K. Schefold: Die Göttersage in der klassischen und hellenistischen Zeit (München 1981) 234-239.

13 Vgl. A. Lombard: Un mythe dans la poésie et dans l'art. L'enlèvement d'Europe (Neuchâtel 1946); H.-R. Hanke: Die Entführung der Europa. Eine ikonographische Untersuchung (Diss. Köln 1963); Ders.: Die Entführung der Europa. Die Fabel Ovids in der europäischen Kunst (Berlin 1967); Die Verführung der Europa. Ausstellungskatalog, Kunstgewerbemuseum Berlin (Frankfurt 1988); S. Salzmann (Hrsg.): Mythos Europa. Europa und der Stier im Zeitalter der industriellen Zivilisation. Ausstellungskatalog Kunsthalle Bremen (Bonn 1988).

14 A. Pope: Titian's Rape of Europe (Cambridge/Mass. 1960); zur Rezeption antiker Vorbilder vgl. C. Vermeule: European Art and Classical Past (Cambridge/Mass. 1964) 85-91 mit Abb. 71. Eine ähnliche Konzeption bietet ein Ölgemälde aus der Schule von Guido Reni im Mittelrheinischen Museum Mainz (Inv. Nr. 212); zu Guido Reni vgl. D. St. Pepper: Guido Reni. A Complete Catalogue of His Works with an Introductory Text (Oxford 1984) Nr. 164 mit Taf. 191 und Nr. 184 mit Taf. 214.

15 Vgl. H. Roeder: The Borders of Filarete's Bronze Doors to St. Peter's, Journal of the Warburg and Courtland Institute 19 (1947) 150-153 mit Taf. 39/40.

16 F. Schottmüller: Der Europa-Teppich im Kaiser-Friedrich-Museum, Jahrbuch der Kgl. Preußischen Kunstsammlungen 37 (1916) 146-154 mit Abb. 1.

17 B.B. Fredericksen: The Cassone Paintings of Francesco di Giorgio (Los Angeles 1969) 43; vgl. Die Verführung der Europa (wie Anm. 13) Nr. 96a mit Abb. V.

18 A. Lombard (wie Anm. 13) 85 und 125, Nr. 120 mit Abb. 26.

19 A. Lombard (wie Anm. 13) 96f. und 126, Nr. 130 mit Abb. 29.

20 W. Boeck: Picasso (Stuttgart 1955) 422 (Abb.); vgl. M. Kampmeyer-Käding: Das verführende Weib, in: Die Verführung der Europa (wie Anm. 13) 188-199.

21 Carnets intimes de G. Braque. Verve VIII Nr. 31/32 (Paris 1955) 40 (Abb.); vgl. Die Verführung der Europa (wie Anm. 13) Nr. 187 (mit Abb.).

22 Lovis Corinth (Hrsg.): Krieg und Kunst. 48 Steinzeichnungen der Berliner Sezession (Berlin 1915) unpaginiert; vgl. Die Verführung der Europa (wie Anm. 13) Nr. 192 mit Abb. S. 196.

23 K. Fußmann: Annäherung eines Malers an einen Mythos, in: Die Verführung der Europa (wie Anm. 13) 228-232 mit Taf. XXIII.

24 Vgl. bes. W. Bühler: Europa (wie Anm. 8) 7-9.

25 Vgl. etwa W. Helck: Die Beziehungen Ägyptens und Vorderasiens zur Ägäis bis ins 7. Jh. v. Chr. (Darmstadt 1979); J. Boardman: Kolonien und Handel der Griechen. Vom späten 9. bis zum 6. Jh. v. Chr. (München 1981) bes. 37-128; S. Deger-Jalkotzy (Hrsg.): Griechenland, die Ägäis und die Levante während der 'Dark Ages' vom 12. bis zum 9. Jh., Symposion Stift Zwettl 1980 (Wien 1983).

26 Zum Bergwerk vgl. Hdt. 6,47; zu Thasos vgl. A.J. Graham: The Foundation of Thasos, ABSA 73 (1978) 61-98; J. Pouilloux: La fondation de Thasos: archéologie, littérature et critique historique, in Rayonnement grec. Hommages à Charles Delvoye (Bruxelles 1982) 91-101; zur phönizischen Präsenz vgl. G.D. Young: The Historical Background of Phoenician Expansion into the Mediterranean in the Early First Millenium B.C. (Diss. Brandeis Univ. 1970); G. Bunnens: L'expansion phénicienne en Méditerranée (Bruxelles/Rome 1979); J.N. Coldstream: Greeks and Phoenicians in the Aegaean, in H.G. Niemeyer (Hrsg.): Phönizier im Westen. Symposion Köln 1979 (Mainz 1982) 261-275; H.G. Niemeyer: Die Phönizier und die Mittelmeerküste im Zeitalter Homers, JRGZ 31 (1984) 1-94.

27 Vgl. bes. D. Fehling: Die Quellenangaben bei Herodot. Studien zur Erzählkunst Herodots (Berlin/New York 1971) 88 und 101-104; N. Ehrhardt: Zur Geschichte der griechischen Handels- und Kolonisationsfahrten im östlichen Mittelmeer im Spiegel von Epos und Periplus-Literatur: Zu Spuren orientalisch-ägäischen Einflusses in Europa während der Bronzezeit. Kolloquium, Mainz 1985, (im Druck).

28 M.C. Astour: Hellenosemitica. An Ethnic and Cultural Study in West Semitic Impact on Mycenaean Greece (Leiden 1965) bes. 113-224; J.-Chr. Billigmeier: Kadmos and the Possibility of a Semitic Presence in Helladic Greece (Diss. Univ. of California, Santa Barbara 1976); R.B. Edwards: Kadmos the Phoenician. A Study in Greek Legends and the Mycenaean Age (Amsterdam 1979).

29 Vgl. A.R. Millard: The Canaanite Linear Alphabet and Its Passage to the Greeks, Kadmos 15 (1976) 130-144; allgemein G. Pfohl (Hrsg.): Das Alphabet. Entstehung und Verbreitung der griechischen Schrift (Darmstadt 1968); H. Graßl: Herodot und die griechische Schrift, Hermes 100 (1972) 169-175; A. Heubeck: Schrift. Archaeologia Homerica III 10 (Göttingen 1979).

30 G. Kratz-Norbisrath: Orgie auf minoisch. Elfriede Egert (54) hat die Zeichenschrift des alten Kreta entschlüsselt, WAZ vom 06. 01. 1990; zu vergleichbaren Nachrichten vgl. E. Grumach: Bibliographie der kretisch-mykenischen Epigraphik (München 1963) 23-30; Suppl. (München 1967) 8f.; neuerdings A. Bradshaw: The Imprinting of the Phaistos Disc, Kadmos 15 (1976), 1-17, vgl. 177; L. Pomerance: The Phaistos Disc (Göteborg 1976); W. Nahm: Zum Diskos von Phaistos II, Kadmos 18 (1979) 1-25.

31 H.G. Wunderlich: Wohin der Stier Europa trug (Reinbek 1972); zum geologischen Aspekt bereits W. Noll: Die minoischen Paläste auf Kreta - Stätten der Lebenden oder der Toten? Antike Welt 2 (1971) 15-20.

32 Vgl. O. Krzyskowska/L. Nixon (Hrsg.): Minoan Society. Proceedings of the Colloquium, Cambridge 1981 (Bristol 1983); R. Hägg/N. Marinatos (Hrsg.): The Function of the Minoan Palaces. Proceedings of the Fourth International Symposium of the Swedish Institute in Athens 1984 (Stockholm/Göteborg 1987).

33 Vgl. H. Schwabl: RE X A 1 (1972) 253-376, s.v. Zeus I. Epiklesen, bes. 325; H. Schwabl/E. Simon u. a.: RE Suppl. XV (1978) 993-1481, s.v. Zeus II/III u. Nachträge, bes. 1208f. (nährende Tiere) und 1058-1063 (Gleichungen mit anderen Gottheiten).

34 Callim. hymn. 1,8-9 (an Zeus); vgl. S. Spyridakis: Zeus is Dead. Euhemeros and Crete, CJ 63 (1968) 337-340; H. Schwabl. u. a.: RE Suppl. XV (1978) 1210.

35 Vgl. M.P. Nilsson: The Minoan - Mycenaean Religion and Its Survival in Greek Religion^2 (Lund 1950) 461f. und 553-556; J.G. Frazer: The Golden Bough. A Study in

Magic and Religion IV 2³ (London 1941) 3-200; J.G. Griffiths: The Origins of Osiris and His Cult (Leiden 1980). Üblicherweise wurde nicht Zeus, sondern Dionysos mit Osiris parallelisiert.

36 Vgl. W. Technau: Die Göttin auf dem Stier, JDAI 52 (1937) 76-103; E. Zahn (wie Anm. 7) 25-39 und 179-181 (Mänaden); M. Robertson (wie Anm. 7) 90.

37 Meist im Zusammenhang mit ihren Söhnen Sarpedon (vgl. Anm. 59) bzw. Minos, aber auch mit ihrem Bruder Kadmos; vgl. M. Robertson (wie Anm. 7) 88f., Nr. 214-225.

38) J.N. Svoronos: Numismatique de la Crète ancienne (Mâcon 1890, ND Paris 1977) 158, Nr. 1; 160, Nr. 25; Abb. bei P.R. Franke/M. Hirmer: Die griechische Münze (München 1964) Nr. 537-538; vgl. E. Zahn (wie Anm. 7) 70-80 und 137-144, Nr. 116-163.

39 J.N. Svoronos (wie Anm. 38) 162, Nr. 35 = P.R. Franke/M. Hirmer (wie Anm. 38) Nr. 539 = E. Zahn (wie Anm. 7) Nr. 129.

40 J.N. Svoronos (s. o.) 168, Nr. 83 = P.R. Franke/M. Hirmer (s. o.) Nr. 540 = E. Zahn (wie Anm. 7) Nr. 139.

41 Vgl. E. Zahn (wie Anm. 7) 71-74; M.P. Nilsson (wie Anm. 35) 389-405 und 550-553; zur Bedeutung der Weide anstelle der Platane vgl. H. Rahner: Griechische Mythen in christlicher Deutung ³ (Zürich 1957) 247-254.

42 Vgl. F. Cumont: Die orientalischen Religionen im römischen Heidentum⁵ (Darmstadt 1969) 43-67 und 94-123 mit 222-233 bzw. 253-277 (Anmerkungen); zur Potnia Theron vgl. J.C. van Leuven: Mycenaean Goddesses Called Potnia, Kadmos 18 (1979) 112-129.

43 Alle Zeugnisse befinden sich jetzt im Archäologischen Museum, Heraklion.

44 Der griechische Mythos wurde vermutlich durch die kretischen Stierspiele inspiriert und findet in der minoischen Religion keine Entsprechung. Die uns bekannte Fassung wurde erst durch Euripides geprägt; vgl. R. Cantarella (Hrsg.): Euripide, I Cretesi (Milano 1964). Der sog. ἱερὸς γάμος könnte eine vorminoische Phase des Kults reflektieren, doch bleibt dies Spekulation; vgl. W. Fauth: Kl. Pauly IV (1972) 540f., s. v. Pasiphae; zur 'Heiligen Hochzeit' (z. B. Hom. Il. 14, 345-351) vgl. A. Klinz: Hieros Gamos (Diss. Halle 1933).

45 H. Diels/W. Kranz (Hrsg.): Die Fragmente der Vorsokratiker. 3 Bde. ⁵ (Berlin 1951) Nr. 12 (Anaximander) A 7. Vgl. H. Berger: Geschichte der wissenschaftlichen Erdkunde der Griechen² (Leipzig 1903) bes. 25-51; J.O. Thomson: History of Ancient Geography (Cambridge 1948); A. Diller: The Tradition of the Minor Greek Geographers (Lancaster 1952); W. Wolska-Conus: RAC X (1978) 155-222, s. v. Geographie (mit Literatur); zu Hekataios von Milet vgl. L. Pearson: Early Ionian Historians (Oxford 1939) 25-108.

46 Vgl. Hdt. 2,16 unter Bezug auf die ionischen Geographen.

47 Vgl. Hdt. 7,10,ß1 (Rede des Artabanos); zur politischen Konzeption Asiens als Herrschaftsgebiet der Achaimeniden vgl. bereits Aeschyl. Pers. 249 und 798f., zum 'Westen' ebd. 230-232; vgl. L. Belloni: I 'Persiani' di Eschilo tra Oriente e Occidente, in M. Sordi (wie Anm. 3) 68-83.

48 Hdt. 4,143,1; 5,12,1; zum Skythenfeldzug vgl. B. Gallotta: Dario e l'Occidente prima delle guerre persiane (Milano 1980).

49 Hdt. 7,185; 1-2; vgl. insgesamt M. Pohlenz: Herodot, der erste Geschichtsschreiber des Abendlandes (Leipzig 1937, ND Darmstadt 1961) bes. 203-207. Philipp II, gab einer Tochter aus seiner letzten Verbindung mit der makedonischen Adelstochter Kleopatra den sprechenden Namen Europa (FGH III p. 161 F 5: Satyros = Athen. 13,557e).

50 Hdt. 7,9.1; vgl. 7,50,4; Hdt. 7,9, γ 1; Zur weiteren Entwicklung vgl. etwa Liv. 34,58,2f. (Rede des Flamininus).

51 [Hesiod] frg. 130 Merkelbach/West, bei Strabo 8,6,6; vgl. oben Anm. 6.

52 Hdt. 8,144,2; zur politischen Akzentuierung etwa Hdt. 6,49,2; ergänzend Plut. Per. 17. Mythologisch dokumentierte sich dieses Gemeinschaftsgefühl der Griechen als Nachkommen des Hellenos, Sohn des Deukalion und der Pyrrha: dessen Söhne Doros, Aiolos und Xuthos, Vater des Achaios und des Ion, bieten einen Reflex der griechischen Dialektgruppen. Vgl. insgesamt F.W. Walbank: The Problem of Greek Nationality, Phoenix 5 (1951) 41-60; J. de Romilly: Panhellénisme et l'union d'Europe, in: The Living Heritage of Greek Antiquity (Paris 1967) 212-230.

53 Hdt. 4,40,1 bzw. 4,45,2; vgl. G. Pfligersdorffer: RAC VI (1966) 964-980, s. v. Europa I (geographisch), bes. 977f. mit weiteren Belegen.

54 Vgl. W. Aly: Die Entdeckung des Westens, Hermes 62 (1927) 299-341 und 485-489; M. Ninck (wie Anm. 4) 179-226; R. Dion: Aspects politiques de la géographie antique (Paris 1977) 189-212; C.F.C. Hawkes: Pytheas. Europe and the Greek Explorers (Oxford 1977). Die Lokalisierung von Thule in Island (Hawkes) oder an der norwegischen Küste (Dion) bleibt umstritten; vgl. auch I. Whitaker: The Problem of Pytheas' Thule, CJ 77 (1981) 148-164.

55 Vgl. H. Berger (wie Anm. 45) 100-118 und 384-441; F. Gisinger: RE Suppl. IV (1924) 604-614, s. v. Geographie (Eratosthenes); zu den mathematischen Grundlagen vgl. B.L. van der Waerden: Die Astronomie der Griechen (Darmstadt 1988).

56 Tac. Agr. 10; vgl. R. Hennig: Die britannischen Inseln im Altertum, Saeculum 3 (1952) 56-69; A.R. Burn: Tacitus on Britain, in T.A. Dorey (Hrsg.): Tacitus (London 1962) 35-61.

57 E. Polaschek: RE Suppl. X (1965) 680-833, s. v. Ptolemaios (als Geograph).

58 Zur Kartographie vgl. O.A.W. Dilke: Greek and Roman Maps (London 1985); A.-D. van den Brincken: Europa in der Kartographie des Mittelalters, AKG 55 (1973) 289-304; zu Mercator vgl. Gerhard Mercator. 1512-1594. Zum 450. Geburtstag, Duisburger Forschungen 6 (Duisburg 1962); A.S. Osley: Mercator (London/New York 1969).

59 Hdt. 4,45,5 (Zitat oben S.); vgl. Aeschyl. frg. 145 Mette: Κᾶρες ἤ Εὑρώπη (zum Tod des Sarpedon, eines dritten Sohnes der Europa); zu Britannien vgl. Arr. anab. 7,1,4 (interessant auch durch die Akzentuierung 'Europa - Asien').

60 [Hippokr.] de aere, aquis locis, bes. 12-24, übers. von W. Capelle: Hippokrates. Fünf auserlesene Schriften (Zürich 1955) 85-120, bes. 106ff.; vgl. F. Jacoby: Zu Hippokrates περὶ ἀέρων ὑδάτων τόπων, Hermes 46 (1911) 518-567; K.E. Müller: Geschichte der antiken Ethnographie und ethnologischen Theoriebildung I (Wiesbaden 1972) bes. 137-144.

61 M.H. von Freeden/C. Lamb: Das Meisterwerk des Giovanni Battista Tiepolo in der Würzburger Residenz (München 1956); vgl. C. Le Corbeiller: Miss America and Her Sisters. Personifications of the Four Parts of the World. Metropolitan Museum Bulletin 19 (1961) 209-223; S. Poeschel: Studien zur Ikonographie der Erdteile in der Kunst des 16.-18. Jhs. (München 1985).

62 R. van Marle: Iconographie de l'art profane au Moyen-Age et à la Renaissance (New York 1971) II 324f. mit Abb. 357; vgl. B. Knipping: De Iconografie van de Contra-Reformatie in de Nederlanden (Hilversum 1940) II 158-166.

63 Cesare Ripa, Iconologia (Rom 1603, ND Hildesheim/New York 1970) 332-339 (Europa, Asia, Africa, America); vgl. oben Anm. 61; E. Mandowsky: Untersuchungen zur Iconologie des Cesare Ripa (Masch. Diss. Hamburg 1934).

64 D. Redig de Campos: Sopra una tavola sconosciuta del secolo undecimo rappresentante il giudizio universale, RPAA 11 (1935) 139-156 (mit Abb.).

65 O. Jahn: Griechische Bilderchroniken (Bonn 1873) Taf. VI M (Umzeichnung); vgl. IG XIV 1296; A. Sadurska: Les tables iliaques (Warszawa 1964) 74-78 mit Taf. XVI f.; J.Ch. Balty: LIMC (wie Anm. 7) II (1984) 858, s. v. Asia Nr. 2. Zur Gegenüberstellung von Asia und Makedonia vgl. K. Fittschen: Zum Figurenfries der Villa von Boscoreale, in B. Andreae/H. Kyrieleis (Hrsg.): Neue Forschungen in Pompeji (Recklinghausen 1975) 93-100 mit Abb. 59-71, bes. Abb. 71.

66 App. b. c. 4,106 (445). Livius (45,33,3) wertete die Feiern nach dem Frieden zwischen Rom und Makedonien in Amphipolis (167 v. Chr.) als Begegnung zwischen Europa und Asien. Weiter westlich, auf der Höhe von Scodra (Scutari) in Albanien verlief die Demarkationslinie der Machtbereiche, die sich Oktavian und Mark Anton als Triumvirn im Frieden von Brundisium (40. v. Chr.) zubilligten (App. b. c. 5,65 [274f.]). Mit geringfügigen Abweichungen wurde diese gedankliche Abgrenzung von Westen und Osten in der Spätantike verwaltungstechnisch praktiziert, schließlich auch politisch umgesetzt: die beiden Pannonien und Dalmatien gehörten zum 'Westreich', Moesia prima, die Praevalitana und Epirus zum 'Ostreich'; vgl. grundlegend A. Pabst: Divisio regni. Der Zerfall des Imperium Romanum in der Sicht der Zeitgenossen (Bonn 1986) bes. 130ff. Abweichend ging Herodian (4,3,4-7), der den (fiktiven) Plan einer Reichsteilung zwischen Caracalla und Geta (211 n. Chr.) berichtet, von den kontinentalen Grenzen Europas und Asiens aus: 'Ganz Europa sollte Antoninus erhalten, das gegenüberliegende Festland Asien Geta gehören; denn schon nach göttlicher Konzeption seien die beiden Kontinente durch das Meer Propontis voneinander geschieden' (Herod. 4,3,5 f.); vgl. G. Alföldy: Der Sturz des Kaisers Geta und die antike Geschichtsschreibung (1972), ND in Ders.: die Krise des Römischen Reiches (Stuttgart 1989) 179-216, bes. 190-193 und 213 (Nachtrag).

67 Lat. Ver. IV 2, p. 248; Not. Dign. Or. XXVI 3 und 10, p. 56f.; vgl. I 72, p. 3; Pol. Silv. Laterc. VI 6, p. 258: Europa, in qua est Constantinopolis prius Licus dicta sive Bizantium. Die Zitate beziehen sich auf O. Seeck (Hrsg.): Notitia Dignitatum (Berlin 1876, ND Frankfurt 1962); vgl. T.D. Barnes: The New Empire of Diocletian and Constantine (Cambridge/Mass. 1982) bes. 201-225. Europa als Name der thrakischen Provinz (vgl. bereits FGrHist 391 F 3: Hegesippos) ist um 325 n. Chr. bezeugt durch CIL VI 1691 = ILS 1240: L. Aradius Val. Proculus v. c. ... consularis pro-

vinciae Europae et Thraciae; zur Person vgl. PLRE I s. v. Proculus 11, dazu auch CIL VIII 24521; IGRR I 789-791. Für die spätere Zeit etwa Amm. 27,5,12 und 22,8,7; HA Aurelianus 17,2; Cod. Theod. 1,6,1 = Cod. Iust. 7,62,23 (361 n. Chr.); Acta conc. oec. 11,7, p. 122f. (Nr. 82); Prokop. aed. 4,9,14 u. 4,11,20; Nov. Iust. 8, Not. gr. 27.

68 Zur geographischen Orientierung vgl. E. Kettenhofen: Östlicher Mittelmeerraum und Mesopotamien. Die Neuordnung des Orients in diokletianisch-konstantinischer Zeit (284-337 n. Chr.). Tübinger Atlas des Vorderen Orients, Blatt B VI 1 (Wiesbaden 1984); G. Zecchini: L'idea di Europa nella cultura del tardo impero, in M. Sordi (wie Anm. 3) 160-173, bes. 165ff.; P. Grattarola: Il concetto di Europa alla fine del mondo antico, ebd. 174-191; J. Koder: Der Begriff Europa als Raumvorstellung in der byzantinischen Historiographie (griech.), in: Byzantium and Europe. First International Byzantine Conference, Delphi 1985 (Athen 1987) and Europe. First International Byzantine Conference, Delphi 1985 (Athen 1987) 63-74; Ders.: Zum Bild des 'Westens' bei den Byzantinern in der frühen Komnenenzeit, in: Deus qui mutat tempora. Festschr. für Alfons Becker (Sigmaringen 1987) 191-201; grundlegend J. Fischer: Oriens – Occidens – Europa. Begriff und Gedanke 'Europa' in der späten Antike und im frühen Mittelalter (Wiesbaden 1957).

69 Immanuel Kant: Idee einer allgemeinen Geschichte in weltbürgerlicher Absicht, in O.H. von der Gablentz (Hrsg.): Immanuel Kant, Politische Schriften (Köln/Opladen 1965) 9-24. Zur weiteren Entwicklung vgl. H. Loebel (Hrsg.): Europa: Vermächtnis und Verpflichtung (Frankfurt 1957); O. Halecki: Europa. Grenzen und Gliederung seiner Geschichte (Darmstadt 1964); F. Jernsson: Das dritte Europa. Die Eopoche der slawischen Stiefkinder? (München 1969).

Europe: from Myth to Geographic Concept*

Leonhard Schumacher

History, and Social Sciences in general, are often, sometimes rightfully, accused of being eurocentered in both their view of the world and their topics of research.[1] The frame topic of the 14th Duisburg Akzente 'Europe's Our House' could support his prejudice because political, economic, and social aspects of the Common Market after 1992 are naturally in deep focus. Historiography however elucidates how Europe has influenced and changed the world, but it also makes clear the impact of non-European influences on Europe. Examples reach from the ancient silk route, Marco Polo, and the potato as our basic food, to religious sects and fundamentalist tendencies within the single church communities. Historiography also makes visible differences in political and social structures, in cultural and mental attitudes. Their peculiarity and strangeness causes cosmopolitan Europeans to react in a scale from surprise, over insecurity to repulse. Paul Westheim's essay "La Calavera - Death in Mexico", recently translated into German (1989, Hanau), is an impressive example of different mentality toward human life and death.

A closer look at the roots of our own 'European' culture brings up a similar feeling of alienation and strangeness: regarding as well the political structures of the so-called 'democratic' Greek Polis as her economic conditions and religious ideas, wich were shaped and expressed by myth in a most peculiar way.[2] A modern point of view ridicules the countless affairs of Zeus, feminists might see them as manifestations of male oppression and exploitation. For the archaic Greeks, myth mainly personalized religious ideas, wich as a system expressed an effort to explain the world. Finally, myth mirrors the identity of the Hellenes in its historical dimension. Heinrich Schliemann and his excavations at Troy, Mycenae, and Cnossos, as they were inspired by the Homeric myths, exemplify the last aspect.

The complex genesis of certain myths usually obstructs an understanding to the carefree reader. Contamination and different historic eras hinder a clear determination of the manifold aspects: personalized religious ideas, efforts to explain the world, and reflection of historic events. But the myth of Europe left a traceable development.

In literature, Europe as a name was first mentioned in Hesiod's 'catalogue of Oceanids' (Theog. 357-359) around 700 BC[2a]: (Tethys bore to Oceanos ... that holy race of daughters:)

> pleasing Petraie, Menestho, and Europe,
> Metis, Eurynome, and crocus robed Telesto,
> Chryseis, Asie, and desirable Calypso' (etc.).

We are interested in only two of Oceanos' daughters: Europe and Asia. As both names are blocked by many others, Hesiod obviously did not intend a juxtaposition, so that a reference to the continents is most unlikely.

No agreement has been reached on the etymology of Europe as name yet, but it is generally denied to be derived from Semitic 'ereb, meaning 'the dark' or 'the land of the setting sun'. Usually the name is derived from (pre-) Greek origins: the feminine gender of the adjective εὐρωπός means accordingly 'looking like εὐρώς', that is 'moisture' or more specifically, 'the dark in the water'. Consequently, Europe would mean 'the dark/ deep water' and would personify the Goddess 'of the deep water'. In analogy, Asia derived from ἄσις (mud) would mean the Goddess 'of the standing, shallow (brackish) water'. According to their father Oceanos, we may consider Asia und Europe as nymphs during the first stage of development around 700 BC.

So we meet the name of Europe, whom we shall confine to, ot that of her masculine equivalent Europos, denominating rivers, mainly in Central and Northern mainland Greece: Boeotia, Epirus, Thessaly, and Macedonia.[4] The river Europos runs through the region of Perrhaibia, flowing into the Peneios just north of Larissa. In Boeotian Lebadeia, Demeter, the Goddess of growth, was worshipped with her by-name Europe. We also know about the cult of a chthonian Earth-Goddess named Europe, guarded by Zeus in an earth cave in Teumessos, Boeotia.[5].

This relation to Zeus suggested association with the well known myth of Europe from the Iliad. To reconcile his wife, Zeus went as far as to compare Hera to his many lovers. His love to her was bigger and more ardent than to Dia, the wife of Ixion, to Danae, Semele, Alcmene, Demeter or Leto, bigger than to Europe, 'the daughter of Phoinix .../ who bore Rhadamanthys, the divine hero, and Minos '(Hom. Il. 14, 321 f.). The same version on Europe's origin is found in the Hesiodic 'Catalogue of Women'[6], without tracing a tie to the Boeotian Europe. These circumstances do not allow for an equation before the 7th or 6th century BC.

The myth is one of the best known themes of Greek and Roman antiquity and has experienced manifold variations in the fine arts up to present times.[7] The story is well known, of course, but may be sketched nevertheless: Zeus, father of the Gods, struck up with love on the pretty princess, changed into a beautiful white bull. Thus transformed, he managed to get close to Europe, who was playing with her girl friends on the shore. Trusting the tame animal the maid petted it and finally climbed onto his back. Zeus took his chance to escape with her over the ocean. Later on, he revealed his identity to beget several sons with Europe.[8]

Visualizations concentrate on phases of the actual abduction. On the (red figured) bell-krater of Tarquinia (around 490 BC), Europe gently holds the bull's left horn.[9] The Edinburgh Painter shows the girl just sitting on the animal's back decorating a (black figured) neck-amphora (early 5th century) (Fig. 1).[10] In the middle of the 6th century BC, a metope on the frieze from the archaic temple Y by Selinunt (Fig. 2)[11] captures the scene in the same manner. The Pompeian fresco from the Casa di Iasone, now on display at the National Museum in Naples, is probably the best known visualization of the myth (Fig. 3).[12] In Augustan time (around 10 AD), the artist created the abduction in tender pastels after an early-Hellenistic model. The painting obviously captures the moment of escape: A topless Europe is shown sitting on top of a light brown bull, while one of her maiden friends tries to stop him. Apparently the artist has focussed the turning point of escape.

Modern versions concentrate on the aspect of Europe on top of the bull.[13] Titian painted (1562) the bull swimming energetically through the open sea.[14] A miniature, we find the motif as early as 1445 AD on the rim frieze of Filarete's bronze-door to St. Peter's Cathedral together with many other mythological representations (Fig. 4).[15] About the same time, a gobelin, designed by Ercole de' Roberti (?) was crafted in Ferrara (?).[16] The artist represented the myth of Europe in a twofold manner: At the left, the royal daughter, surrounded by her friends, has just got on the top of the bull; at the right, the bull escapes with his prey over the ocean. The same sequence of images is captured in a Cassone tablet from the dowry chest of an Italian maid of noble birth (about 1480 AD) (Fig. 5).[17] The sequence was complemented by a visualization of Zeus, who reveals himself to Europe in a young aristocrat's body. At the beginning of the 19th century, Anne Louis Girodet stressed this double role of Zeus as both a man and a bull in his illustrated translation of the Greek poet Anacreon (1825).[18]

We also have to limit ourselves to very few examples of the multitude of 20th century representations of the myth. Felix Vallotton's (1908) massive version of a woman creeping close to a bull, crossing the ocean, has an almost cosmic character.[19] Picasso (1946) created a dominant Europe throning on the bull's neck and 'steering' him firmly by the horn.[20] George Bracque's (undated) pen-and-ink-drawing stands out for its multidimensional perspective, that alludes to the close relationship between Europe and the bull.[21] A lithography of Gino von Finetti (1915) shows a graceful woman of the demi-world lasciviously enjoying her ride on a racing bull, wherever it may lead her.[22] In the war year of 1915, the Berlin Secessionist produced Europe most impressively as an allegory of morbid vitality facing as risky future (Fig. 6). Last not least, I want to mention a water-color painting of the Berlin artist Klaus Fussmann (1987) as one of the most recent examples of the theme.[23] The ingenious painting also stands out for its interpretation given by the artist himself.

Setting of the abduction in the ancient myth is always Phoenicia: The speaking name of Phoinix as the girl's father in Homer's Iliad supports this trait. In a later tradition, the maid is also identified as daughter of Agenor, king of Tyre or Sidon. Both versions indicate that the myth of Europe developed from contacts between Phoenicians in today's Lebanon and Greeks or supposed these connections. According to the later tradition, Agenor has several sons beside his daughter Europe, who all had speaking names: Phoinix (Phoenicia), Cilix (Cilicia), Cadmus, the founding hero of Thebes (Cadmeia), Thasos, the hero of the homonymous island in the Northern Aegean Sea, and Phineus, whom the myth of the Argonauts terms king in Thrace. According to the myth of Europe, the girl's father sent out his sons to find their sister, but they never returned home.[24]

In general, mythology here offers a reflex of the manyfold relations and the interchanging influences between the Phoenician and the Greek world, especially during the so-called 'Dark Ages' (12th to 8th century BC).[25] The problem can only be sketched in two representative examples. Both are recorded by Herodot and relate to the Phoenician presence in the Aegean Sea. The first text deals with the cult of Heracles, which Herodot as historian was interested in.

'Wishing to get clear knowledge (of Heracles) I even took a ship to Tyre in Phoenicia, because I had heard that there was a temple of Him. I found it, richly decorated with many sacred offerings... At Tyre I also visited a second temple of Heracles, called the Thasian. So I went to Thasos, where I found a temple of Heracles built by the Phoenicians, who founded Thasos when they voyaged in search of Europe' (Hdt. 2, 44, 1-4).

Despite a further hint of Herodot, telling of Phoenicians who discovered a mine on the island, and despite the archeological traces of Phoenician activities in the Northern Aegean,[26] the historic content of his account has experienced much scepticism lately.[27] Nevertheless we can pinpoint the tradition as a mythological reflex of the relations between Phoenicians and the Greek islands.

The same applies for Herodot's ideas on the development of Greek letters from an adaptation of the Phoenician alphabet:[28]

'Those Phoenicians, who came with Cadmus (to Hellas),'... - Herodot (5, 58-59) tells us - 'at their settlement (in Boeotia: Thebes / Cadmeia), brought many sciences and arts to the Hellenes, mainly the alphabet ... In the beginning, (the people of Cadmus) used the same characters as the other Phoenicians, but later the form of their letters altered with changes in their language. The Greek Ionians, who at this time dwelt round the Cadmus people, having been taught the letters by the Phoenicians used them with few changes of form and gave them the name of 'Phoenician' (characters) - Φοινικήια: τὰ τῶν Φοινίκων γράμματα. This was indeed but just, because the Phoenicians had brought them into Hellas ... I have seen myself Cadmeian letters in the temple of Ismenian Apollo at Thebes of Boeotia ...'

We do not need to focus on the development of the Greek alphabet,[29] but the characters of the archaic times are formally equivalent to older Semitic signs. Single letters got new vowel sounds: the Semitic 'aleph' (cattle), sensed as a consonant, for example, became the Greek ἄλφα with the vowel sound 'a'. Our term 'alphabet' mirrors this genesis of writing recorded by Herodot in the myth of Cadmus. The deciphering of the famous 'disc of Phaistos' by a Duisburg teacher went through the press recently.[30] The method reported employs a reading based on Semitic letters. Whether its results are satisfying or not, the kind of decipherment fits in with our context.

The round clay disc covered on both sides with letters and hieroglyphic signs was found in the Minoan Palace of Phaistos in Southern Crete. As is well known, Crete was the island, where Zeus had abducted Europe mythologically, or to use the popular title of Hans-Georg Wunderlich "Where the Bull brought Europe to".[31] His thesis of the palaces' function of giant necropoles (cities of the dead) can be disregarded altogether. The newly opened exhibition on Minoan Crete at the Niederrhein Museum will supply sufficient information on the palaces of Phaistos, Cnossus, Hagia Triada, Zacros, or Archanes as centers of social, political, religious, and economic life of the Minoan civilization.[32]

Due to his function as a junction between Egypt, Phoenicia and Greece, Crete is rightfully considered the cradle of European culture. Myth describes Zeus - Κρηταγενής - being nourished by the she-goat Amaltheia and the sacred bees in a cave on Mount Ida or Dicte. This multifunctional weather and heaven God indicates as much oriental influence (El, Hadad, Baalim) as his epicleses.[33] The later tradition of his grave in Crete established the Cretans' so-called character as arch-liars,[34] and seems the result of a syncretistic assimilation of the Greek God to Egyptian Osiris as the God of vegetative being and decay.[35]

The general tradition of Europe's abduction to Crete, where Zeus loved her in a cave on Mount Ida or in the neighborhood of Gortyn, makes visible the combination of the myth with original local cults. Our ideas of Europe are shaped by the works of fine art, and we thus generally link the myth to a female on top of a bull. In antiquity, the motif was not limited to this visualization. A female sitting on top of a bull did not necessarily express Europe,[36] and vice versa Europe is also identifiable without the bull.[37] The center of the Cretan cult of Europe was Gortyn on the river Lernaois in the Mesara, where the princess is said to have loved Zeus under a plane-tree. In the 5th century BC coins of the city show the common version of the girl on top of the bull.[38] During the 4th century BC though, a woman sitting in a tree top (willow) has to be identified as Europe, too.[39] Later on, a stater (around 300 BC) shows Zeus, as an eagle with wide opened wings, making love to Europe (Fig. 7).[40] The corresponding bull is shown on the reverse.

These versions hint at the roots of the myth as we have met them in Bocotia and with Hesiod. Europe here is considered a tree nymphe or the Goddess of growth. In combination with the bull she is to be understood as Πότνια ταυρῶν - queen of the bulls - or more generally as Πότνια θηρῶν, - mistress of the animals.[41] Again ties to the oriental cults of Astarte, Mâ Bellona, Mater Deum Magna Idaea clear up.[42] As commonly known, the bull was emphasized in Minoan cult. The many 16th/15th centuries representations from the Main Palace of Cnossus - so the painted high-relief from the North Entrance or the libation vessel of steatite from the Minor Palace - prove this as much as the Cretan bull-jumping-contests, as they are visualized in the famous fresco showing the different stages of the acrobat's up- and downswing.[43] In this context, we remind of the myth of Pasiphae, who made love to an oceanic bull (ἱερὸς γάμος) to bear Minotaur.[44] The multiple creation of the cult cannot be discussed in detail, but the myth of Europe can pinpointed as having contaminated elements of Oriental, Minoan, and Greek religion reflecting the interchanging influences of different cultures.

The earliest hint to Europe as a geographic name date around 600 BC with the Homeric Hymn to Pythian Apollo of Delphi. In substance, the conception coincides, as we have seen, with the spread of the archaic cult of Europe in Central and Northern mainland Greece. These districts are summarized under the term of Europe. They are equally differed from other regions, such as the Peloponnese and the Greek Islands: Greeks from everywhere should visit the temple of Delphic Apollo to employ His oracles,

'all men who dwell on fertile Peloponnesos, as those of Europe and throughout the sea-girt islands'.
([Hom.] hymn to Apollo 290 sq.)

This distinction exactly documents that Europe did not describe the continent yet, but only mainland Greece except the Peloponnese. Only by the end of the 6th century, this concept changed and became popular in connection with the Persian Wars. Even Herodot (4, 45, 4-5) didn't know how to trace the beginnings of this development.

'As for Europe, no men have any knowledge, whether it be surrounded or not by the sea, nor whence it took its name, nor it is clear who gave the name, unless we are to say, that the land took its name from the Tyrian Europe ... But it is plain, that this Europe was of Asiatic birth, and never came to this land which the Greeks now call Europe - ἐς τὴν γῆν ταύτην, ἥτις νῦν ὑπὸ Ἑλλήνων Εὐρώπη καλέεται. On the contrary, Europe came from Phoenice to Crete, and from there to Lycia.'

About in the middle of the 6th century, the first world map was drawn by Anaximander, a student of Milesian Thales. The map was detailed by Hecataeus of Milet around 500 BC.[45] Based on the conception of the earth as a circular plane surrounded by the ocean, Hecataeus took the Mediterranian as central axis extended to the Black and the Caspian Sea in the east. This central axis divided Europe in the north from Asia in the south; Libya/Africa was understood as part of Asia. The name of Europe for the northern continent likely resulted from being transferred as a geographic term naming the region of Central Greece to the entire neighboring land in the north and west (pars pro toto). According to Herodot (1, 4, 4), who later distinguished Africa (Libya) as a third continent,[46] Asia was the dominion of the Achemenids: 'The Persians claim Asia for their own and that foreign nations, that dwell in it. Europa and the Greek country they hold to separate from them.' The Propontis (Sea of Marmora) was the natural border flanked by the Hellespont or the Dardanelles in the south, by the Bosphorus in the north.

In this context, it is remarkable that Herodot used Europe as geographic name specifically for the land closest to Persian territory, namely the regions north and west the Propontis. The historian (7, 8, ß1) described King Xerxes in a war council explaining his offensive against Greece with the following words: 'It is my intent to bridge the Hellespont and to lead my army through Europe against Greece'- μέλλω ξεύξας τὸν Ἑλλήσποντον ἐλᾶν στρατὸν διὰ τῆς Εὐρώπης ἐπὶ τὴν Ἑλλάδα.[47] This use limits the name of Europe to Northern Greece, we will refer to this point later on. Herodot employs this usage telling us that Darius I, after his abortive campaign against the Scythians, left Megabazus as strategos in Europe, namely in Thrace to relocate the Paeonians ἐκ τῆς Εὐρώπης ἐς τὴν Ἀσίαν.[48]

Herodot thus understands Europe in a limited way as the region of Thrace possibly including parts of Macedonia. Later on, describing the military review of Xerxes, he extends the name to the whole of Northern Greece including Thessaly in clear difference to Hellas.[49] On the other hand the historian uses Europe as a name of the entire continent, when he has Xerxes' general Mardonius tell the war council about the Ionians in Europe - Ἴωναι οἱ ἐν τῇ Εὐρώπῃ. Xerxes was about to head his entire army from Asia - πλῆθος τὸ ἐκ τῆς Ἀσίης - against them.[50] In the course of this conflict between the Persian Empire and the Greeks, the polarization of Asia and Europe as a contest between East and West became commonplace. The victories of Salamis and Plataea stylized Greece as Europe's saviour from Oriental despotism. By the way we should remember, that the Greeks had been feeling as a Hellenic community beyond continental boundaries since the beginning of the 7th century BC.[51] Within certain limits we may even talk about Hellenic nationalism, manifested in family ties, identical language, common religion, and comparable customs of all Greeks,[52] all who, of course, were politically structured as a multitude of sovereign Poleis. This aspect is especially interesting in face of the current discussion about a central German state.

For Herodot, the legendary river Araxes in the utmost east outlined the boundary of Europe and Asia. Mostly however, the river Tanais (Don) or the Colchic Phasis, south of the Caucasus, were treated as the limit of the continents.[53] The historian could not make any remarks abouth the western boundaries of Europe. Around 300 BC, the expedition of Pytheas of Massilia (Marseilles) to the legendary Thule shed more light on the matter.[54] Eratosthenes incorporated these insights in his map of the world.[55] In Roman times, the results were partly confirmed by Iulius Agricola during his reconnaissance cruise to the Orkneys.[56] Later on, about the mid 2nd century AD, the mathematician, astronomer and geographer Claudius Ptolemy summarized the knowledge in his "Introduction to Geography" - γεωγραφικὴ ὑπήγησις.[57] His image of the world, as far as it was known, remained dominant during the Middle Ages until early Modern Times. The discovery of America in search of a western seaway to India, resulted from calculations done by Ptolemy. Only Gerhard Mercator's techniques of projection created a new basis of scientific cartography.[58] This incredibly interesting matter cannot even be sketched here.

As early as in the 5th century BC, Europe has been established as name of the continent describing the regions from the Atlantic Ocean in the west to the Don in the east with Bosphorus and Dardanelles as southern extensions. The Island of Crete was only understood as part of Europe after Herodot.[59] The geographic disctinction early has shaped the image of the inhabitants of this continent typologically. Europeans are usually portrayed in pointed antithesis to the character of the Asians. As early as in the pseudo-Hippocratic treatise "About the Environment", this distinction is explained anthropologically and not historically.[60] As a result of climatic and material conditions, Asians were generally easier going, gentler and more pacific thane the Europeans, who were characterized as active, rough and aggressive:

'The regular changes of season and weather cause boldness destroying tameness and tenderness. That is why I consider the Europeans more courageous than Asians. For uniformity (of the steady climate) supports laziness and irresponsibility. A country of repetitive changes and frequent variations though, strengthens body and mind. Indifference and phlegma develop to cowardice, training and endurance of hardships develop braveness' (Ps. Hippocr. aer. 23, p.167 Kühlewein).

This typology bears its consequences for the physical constitution of the people, though the characterization also reflects regional differences within the continents. In general, Europeans are described as taller and more mascular, the Asians as petite and delicate.

We can recapture this typology with regards to the image of Europe as personification of the continent. The staircase design of the Wuerzburg residency by Giovanni Battista Tiepolo (1751/53) can be considered as the best known allegory.[61] His image of the world shows the now known four continents as females, placed on a significant animal: America with a feather crown on a giant alligator, Africa on a dromedary, Asia on an Indian elephant, and Europe on the mythological bull (Fig. 8). Europe appears matronly, compared to a petite Asia; both Asia and Europe are shown in high-necked dresses, whereas the continents of the 'Third World' are topless.

Typologically most interesting seems the copperplate print by Philip Galle (16th century AD), who symbolized a Valkyrian Europe with scepter and crown, claiming political power.[62] Cesare Ripa captured a similar personification of Europe as 'Queen of the World' with a crown in his "Iconologia" (1603). The bull is replaced by the horse, underlining the royal position of the European continent (Fig. 9).[63] Iconologically, the bull did not have a part in the early personifications of Europe as a continent. Sure, a dipinto on a limewashed canvas (1040/80 AD) shows a female on a bull.[64] Yet, this allegory within the visualized 'Last Judgement' does not display Europe, but the 'Land' in contrast to the 'Sea', symbolized by a Nereid on a sea dragon.

Classical antiquity has left only one certain allegory of the continent. The relief of the Palazzo Chigi (1st century BC) offers two female personifications dressed with the chiton, Europe at the left and Asia at the right, both with mural crowns, carrying a shield with a battle scene (Fig. 10).[65] The identification follows from the inscription, characterizing the battle as conflict between Orient and Occident, fought near Gaugamela/Arbela, where Alexander beat the Great King Darius (III).

In substance, we deal with the conflict between East and West, Europe and Asia, as it has been varied since the Persian Wars in many ideological manifestations. The geographic boundaries were considered secondary, based on the specific situation. Appian, for example, localized the battlefield of Philippi,[66] where Brutus and Cassius died 42 BC, close to the main pass between Europe and Asia, about one mile away from the δίοδος ἐς τὴν Ἀσίαν τε καὶ Εὐρώπην. According to this version, East and West confronted near Kavalla, in today's province of Macedonia.

Following the further development of the geographic term, it is surprising, that due to Diocletian's administrative reforms, the name of Europe was attached to one of the smallest provinces of the Roman Empire,[67] namely the region next to Byzantium neighboring with Asian territory (Fig. 11).[68] This phenomenon of territorial limitation or consumption of Europe as a geographic term we met already with Herodot. In late antiquity, Europe as province of the Thracian diocese was thus located in the exposed part of the homonymous continent, bearing the name of the continent itself. Linguistically, we can categorize this result as a form of catachresis.

With minor expansion, the territory of this post-Diocletianic province is part of today's Turkey. Depending on the political viewpoint, this could read as the last Asian front in Europe. In the face of the Common Market, I would rather like to understand this result of a long historic process as a proof of Turkey's capacity to be adapted or integrated into the European Community. Continental boundaries within the Roman Empire were unimportant due to its universal concept of validity. Disconsidering the ideological components, this aspect offers definitely positive perspectives in the sense of Kant's "Idea of a General History in Cosmopolitan Intention".[69]

---

*Lecture read at the 14th Duisburg Akzente 'Europe's Our House' (24. 4. 1990); footnotes were added for publication, but visuals could be reproduced on a limited scale only.

L'EUROPE: Du mythe au concept géographique*

Leonhard Schumacher

D'une manière générale, historiens et sociologues se voient reprocher, et quelques fois à juste tire, l'euro-centrisme de leur vision du monde, l'euro-centrisme des questions qu'ils abordent[1]. "L'Europe - Notre foyer" thème cadre des "Accents" de Duisbourg, cette année, pourrait alimenter cette critique. Il est évident que les perspectives du marché commun de 1992, leurs aspects politiques, économiques et sociaux seront le thème essentiel de nos préoccupations et cependant l'aspect historique fait apparaître de façon toute aussi évidente que, si l'Europe a influencé et transformé le reste du monde, elle n'en a pas moins été, elle-même, soumise, dans une large mesure, à des influences extra-européennes. Ces dernières vont, succintement parlant, de l'antique route de la soie en passant par Marco Polo, jusqu'à la pomme de terre, notre aliment de base, et jusqu'aux sectes ou aux courants fondamentalistes au sein des communautés religieuses. Dans un même temps, cependant, des différences de structures sociales et politiques, des différences dans les domaines culturels, dans celui des modes de pensées, s'affirment dont l'originalité et l'exotisme peuvent à l'occasion, déranger, dérouter ou repousser l'Européen cosmopolite. L'essai traduit il y a peu de temps en allemand, "La Cavalera - La Mort au Mexique" (Hanau 1989) fournit un exemple impressionnant de différences de mentalités, de différences du système de valeurs à l'égard de la vie et de la mort.

Dès que nous nous mettons à les considérer de plus près, les racines de notre propre culture nous semblent déjà exotiques ou du moins étrangères: Les mécanismes, soi-disant démocratiques, de la Cité Grecque, de la Polis, ses données économiques ou son imaginaire religieux, empreints qu'ils sont du Mythe, tout comme le fait qu'ils se manifestent par les mythes[2]. On peut bien sûr de notre point de vue d'hommes modernes sourire des innombrables aventures amoureuses de Zeus; les féministes peuvent les stigmatiser en tant que manifestations évidentes de mécanismes d'oppression et d'exploitation masculins d'une société patriarcale. Pour les Grecs archaïques le Mythe était avant tout la personnification de concepts religieux, l'expression en tant que système d'une interprétation de l'univers et finalement le reflet de leur identité dans sa dimension historique. Illustrons provisoirement ce dernier aspect en évoquant les fouilles de Troie, de Mycène et de Cnossos que les mythes homériens inspirèrent à Heinrich Schliemann.

Pour le lecteur non-averti, en règle générale, la génèse complexe d'un mythe particulier est quelque chose de difficile à comprendre. Des interférences entre ses différents aspects, personnification de concepts religieux, interprétation de l'univers et reflets d'événements historiques, d'autant plus que différentes époques historiques entrent en jeu, en rendent la différentiation précise et nette, quelques fois ardue ou même impossible. Dans le cas du mythe d'Europe, nous sommes en mesure toutefois d'en reconstruire assez clairement le processus d'évolution.

On trouve le nom d'Europe cité pour la première fois en littérature dans le catalogue des Océanides de la Théogonie d'Hésiode (357 - 359) vers l'an 700 av. JC.[2a] (Téthys donna à Océan des filles de sang divin:) Pétrée l'attirante, Ménesthô et Europe, Métis, Eurynomé et Télestô à la tunique de couleur de crocus, Chryséis, Asie et Calypso, celle qu'éveille le désir' (etc).

Parmi ces filles d'Océan, seules deux ici nous intéressent: Europe et Asie. Etant donné que ces deux noms se trouvent espacés dans une énumération, il semble qu'Hésiode n'ait pas voulu les opposer et donc qu'une référence aux deux continents du même nom soit exclue.

L'étymologie du nom Europe[3] n'a pas encore été retracée de façon unanime, elle est toujours l'objet de polémiques, cependant on rejète totalement une origine sémite: 'ereb' dans le sens de 'sombre', voire 'pays du soleil couchant', au profit d'une origine (pré-)héllénique: la forme féminine de l'adjectif $εὐρωπός$ signifiant 'ressemblant à $εὐρώς$ tout en l'interprétant dans son sens général de 'humidité' ou plus restreint de 'ce qui est sombre dans les eaux'. En conséquence, Europe signifierait 'les eaux sombres, les eaux profondes', personnifierait la Déesse des 'eaux profondes'. Par opposition Asie signifierait, à partir de $ἄσις$ (la boue), la Déesse des 'eaux basses, des eaux dormantes, stagnantes'. En filles dignes de leur père Océan, Europe et Asie dans la première phase de l'évolution du mythe, vers 700 av. JC, sont des nymphes.

C'est dans ce sens que nous trouvons le nom d'Europe dont nous entendons nous occuper ici, ou son équivalent masculin Europos désignant des rivières essentiellement en Grèce centrale et septentrionale: en Béotie, en Epire, en Thessalie, en Macédoine[4]. En Perrhaibie, nous trouvons l'Europos que se jète dans le Pénée au nord de Larisa. A Lébadée en Béotie, on honorait Déméter en lui accolant l'épithète d'Europe comme divinité de la croissance, à Teumesse en Béotie aussi, on trouve le témoignage d'un culte rendu à une Déesse chthonienne de la terre, appelée Europe, sur laquelle Zeus veilla dans une grotte[5].

Cette mention de Zeus nous amène au mythe beaucoup plus connu d'Europe dans l'Iliade. Le père des dieux n'hésita pas pour se réconcilier avec Héra, son épouse, à dresser des comparaisons entre toutes ses 'maîtresses'. Son amour pour Héra était plus fort que celui éprouvé pour Dia, l'épouse d'Ixion, pour Danaé, Sémélé, Alcmène, Déméter ou Latone, mais aussi plus fort que celui qu'il avait éprouvé pour Europe 'la fille de Phénix .../ qui donna le jour à Rhadamante, le héro divin, et à Minos' (Hom. Il. XIV 321 s.) La même version de la généalogie d'Europe se trouve dans le "Catalogue des Femmes" attribué à Hésiode[6] sans que toute fois on n'y fasse allusion à l'Europe béotienne. Dans ces conditions il semblerait qu'une harmonisation du mythe ait eu lieu seulement au 7ème ou 6ème siècle avant notre ère.

Ce mythe compte parmi les thèmes les plus connus de l'antiquité gréco-romaine et les arts figuratifs en ont donné de nombreuses versions[7]. Considérons le thème comme connu et contentons-nous d'en esquisser brièvement l'histoire: Zeus, le père des dieux s'éprend de la belle Europe, fille de roi, se métamorphose en un magnifique taureau blanc. C'est sous cette forme qu'il s'approche d'Europe alors qu'elle joue sur la grève avec ses compagnes. La jeune fille n'éprouve aucune crainte devant ce doux animal, le caresse et finalement bondit sur son dos. C'est alors que le taureau l'enlève et la conduit de l'autre côté de la mer. Plus tard, il lui découvre sa véritable identité et elle lui donnera plusieurs fils[8].

Les représentations picturales se concentrent sur la phase de l'enlèvement. Sur le cratère en cloche de Tarquinies (à figures rouges) on peut voir Europe diriger le taureau par sa corne gauche[9], de façon précieuse, (vers 490 av. JC), tandis que le peintre d'Edinbourg représente à figures noires sur un amphore à col (début du 5ème siècle) la jeune fille alors qu'elle a déjà pris place sur le dos du taureau (fig. 1)[10]. La même scène se trouve sur la métope de la frise du Temple archaïque Y de Sélinonte au milieu du 6ème siècle (fig. 2)[11]. La plus connue de toutes est peut-être la fresque pompéienne provenant de la Casa di Iasone qui peut maintenant être admirée au Musée National de Naples (fig. 3)[12]. L'artiste de l'époque Augustéenne s'inspirant d'un exemple hellénistique a représenté l'enlèvement dans des teintes pastèles. Europe, la partie supérieure du corps dénudée, se tient déjà sur le dos d'un taureau brun clair que l'une de ses compagnes essaie de retenir. Il s'agit évidemment ici de fixer le moment de la fuite.

Les versions modernes tournent principalement autour de la scène centrale de la jeune fille sur le dos du taureau[13] qui est entrain, comme chez Le Titien (1562) de traverser la mer d'une nage puissante[14]. On trouve déjà ce sujet en miniature sur la frise de bordure du portail médian en bronze de la Basilique Saint-Piere (1445) aux côtés d'autres représentations mythologiques (fig. 4)[15]. A Ferrare (?), une tapisserie de la même époque, d'après un carton de Ercole de Roberti (?)[16] divise le mythe d'Europe en deux épisodes: à gauche, la fille du roi au milieu de ses compagnes de jeu, vient de monter sur le dos du taureau qui, à droite, prend la fuite, emportant sa proie au-delà de la mer. Un panneau de cassone (fig. 5), coffre de mariée d'une noble italienne (1480)[17], représente la même séquence et finalement le moment où Zeus se présente à Europe sous les traits d'un jeune homme. Cette double apparence de Zeus-taureau, Zeus-homme, est le thème auquel AnneLouis Girodet s'est consacré en illustrant la traduction du poète grec Anacréon (1825)[18].

En ce qui concerne le vingtième siècle, étant donné la profusion de représentations de ce mythe, nous allons devoir nous limiter à quelques exemples. La version massive d'une jeune femme enlacée à un taureau nageant en mer de Félix Vallotton (1908) a presque un côté cosmique[19]. Chez Picasso (1946), c'est une Europe dominante qui trône sur le cou du taureau qu'elle dirige d'une main énergique par la corne[20]. Le dessin à la plume de Georges Braque (non daté) se singularise par sa perspective multi-dimensionnelle et le fait qu'il laisse entrevoir une relation intime entre jeune femme et taureau[21]. Le taureau au galop de la lithographie de Gino von Finetti (1915)[22] porte, lui, une femme du demi-monde qui, gracieuse et lascive, jouit de cette calvacade où qu'elle puisse la conduire (fig. 6). La dernière version que je connaisse de ce motif est une aquarelle du peintre Berlinois Klaus Fussmann (1987). Elle mérite, rien qu'en raison de l'interprétation personnelle du peintre, une attention toute particulière[23].

Le lieu de l'enlèvement dans le mythe antique est évidemment la Phénicie, comme l'implique le nom de Phénix duquel Homère désigne le père d'Europe. Dans des versions plus récentes la jeune fille est évoquée comme étant la fille d'Agénor, roi de Tyr ou de Sidon. Ces deux variantes impliquent un contact entre Phéniciens peuplant l'actuel Liban et Grecs. Si nous suivons la deuxième version, Agénor avait eu en plus de sa fille Europe, plusieurs fils qui tous portent des noms significatifs: Phénix (Phénicie), Cilix (Cilicie), Cadmos, le héro fondateur de Thèbes (Cadméée), Thasos, le héro de l'île homonyme en mer Egée septentrionale, et Phinée qui dans la légende des Argonautes est mentionné en tant que roi de Thrace. Dans le mythe, leur père les envoie à la recherche de leur soeur, mais ils ne reviendront jamais dans leur patrie[24].

En somme la mythologie reflète les relations multiples et les influences réciproques entre le monde grec et le monde phénicien pendant l'époque obscure nommée 'Dark Ages' (12ème - 8ème siècle av. JC)[25]. Nous n'évoquerons ce thème qu'en considérant deux exemples représentatifs. Tous deux se réfèrent à la présence de Phéniciens en mer Egée et sont rapportés par Hérodote. Dans le premier texte, il s'agit du culte d'Héraclès qui intéressait alors l'historien.

'Pour en savoir plus (sur Héraclès) je me rendis même à Tyr, en Phénicie, parce que j'avais entendu dire qu'il y avait un temple dédié à Héraclès. Je l'y trouvai, richement orné et rempli d'offrandes. A Tyr j'ai visité un autre temple d'Héraclès qui portait l'épithète de Thasos. C'est ainsi que je partis pour Thasos et y trouvai un temple construit par les Phéniciens. A la recherche d'Europe ils avaient fondé Thasos' (Hérodote, 2, 44, 1 - 4).

Malgré une autre mention chez Hérodote de la découverte d'une mine installée par les Phéniciens, sur l'île, et de traces archéologiques d'activités phéniciennes en mer Egée septentrionale[26], la valeur historique de son récit éveille chez les chercheurs actuels un certain scepticisme[27]; cependant il semble légitime de retenir que les faits rapportés par Hérodote montrent que le mythe reflète l'existence de relations entre les Phéniciens et les îles grecques.

Il en va de même de la façon dont Hérodote voit dans l'apparition de l'écriture grecque, l'adaptation de l'alphabet phénicien:[28]

'Les Phéniciens arrivés avec Cadmos (en Grèce', raconte Hérodote(5, 58 - 59), 'ont apporté, en s'y installant (en Béotie) (Thèbes = Cadmée), aux Grecs, leurs arts et leurs sciences en particulier celui de l'écriture lettrée. Au début les Cadméens utilisaient les mêmes signes que les autres Phéniciens. Plus tard, simultanément à leur langue, leur écriture se transforma. La tribu grecque des Ioniens, à cette époque, proche voisine, se fit enseigner les signes graphiques des Phéniciens les changea un peu et les désigna sous le nom de "Phéniciens" - *Φοινικήια: τὰ τῶν Φοινίκων γράμματα*. Ce qui était tout à fait justifié puisque les Phéniciens les avaient introduits... J'ai vu de mes propres yeux des signes de cette époque dans le sanctuaire d'Apollon-Isménios à Thèbes en Béotie...'

Il n'est nul besoin d'entrer dans les détails concernant l'apparition de l'écriture grecque[29], notons simplement que la forme des signes archaïques correspond en grande partie à celle des signes de l'alphabet du sémite ancien, que, toutefois, certains signes se virent doter de nouvelles valeurs phonétiques de voyelles: le caractère 'aleph' (le boeuf), senti comme consonne en sémite se transforma en grec en *ἄλφα*, prit donc la valeur de la voyelle a. Notre terminologie alphabétique reflète la génèse de cette écriture dont Hérodote rapporte l'essentiel de façon correcte, dans son récit du mythe de Cadmos. La presse a dernièrement fait état du 'déchiffrement' du célèbre 'disque de Phaistos' par une enseignante de Duisbourg[30]. La méthode employée (que son résultat soit correct ou non) s'intègre dans le contexte que nous venons de décrire, de lecture à partir de signes sémites.

Le disque d'argile couvert de signes et de hiéroglyphes a été trouvé dans le palais minoen de Phaistos dans le sud de la Crète. Nous savons que la Crète est l'île où Zeus conduisit Europe après l'avoir enlevée et pour reprendre le titre populaire de Hans-Georg Wunderlich "Où le taureau apporta Europe"[31]. Laissons de côté sa thèse interprétant la fonction des palais minoens comme étant des nécropoles immenses, des villes pour les morts. L'exposition que nous inaugurons aujourd'hui dans les Musée du Niederrhein informe suffisamment sur les fonctions sociales, politiques, économiques et religieuses des palais de Phaistos, Cnossos, Mallia, Haghia Triada, Zacros ou Archanes, centres de la vie culturelle crétoise[32].

Située à la rencontre de l'Egypte, de la Phénicie, de la Grèce, la Crète a la juste réputation d'avoir été le berceau de la culture européenne. Dans le mythe, c'est ici que Zeus - *Κρηταγενής* - fut nourri dans une grotte du Mont Ida ou Dicté du lait de la chèvre Amalthée et du miel des abeilles sacrées. Les fonctions multiples de ce Dieu du ciel et des phénomènes météorologiques, font apparaître de même que la lecture des épopées qui lui sont consacrées également des influences orientales (El, Hadad, Baalim).[33] La tradition ultérieure qui voulut que sa tombe se trouvât en Crète et qui valut au Crétois leur réputation de menteurs[34] devrait être le résultat d'une assimilation syncrétique du Dieu avec Osiris, l'Egyptien, dieu des puissances végétantes, du périssable.[35]

La tradition de l'enlèvement d'Europe, de son arrivée en Crète où Zeus s'unit à elle soit sur le Mont Ida soit près de Gortyne, fait apparaître une fusion du mythe et de cultes locaux originaux. Dans notre imagination, imprégnée qu'elle est de témoignages de l'art figuratif, nous associons le mythe d'Europe à la femme assise sur le dos du taureau. Dans l'antiquité, le motif n'est vu aucunement si précisément: une femme assise à cheval sur un taureau n'est pas obligatoirement identifiée à Europe[36] et vice versa, Europe peut être identifiée sans la présence du taureau.[37] Le centre du culte crétois rendu à Europe devrait être Gortyne sur le Lernaios dans la plaine de Mesara, là où la princesse s'est donnée, sous un platane, au père des dieux. Au 5ème siècle av. JC, des monnaies de cette ville représentent la figure traditionnelle de la femme au taureau[38] mais on peut également identifier Europe dans la silhouette de cette jeune femme du 4ème siècle, assise sur la couronne d'un saule.[39] Sur un statère plus récent (300 av. JC), on la voit s'unir à Zeus a pris la forme d'un aigle aux ailes largement déployées (fig. 7).[40] Dans les deux cas cependant, le taureau est représenté sur le revers de la monnaie.

En compagnie du taureau c'est la *Πότνια ταυρῶν*, celle qui exerce son autorité sur le fauve, ou d'une façon plus générale la *Πότνια θηρῶν*, celle qui sait se faire obéir des animaux.[41] Nous voyons ici aussi apparaître des traits communs aux cultes orientaux de Astarte, Mâ Bellone, Mater Deum Magna Idaea.[42] Dans le culte minoen, le taureau joue un rôle capital, comme nous le savons. Les nombreuses représentations du 16ème et 15ème siècles trouvées dans le palais de Cnossos, comme, par exemple, le haut-relief peint sur le portique nord ou le rhyton de stéatite provenant du petit palais, tout comme les tauromachies crétoises telles qu'elles sont représentées par exemple sur une fresque montrant les diverses phases acrobatiques de ce sport[43], en sont une preuve tangible. Rappelons, dans ce contexte, le mythe de Pasiphaé qui après s'être unie au taureau émergeant de l'ocean (*ἱερὸς γάμος*) donna le jour au Minotaure[44]. Nous ne pouvons ici traiter les différents niveaux de la naissance de ce culte mais nous nous devons de noter que le mythe d'Europe comprend des éléments orientaux, minoens et grecs et qu'il reflète les influences réciproques de ces diverses cultures.

La mention la plus ancienne d'Europe utilisée en tant que terme géographique se trouve dans l'hymne à l'Apollon de Delphes attribué à Homère (600 av. JC), qui implique un recoupement avec l'idée déjà esquissée d'une diffusion du culte archaïque rendu à Europe dans le nord et le centre de la Grèce. Ce sont ces mêmes régions qui y sont désignées sous le terme d'Europe et ainsi nettement séparées des autres régions mentionnées: le Péloponnèse, les îles Grecques. De partout, les Grecs doivent se rendre au Temple de l'Apollon de Delphes pour consulter l'oracle:

'Tous, ceux qui vivent dans le riche Péloponnèse, ceux qui habitent l'Europe et les îles ceintes de la mer' ((Hom)) hymne à Apollon 290 s.)

Cette façon de différencier entre les régions montre clairement qu'Europe ne désigne ici pas encore un continent mais la partie continentale de la Grèce à l'exception du Péloponnèse. C'est seulement vers la fin du 8ème siècle que la signification s'élargit et que l'emploi du terme se répand, dans le contexte des guerres Médiques. Les origines de cette évolution étaient déjà pour Hérodote (4, 45, 4-5) un mystère:

'A propos de l'Europe nul ne sait si elle

est entourée de mers, ni d'où elle tient sont nom, nul ne sait non plus qui le lui imposa à moins que nous ne soyons prêts à accepter qu'elle le reçût de la Tyrienne Europa... Mais selon toute évidence cette Europa - là était originaire d'Asie et ne foula jamais le sol de ce que les Grecs nomment présentement Europe - ἐς τὴν γῆν ταύτην, ἥτις νῦν ὑπὸ Ἑλλήνων Εὐρώπη καλέεται. Bien plus, elle est venue de Phénicie en Crète et de là a atteint la Lycie.'

La première carte fut dessinée par Anaximandre, disciple de Thalès, vers le milieu du 6ème siècle, puis élaborée de manière plus détaillée par Hécatée de Milet vers l'an 500 av. JC.[45] partant d'un disque terrestre, baigné par Océan qui l'entoure, le géographe prit la Méditerranée comme axe central, se prolongeant par la Mer Noire et la Mer Caspienne à l'est. Cet axe central sépare l'Europe au nord de l'Asie au sud, la Lybie, c'est à dire l'Afrique, étant vue comme appartenant à l'Asie. La désignation du continent au nord sous le terme d'Europe résulterait vraisemblablement d'un transfert du nom employé pour désigner la Grèce centrale à toutes les régions limitrophes au nord et à l'ouest (pars pro toto). L'Asie, selon Hérodote (1, 4, 4) qui plus tard verra la Libye ou l'Afrique comme un troisième continent[46], constitue le territoire des Achéménides: 'Les Perses considèrent comme à eux l'Asie et les peuples barbares qui l'habitent, mais ils tiennent l'Europe et le monde Grec pour un pays à part.' La frontière naturelle est formée par la Propontide (la Mer de Marmara), avec l'Hellespont (les Dardanelles) au sud et le Bosphore au nord.

Il est étonnant, dans ce contexte, que le terme d'Europe soit employé par Héodote plus spécialement pour désigner la région proche du territoire Perse, c'est à dire la région située au nord et à l'ouest de la Propontide. Ainsi cet historien (7, 8, §1) fait dire au Grand Roi Xerxès, en conseil de guerre, alors qu'il explique son offensive contre la Grèce, la remarque suivante: 'J'ai intention de jeter un pont sur l'Hellespont et puis je vais conduire mon armée à travers l'Europe contre la Grèce - μέλλω ξεύξας τὸν Ἑλλήσποντον ἐλᾶν στρατὸν διὰ τῆς Εὐρώπης ἐπὶ τὴν Ἑλλάδα.[47] Cette application restreinte du terme d'Europe à la Grèce septentrionale se trouve à plusieurs reprises chez Hérodote, nous y reviendrons, même si ce n'est pas toujours aussi explicitement: c'est ainsi que Darius I après l'échec de sa campagne contre les Scythes laisse Megabazos comme statège en Europe, concrètement en Thrace, où il doit déplacer les Péoniens ἐκ τῆς Εὐρώπης ἐς τὴν Ἀσίαν.[48]

Lorsque Hérodote emploie le terme d'Europe dans son sens restreint, il l'applique à la région habitée par les Thraces, peut-être y inclut-il une partie de la Macédoine, l'élargit à toute la Grèce septentrionale y compris à la Thessalie, lorsqu'il s'agit pour lui de décrire les prouesses guerrières de Xerxès, pour séparer clairement ces régions de 'Hellas', la Grèce, le pays des Héllènes[49]; d'autre part, il l'applique également à tout le continent quand il met dans la bouche du général Mardonios, au conseil de guerre de Xerxès, les mots suivants: 'Les Ioniens établis en Europe - Ἴωναι οἱ ἐν τῇ Εὐρώπῃ - contre lesquels le Grand Roi va conduire toutes ses troupes de l'Asie - πλῆθος τὸ ἐκ τῆς Ἀσίης.[50] A la suite des conflits opposant l'Empire Perse et la Grèce, on voit apparaître la polarisation entre l'Asie et l'Europe, conflit qui se résume comme conflit est-ouest. Les victoires de Marathon, Salamine, Platées donnaient aux Grecs le halo des vainqueurs, des sauveurs de l'Europe face au despotisme oriental. Remarquons au passage que les Grecs se sentaient, depuis le début du 7ème siècle, par delà les limites continentales, membres d'une communauté hellénique.[51] A quelques restrictions près, on pourrait même parler d'une conscience nationale hellénique qui se manifeste par des liens de parenté, la même langue, une religion commune, des moeurs comparables à tous les Grecs[52] bien qu'ils soient, politiquement parlant, citoyens d'une multitude de Cités souveraines (Poleis). Dans le cadre de la discussion, brûlante d'actualité, concernant l'existence d'un état allemand centraliste, cet aspect ne manque pas d'intérêt.

Chez Hérodote, la frontière naturelle à l'extrème est, est le légendaire Araxe frontière entre l'Asie et l'Europe; puis le Tanaïs (le Don) voire le Phase en Colchide au sud du Caucase.[53] L'historien ne fait aucune mention d'un élargissement du continent vers l'ouest ni vers le nord. C'est après le voyage de Pythéas de Marseille à la Thulé légendaire vers l'an 300 av. JC que des représentations plus précises prennent forme.[54] Eratosthène en donnera une représentation cartographique.[55] A l'époque romaine une expédition de reconnaissance vers les Orcades conduite par Iulius Agricola en confirmera partiellement les données.[56] Vers le milieu du 2ème siècle de notre ère, le mathématicien, astronome et géographe Claude Ptolémée dans son "Introduction à la géographie" - γεωγραφικὴ ὑπήγησις - résuma la somme des connaissances acquises jusque - à.[57] Ces connaissances, autant qu'on le sache, restèrent acceptées et reconnues pendant tout le moyen-âge, jusqu'au début des temps modernes. La découverte de l'Amérique, alors qu'on cherchait une voie de passage pour atteindre les Indes par l'Ouest, résulte de calculs effectués sur la base des données de Ptolémée. Ce n'est qu'avec Gérard Mercator et sa nouvelle technique de projection que les bases d'une cartographie scientifique furent jetées.[58] Ce développement extrêmement intéressant ne fait malheureusement pas partie de notre sujet et nous ne pourrons l'aborder ici.

L'Europe, ce nom de continent, s'était déjà affirmé au 5ème siècle av. JC et désignait la région allant de l'Atlantique au Don en passant par le prolongement du Bosphore et des Dardanelles. La Crète se retrouva, d'ailleurs, seulement après la mort d'Hérodote, rattachée à l'Europe.[59] Très tôt, ces limites géographiques ont eu des conséquences sur la manière d'envisager une typologie des habitants du continent, à faire ressortir une antithèse entre européens et asiatiques. Déjà dans le texte pseudo-hippocratique "De l'environnement" on voit apparaître ce contraste établi non pas historiquement mais anthropologiquement.[60] En raison de conditions climatiques et matérielles, les asiatiques sont bien plus équilibrés, plus doux et plus pacifiques que les européens, qui eux sont actifs, rudes, et guerriers:

'Les changements répétés de saisons et de temps' (selon ps. Hippocrate aër. 23, p. I 67 Kühlewein) 'activent la rudesse et affaiblissent la douceur et l'aménité; c'est pourquoi je crois les Européens plus courageux que les Asiatiques. Car dans cette éternelle uniformité (de conditions climatiques) naissent légèreté et paresse tandis que dans les contrées soumises à des changements brusques et répétés, se développent force de tempérament et d'esprit. De la tranquillité paresseuse et de l'indifférence vient la lacheté alors que l'endurcissement et l'habitude à supporter sa peine engendrent le courage.'

Cette typologie est aussi riche en conséquences pour la constitution physique des êtres humains et le texte tient compte des différences régionales à l'intérieur de chaque continent. De façon généale, à quelques rares exceptions près, les Européens seraient plutôt de haute stature, les Asiatiques minces et petits.

Il est possible de retrouver des traits de cette typologie dans les personnifications d'Europe. L'allégorie certes la plus connue devrait être celle de l'escalier de la Résidence de Würzburg par Giovanni Battista Tiepolo (1751/53).[61] Son 'univers' présente les quatre continents sous des formes féminines respectivement juchées sur un animal symbolique: Amérique coiffée d'une couronne emplumée se trouve sur un alligator, Afrique sur le dromadaire, Asie sur un éléphant des Indes et finalement Europe sur son taureau mythique (fig. 8), contrastant par son apparence massive avec Asie représentée, elle, élancée. Asie et Europe portent des tuniques montantes tandis que les continents du 'tiers monde' ont le buste nu.

La gravure de Philippe Galle symbolisant l'impérialisme de l'Europe sous la forme d'une Walkyrie couronnée, un sceptre à la main,[62] nous offre égalementf une vue intéressante de cette typologie. Semblablement, Césare Ripa réalisa une personnification d'Europe, Reine du Monde, dans son "Iconologie" (1603). Le taureau y a été remplacé par un cheval qui doit avoir la fonction de souligner la position royale que tient le continent européen (fig. 9)[63] Dans l'iconologie ayant trait à la personnification primitive du continent européen, le taureau du mythe ne jouait aucun rôle. On voit bien une forme féminine sur un taureau[64] sur une détrempe sur toile enchaulée (1040 - 80), dans le cadre du jugement universel, mais il s'agit ici non pas d'Europe mais d'une allégorie de la terre opposé à la mer qui, elle-même, est symbolisée par une néréide sur un dragon marin.

De l'époque antique il ne nous est parvenu qu'un seul témoignage certain se rapportant au continent: Le relief du Palais Chigi (1er siècle av. JC) présente une allégorie d'Europe à gauche et d'Asie à droite, toutes deux couronnées et portant le chiton, arborant un boucllerd, illustré d'une scène de bataille (fig. 10).[65] L'identification en est possible grâce à l'inscription qui caractérise cette scène comme celle d'un conflit opposant l'orient à l'occident; concrètement, il s'agit de la bataille de Gaugamela-Arbela, où Alexandre remporta la victoire sur la Grand Roi Darius (III).

En substance il s'agit d'un conflit opposant l'Est à l'Ouest, l'Europe vers l'Asie tel qu'il a été encore et encore représenté avec de nombreuses variations idéologiques depuis les guerres Médiques. Les frontières géographiques, selon les situations, ne sont appréhendées que superficiellement, qu'en tant que données secondaires. C'est ainsi qu'Appien localise le champ de bataille de Philippes,[66] où Brutus et Cassius trouvèrent la mort en 42 av. JC, près du col principal entre l'Asie et l'Europe, à huit stades (environ 1,5 km) du δίοδος ἐς τὴν Ἀσίαν τε καὶ Εὐρώπην. D'après cette version d'Appien, il est évident que l'Est et l'Ouest seraient mesurés à la hauteur de Kavala en Macédoine.

En conclusion, survolons à nouveau la terminologie géographique: il est étonnant de remarquer que dans la classification entraînée par la réorganisation dioclétienne, Europe désigne une des plus petites provinces romaines,[67] la région située immédiatement dans l'arrière pays de Byzance, région qui est directement limitrophe de l'Asie (fig. 11).[68] Ce phénomène de restriction territoriale de ce qu'on désigne sous le terme d'Europe, nous l'avons déjà rencontré chez Hérodote. La Province Europe de la basse antiquité, partie du diocèse de Thrace, est la partie la plus exposée du continent dont elle porte le nom. On pourrait interpréter sémantiquement ce phénomène comme une forme de catachrèse.

Sans avoir besoin de l'étendre beaucoup plus, le territoire de la Province de la basse antiquité désigné sous le nom d'Europe appartient territorialement à la Turquie. Selon les opinions politiques, on pourrait juger d'un résultat d'un long développement historique comme le dernier bastion de l'Asie en Europe. Considérant l'évolution de la Communauté Européenne, je me permettrai d'y voir un signe vers une intégration ou association possible de la Turquie. L'idéologie politique des Romains et leur conception ambitieuse de pouvoir universel laissaient de côté toutes les données concernant les frontières continentales, européennes, asiatiques ou africaines. Cet aspect peut offrir des perspectives positives, si on renie tous les éléments idéologiques et si on le prend au sens de ce que Kant a nommé: "Idée d'une histoire générale intentionellement cosmopolite".[69]

*Exposé tenu dans le cadre des "Accents" de Duisbourg "L'Europe, notre foyer" (24. 4. 1990); les notes ont été ajoutées au manuscript à l'impression, les illustrations n'ont pû être reproduites que dans un nombre limité.

Archäologischer Teil

Kreta. Das Erwachen Europas – aus archäologischer Sicht

Wolfgang Schiering

Die phönikische Königstochter Europa wird in der Sage von Zeus, der sich in einen zahmen weißen Stier verwandelt hat, angelockt und, als sie sich vertrauensvoll auf dessen Rücken setzt, übers Meer nach Kreta entführt. Die drei Söhne, die sie dort dem Göttervater gebar, hießen Minos, Rhadamanthys und Sarpedon. Minos wurde König von Knossos, Rhadamanthys Herrscher von Phaistos. Europa gab ihren Namen zwar dem ganzen Kontinent, doch steht Kreta nicht nur in dieser griechischen Sage, die wie kaum eine andere die antike und die neuere Kunst (bis zu Max Beckmann) beschäftigt hat, sondern auch archäologisch und historisch am Anfang der europäischen Geschichte.

Kreta meint in diesem Zusammenhang das nach dem Sohn von Zeus und Europa heute „minoisch" genannte Kreta, dessen Blütezeit in der zweiten Hälfte des 3. Jahrtausends einsetzte und einen ersten Höhepunkt im 19. Jahrhundert, einen zweiten im 17. und 16. Jahrhundert hatte. Die Insel spielte freilich, was nicht vergessen werden soll, auch später, als dorische Griechen ihre Herren waren und nach der Überlieferung hundert Städte zum Erblühen brachten, kulturell wieder eine bedeutende Rolle. Im 8. und 7. Jahrhundert v. Chr., der sog. orientalisierenden Epoche Griechenlands, erfüllte Kreta nämlich nicht nur eine führende Mittlerrolle zwischen dem Orient (Nordsyrien – Phönikien) und Griechenland, sondern es übernahm im 7. Jahrhundert auch eine herausragende Stellung bei der Entstehung der frühgriechischen Plastik, die in der antiken Literatur mit einem neuen, zweiten Daidalos in Verbindung gebracht wurde. Aber auch noch viel später, in byzantinischer Zeit, bis hin zum Kreter El Greco (Theotokopoulos) hatte das vom Apostel Paulus so unfreundlich bedachte Kreta einen europäischen Rang.

Kommen wir zum ersten Daidalos, dem Tausendkünstler des Königs Minos zurück. Er war es, der nach der Sage das Labyrinth in Knossos gebaut hat. Wir wissen längst, daß

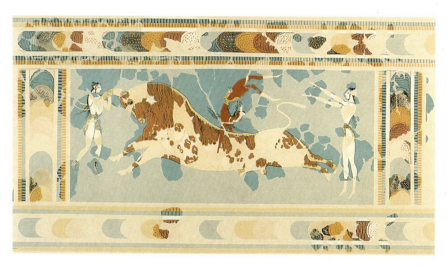

12 Stierspielfresko aus Knossos. Um 1500 v. Chr. Heraklion, Archäologisches Museum.

diese sagenhafte Wohnstatt des aus einer unnatürlichen Verbindung der Minosgattin Pasiphae mit einem Stier Poseidons hervorgegangenen Minotauros auf den Palast der Herren von Knossos zurückgeht, den der englische Archäologe Sir Arthur Evans zu Beginn unseres Jahrhunderts in der Nähe des heutigen Heraklion ausgegraben und teilweise rekonstruiert hat. Unsere Kenntnis aber vom Zeusstier der Europa, vom Poseidonstier der Pasiphae und vom Stiermenschen Minotauros weist auch schon ohne entsprechende archäologische Funde auf eine außerordentliche Bedeutung des Stieres in den religiösen Vorstellungen der minoischen Kreter hin. Die Funde bestätigen einen Stierkult nicht nur durch viele Darstellungen des letztlich wohl immer geheimnisvoll bleibenden kretischen Stierspringens (Abb. 12), sondern auch durch zahllose andere Stier- und Stiermenschdarstellungen (Abb. 13), durch mehr oder weniger abstrakt wiedergegebene Stierhörner sowie große und kleine Nachahmungen und Darstellungen der Doppelaxt, mit der das Stieropfer vollzogen worden ist.

Das minoische Kreta entwickelte die erste Hochkultur Europas, die mit einem hierarchisch aufgebauten und bürokratisch organisierten, mehr und mehr zentralistischen Wirtschafts- und Verwaltungssystem sowie festen, engstens miteinander verquickten religiösen und herrschaftlichen Ordnungen den Hochkulturen Ägyptens und des Vorderen Orients zu vergleichen und an die Seite zu stellen ist. Auch diese umfassende Aussage läßt sich durch ausgegrabene Bauten und mit Hilfe unzähliger Funde archäologisch belegen. Von den architektonischen Zeugnissen geben die Überreste der Paläste in Knossos, Phaistos, Mallia und Kato Zakros die meisten Auskünfte. Wichtige Quellen sind auch die sog. Villen (Gutshöfe), die eine Art Zwischenstellung zwischen den Palästen und den städtischen oder ländlichen Siedlungen einnehmen: Hagia Triada, Tylissos, Vathypetron etc. Die Städte, welche die Paläste umgaben, müssen noch besser erforscht werden. Sie liefern aber auch heute schon wichtige Anhaltspunkte, so daß man sich vorsichtig ein Bild etwa von den Beziehungen zwischen Stadt und Palast machen kann. Aussagen über den Wohlstand der Städte, über technische Leistungen, Werkstätten, Verwaltungsarbeiten, Hafenanlagen und Kultisches lassen auch Stadtgrabungen zu, für die ein Palast oder ein palastartiges Zentrum bisher noch fehlt. Hinzu kommen schließlich zahlreiche kleinere Anlagen von meist landwirtschaftlichem Charakter. Nicht zu verges-

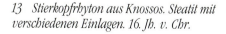

13 Stierkopfrhyton aus Knossos. Steatit mit verschiedenen Einlagen. 16. Jh. v. Chr.

14 Grundriß des Palastes von Mallia (nach C. Tiré–H. van Effenterre).

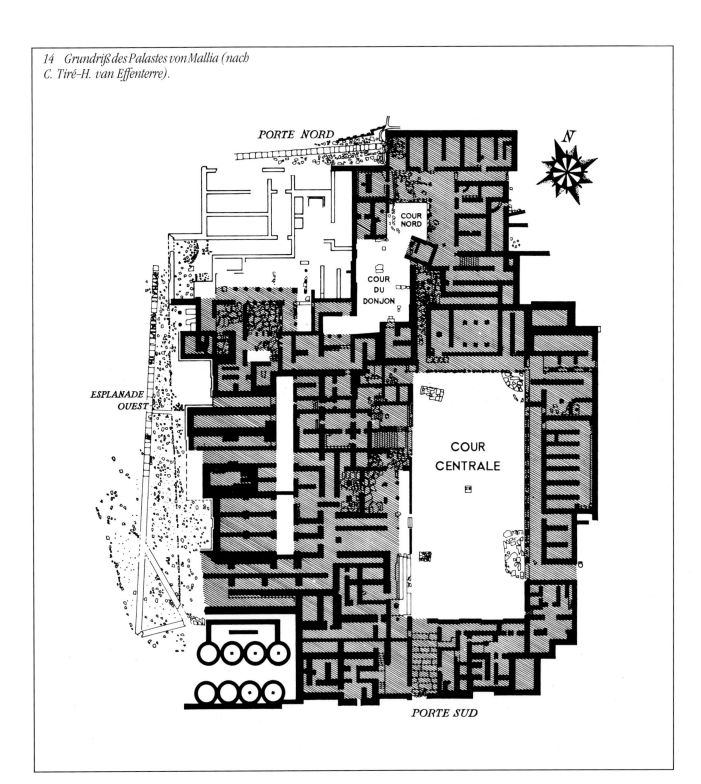

sen sind aber auch Gräber, die gelegentlich besser und vollständiger überliefert sind als die zugehörigen, nicht selten sogar noch ganz unbekannten Siedlungen. Von diesen Gräbern erhellen vor allem große Familienanlagen, sowohl frühe Rundbauten des 3. und frühen 2. Jahrtausends als auch stattliche fürstliche Grabbauten wie das sog. Tempelgrab bei Knossos, unsere Kenntnisse der gesellschaftlichen Strukturen des minoischen Kreta.

Zu unserem Wissen über die Lebensvorgänge in den Palästen (Abb. 14), Villen und Häusern der minoischen Kreter verhelfen die baulichen Anlagen selbst (Höfe, Wege und Treppen, Hallen, Schreine und Kultbecken, Magazine und Werkstätten), aber auch Überreste von Wandschmuck (Fresken und Stuckreliefs) und Mobiliar (Throne und anderes Mobliar, Ton- und Steingefäße). Interessanterweise können auch vergleichsweise bescheidene Häuser Einrichtungen aufweisen (Hof, Halle, Kultbecken, Obergeschoß), die den qualitativen Abstand zu Villa und Palast verringern und das Leben hier und dort mehr graduell als grundsätzlich unterscheiden lassen. In der unter deutlichen kretisch-minoischen Einflüssen entstandenen Stadt bei Akrotiri auf Thera waren sogar alle Wohnhäuser mit Fresken ausgemalt. Die teils kultischen Themen erinnern dort an die von kretischen Palästen oder Villen bekannten Darstellungen. Kultisches und Repräsentatives findet sich also über Palast und Villa hinaus auch in den Siedlungen in auffallend enger Verbindung. Privates scheint in Wohnhäusern allerdings leichter erkennbar zu sein als in den Palästen, wo selbst Küchen nur schwer auszumachen sind.

Auf den profanen, bürokratisch bestimmten Alltag in den Palästen und Villen weisen außer architektonischen Einrichtungen, wie den vielen Magazinen, Lagerräumen, Schatzkammern, Ölmühlen, Weinpressen, Vorratsgefäßen etc., die Schrift- und Siegelerzeugnisse hin, die Einblicke in die bürokratischen Verwaltungsformen geben. Den kultischen Bereich erschließen in den Palästen, Villen, Wohnhäusern wie auch in den monumentalen Gräbern verschiedenartige Kulträume, die sich baulich oder von ihrem Inventar her (Kultgeräte, Kultsymbole, Darstellungen) als solche ausweisen. Draußen sind es Heiligtümer auf Berggipfeln oder in Kulthöhlen.

Die wirtschaftliche, politische und religiöse Ordnung ist in der kretisch-minoischen Kultur wahrscheinlich weder einseitig nur aus familiärem Wachstum und sozialen oder politischen Veränderungen entstanden, wie sie aus der Siedlungsgeschichte der zweiten Hälfte des 3. Jahrtausends abgelesen werden können, noch einseitig durch äußere Einflüsse aus

15 *Fayencestatuette einer Göttin oder Priesterin aus Knossos. 17. Jh. v. Chr. Heraklion, Archäologisches Museum.*

Ägypten und dem Vorderen Orient. Die innere Expansion hat, von der Inselsituation und der geographischen Lage unterstützt, vielmehr zwangsläufig auch zu einer äußeren, übrigens auch nach Norden (Kykladen) und Westen (Liparische Inseln) gerichteten Expansion geführt, aus deren Kontakten die weniger kriegerischen als seetüchtigen und von Hause aus zum Handel begabten Kreter erst zu begierigen Schülern, dann zu Partnern der älteren Kulturländer geworden sind.

Im Mittelpunkt des kretischen Wirtschafts- und Handelssystems stand offensichtlich die Magazinwirtschaft, d. h. allem voran eine Naturalienwirtschaft mit Erzeugnissen, die in großen Tonpithoi, in versenkten Steinkisten oder in geeigneten Gefäßen aufbewahrt worden sind (Getreide, Honig, Oliven, Öl, Wein). Eine sehr wichtige Rolle muß daneben die für Schiffs- und Hausbau unentbehrliche Holzwirtschaft gespielt haben. Auch die Produkte einer heimischen Metallindustrie (von einfachen Geräten über Waffen bis zu kunstvollen Gefäßen etc.) gehörten mit dem notwendigen, weitgehend importierten Rohmaterial in den Bereich der Magazinwirtschaft, ebenso Töpfereien, Werkstätten für steinerne Geräte (Lampen) und Gefäße, wie sie sich in den Palästen von Knossos und Kato Zakros durch Materialfunde lokalisieren lassen, weiterhin Manufakturen, die mit edlem Material (Elfenbein und Edelmetallen) gearbeitet haben, Material, das wie Kupfer usw. auch nur als Rohstoff magaziniert und gehandelt wurde. Nicht zu vergessen ist schließlich das weite Gebiet der Textilverarbeitung bis hin zur kostbaren privaten und kultischen Kleidermode der minoischen Frau (Abb. 15, 16). Magazinierung einheimischer und importierter Roh- und Fertigprodukte, eigene Verarbeitung im Palastbereich und Handel müssen eng ineinandergegriffen haben.

Die Bindung einer derart komplexen Magazin- und Handelswirtschaft an die Paläste und die großen „Villen" (Gutshöfe) illustrieren

16 „La Petite Parisienne". Freskofragment aus Knossos. 15. Jh. v. Chr. Heraklion, Archäologisches Museum.

Funde und Darstellungen, die Einblick in das Leben der minoischen Gesellschaft geben. Was Darstellungen wie das knossische Freskofragment der sog. Petite Parisienne (Abb. 16) dem heutigen Betrachter zeigen, ist weniger eine „Hofkunst" um des „Hofes", des Kultes oder gar der Kunst willen als der gleichsam natürliche, in künstlerische Formen gebrachte Aus- und Überfluß einer höchst erfolgreichen Wirtschaftsform, deren glückliche Handhabung sich offenbar auf einen recht breiten Kreis der Bevölkerung niedergeschlagen hat. Solche Auswirkungen einer florierenden Wirtschaft, die ohne einen einträglichen und die eigenen Lebensformen zugleich stimulierenden Außenhandel kaum denkbar wäre, hat es schon in der „Vorpalastzeit" der zweiten Hälfte des 3. Jahrtausends gegeben, als z. B. reiche Bewohner von Mochlos ihren Toten Totenhäuser errichtet und kostbare Grabgaben mitgegeben haben. Höhepunkte dessen, was man als

17 Goldener Anhänger mit zwei Bienen aus der Nekropole von Mallia. 19. Jh. v. Chr. Heraklion, Archäologisches Museum.

„höfische Kunst" bezeichnen könnte, zeigen für die „Altpalastzeit" des 19. Jahrhunderts der aus der Nekropole von Mallia stammende goldene Anhänger mit zwei Bienen (Abb. 17), für das 17. Jahrhundert der gleichfalls in Mallia gefundene Szepterkopf aus Steatit, der zur einen Hälfte Panther, zur anderen Axt ist (Abb. 18) oder für die „Jungpalastzeit" des 16. Jahrhunderts ein gleichfalls aus Speckstein geschnittener Stierkopf, der im Palast von Knossos als kostbares Spendegefäß verwendet worden ist (Abb. 13).

Bei einer Kultur, in der Leben und Kult so eng miteinander verflochten waren, ist es auch in der Kunst nicht immer leicht, die ursprünglich profanen oder kultischen Zwecke der Funde zu unterscheiden. Das zeigt sich et-

18 Kopf eines Szepters aus Schiefer in Pantherform aus Mallia. 17. Jh. v. Chr. Heraklion, Archäologisches Museum.

wa auch im Bereich des von Haus aus profanen Siegelwesens. Siegel mit kultischen Darstellungen nehmen nämlich einen verhältnismäßig breiten Raum ein (Abb. 19). Von den zahllosen anderen Siegeln möchte man allerdings, wie von dem Bienenanhänger in Mallia (Abb. 17) annehmen, daß sie auch dann zunächst einmal im Leben gebraucht wurden, wenn sie schließlich als Grabgaben in Gräber gekommen sind.

Die interessantesten Auskünfte über Leben und Kult geben - wie schon deutlich wurde - die ausgegrabenen Ruinen der Paläste (Abb. 14. u. 20). Diese weisen viele Gemeinsamkeiten auf; so vor allem den Zentralhof als Mittelpunkt des Palastes. Von ihm aus waren - ähnlich wie vom Hof unserer Burgen oder Schlösser - alle Teile des Palastes zu erreichen. Er hatte aber auch als Hof an sich viele Aufgaben zu erfüllen, von denen zumindest die eindeutig nachweisbaren kultischen Funktionen in unseren Burgen und Schlössern keine Parallele hatten. Für das minoische Stierspringen dürften die Zentralhöfe nicht lang genug gewesen sein. Andere (kultische) Spiele und Aufführungen hat es dort aber gewiß gegeben, wie ein bekanntes, freilich stark restauriertes Fresko nahelegt (Abb. 21). Für weitere kultische und profane Begegnungen hatten die Paläste den Westhof auf der Eingangsseite. Dorthin kamen die Leute aus der Stadt, um an bestimmten Veranstaltungen teilzunehmen, für welche die Paläste von Knossos und Phaistos zusätzlich auch noch den Bereich hatten, den die Ausgräber wegen der freigelegten Schautreppen als Theaterareal bezeichnet haben. Auf den Westhof und in den Westflügel wurden aber auch die Naturalien für große runde Silos (auf dem Platz) und für die Pithoi und Steinkisten (in den Magazinen) gebracht, Anlässe zugleich für Erntefeiern mit kultischem Charakter. Die Westfassaden der Paläste waren in Aufbau und Gliederung als stadtseitige Palastfronten mit voller Absicht besonders attraktiv und repräsentativ. Die minoische Palastarchitektur war nämlich gewiß nicht - wie man früher glauben wollte - Zufallsergebnis einer „agglutinierenden" Bauweise (vgl. unten).

Wie deutlich sich eine erste europäische Architektur in der Gestaltung der minoischen Paläste angebahnt hat, die sich mit entsprechenden, den kretischen Architekten nicht unbekannten Bauten des Vorderen Orients messen konnte, das zeigt eindrücklicher noch als die erwähnten Front- und Hofseiten der gewichtigen Westflügel die Nordfassade im Zentralhof von Phaistos (Abb. 22). Mit der durch ein Tor, flankierende Säulen und Nischen betonten Mitte und einer (absichtlich) nur ein wenig abweichenden Symmetrie über die ganze Breite nimmt sie mykenisches und das heißt frühes griechisches Bauen, wie es die monumentale Fassade des „Atreusgrabes" in Mykene

19 Siegelring mit Kultszene. Grabfund von Isopata/Knossos. 15. Jh. v. Chr.

zeigt, bereits vorweg. Auch sonst ist – wie unten noch gezeigt werden soll – Ordnung als künstlerisches Prinzip nicht erst im Mykenischen, sondern bereits im Minoischen unschwer aufzuspüren.

Zunächst aber gilt es festzuhalten, welche anderen Leistungen von der minoischen über die mykenische an die europäische Kultur weitergegeben worden sind. Im technischen Bereich wird man zunächst Ingenieurleistungen nennen, wie Straßen-, Brücken-, Wagen- und Schiffbau, aber auch die von den Palästen und „Villen" bekannte Kanalisation (einschließlich WC). Eindrucksvolle Schiffsdarstellungen, z. B. in einem schönen Wandfresko von Akrotiri auf Thera (Abb. 23), verdeutlichen zusammen mit wenigstens einer neuerdings bekannt gewordenen monumentalen Schiffshalle in

20 Teilansicht des Palastes von Phaistos mit Blick auf die sog. Schautreppe, das Eingangspropylon und den Palasthof (unten).

21 Miniaturfresko aus Knossos mit (kultischer) Versammlung und dreiteiligem Heiligtum. Um 1500 v. Chr. (oben).

23 Schiffsdarstellungen auf einem Fresko aus Akrotiri/Thera. 17./16. Jh. v. Chr.

Kommos auf Kreta und mit all den vielen bekannten und unbekannten technischen und seemännischen Voraussetzungen für die in der späteren griechischen Geschichte (Thukydides) gerühmte Seeherrschaft („Thalassokratie") des Minos den von den mykenischen Griechen übernommenen hohen technischen Standard des ganzen minoischen Seewesens.

Es ist kein Zufall, daß man später in der mythisch verbrämten Gestalt des Daidalos nicht nur den Künstler, sondern wenigstens ebensosehr den Techniker und Erfinder sah, der stellvertretend für alle Technik und Erfindungs-

22 Die Nordfassade des Palasthofes von Phaistos im heutigen Zustand.

kunst des minoischen Kreta stand. Archäologisch können wir Erfindungen oder Vervollkommnungen in der Freskotechnik, im töpferischen Bereich (Temperaturen der Brennöfen, weiße Farbe der sog. Kamaresvasen aus Talk), in der Metallindustrie, in den Werkstätten der Siegelschneider (schnell rotierender „Zeiger") oder bei den Goldschmieden (Filigran, Granulation) nachweisen. Fast alle diese Errungenschaften sind an das mykenische Griechenland weitergegeben worden. Erfinderisch kann man auch nennen, was die minoische Mode, d. h. die Damenmode (Abb. 15, 16) hervorgebracht und dann in der mykenischen Kultur verbreitet hat. Für diese Haute Couture gab es technische Voraussetzungen, wie das Fertigen, Färben und Verzieren der Stoffe, als künstlerische Voraussetzung aber die erfinderische Gestaltung. Das Stierspringen, das zu den minoischen Kultspielen gehörte und im Mykenischen später nicht unbekannt blieb, ist gleichfalls eine Erfindung, so schwierig im Erwerben der erforderlichen Technik, daß spanische Stierkämpfer heute ratlos sind. Ein Prunkschwert aus Mallia kann mit anderen minoischen Schwertern für die minoische Waffen- und Rüstungskunst stehen. Wir kennen aber auch bronzene Helme für den minoischen Krieger. Deshalb kann man sagen, daß das minoische Kreta selbst auf dem Gebiet, das nicht ohne weiteres mit unbefestigten Städten, „Villen" und Palästen, mit unseren Vorstellungen also vom „minoischen Frieden" vereinbar scheint, das Interesse der bekanntlich kampfesfreudigen mykenischen Griechen wecken konnte.

Mit dem bürokratisch organisierten minoischen Verwaltungs- und Wirtschaftssystem sind dank der minoischen Expansion nicht nur architektonische Einheiten wie Repräsentationsräume und Magazine von Kreta auf Inseln der Ägäis, (Thera, Melos, Keos), auf einzelne Städte an der kleinasiatischen Westküste und vor allem auf das griechische Festland übertragen worden, sondern auch die Schreibpraxis und der Gebrauch von Siegeln. Aufgrund eines großen Archivs beschrifteter Tontäfelchen konnten sich mykenische Palastverwaltungen, wie die von Pylos etwa, mit entsprechenden älteren minoischen Einrichtungen, aber

auch mit solchen Ägyptens und des Vorderen Orients vergleichen. Das minoische Kreta hatte schon in der ersten Hälfte des zweiten Jahrtausends Hieroglyphen und auch ein lineares Schriftsystem entwickelt. Keine dieser Schriften kann bis jetzt gelesen werden. Aus der minoischen Linear-A-Schrift aber hat sich die von M. Ventris und J. Chadwick entzifferte und als Schrift einer frühen griechischen Sprache erkannte mykenische Linear-B-Schrift entwickelt. Daß Kreta den entscheidenden Anstoß zu dieser Silbenschrift gegeben hat, die von mykenischen Griechen übrigens auch im nachminoischen Palast von Knossos verwendet worden ist, gehört – auf Europa bezogen – zu den bedeutendsten kulturellen Leistungen des Alten Kreta.

Der griechische Tempel als die wichtigste Wurzel der europäischen Sakralarchitektur hat seinen Ursprung im „Megaron" der mykenischen Baukunst gehabt. Doch gab auch Kreta im Bereich des sakralen Bauens, und zwar mit größeren und kleineren Kulträumen oder mit den sog. Kultfassaden, Anstöße, die weitergewirkt haben. Daß wichtige minoische Kultfeiern in Höfen, im Freien, auf Bergen und in Kulthöhlen stattgefunden haben, wurde oben schon angesprochen. Ebensowenig wie das Megaron, das zu stolzen mykenischen Palastzentren (Tiryns, Pylos usw.) wurde, sind die gewaltigen Wehrmauern aus meist vielkantig zugerichteten großen Blöcken von Kreta aufs griechische Festland gekommen. Diese „kyklopischen Mauern" haben – im Unterschied zum Megaron – in ihrer typischen Form allerdings auch nicht direkt auf die Entwicklung im späteren Griechenland eingewirkt.

Kommen wir abschließend noch einmal auf künstlerische Ordnungsprinzipien zurück, wie wir sie in der minoischen Palastarchitektur (Abb. 14) schon beobachtet haben. Als Beispiele seien ausgewählt der goldene Bienenanhänger aus Mallia (Abb. 17), das Lilienfresko von Amnissos (Abb. 24) und die linsenförmige Tonflasche mit dem Oktopus aus Palaikastro (Abb. 25). Allen drei Darstellungen gemeinsam ist eine symmetrische Anlage: zwei Bienen, drei Lilienstengel, acht Fangarme. Abweichungen von der Symmetrie läßt am schnellsten das Oktopusbild erkennen. Bei genauerem Hinsehen werden Asymmetrien in den kleineren Formen (Knospen, Blüten) des Freskos jedoch ebenso deutlich wie in den eigenwilligen Bewegungen der Fangarme des Oktopus. Allein die Körper und Flügel der Bienen scheinen einander spiegelsymmetrisch genau zu entsprechen. Hier ist es aber vor allem die mit konzentrisch verlaufender Granulation übersäte konvexe Scheibe zwischen den Bienen, deren Position deutlich nach rechts verschoben ist. Außerdem finden sich der kugelförmige „Käfig" über den Bienenköpfen und der Aufhänger darüber nicht im Gleichgewicht mit den Bienen. Ich möchte schließlich auch bezweifeln, daß die drei scheibenförmigen Anhänger – was möglich gewesen wäre – ursprünglich einmal exakt symmetrisch herunterhingen. Also sind alle drei Motive, wie unzählige andere Beispiele in der minoischen Kunst, zugleich geordnet und frei, ruhig und bewegt. Es drängen sich Begriffe wie „freie Ordnung", „geordnete Freiheit", „Bewegung in der Ruhe" oder „Ruhe in der Bewegung" auf. Um dieses Phänomen konkreter fassen zu können, wählen wir von unseren drei Motiven den Oktopus auf der linsenförmigen Tonflasche von Palaikastro (Abb. 25) aus, bei dem die Prinzipien Freiheit und Bewegung eine größere Rolle zu spielen scheinen als die Prinzipien Ordnung und Ruhe.

Auf dem Gefäß ist der Oktopus zweimal dargestellt, einmal auf der einen, einmal auf der anderen Seite. Doch es handelt sich nicht um eine kontinuierliche Darstellung, die man

24 Lilienfresko aus Amnissos. 17./16. Jh. v. Chr. Heraklion, Archäologisches Museum.

25 Tonflasche mit Oktopus-Bemalung aus Palaikastro/Ostkreta. 17./16. Jh. v. Chr. Heraklion, Archäologisches Museum.

ein „Meeresbild" nennen könnte. Auch die vielen Korallen, die Meeresschnecken oder die Seeigel zwischen den Fangarmen des Oktopus sind nicht dazu da, ein Bild vom Leben des Meeres zu wecken, sondern sie sind additiv eingestreut und passen sich – mehr formale als inhaltliche Elemente – im Sinne des „horror vacui" den freien Zwischenräumen an. Der Betrachter sieht auf dieser Flasche, die zwei Seiten hat, also zwei Ausschnitte je als etwas Ganzes und nicht beide Seiten zusammen als ein naturalistisches Bild mit zwei Oktopoden und einer Vielzahl anderer Meeresbewohner. Ausgangspunkt des minoischen Vasenmalers war die Natur also nicht als Einheit, sondern nur als Anreiz zur Verwirklichung einer künstlerischen Vorstellung, die sich in der Vasenmalerei der ersten Hälfte des 2. Jahrtausends in teils großartigen ungegenständlichen Formen (Spiralkompositionen etc.) entwickelt hat (sog. Kamaresstil). Statt solcher ungegenständlichen, jedenfalls nicht sicher benennbaren Ornamente haben die Vasenmaler jetzt u. a. den Oktopus verwendet, weil dieser als eine natürliche Form ideal geeignet war, die Aussage älterer Ornamente zu übernehmen. Eine Interpretation, der Oktopus sei dargestellt, als würde er schnell am Betrachter vorüberhuschen, läßt sich mit Kenntnis moderner Unterwasserfotografie nicht mehr halten. Sie ist heute durch eine Anschauung zu ersetzen, die den Zeichner viel weniger das Leben des Oktopus beobachten, als den gefangenen oder toten Oktopus studieren und dank der künstlerischen Phantasie so ordnen läßt, wie er den überkommenen gestalterischen Vorstellungen entsprach. Nicht Natur, sondern Kunst dominiert, natürliche Bewegung ist in Ruhe gebracht und künstlerischer Bewegung unterworfen, natürliche Freiheit ist künstlerisch geordnet.

So ist ein Motiv entstanden, das verdoppelt, ja beliebig vermehrt werden konnte – wie die Lilien von Amnissos (Abb. 24), fliegende Fische auf einem Fresko aus Melos, die Korallen unseres Oktopusbildes, aber auch die Bau- und Raumelemente der minoischen Architektur. Was die minoischen Künstler dabei im Sinne hatten, war nicht ein Ganzes im späteren und heutigen Sinn, sondern die Summe wohldurchdachter und überlegt aneinandergefügter Teile. Der Minoer sah das Ganze im Teil allein, oder aber in einer Summe des Teils, bzw. der Teile. In letzterem Falle war das Prinzip der Zusammensetzung abermals künstlerischen Ordnungen unterworfen, die als Reihung, als endlicher oder unendlicher Rapport, als symmetrische oder konzentrische Ordnung usw. der jeweiligen Aufgabe angepaßt wurde. Agglutinieren, ein Begriff, den man früher gern für die minoische Baukunst gebraucht hat (vgl. oben), kann für dieses Zusammenwachsen von Teilen stehen, wenn man dabei weniger an natürliche, scheinbar unkontrollierte Verbindungen von Teilen, als an ein bewußtes, geordnetes „Anleimen" (agglutinare) denkt.

Es ist nur selbstverständlich, daß eine Kultur, in deren künstlerischen Aussagen Prinzipien der Ordnung von so grundsätzlicher Bedeutung waren, Ordnung auch in politischer, wirtschaftlicher und religiöser Hinsicht in den Vordergrund ihrer Existenz gestellt hat. Ein ausgeprägter Sinn für Ordnung war also ohne Zweifel eine wesentliche Voraussetzung für die starke Wirkung, die vom minoischen Kreta auf die weitere Entwicklung der griechischen und europäischen Kultur ausgegangen ist.

Die minoische Kultur Kretas: Versuch eines historischen Abrisses

Wolf-Dietrich Niemeier

Die nach Minos, dem mythischen Herrscher von Knossos, minoisch genannte bronzezeitliche Hochkultur Kretas gehört zu jenen Kulturen, aus denen wir über keine lesbaren schriftlichen Quellen verfügen (die minoischen Schriftsysteme sind noch nicht entziffert) und über die wir nur indirekt aus Schriftquellen benachbarter Kulturen hören. Für den Versuch einer Rekonstruktion der Geschichte Kretas in der Bronzezeit sind wir daher fast ausschließlich auf die Interpretation archäologischer Befunde und Funde angewiesen, was kein einfaches und ein nicht immer zu eindeutigen Ergebnissen führendes Unterfangen ist. Die folgende Skizze muß daher in der Kürze des zur Verfügung stehenden Raumes nicht selten vereinfachen und außerdem auf eine Diskussion methodischer Probleme weitgehend verzichten.

Kretas geographische Position bildete eine der wesentlichen Voraussetzungen dafür, daß sich auf dieser Insel die erste Hochkultur westlich der älteren Hochkulturen des Vorderen Orients und Ägyptens entwickeln konnte. Die Insellage bot durch den natürlichen Schutz des Meeres gegen feindliche Invasionen günstige Voraussetzungen für eine kontinuierliche, weitgehend ungestörte Kulturentwicklung. Mit der Entwicklung der Schiffahrt wurde dann das Meer andererseits zu einem wichtigen Kommunikationsmittel mit der Außenwelt (Abb. 23). Die günstige Lage Kretas in etwa gleicher Entfernung von den drei anrainenden Kontinenten Afrika, Asien und Europa ließ die drittgrößte Insel des Mittelmeeres zu einem Sprungbrett zwischen diesen Erdteilen werden.

Nachdem in der Altsteinzeit, in der Kreta wegen des damals sehr viel niedrigeren Meeresspiegels von der Peloponnes ohne große Probleme mit einfachen Booten oder Flößen erreicht werden konnte, einzelne Jäger- und Sammlerhorden die Insel aufgesucht hatten, kamen in der Jungsteinzeit, bald nach 7.000 v. Chr. die ersten permanenten Siedler und ließen sich an der Stelle des späteren 'Palastes' von Knossos nieder. Diese Siedler stammten aus Kleinasien, von wo sie schon eine voll entwickelte gemischte Landwirtschaft mit Ackerbau und Viehzucht mitbrachten. Für die Herstellung von Steinwerkzeugen importierten sie bereits Obsidian (schwarzes, glasartiges Vulkangestein) von der Kykladeninsel Melos.

Anfangs bestand die Bevölkerung des jungsteinzeitlichen Kreta aus wenigen Sippenverbänden, die weit verstreut in offenen Siedlungsplätzen mit Lehmhäusern, aber auch in Höhlen wohnten. Nur allmählich stieg die Bevölkerungszahl an, und erst am Ende der Jungsteinzeit (ca. 4.300 - 3.330 v. Chr.) ist eine deutliche Ausweitung in Anzahl und Verbreitung der Siedlungsplätze festzustellen. Die Siedlung von Knossos besaß damals eine Ausdehnung von ca. 4 ha., was auf eine Bevölkerungszahl von über 1.000 schließen läßt. Wie ethnologische Parallelen zeigen, muß man daher bereits mit der Existenz einer institutionalisierten hierarchischen Gliederung der Gesellschaft rechnen. Hierfür sprechen auch die wenigen exotischen Prestigeobjekte, welche zu jener Zeit nach Knossos kamen: Steingefäße aus Ägypten und Elfenbein aus Syrien.

Für die Siedlungen der frühminoischen Epoche oder Vorpalastzeit (ca. 3.300 - 2.100 v. Chr.) verfügen wir nur über äußerst spärliche Informationen. Bei den wenigen freigelegten Beispielen (Myrtos, Vasiliki) handelt es sich um kleine, ländliche Siedlungen. Architekturreste und Keramikfunde dieser Zeit unter den späteren Palastzentren von Knossos, Phaistos und Malia zeigen jedoch an, daß sich dort bereits recht große Siedlungen befanden. Knossos, die größte von ihnen, nahm im späteren Teil der frühminoischen Epoche bereits eine Fläche von fast 5 ha. ein und hatte zwischen ca. 1.300 und 1.900 Einwohner.

Neben der Größe der Siedlungen, die notwendigerweise die Existenz einer sozialen Schichtung voraussetzt, gibt es hierfür auch weitere Indizien. So besitzen wir Hinweise auf eine differenzierte Arbeitsteilung und spezialisiertes Handwerkertum im vorpalastzeitlichen Kreta. Die um die Mitte des 3. vorchristlichen Jahrtausends auf der gesamten Insel verbreiteten Tongefäße des (nach dem ersten Fundort) sog. Vasiliki-Stils (Abb. 26) sind von so hoher töpferischer Qualität, und ihre reizvollen Dekorationen beruhen auf derart komplizierten

26 Napf und Schnabelkanne mit geflammter Oberfläche (sog. Vasiliki-Stil). Um 2500 v. Chr. Heraklion, Archäologisches Museum.

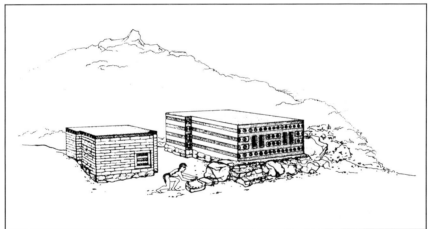

Verfahren (Reduktion, partielle Reoxydation beim Brand), daß sie nur in spezialisierten Produktionszentren hergestellt worden sein können. Ähnliche Entwicklungen sind für die Metallurgie, für die Herstellung von Steingefäßen und Siegeln festzustellen.

In den Bestattungssitten dieser Zeit zeichnet sich bereits deutlich eine soziale Hierarchie ab. So finden sich neben den gebauten Gräbern einer ökonomisch privilegierten Gruppe – in Südkreta Rundgräber mit rechtwinkligen Annexen (Abb. 27), in Nord- und Ostkreta vornehmlich Hausgräber (Abb. 28) – in den gleichen Nekropolen einfache Erdbestattungen sowie bescheidene Beisetzungen in Pithoi (Vorratsgefäßen) und Steinkisten. Die gebauten Rund- und Hausgräber heben sich auch im Reichtum ihrer Grabbeigaben deutlich von den einfacheren Bestattungen ab. Insbesondere in den Elitegräbern von Mochlos und Gournia in Ostkreta ist eine Konzentration von kostbaren Objekten festzustellen. Einige von ihnen können aufgrund zeitgleicher Parallelen im Vorderen Orient als Autoritätssymbole interpretiert werden, wie etwa goldene Diademe (Abb. 29).

Vor den Gräbern mit reicher Ausstattung liegen zumeist gepflasterte Plätze und stehen Altäre (Abb. 28). Diese und die Funde von Kultobjekten auf ihnen zeigen an, daß die betreffenden Gräber den Mittelpunkt ritueller Handlungen bildeten, d.h. daß die hier bestattete Elite auch eine religiöse Funktion hatte. Dies spricht für die Existenz dessen, was man in der Ethnologie 'Häuptlingstümer' nennt. Häuptlingstümer sind in der Regel Theokratien (Gottesherrschaften, d.h. Herrschaftsformen, bei denen eine religiöse Hierarchie an der Spitze der Gesellschaft steht), in denen die Ahnenverehrung der 'Häuptlinge' eine bedeuten-

27 Rekonstruierte Ansicht des Rundgrabes von Apesokari/Mesara (nach S. Hood).

28 Rekonstruktion von Hausgräbern aus Gournia/Ostkreta (nach J. Soles).

29 Golddiadem aus Mochlos/Ostkreta. Um 2500 v. Chr.

de Rolle spielt. Mit diesem theokratischen System in Zusammenhang steht auch die Entwicklung einer religiösen Bilderwelt. In der Vorpalastzeit treten die berühmten minoischen Kultsymbole der Doppelaxt und der 'Kulthörner' erstmals auf, und wir besitzen aus ihr die ersten Darstellungen von Gottheiten (Abb. 30).

In der Vorpalastzeit entwickelten sich Handelskontakte zwischen Kreta und den anderen Regionen des ägäischen Meeres: Wir kennen Importe von den Kykladen und vom griechischen Festland auf Kreta und umgekehrt. Um die Mitte des 3. vorchristlichen Jahrtausends wurde auch die erste kretische Niederlassung außerhalb der Insel gegründet, die von Kastri auf Kythera, welche als Anlaufhafen für eine Handelsroute zwischen Westkreta und der Peloponnes diente. Fernhandelsbeziehungen mit Ägypten, Zypern und der Levante in dieser Zeit bezeugen die Funde von ägyptischen Steingefäßen, syro-palästinensischen Rollsiegeln und an exotischen Rohmaterialien Elfenbein und Straußeneier im vorpalastzeitlichen Kreta sowie von kretischen Dolchen in zyprischen Gräbern. Diese Objekte waren aber sicherlich nur Beiprodukte eines Handels mit anderen Waren, über die wir z. T. nur spekulieren können.

Ein Hauptziel des kretischen Außenhandels muß in jedem Fall die Erlangung der nun sehr wichtigen Metalle gewesen sein, die auf der Insel nicht oder nur unzureichend vorhanden waren. Blei und Silber wurden von der Kykladeninsel Siphnos und aus Laurion in Attika importiert, wie naturwissenschaftliche Analysen gezeigt haben. Bei den anderen Metallen ist die Herkunft bisher nicht so klar zu bestimmen. Kupfer kam möglicherweise auch aus Laurion, aus Lakonien (womit vielleicht die 'Kolonie' auf Kythera zu erklären wäre) und aus Zypern, Gold aus Makedonien, Nordwest-Anatolien (Troja) oder Ägypten. Sicherlich aus einer außerägäischen Quelle stammte das Zinn, das neben der in der Vorpalastzeit noch überwiegenden Arsenbronze bereits zur Herstellung der widerstandsfähigeren Zinnbronze verwendet wurde. Möglicherweise wurde es über Nordwest-Anatolien importiert, wo wir

30 Tongefäß in der Gestalt einer Göttin aus Myrtos/Ostkreta. Um 2500 v. Chr. Aghios Nikolaos, Archäologisches Museum.

in Troja schon um 3.000 v. Chr. Zinnbronze kennen, die dann dort um die Mitte des 3. Jahrtausends besonders häufig begegnet. Der ursprüngliche Herkunftsort des Zinns war aller Wahrscheinlichkeit nach schon damals das heutige Afghanistan (siehe unten).

Der Metallmangel und die dadurch bedingte Organisation eines Außenhandels zur Erlangung der begehrten Metalle stellte allem Anschein nach einen wesentlichen Stimulus für die Entwicklung staatlicher Organisationen und damit einer Hochkultur auf Kreta dar, eine Parallele zu den älteren Hochkulturen Ägyptens und Mesopotamiens, die ebenfalls arm an Bodenschätzen waren.

Über die letzten Phasen der Entwicklung, die schließlich um 2.000 v. Chr., zu Beginn der sog. Altpalastzeit, zur Entstehung urbaner Zentren und der ersten (der 'Alten') 'Paläste' auf Kreta führte, besitzen wir wegen der starken Störungen der betreffenden Schichten durch die umfassende Überbauung in der Altpalastzeit nur sehr wenige Informationen. Die kürzlich erfolgte Identifizierung von 'Protopalästen' aus dem späten 3. Jahrtausend unter den 'Palästen' von Knossos und Malia zeigt an,

31 Knossos, sog. Königliche Straße zwischen dem Großen und Kleinen Palast.

32 Der neue Palast von Mallia in rekonstruierter Ansicht (nach J. W. Graham).

34 Tontäfelchen mit Schriftzeichen der minoischen Linear A-Schrift aus Aghia Triada.

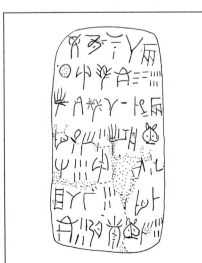

daß die Änderungen zu Beginn der Altpalastzeit nicht so abrupt waren, wie es auf den ersten Blick scheinen mag.

Warum war es gerade Kreta, auf dem die erste Hochkultur westlich der älteren Hochkulturen Ägyptens und des Vorderen Orients entstand? Wenn wir uns im 3. vorchristlichen Jahrtausend im ägäischen Raum umschauen, so finden wir zu dieser Zeit drei Kulturkreise, die zumindest das gleiche Niveau wie der kretisch-minoische erreicht hatten: den sog. frühhelladischen in Mittelgriechenland und auf der Peloponnes, den frühkykladischen auf den zentralen Inseln der Ägäis und den nordwestägäischen an der Nordwestküste Kleinasiens und auf den dieser vorgelagerten Inseln. Mit ihren z. T. großen Siedlungen mit geplanten Wegenetzen (z. B. Manika auf Euböa mit einer Fläche von 50 ha., Poliochni auf Lemnos) und fast schon palastartigen Zentralgebäuden (z. B. Lerna, Troja) und hervorragenden Kunstproduktion (z. B. 'Kykladenidole') standen sie alle um die Mitte des 3. vorchristlichen Jahrtausends sozusagen auf dem Sprung zur Hochkultur. In der zweiten Hälfte des 3. Jahrtausends aber fand diese Entwicklung ein recht abruptes Ende in allenthalben festzustellenden gewaltsamen Zerstörungen. Nach den archäologischen Zeugnissen sind diese auf neue Bevölkerungsgruppen zurückzuführen, die aus Anatolien und vom Balkan in den ägäischen Raum eindrangen. Kreta wurde allem Anschein nach von diesen Zuwanderungen nicht betroffen und erlebte deshalb im Gegensatz zu den anderen Regionen der Ägäis in dieser Zeit keinen kulturellen Bruch und Niedergang. Auf diese Weise konnte es sich kontinuierlich weiterentwickeln, die Kontakte mit den Hochkulturen des östlichen Mittelmeers weiter intensivieren und als die soziale Entwicklung auf der Insel entsprechend weit fortgeschritten war, wesentliche Anregungen durch diese Hochkulturen empfangen und in zumeist sehr eigener, selbständiger Weise verarbeiten.

Um 2.000 v. Chr. also wurden die ersten Städte auf Kreta gegründet. Zu dieser Zeit erreichte Knossos eine Größe, die bis zum Ende der minoischen Kultur kaum übertroffen wurde. Es bedeckte eine Fläche von mindestens 45 ha. und hatte eine Einwohnerzahl von zumindest 11.000 – 18.000. Malia und Phaistos waren nicht sehr viel kleiner. Diese Städte wiesen gut organisierte Pläne mit gepflasterten Straßen auf (Abb. 31).

Im Mittelpunkt dieser städtischen Siedlungen lag jeweils ein monumentaler Zentralbau, den wir – seitdem Arthur Evans glaubte, in Knossos den Palast des mythischen Herrschers Minos gefunden zu haben – als 'Palast' zu bezeichnen pflegen (Abb. 32). Eine Reihe von Entwurfs- und Bautechniken dieser 'Paläste' sind von ägyptischen und/oder vorderasiatischen Vorbildern übernommen: fast exakte Nord-Süd-Orientierung, Orthostaten (aufrecht stehende große Kalksteinblöcke als Basis der Außenfassaden), Quaderbauweise. Mit seinen um einen großen Zentralhof arrangierten Flügeln und einem weiteren großen Platz, der jeweils vor der Westfassade liegt, stellt dieser Architekturtyp jedoch insgesamt eine eigene kretische Entwicklung dar. Die 'Alten Paläste' wurden um 1.700 v. Chr. durch eine Erdbebenkatastrophe zerstört, aber sehr schnell und z. T. prächtiger als 'Neue Paläste' wieder aufgebaut.

Als Evans zu Beginn unseres Jahrhunderts Knossos freilegte, regierte in Großbritannien noch die Königin Victoria, und es waren zeitgenössische Vorstellungen, die damals im wesentlichen das Bild von der Funktion der minoischen 'Paläste' prägten. Aus dem archäologischen Befund läßt sich jedoch eine funktionale Vielfalt für diese monumentalen Zentralbauten ermitteln:

1. Eine nach dem Vorbild der altorientalischen Kulturen entwickelte Administration, wie nicht nur die mit Siegelabdrücken versehenen tönernen Versiegelungen (Abb. 33) verschiedener Objekte (Tür- und Kistengriffe, Gefäße) zeigen, sondern auch die Benutzung der neu eingeführten Schrift ('Kretische Hieroglyphenschrift', 'Linear A') für bürokratische Zwecke (Tontafeln) (Abb. 34).

2. Religion und Ritual, worauf zahlreiche Räume mit eindeutig religiös-rituellem Charakter, zahlreiche Kultobjekte und - in der Neupalastzeit - das religiös-rituelle Bildprogramm der Wandmalereien des 'Palastes' von Knossos (Abb. 21) hinweisen.

3. Vorratshaltung, die - wie die ausgedehnten Magazintrakte (Abb. 35) und die großen, in die Westhöfe der Paläste von Knossos und Phaistos eingetieften Getreidesilos zeigen - den Eigenbedarf des 'Palastes' und seiner Bewohner bei weitem überstieg.

Diese Funktionsvielfalt hat Paul Halstead mit britischem Humor veranschaulicht, indem er meinte, ein minoischer 'Palast' habe unter einem Dach die Equivalente von Buckingham Palace, Whitehall, Westminster Abbey und möglicherweise sogar Wembley Stadium vereinigt. Mit letzterem soll dabei wohl auf den minoischen Stiersprung (Abb. 12) angespielt werden. Bei diesem sicherlich nicht ungefährlichen 'Sport' handelt es sich allerdings höchstwahrscheinlich um einen mit dem Stieropfer verbundenen religiösen Ritus.

Die überproportionale Vorratshaltung der 'Paläste' spricht wie die sich in den Versiegelungen und Tontafeln manifestierende Bürokratie für die Wirtschaftsform der Redistribution (unter Redistribution versteht man einen Austauschmodus, bei welchem Güter und Dienstleistungen einem Verwaltungszentrum abgeliefert werden und von diesem wieder – in anderer Verteilung – ausgegeben werden). Dieses Wirtschaftssystem ermöglicht Handwerkern die Spezialisierung, da sie über die Redistribution von ihrer Gesellschaft bzw. deren Führung unterhalten werden und nicht mehr ihre eigene Nahrung produzieren müssen.

Die durch die Redistribution ermöglichte qualitative Intensivierung der handwerklichen Produktion führt zur Herstellung äußerst qualitätsvoller Prestigeobjekte. In der Metallurgie sind insbesondere die Leistungen in der Waffentechnologie (Langschwerter, fortschrittliche Lanzenspitzentypen) zu nennen, die zusammen mit der Schaffung einer zu dieser Zeit in der Ägäis konkurrenzlosen Flotte die Voraussetzung für die kretische Expansion in der Ägäis bildete. Aus Metall (Bronze, Silber, Gold) wurden auch kostbare Gefäße hergestellt, die Goldschmiede führten aus dem Vorderen Orient die Techniken des Filigran und der Granulation ein (Abb. 17). Kretische Me-

33 Mallia. Tonabdrücke von Siegeln mit Zeichen der „Kretischen Hieroglyphenschrift". Um 1800 v. Chr.

35 Knossos, Großer Palast. Blick in die Magazine im Erdgeschoß des Westflügels.

tallgefäße und Prunkwaffen waren begehrte Exportartikel. Sie werden im 18. Jh. v. Chr. im Tontafelarchiv des Palastes von Mari am mittleren Euphrat erwähnt. Minoische Silbergefäße sind in etwa gleichzeitigen Königsgräbern in Byblos im heutigen Libanon gefunden worden. In der Neupalastzeit wurden kretische Edelmetallgefäße und Waffen auch auf das griechische Festland exportiert, wie u. a. die Funde aus den Schachtgräbern von Mykene zeigen, außerdem nach Ägypten, wo in thebanischen Beamtengräbern Keftiu (Kreter) dargestellt sind, die solche Objekte tragen (Abb. 36).

In der Keramiktechnik wurde zu Beginn der Altpalastzeit die rotierende Töpferscheibe eingeführt und u. a. mit ihrer Hilfe die nach dem ersten Fundort sog. Kamares-Ware entwickelt (Abb. 37). Die Gefäße dieser in den Palastzentren hergestellten, teilweise extrem dünnwandigen ('Eierschalenware') Gattung

36 Theben/Ägypten. Fresko im Grab des Senmut mit der Darstellung kretischer Gesandter, die „spätminoische" Gefäße tragen.

37 Schnabelkrug im sog. Kamares-Stil aus dem Alten Palast von Phaistos. Um 1800/1700 v. Chr. Heraklion, Archäologisches Museum.

gehören zweifellos zu dem Schönsten, was menschliche Töpferkunst überhaupt je hervorgebracht hat, und war in der Levante und in Ägypten ungefähr so begehrt wie chinesisches Porzellan im Europa des 18. nachchristlichen Jahrhunderts.

Auf Kreta wurde zu Beginn der Altpalastzeit die Freskotechnik (die Malerei auf frisch aufgetragenen, noch feuchten Kalkputz) erfunden und zu Beginn der Neupalastzeit auch in die Levante exportiert. In den Palästen der kanaanitischen Herrscher von Alalach und Tel Kabri (Rechob) fanden sich unter der Leitung von kretischen Künstlern ausgeführte Freskodekorationen an den Wänden bzw. auf dem Fußboden eines zeremoniellen Saales.

Übernahmen die Kreter also anfangs Anregungen von den Kulturen des Vorderen Orients und Ägyptens, so waren sie doch bald nicht nur mehr der allein nehmende Teil, sondern entwickelten sich rasch zu einem gleichberechtigten Partner jener älteren Hochkulturen. Besonders ihre künstlerischen Produkte standen dort in hohem Ansehen, was sich u. a. darin spiegelt, daß in der Vorstellung der Kanaaniter der Gott der Künste nach den mythischen Texten von Ugarit aus Kaphtor (Kreta) stammte.

Die engen Beziehungen zwischen dem mi-

noischen Kreta und der Kanaanitischen Kultur der Levanteküste erklärt sich u. a. aus dem wirtschaftlich so wichtigen Metallhandel. Das für die Herstellung von Bronze notwendige Zinn war Mangelware. Auf einer Tontafel aus dem Archiv des Palastes von Mari erfahren wir von einem kretischen Händler, der in Ugarit von Agenten des Palastes von Mari Zinn kauft. Der Kreter verfügt für die Verhandlungen auch über einen Dolmetscher. Auf einer anderen Tafel ist verzeichnet, daß das Zinn mit Karawanen aus der Region des heutigen Afghanistan herantransportiert und über Zwischenhändler in Mesopotamien an den Palast von Mari geliefert wurde.

Kehren wir nach Kreta zurück, so ist noch darauf einzugehen, daß auf der Insel zu Beginn der Altpalastzeit die ersten politischen Organisationen westlich des Vorderen Orients und Ägyptens gegründet wurden, die man als 'Staaten' bezeichnen kann. In diesem Zusammenhang wirkt sich das anfangs angesprochene Fehlen lesbarer schriftlicher Quellen natürlich besonders erschwerend aus. Es läßt sich jedoch rekonstruieren, daß zu jedem der urbanen Zentren ein Hinterland, ein Territorium gehörte. Hinweise hierfür geben u. a. die gleichzeitig mit den ersten 'Palästen' errichteten Gipfelheiligtümer, welche die gesamte In-

sel überziehen. Innerhalb dieser Gipfelheiligtümer zeichnet sich eine Hierarchie ab, mit einem in der Nähe eines 'Palastes' und urbanen Zentrums gelegenen und mit diesem in enger Verbindung stehenden Hauptheiligtum und einer Reihe kleinerer Gipfelheiligtümer, die mit dem jeweiligen Hauptheiligtum Blickkontakt haben. Neben diesen Indizien ergeben auch regionale Keramikstile und die Verbreitung bestimmter Artefakte (Siegel einer bestimmten Palastwerkstatt etc.) Hinweise auf die territoriale Gliederung des minoischen Kreta.

Insgesamt zeichnet sich auf diese Weise für Kreta in der Alt- und Neupalastzeit ein Siedlungsmuster mit ca. sechs urbanen und 'palatialen' Zentren ab (Abb. 38), die in einem durchschnittlichen Abstand von 35 - 40 km voneinander entfernt liegen und zu denen jeweils ein Territorium von etwa 1.000 - 1.500 km² gehört. Damit folgt die politische Organisation des minoischen Kreta allem Anschein nach einem Modell, das der britische Archäologe Colin Renfrew als 'early state module' definiert hat und das für viele frühe Staatsbildungen charakteristisch ist, so z. B. für jene der Sumerer, Etrusker und Maya, aber auch für die mykenische Kultur des griechischen Festlandes und die Entstehung des griechischen Stadtstaates, der Polis. In all diesen Beispielen treffen wir eine Reihe kleiner, politisch voneinander unabhängiger staatlicher Organisationen an, die keine politische, aber eine kulturelle und ethnische Einheit bildeten.

Spätestens in der Neupalastzeit weisen die einzelnen Territorien eine klare Siedlungshierarchie mit dem jeweiligen 'Palast' untergeordneten Subzentren (Siedlungen, 'Villen') auf. Ob das minoische Kreta eine zentral ver-

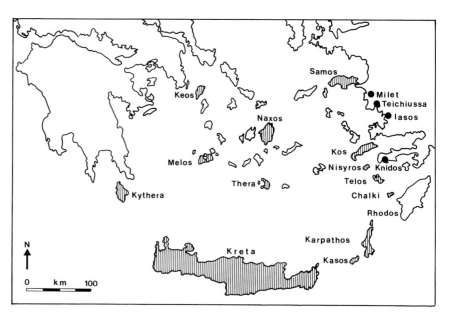

39 Karte der Ägäis mit dem minoischen Einflußbereich zur Zeit der Neuen Paläste.

38 Karte des minoischen Kreta mit schematisch eingezeichneten, hypothetischen politischen Einheiten, nach J. F. Cherry mit Änderungen. Die „Palast"-Zentren sind durch Quadrate wiedergegeben, andere wichtige Plätze („Villen", Siedlungen) mit Punkten.

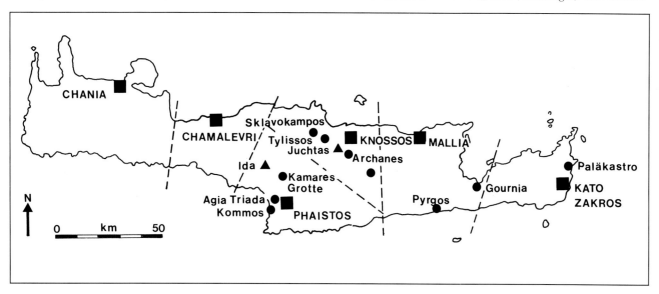

waltete politische Einheit war, ist aus dem archäologischen Befund allein nicht mit letzter Sicherheit zu klären. Zumindest in der Altpalastzeit formte es wohl eher eine Art von Städtebund, wie wir ihn aus dem Alten Orient (Sumer) und aus Etrurien kennen. Nur in der Neupalastzeit (ca. 1.700 - 1.500) hat Knossos anscheinend die Zentralgewalt über die gesamte Insel ausgeübt. Als Indizien hierfür könnten die Tonabdrücke von Siegeln der knossischen Administration an einer Reihe von kretischen Fundplätzen gewertet werden, außerdem die ägyptischen Zeugnisse für einen größeren kretischen Staat (siehe unten).

Nachdem bereits in der Vorpalastzeit die minoische 'Kolonie' von Kastri auf Kythera gegründet worden war, dehnten die Kreter in der Altpalastzeit ihr Territorium in größerem Maße außerhalb ihrer Insel aus. Weitere 'Kolonien' wurden auf den Inseln der Ostägäis (Kasos, Karpathos, Rhodos, Samos) und an der kleinasiatischen Küste (Knidos, Iasos) angelegt. Sie dienten aller Wahrscheinlichkeit nach der Sicherung der Handelswege. In der Neupalastzeit zählten dann noch weitere Plätze in der östlichen Ägäis (u. a. Telos, Kos, Milet) sowie eine Reihe von Inseln der Kykladen (Thera, Melos, Keos, Naxos) zum Machtbereich des minoischen Kreta (Abb. 39). Dies spiegelt sich in ägyptischen Quellen aus der Zeit Tuthmosis III. wieder, in denen von Keftiu (Kreta) und den Inseln in der Mitte der großen grünen See" die Rede ist, d. h. von Kreta als Zentrum eines Inselreiches. An die Existenz dieses Inselreiches erinnerte sich in historischer Zeit noch die griechische Tradition. So schrieb Thukydides, der große athenische Historiker des 5. Jh. v. Chr. (I. iv): „Minos nämlich war der erste, von dem wir Kunde haben, daß er eine Flotte baute, das heute hellenische Meer weithin beherrschte, die Kykladen eroberte und meistenteils zuerst besiedelte, wobei er die Karer verdrängte und seine eigenen Söhne als Statthalter einsetzte".

Ein Problem stellt die Herrschaftsform im minoischen Kreta dar. Die typische altorientalische Stadt ist durch die Dualität und nicht selten auch Rivalität von Tempel und Palast geprägt. In den Städten des minoischen Kreta gibt es dagegen aber immer nur einen monumentalen Zentralbau, den 'Palast', der - wie gesagt - neben der Administration und Vorratshaltung auch immer eine sehr stark ausgeprägte religiös-rituelle Komponente zeigt. Die kretischen 'Paläste' haben deshalb allem Anschein nach in sich die Funktionen des Sitzes der zentralen Administration und des urbanen religiösen Zentrums vereinigt. Man könnte sie daher als 'Palasttempel' oder 'Tempelpaläste' bezeichnen.

Hinzu kommt ein weiteres überraschendes Charakteristikum der minoischen Kultur: das vollkommene Fehlen von Herrscherdarstellungen, die ja eine charakteristische Erscheinung der Kunst des Alten Orients und Ägyptens sind. Die politische Funktion der Bildkunst im minoischen Kreta dagegen war es allem Anschein nach nicht, Propaganda für einen Herrscher zu machen, sondern sie propagierte Kult und Ritual, welche nach den Bildzeugnissen (Abb. 19) in der minoischen Kultur einen hohen Stellenwert besaßen. Der Verhaltensforscher Konrad Lorenz hat gezeigt, daß Ritualisierung dazu imstande ist, Agressionen einzudämmen und sozialen Zusammenhalt zu schaffen. Eine religiös begründete ideologische Machtbasis kann auch dazu dienen, anstelle eines 'Erzwingungsstabes' die Unterstützung der herrschenden Gruppe durch die Bevölkerung zu sichern. Und dies scheint das Geheimnis zu sein, das hinter der im Vergleich zu den Kulturen des Vorderen Orients merkwürdigen Tatsache steht, daß die 'Paläste' unbefestigt in den ebenfalls unbefestigten minoischen Städten liegen, ja, daß man manchmal gar nicht sagen kann, wo die Stadt aufhört und der 'Palast' beginnt. Es herrschte also innerer sozialer Friede, der auf der religiösen Autorität der Führungsschicht sowie sicherlich auch auf dem Wohlstand der Bevölkerung beruhte. Äußere Feinde brauchte man wegen der Insellage und der starken Flotte zunächst nicht zu fürchten.

Im Gegensatz zu den Hochkulturen Ägyptens und des Vorderen Orients scheinen also im palastzeitlichen Kreta - wie schon in der Vorpalastzeit - die politische und die religiöse Führungsschicht identisch gewesen zu sein. Diese Ausnahme hängt vielleicht mit der Insellage zusammen, denn wie der britische Archäologe John Evans festgestellt hat, „zeigen Inselgemeinschaften eine Tendenz in Richtung auf eine übertriebene Entwicklung eines Aspektes ihrer Kultur, der oft mit dem zeremoniellen Bereich verbunden ist".

Nach dem Aufstieg während der Altpalastzeit (ca. 2.000 - 1.700 v. Chr.) war das minoische Kreta in der Neupalastzeit (ca. 1.700 - 1.500 v. Chr.) auf dem Höhepunkt seiner politischen und ökonomischen Macht. Auch der Ausbruch des Thera-Vulkans, den man früher für den Untergang der minoischen Kultur verantwortlich gemacht hat, bedeutete hierbei allem Anschein nach keine wesentliche Unterbrechung. Wie wir jetzt durch naturwissenschaftliche Datierungsmethoden wissen, erfolgte diese Eruption um 1.625 v. Chr., also mehr als 100 Jahre vor den Zerstörungen auf Kreta. Dort, wo der Aschenregen niederging, in Ostkreta und auf den Inseln der östlichen Ägäis, räumte man in den minoischen Siedlungen die Asche schnell zur Seite und begann sogleich mit dem Wiederaufbau.

Um 1.500 v. Chr. aber ereignete sich auf Kreta eine Reihe von Zerstörungen, nach denen die politische Ordnung völlig verändert war. Alle 'Paläste' mit Ausnahme desjenigen von Knossos waren zerstört und wurden nie wieder aufgebaut, ebenso die als 'Herrenhäuser' oder 'Villen' bezeichneten Filialen der Palastadministrationen. Es gibt Hinweise darauf, daß die betreffenden Zerstörungen oder zumindest einige von ihnen mit Erdbeben in Verbindung standen. Erdbeben allein aber können nicht die einzige Ursache für die umwälzenden politischen Veränderungen gebildet haben, die sich in der archäologischen Hinterlassenschaft widerspiegeln. Nachdem die 'Paläste' um 1.700 v. Chr. zum ersten Mal in einer Erdbebenkatastrophe zerstört worden waren, hatte man sie ja sogleich wieder aufgebaut. Warum war es diesmal ganz anders?

Die Tatsache, daß Knossos als einziger 'Palast' die Zerstörungen unbeschadet überstand, spricht am ehesten für innerkretische Auseinandersetzungen. Die Zentralisierung der Administration und die Monopolisierung des Handels durch die Herrscher von Knossos war den anderen 'Palästen' möglicherweise zu weit gegangen und hat wohl zur Rebellion gegen Knossos geführt, die von diesem jedoch erfolgreich niedergeschlagen wurde. Derartige Ereignisse stehen vielleicht hinter der mythologischen Überlieferung, nach der Minos von Knossos mit Sarpedon, dem Herrscher von Lyktos (Malia?), eine bewaffnete Auseinandersetzung hatte, außerdem auch mit Rhadamanthys, dem Herrscher von Phaistos, in Streit geriet und beide mitsamt ihren Gefolgsleuten von der Insel vertrieb.

Diese inneren Auseinandersetzungen schwächten Kreta aber entscheidend, und diese Schwächung führte schließlich zum Untergang der selbständigen minoischen Kultur. Um 1.500 v. Chr. brachten Mykener vom griechischen Festland die minoischen Siedlungen auf den Kykladen an sich, ein knappes Jahrhundert später eroberten sie auch die minoischen Niederlassungen in der östlichen Ägäis und Kreta selbst. Sie bauten den teilweise zerstörten 'Palast' von Knossos wieder auf, um von dort zentral den größeren Teil der Insel zu regieren. Für ihre Administration entwickelten sie dabei, sicherlich mit Hilfe minoischer Schreiber, aus der kretischen Linear A-Schrift mit Linear B eine eigene Schrift für ihre Sprache, die – wie wir seit der Entzifferung von Linear B durch den britischen Forscher Michael Ventris wissen – bereits griechisch war.

Von der einstigen Vorherrschaft der Kreter im ägäischen Raum blieb nur die Legende. Und diese Legende erzählt uns grausame Geschichten wie die vom Minotauros, dieser von Minos' Frau Pasiphae und einem Stier gezeugten Mißgeburt, welcher athenische Jungfrauen und Jünglinge als Tribut zum Fraß vorgeworfen wurden, bis es schließlich Theseus gelang, mit Hilfe von Minos' Tochter Ariadne das gräßliche Ungeheuer zu töten. Dies ist aber die von den Siegern tradierte Legende, und Verlierer kommen in der Überlieferung der Sieger immer schlecht weg. Nicht besser erging es in dieser Hinsicht später den Etruskern und den Karthagern durch ihre Bezwinger, die Römer.

Durch die archäologischen Entdeckungen auf Kreta seit dem Beginn unseres Jahrhunderts ist jedoch deutlich geworden, daß die Insel in der Bronzezeit eine in allen Bereichen hochkultivierte Gesellschaft beheimatete, der die mykenischen Griechen viel verdankten. Ohne dieses Vorbild ist die Entstehung der mykenischen Kultur im 17. Jhd. v. Chr. überhaupt nicht denkbar, und nach der Eroberung Kretas durch die Mykener um 1.400 v. Chr. wurde die Prägung der Hofkultur in den mykenischen Burgen und Residenzen durch das Vorbild des minoischen Kreta noch stärker. Die Träger der mykenischen Kultur aber waren die direkten Vorfahren der Griechen, welche die Kultur Europas bis in unsere Zeit nachhaltig beeinflußt haben. Die gängige Bezeichnung des minoischen Kreta als der ersten Hochkultur Europas ist eigentlich anachronistisch. Die Minoer sahen sich natürlich nicht als Europäer, sondern bildeten das jüngste Mitglied einer Gemeinschaft von Hochkulturen, die sich nach Osten bis zu den Tälern des Nil sowie des Euphrat und Tigris erstreckte. Durch die Schaffung einer durch die dortigen Vorbilder angeregten, aber doch eigenständigen Hochkultur und der Weitergabe der kulturellen Errungenschaften auf das griechische Festland schuf Kreta wesentliche Voraussetzungen für alle weiteren Entwicklungen. Und hierin liegt die europäische Bedeutung der minoischen Kultur.

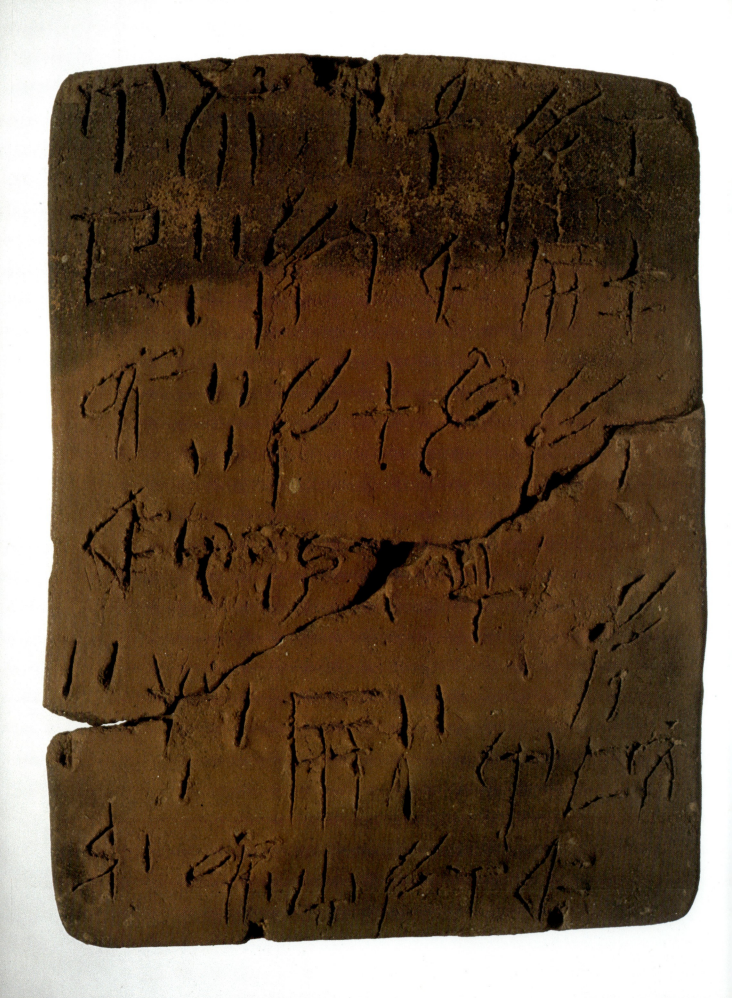

Minoische Archäologie in Westkreta

Yannis Tzédakis

Kreta, die größte griechische Insel, die im äußersten Süden des Landes liegt, ist bereits seit der Jungsteinzeit einer der bedeutendsten strategischen Punkte der mediterranen Welt.

Das Gebiet Westkretas umfaßt mit den Regierungsbezirken Chania und Rethymnon fast die halbe Fläche der Insel. Der Ida oder Psiloritis, mit 2456 m das höchste Gebirge Kretas, bildet die natürliche Grenze im Osten, während die bis zu 2453 m aufsteigenden Levka Ori, die „Weißen Berge", den Bezirk Chania beherrschen. Von den Umweltbedingungen, unter denen die Menschen der neolithischen und minoischen Epoche lebten, dem Klima und der Vegetation, können wir uns ein ziemlich klares Bild machen, wenn wir die Bodengestalt Westkretas betrachten und davon ausgehen, daß das Gebiet früher einen zweifellos reichen Baumbestand hatte und die jetzt noch fließenden Quellen auch damals schon Wasser führten. Heute gilt es allgemein als sicher, daß sich Klima und Lebensbedingungen in den beiden Perioden nicht wesentlich unterschieden haben.

Durch die ersten Ausgrabungen in Knossos, Phaistos, Tylissos, Malia, Gournia, Palaikastro und andernorts, Stätten von großer Bedeutung mit überaus reichen Funden von hervorragender Qualität, konzentrierte sich das Interesse der Archäologen auf Ost- und Mittelkreta. Nach dem „heroischen Zeitalter" der frühen kretischen Archäologie mit Forschern wie Evans, Chatzidakis und Pernier beschäftigten sich alle griechischen und ausländischen Archäologen ausschließlich mit Ost- und Mittelkreta, den Westen jedoch besuchten oder erforschten sie nur gelegentlich (gemeint ist die prähistorische Epoche).

Die Gründe für dieses mangelnde wissenschaftliche Interesse an Westkreta liegt vielleicht darin, daß die Theorie des englischen Archäologen Pendlebury allgemein akzeptiert wurde, im Westen Kretas habe es wegen der rauhen Natur des unwegsamen Ida-Gebirges bis zur endgültigen Zerstörung von Knossos 1375 v. Chr. so gut wie keine neolithische und minoische Kulturentwicklung gegeben. Erst nach der Vernichtung der Zentralgewalt in Knossos seien die Minoer gezwungen gewesen, das Gebiet westlich des Ida zu erkunden, in dem es vorher nur vereinzelte Stützpunkte gegeben habe. Diese Ansicht versucht Pendlebury in seinem Buch durch die Vorlage des archäologischen Materials zu begründen. In anderen Schriften spricht es von mißlungenen Versuchen, Siedlungen zu gründen sowie von Fischerdörfern.

Während des Zweiten Weltkrieges führten die Deutschen ohne Genehmigung an verschiedenen Orten der Insel und besonders in Westkreta Ausgrabungen durch, deren Ergebnisse sie 1951 veröffentlichten. Entsprechend können wir sagen, daß deutsche Archäologen als erste diesen Teil der Insel erforscht haben. Die generelle Einstellung der spezialisierten „Kretologen" gegenüber Westkreta und seiner Rolle in der Entwicklung der neolithischen und minoischen Kultur der Insel wurde jedoch von der Veröffentlichung des neugefundenen Materials und den archäologischen Beobachtungen der Deutschen nicht beeinflußt. In seiner Besprechung des Buches von Fr. Matz über die deutschen Ausgrabungen während des Krieges untersucht der englische Archäologe S. Hood die minoische Stätte von Chania, doch führte dies erst viele Jahre später, zwischen 1962 und 1965, zur weiteren Erforschung Westkretas.

In dieser Zeit wurde von Ventris und Chadwick die Linear-B-Schrift entziffert. Unter den Ortsbezeichnungen finden wir den Namen Ku-do-ni-ja und a-pa-ta-wa, die Kydonia bzw. Aptara entsprechen; da die Texte der Schrifttäfelchen, die sich auf Verwaltungsangelegenheiten beziehen, aus der Zeit vor der endgültigen Zerstörung des Palastes von Knossos stammen, kann damit die Existenz dieser beiden Städte während der minoischen Epoche nicht mehr bezweifelt werden. Anscheinend wurden diese Einzelheiten in der allgemeinen Verwirrung vergessen, die die Erkenntnis der beiden englischen Forscher verursachte, deren Entdeckungen zur Herkunft und Art der Sprache dieser Texte unser Geschichtsbild wesentlich verändert hat.

Hier müssen wir den großen Beitrag von Prof. P. Faure erwähnen, der viele Jahre lang die Höhlen in ganz Kreta erforscht und dabei wichtiges Material zusammengetragen hat. Mögen seine Datierungen der gefundenen Gefäße und Scherben nicht immer ganz richtig sein und seine Theorien mitunter eigentümlich anmuten, so sind seine Bücher und Artikel für die Geschichte der Achäologie Westkretas doch von grundlegender Bedeutung; es sind Pionierarbeiten und sollen auch als solche betrachtet werden.

Die Einrichtung einer Ephorie für Altertümer in Westkreta im Jahre 1964, die es bis dahin in der Geschichte des Griechischen Archäologischen Dienstes nicht gegeben hatte, und die Aufstellung eines Funktionsrahmens schufen die Vorraussetzungen zur Erforschung dieses Gebietes. Dazu sollten die schriftlichen Quellen herangezogen, Bodenuntersuchungen vorgenommen und systematische Ausgrabungen durchgeführt werden. Der Leitgedanke, der hinter dieser Forschungstätigkeit stand, war die grundsätzliche Überzeugung, daß weder ein Gebirge, noch die unwirtliche Natur die Menschen der neolithischen und minoischen Epoche daran hindern konnte, sich in dem überaus fruchtbaren Gebiet Westkretas anzusiedeln und auszubreiten.

Die letzten 25 Jahre sind für das westliche Kreta zu einem „eindrucksvollen Beginn einer glänzenden Zukunft" geworden. Die Ergebnisse der systematischen Ausgrabungen, von denen einige noch im Gange sind, haben die Anschauungen von der Ausbreitung der neolithischen und minoischen Kultur auf der Insel radikal verändert, und auf der archäologischen Karte Westkretas nimmt die Zahl der minoischen Stätten ständig zu.

Die Veröffentlichungen der letzten Jahre in der Fach- und populärwissenschaftlichen Literatur haben einigen Archäologen, vor allem griechischen, zu der Behauptung Anlaß gegeben, es werde bewußt der Versuch gemacht, die Bedeutung großer Wissenschaftler, die auf Kreta gearbeitet haben oder noch arbeiten, zu mindern. Ich glaube, daß dies eine irrige Annahme ist, die auf einer übermäßigen Empfindlichkeit gegenüber wirklich großen For-

Vergl. Kat.-Nr. 8.

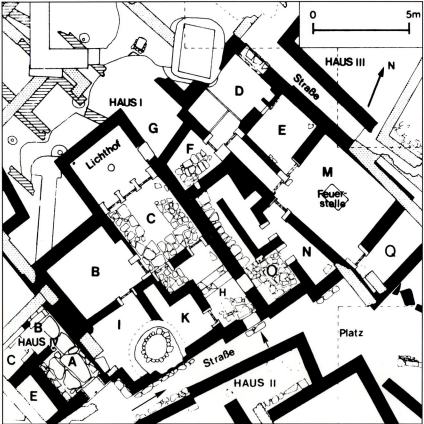

schern beruht, einer Empfindlichkeit, die wir alle der Wissenschaft und den Kollegen gegenüber haben. Die seit 1964/65 gemachten Funde werden nicht unter Verschluß gehalten und damit für die Kollegen unzugänglich gemacht, sondern können ganz im Gegenteil von allen eingesehen werden. Sie sind es der Mühe wert, und schließlich ist auch das Prestige der Ausgräber durch diese Öffentlichkeit gestiegen.

Es ist demnach sehr merkwürdig, daß sich verschiedene Aufsätze und Artikel vom Ende der siebziger Jahre, die sich mit dem neolithischen und minoischen Kreta beschäftigen, immer noch auf die Bibliographie stützen, die fast noch aus der Zeit vor dem letzten Kriege stammt. Gewiß sind die zitierten Archäologen bekannter als die damaligen griechischen und ausländischen Ausgräber in Westkreta. Das jedoch, was die Wissenschaft weiterbringt, ist nicht der Name eines Forschers, sondern das Ergebnis seiner Arbeit, und wenn damit eine bisher allgemein anerkannte Theorie umstürzt, zeigt das fortdauernde Beharren darauf zumindest einen Mangel an wissenschaftlicher Information.

Westkreta steht also allen Forschern offen, und allen, die hier gearbeitet haben oder noch arbeiten, ist das Glück und die Freude zuteil geworden, bedeutende Überreste der neolithischen und minoischen Kultur zu entdecken, die bezeugen, daß die Insel eine kulturelle Einheit darstellte, ohne natürliche oder künstliche Grenzen.

Welche Bedeutung haben nun aber die Funde der Ausgrabungen in Westkreta für die wissenschaftliche Forschung und welchen Beitrag haben sie zum richtigeren und besseren Verständnis der einheitlichen neolithischen und minoischen Kultur auf der ganzen Insel geleistet?

Die Höhle bei Gerani im Regierungsbezirk Rethymnon hat ein ziemlich klares Bild vermittelt vom täglichen Leben und Aktivitäten einer kleinen menschlichen Gemeinschaft,

Chania-Kastelli. Überblick der griechisch-schwedischen Grabungen mit Übersichtsplan (nach Y. Tzédakis - E. Hallager).

und zwar fast für den gesamten Zeitraum der neolithischen Epoche. Die Grabungsfunde, die Untersuchung der einzelnen Schichten und der darin enthaltenen Fundstücke (Gegenstände aus Stein, Ton, Bein und Tierknochen) zeigen uns, daß die Bewohner hier wegen ihrer saisonbedingten Arbeiten in der Landwirtschaft, Fischerei, Viehzucht und Jagd nicht ständig leben, sondern nur zeitweise, und daß sie ihren ständigen Wohnsitz an einem anderen Ort hatten, der allerdings bisher nicht festgestellt werden konnte. Daß die Menschen hier nur zeitweise wohnten, geht aus der Art der gefundenen Gefäße hervor, unter denen große Vorratskrüge fehlen, sowie aus dem Gesamtkomplex der übrigen Fundstücke wie Statuetten und Werkzeugen. In den Zeitabschnitten, in denen die Menschen die Höhle bewohnten, unterhielten sie mit Sicherheit eine Werkstatt für Werkzeuge aus Bein. Denn außer fertigen wurden auch viele halbfertige Stücke und vor allem Rohmaterial gefunden: Tierknochen, darunter auch Knochen von Hirschen.

Diese Höhle wurde in der späten Jungsteinzeit verlassen, wahrscheinlich weil der Eingang verschüttet wurde. Deshalb ist sie eine der wenigen Höhlen mit rein neolithischen Schichten ohne spätere Überlagerungen. Entdeckt wurde die Höhle bekanntlich 1969 bei

Funde aus den Grabungen in Chania: Siegelabdruck (Kat.-Nr. 1), Linear A-Schrifttäfelchen, Gefäß mit Deckel (Kat.-Nr. 15).

Bauarbeiten an der neuen Nationalstraße zwischen Chania und Rethymnon.

Im Gegensatz dazu erbrachten die Ausgrabungen in den Höhlen auf der Halbinsel von Chania und besonders in den Grotten auf der Hochebene Keramion – Koumarospilio und Platyvola – reiche Keramikfunde aus dem späten Neolithikum, der Übergangszeit zum Frühminoikum sowie aus der frühminoischen Zeit. Wenn sich auch die Schichten nicht klar voneinander trennen lassen, sind sie doch sehr aufschlußreich. Etwas näher möchte ich auf Gefäße mit Ritzdekor aus der Periode FM II eingehen. Das Herstellungszentrum, aus der diese Keramik stammt, scheint eines der bedeutendsten der Insel gewesen zu sein. Besonders bemerkenswert ist, daß diese Tongefäße Nachahmungen von Steinvorbildern sind. Diese Tatsache, das Vorkommen eingeführter und imitierter helladischer Schnabeltassen der Periode FH II und die Gräber vom frühkykladischen Typ der Nekropole von Nea Roumata sind sichere Zeugnisse dafür, daß zwischen diesem Teil Kretas, dem helladischen Raum und den Kykladen Verkehrsverbindungen und andere Beziehungen bestanden.

Die Lage der Nekropole von Nea Roumata an den Ausläufern der Levka Ori mehr als 16 km landeinwärts zwingt uns zur Skepsis gegenüber der bekannten Theorie, daß in der frühkykladischen Periode die Siedlungen mit Ihren Friedhöfen am Meer oder unweit der Küste angelegt worden sind.

Chania-Kastelli. Detail der Grabung. Vergl. Abb. S. 58.

Wichtige Forschungsprojekte, die die ausgehende neolithische und die frühminoische Periode betreffen, sind:
1. das griechisch-italienische von Nerokourou
2. das griechisch-englische von Debla
3. das griechisch-schwedische von Kastelli/Chania.

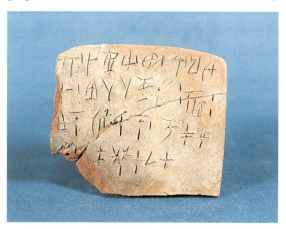
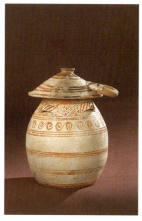

Es ist bekannt, daß die Beziehungen zwischen den Bewohnern Kretas, des griechischen Festlandes, der ägäischen Inseln und der Kleinasiatischen Küste sowie Ihre Herkunft eines der großen Probleme der ägäischen Archäologie sind, mit einander widersprechenden Theorien, die dem jeweiligen Interessengebiet einzelner Forscher entsprechen.

Die Beziehungen zwischen den Kulturzentren des östlichen Mittelmeerraumes, die wie wir wissen, seit neolithischer Zeit bestanden haben, werden ohne Unterbrechung fortgeführt. Dabei unterhält Chania besonders zu Kythera enge Beziehungen. Die dortigen englischen Ausgrabungen haben gezeigt, daß die Siedlung bei Kastri an der Wende von der frühen zur mittleren Bronzezeit von Minoern angelegt wurde. Stammten die Kolonisten etwa aus der Gegend von Chania? Dies ist vor allem deshalb wahrscheinlich, weil Gefäße des frühen Barbotine-Stils hier häufiger vorkommen als in anderen minoischen Zentren.

Wo aber gibt es Zeugnisse der mittelminoischen Zeit im Umkreis von Chania? Entdeckt wurden bereits eine bedeutende Siedlung in Kastelli, dem Stadtteil oberhalb des Hafens in Chania, Überreste dichter Besiedlung auf der Halbinsel von Chania, auf dem Plateau von Keramion und in der Gegend von Drapania bei Kissamos. Die Menschen jener Zeit benutzten Höhlen wie die bei Perivolia und Gipfelheiligtümer wie die von Sklopa und Drapanos für religiöse Zeremonien.

Die Siedlung von Kastelli, Chania, die zunächst provinziellen Charakter hatte, unterhielt Beziehungen zu den großen Zentren. Sie erlebte eine rasche Entwicklung und wandelte sich zu Beginn der Zeit der Zweiten Paläste zu einer bedeutenden Stadt, die in der Phase SM I ihre höchste Blüte erreichte. Häuser, Straßenzüge und Plätze wurden nach dem damals gültigen städtebaulichen System angelegt. Verwaltet wurde die Stadt von einer wohlorgani-

Armeni/Rethymnon. Oben: Spätminoische Nekropole mit zahlreichen Kammergräbern. Unten: Tonsarkophag, mit Papyrusstauden bemalt (Kat.-Nr. 170).

sierten Bürokratie, wie es aus den Archiven mit Schrifttäfelchen und Siegeln mit Linear-B-Schrift hervorgeht. Außerdem produzierte sie eigene Keramik, unter anderem die bekannten Becher im sog. alternierenden Stil, die auch exportiert wurden.

Dies sind einige der charakteristischen Merkmale, die die kulturelle Bedeutung der Stadt kennzeichnen. Ob sie nun Kydonia hieß oder nicht, ist meiner Meinung nach unwesentlich, obwohl es natürlich interessant wäre, wenn sich dies beweisen ließe.

In dieser Periode war auch die Souda-Ebene dicht besiedelt. Dies geht deutlich aus der Anzahl der minoischen Häuser hervor, die durch die griechisch-italienischen Ausgrabungen 1977–1979 und spätere griechische Rettungsgrabungen zutagegekommen sind.

An dieser Stelle seien die griechischen Ausgrabungen bei Monastiraki erwähnt, wo ein großer Komplex von Magazinen und Werkstätten freigelegt worden ist. Die monumentale Architektur, die Existenz einer Kultstätte, für die es Anhaltspunkte gibt, sowie Archive mit Siegelabdrücken lassen darauf schließen, daß es sich hier um eine palastartige Anlage handelt.

Etwa in dieselbe Zeit wird die Stätte von Apodoulou datiert, die von einem griechisch-

Funde aus Armeni: Halskette (Kat.-Nr. 17) und bemalter Tonsarkophag (Kat.-Nr. 171). Statuette (Kat.-Nr. 128) vom Vrysinas-Berg.

italienischen Forscherteam freigelegt wird; hier wurde eine große Anzahl von Gebrauchs- und Vorratsgefäßen entdeckt.

Wenden wir uns nun wieder Chania und der minoischen Siedlung von Kastelli zu: die Theorie, daß sich die Phase SM II, wenn überhaupt, nur in Knossos nachweisen ließe, ist inzwischen überholt. Denn auch aus dieser Zeit gibt es inzwischen Gebäudereste und andere Funde, bis jetzt zwar nur wenige, aber doch sehr charakteristische Zeugnisse. Es hat einige Zeit gekostet, unsere Kollegen davon zu überzeugen, aber wir glauben, daß wir es mit gutem Recht getan haben.

Nach der endgültigen Zerstörung des Palastes von Knossos erreichte das minoische Kydonia seine höchste Blüte, die bis in die Phase SM III C andauerte. In dieser Zeit unterhielt Kydonia Beziehungen bis nach Zypern und Palästina. Es exportierte seine Keramik – die bekannten einheimischen Gefäße mit weißlichem Überzug – in alle Bereiche Kretas, nach Griechenland und Zypern. Jüngste Forschungen haben sogar ergeben, daß die bekannten Bügelkannen mit Linear-B-Schriftzeichen, die für den Warentransport benutzt wurden und im helladischen Raum in großer Anzahl vorkommen, aus Chania stammen. So können wir sagen, daß zumindest der westkretische Außenhandel vom Herrscher, dem „wa-nax", von Kydonia aus kontrolliert wurde.

Ein bedeutendes Merkmal ist im übrigen, daß in Kastelli keine Zerstörungsschicht der

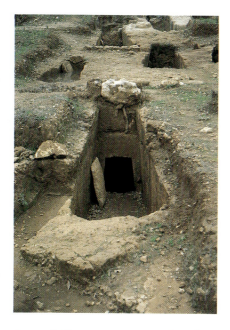

Armeni/Rethymnon. Spätminoisches Kammergrab mit Verschlußstein.

Phase SM III A festgestellt wurde, sondern lediglich eine von geringer Ausdehnung zu Beginn der Phase SM III B. Die aus dieser Periode stammende, handgeformte Keramik liefert Anhaltspunkte dafür, daß Kydonia sehr wahrscheinlich auch zu städtischen Zentren auf Sizilien und Sardinien Beziehungen unterhielt. An dieser Stelle ist es notwendig, kurz gefaßt etwas über die mykenische Eroberung Kretas

61

und die Ausbreitung der mykenischen Kultur auf der Insel zu sagen. Abgesehen von der Sprache, die auf Täfelchen und Gefäßen erscheint, und die in allen bisher bekannten kretischen Zentren der Nachpalastzeit mehr oder weniger gut belegt ist, gibt es hierfür kaum ausreichendes Beweismaterial, und zwar weder in der Architektur, noch in der Keramik. Vom Gesamtbestand der Keramikfunde sind nur etwa 5% mykenische Importe oder Imitationen einheimischer Werkstätten. Dagegen entsprechen die einheimischen Gefäße sowohl in der Form wie im Dekor der minoischen Tradition und übernehmen nur ganz wenige Elemente aus dem mykenischen Repertoire.

Bemerkenswert sind die importierten Kästchen und sonstigen Gegenstände aus Elfenbein, von denen man annimmt, daß ihre Herkunft oder zumindest ihr Stil mykenisch ist. Bis jedoch das Problem in seiner ganzen Reichweite gelöst werden kann und die von allen erwünschte objektive Wahrheit gefunden ist, bleibt noch ein langer Weg.

Ich bin deshalb auch überaus vorsichtig mit der Verwendung des Begriffs „mykenisches Kreta" bzw. der sich ebenfalls anbietenden, aber inhaltslosen Bezeichnung „kretisch-mykenische Epoche" und ziehe den einfacheren und herkömmlichen Ausdruck „spätminoische Periode" vor.

Bügelkannen mit Linear-B-Schriftzeichen wurden auch außerhalb der Siedlung von Chania an Orten gefunden, wo man sie wohl kaum vermutet hätte: in der Höhle von Perivolia und in einem Kuppelgrab bei Armeni im Regierungsbezirk Rethymnon.

Die Nekropole der Phase SM III beim Dorf Armeni besteht aus Gruppen von Kammergräbern und einem kleinen Kuppelgrab. (Bis heute wurden 207 Gräber freigelegt).

Da die Gräber außerhalb eines heute besiedelten Gebietes liegen, besteht hier zum ersten Mal die Möglichkeit, einen Friedhof dieser Epoche ungestört zu untersuchen und vollständig freizulegen. So haben die Ausgrabungen überaus wichtige Erkenntnisse erbracht. Die Nekropole wurde von den Bewohnern der bislang unbekannten Stadt an einem ausgewählten Ort angelegt, und zwar nach Plan. Das geht aus Art und Weise der vorbereitenden Arbeiten hervor: der Abarbeitung des gewachsenen Felsens, der Gliederung in Gruppen von kleinen und großen Gräbern und der Anlage von Zugängen zu den einzelnen Grabkomplexen.

Architektonisch bestehen die Gräber, die alle nach Nordosten ausgerichtet sind, aus einer einfachen, abwärts geneigten Rampe, einem Gang und einer Kammer mit halbkreisförmigem oder viereckigem Grundriß. Einige Gräber haben aber auch eine Treppe, eine große viereckige Kammer mit einem Stützpfeiler in der Mitte bzw. im hinteren Teil des Raumes sowie eine Wandbank. Von zwei Gräbern wurden Stelen gefunden, die natürlich nicht mehr an ihrem Platz standen, deren Bestimmung als Grabdenkmäler jedoch mit Sicherheit anzunehmen ist.

Gefunden wurden außer den Tonsarkophagen, die oft religiöse Darstellungen tragen, Keramik, zahlreiche Waffen und Schmuckstücke aus Bronze, Siegelsteine aus Halbedelsteinen, ein Eberzahnhelm, ein Strohkörbchen und eine mit Linear-B beschriftete Bügelkanne mit dem Namen wi-na-jo, der auch auf einem ähnlichen Gefäß aus Knossos und auf Linear-B-Schrifttäfelchen vorkommt. Vielleicht ist dies der erste Tote der minoischen Zeit, dessen Namen wir kennen.

Aus welchen Gründen aber wurde um 1375 v. Chr. die zur Nekropole gehörige Stadt gegründet, die etwa sechs Generationen lang bis 1200 v. Chr. bestand, wie aus den Gräberfunden hervorgeht, und die ziemlich groß gewesen sein muß, wenn wir berücksichtigen, daß über 50 Gräber bisher noch nicht freigelegt wurden?

Eine endgültige Antwort darauf kann erst gegeben werden, wenn die Stadt gefunden und weitgehend erforscht sein wird. Zu einer vorläufigen Erklärung kommt man jedoch, wenn man in Betracht zieht, daß in den Gräbern zahlreiche hervorragende Bronzegegenstände gefunden wurden und daß verhältnismäßig nahe bei der Nekropole ein Kupferbergwerk liegt, das allerdings nicht mit Sicherheit in der Periode SM III in Betrieb war.

So kann es also sein, daß bei Armeni eine Industriestadt lag, zumal Kreta, wie wir wissen, in dieser Periode kein Kupfer mehr aus Zypern einführte. Die zukünftigen Forschungen werden zeigen, ob diese Theorie der Wirklichkeit entspricht oder nicht.

Crete. Europe's awaking- an archeological view

Wolfgang Schiering

Legend has it that Zeus disguised as a tame white bull to get close to the Phoenician princess Europa; when she trustingly sat down on his back, he took his chance to abduct her to Crete where she gave birth to three of Zeus' sons: Minos, Rhadamanthys and Sarpedon. Minos became king of Knossos, Rhadamanthys of Phaistos and Europa gave her name to our whole continent. The legend of Europa was again and again theme of ancient and modern art and the princess' residency, Crete, has its place as the cradle of European history not only in this Greek myth, but also archeologically and historically.

In this context we talk about the Minoan Crete, named after Europa's and Zeus' son, beginning its life in the first half of the 3rd millennium. A first cultural climax in the 19th century BC was followed by a second in the 17th and 16th century BC. When later on Dorian Greeks - who are said to have caused the flourishing of one-hundred cities - ruled over the island, Crete again took on a main cultural rol. During the 8th and 7th century BC, the so-called Orientalizing Period of Greece, Crete was the leading mediator between orient (North Syria and Phoenicia) and Greece. In the 7th century, the island also dominated the emergence of early Greek sculpture wich is related to a new, second Daidalos in ancient literature. Crete maintained its European status until Byzantine time and the painter El Greco, even though St. Paul had given it a bad reputation.

Let's have a look at the first Daidalos, King Minos' allround artist. Legend has it that he built the labyrinth of Knossos. It is common knowledge, that the legendary residence of Minotaur, son of Minos' wife Pasiphae and one of Poseidon's bulls, is based on the King of Knossos' palace. In the beginning of our century, the English archaeologist Sir Arthur Evans excavated and partly reconstructed the palace near nowadays Heraklion. Even if there were no supporting finds, our knowledge about Europa's Zeus bull, Pasiphae's Poseidon bull, and the bull-human Minotaur make evident the outstanding position of the bull in Minoan religious ideas. Finds of numerous visualizations of the mysterious Cretan bull-jump, other bulls and bull-humans prove a bull cult (fig. 12 and 13). The bull horns are shown in a more or less abstracted way in connection with the double axe which was used to sacrifice the bull.

Minoan Crete developed Europe's first advanced civilization and holds comparison with hierarchic structures and bureaucratic organizations of the advanced civilizations of Egypt and the near East. Minoan Crete exceedingly centralized its economic and administrative system and also strictly interrelated its religious and executive order. Such massive statement finds ample proof in excavated building and countless archeological finds. The palaces of Knossos, Phaistos, Mallia und Kato Zakros are most informative on an architectural level. The so-called villas (estates) are also important source and they represent an inbetween of palaces and urban or rural settlements: Hagia Triada, Tylissos, Vathypetron etc. More research has to be done on the cities surrounding the palaces. Nevertheless they have conveyed some important indications wich allow for a careful picture of how the relations between palace and city might have been. Excavations of those cities, where no palace-like centre could be located, also allow for statements about the cities wealth and technological advance, about manufactures, administration, harbours and ritual. Tombs can also be of special value, because they sometimes are archaeologically better known than contemporary settlements they belonged to. Important insights into social structures of the Minoan Crete are allowed for mainly by big family graves and early Tholoi of the 3rd and early 2nd millennium. Impressive aristocratic graves such as the so-called temple tomb near Knossos offer further understanding.

Our knowledge about the life style in Minoan palaces (fig. 14), villas and houses is based as well on the excavated architecture (courts, streets and stairs, halls, shrines and ritual basins, storerooms, and workshops as on the evidence of wall decorations (frescos and stucco work) and furniture (thrones and other furniture, terracotta and stone vessels). It is interesting that comparatively modest houses had installations (court, hall, ritual basin, first floor) wich reduce the quality gap between house, villa and palace and distinguish between life-style here and there more gradually than generally. Frescos were painted into all private housing of the city near Akrotiri on Thera which developed under significant Cretan-Minoan influence. Cult and representation are found in a remarkably close connection not only in palaces and villas but also in the settlements. Private items seem to be easier to identify in houses than in the palaces where it is difficult to identify even a kitchen.

Apart from architectural installations, such as many storerooms, treasuries, oil-mills, wine-presses, storage vessels, finds of writings and seals supply information about profane daily palace routine which was dominated by bureaucracy. Different ritual rooms recognizable by their architecture or furnishing (ritual-objects, ritual symbols, representations) give important insights into the ritual sphere. In the open, there are sacred places on mountain tops or in caves.

The development of economic, political and religious structure of the Minoan Crete most likely is not caused by family growth or social and political changes alone, as shown by settlement history of the 3rd millenium. It is also unlikely that this development is only based on exterior influences from Egypt and the Near East. The interior expansion was supported by island situation and geographic setting. A consequent exterior expansion also directed toward the North (Cyclades) and West (Lipari Islands). The contacts resulting from this expansion made the Cretans - who were less aggressive than seaworthy and mercantile - first the pupils and than the partners of the older advanced civilizations.

The centre of the Minoan economic and trading systems was obviously a "magazine economy" with products stored in clay pithoi in imbedded stone boxes or in special jars (grain, honey, olives, oil, wine). Timber trade, basis of ship- and house construction must have been paramount, too. The products of a local metallurgy (simple tools, weapons or luxurious vessels and respective, mostly imported raw materials, are part of the magazine economy. Earthen ware, workshops for stone products (lamps) and bowls, were found in the palaces of Knossos and Kato Zakros. Manufactures used precious materials (ivory and precious metals) wich were stored and traded as raw materials like copper. They all are part of this magazine economy. The area of textile production, such as the expensive private and ritual dresses for Minoan women (fig. 15, 16) and the storage of local and imported raw and ready mate items were also included. Processing in the palaces must habe been interconnected closely to the trade.

Finds and representations wich give us insights into the life of the Minoan society illustrate the ties between trade and economy on the one hand and palaces and villas on the other. Representations, such as the Knossos fresco fragment of the so-called Petite Parisienne (fig. 16.) demonstrate by no means any kind of "court art" produced for the court, the ritual or even the arts. In contrast, they are a natural, elaborately structured consequence and expression of a highly successful economic system shared by large parts of the populations. Already in the prepalatial period, second half of the 3rd millenium, such consequences of a flowering economy, in need for profitable and stimulating foreign trade, were apparent when the rich people of Mochlos built houses for their dead furnished with expensive gifts. Climaxes of what could be called "court art", are for the 19th century BC the golden bee pendant from Mallia (fig. 17), for the 17th century the scepter head from steatite with one halt sculptured as a panther and the other as an axe (fig. 18), and for the 16th century a bull's head, also crafted from steatite, wich was used in the Knossos palace as a precious vase for donations (fig. 13).

A culture that so closely interelated daily life and ritual naturally obstructs the distinction between the profane or the ritual applications of its art. This can be illustrated with the naturally profane sealing. Seals with ritual representations are relatively common (fig. 19). The countless other seals and the bee pendant from Mallia (fig. 17), seem to have been in daily use before. they came into ritual use as tomb gifts.

Excavated ruins of the palaces obviously give the most interesting information about daily life and ritual (fig. 20). They have many things in common such as a central court as centre of the palaces. Similar to our castles and chateaus, all parts of the palace could be reached from these central courts. Their ritual function is not paralleled by our castles and chateaus. These central courts seem too short for the Minoan bull-leaping but they were surely the setting of other (ritual) games and activities, as shown on a well known and heavily restored fresco. The west courts on the entrance side of the palaces were used for further ritual and profane activities. City people used to come to these west courts to participate in certain functions. The palaces of Knossos and Phaistos had a further area wich was called "theater area" by the excavators due to a theater-like tribune. When natural produce for the big round silos (on the plaza) and for the pithoi and stone boxes (in the storerooms) were brought to the western court and into the west wing of the palace, it gave reason for thanksgivings with ritual character. The palaces' western facades were designed in an especially attractive and representative manner because they faced the cities. The Minoan palace architecture was not – as believed earlier – the random result of an agglomerating way of construction (see below).

Phaistos' Northern facade of the central court shows, more clearly than the aforementioned facades of the impressive west wings, the foundations of a first European architecture (fig. 22). The middle is accentuated with a door, flanked by columns and niches with a symmetry that diverges just a bit over the whole broadth. These arrangements constitute an architecture wich anticipates Mycenaean (i.e. early Greek) architecture, as for example the so-called treasury of Atreus in Mycenae.

Later on we will explain that order as an element of art is apparent already in Minoan art.

It is necessary to pin down the other Minoan progresses that were transferred from Minoan over Mycenae to European culture. In an Cretan technology, engineering has the first place. The Cretans built streets, bridges, cars and ships but they also built a network of canalization that villa and palaces were connected with inclusively water toilets. Numerous finds illustrate the importance of minoan shipping impressive visualizations of ships, such as on a beautiful wall fresco from Akrotiri on Thera (fig. 23) and one giant hall at Kommos (South Crete) wich was identified as a ship dock only recently. These and many other advances in technology of navigation provided the basis for minoan sea supremacy. This "thalassocracy" of Minos was praised by Thukydides, the Greek historian, after it had been adapted by the mycenaen greeks.

Daidalos. the mythic character, was later seen as both artist and engineer representing Minoan technology and creativity. There is archaeological proof for the Cretans' creativity in the areas of fresco technique, pottery (high temperatures, white paint on the so-called Kamares vases made of talc), metallurgy, sealing (quickly rotating drill), jewellery (filigree, granulation). Nearly all these advances were passed on to Mycenean Greece. Creativity was also involved in the area of Minoan lady's fashion which later became popular in Mycenae (fig. 15, 16). This haute couture demanded technical skills such as production, dying and decoration of the fabrics and it also demanded an imaginative design. The techniques of the bull-leaping, which as part of ritual Minoan games were also passed on to Mycenae, are so hard to acquire that today's Spanish bull fighters are perplexed. A splender sword from Mallia and other Minan swords are examples of Minoan weapon technique. We also know of bronze helmets for Minoan soldiers. Even this area which is hard to relate to our idea of 'Minoan peace' (cities, palaces and villas without fortifications) must have caught Mycenaeans' interest who were known to be aggressive.

Due to a bureaucratically organized Minoan administrative and economic system and the Minoan expansion, architecture (representational rooms, storerooms) and the use of writing and sealing was brought from Crete to Aegean Islands (Thera, Melos, Keos), to single cities of Asia Minor's coast and to mainland Greece. Big archives of clay tablets in Mycenean palace administrations, such as those in Pylos, make them comparable to older Minoan, but also to Egyptian and Near Eastern institutions. Minoan Crete had developed hieroglyphes and a linear writing system by the first half of the 2nd millenium. Even today none of these writings can be read. M. Ventris and J. Chadwick deciphered to the Mycenean Linear B writing and identified it as an early Greek language. Linear B was derived from the Minoan Linear A. Crete made the decisive step toward this writing, based on syllables, wich was still in use in the postminoan palace of Knossos. In relation to Europe, this writing is one the main cultural advances of the Minoan civilization.

The main root of European sacral architecture is the Greek temple wich had its origin in the Mycenaean "megaron". Crete influenced the architectural development with smaller sacred rooms and the important Minoan ritual activities took place in the open air, in courts, on mountaintops or in ritual caves. Neither the megaron which became the proud center of Mycenaean palaces (Tiryns, Pylos) nor the giant walls wich usually consisted of polygonal big blocks did come from Crete to the Greek mainland. It is true, these Cyclopic walls, in their typical form, did not directly influence the development of the later Greece.

Let us finally return to the element of order as an element of art as we could discover it in the architecture of Minoan palaces (fig. 14, 22). The golden bee pendant of Mallia (fig. 17), the lily fresco (fig. 24) of Amnissos and the lentil shaped clay bottle with octopus from Palaikastro (fig. 25) are picked as examples. All three representations have a symmetric design: two bees, three lily stems, eight tentacles. Symmetry divergences are found easily within the image of the octopus. A closer look reveals asymmetries in the smaller forms (buds, blossoms) of the fresco similar to the peculiar movements of the tentacles. Only the bodies and wings of the bees seem to be symmetric to each other. In this case it is the convex disk covered with a concentric granulation between the bees whose position is obviously shifted to the right. Apart from that the globular cage above the bees heads and the tap are not in symmetry with the bees. Finally I would also denounce that the three small discs of the pendant orginally were in exact symmetry. Thus all three motifs are ordered and free, quiet and in motion, like countless other examples of Minoan art. Terms like "free order", "ordered freedom", "movement in the stillness" or "stillness in the movement" come to mind. The octopus on the lentil shaped clay bottle of Palaikastro is an excellent example of this phenomenon which embodies the elements of freedom and movement in a more apparent way than the elements of order and stillness (fig. 25).

The octopus is represented twice on the bottle, once on each side. But it is not a continuous picture which could be called a visualization of the sea. The many corals, the sea-snails or the sea-hedgehog between the tentacles do not exist to give a picture of the life under water but are added more as elements of form than elements of content to cover the "horror vacui" of the empty spaces. The spectator of this two sided bottle sees two sections as two independent units and not as both sides together as a naturalistic picture of two octopuses and other creatures of the sea. For Minoan vase painters nature was not a unity, but a stimulus to realize the artist's creative imagination which manifested itself in the vase painting of the first half of the 2nd millenium and developed to partly gorgeous, abstract forms (spiral compositions, so-called Kamares ware). Instead of these abstract ornaments, the vase painters had now selected the octopus, because as a natural form the octopus ideally expressed the content of older ornaments. An interpretation claiming, the octopus is visualized as if it was passing by quickly under water, becomes obsolete in the face of underwaterphotography. Today, it is replaced by another view which considers the artist not as rendering the life of the octopus but as studying an imprisoned or dead octopus. The artist's creativity gave order, according to traditional design concepts to the portrayal of the octopus. Not nature, but art dominates, natural movement is brought to a stand and subordinated to artistic movement, natural freedom is designed artistically.

Thus a motif developed that could be doubled or reproduced in any number -as the lilies of Amnissos (fig. 24), flying fishes on a fresco from Melos, the corals of our octopus picture but also the construction and room elements of Minoan architecture. The concept of the Minoan artist was thus not a whole in the later or modern sense but the sum of exactly calculated and combined parts. The Minoans saw the whole in each single part or in the sum of parts. In the latter case, the element of combination was dominated again by artistic orders: repetition, ending and unending rapport, symmetric or concentric order were adapted to artistic functions. Agglomeration, a term which was in common use for Minoan architecture, suits to describe this process of growing together of parts if we think less of a natural, seemingly uncontrolled relation of parts but more of an organized, designed 'gluing together' (agglutinare).

If the artistic statements of a culture are dominated so distinctly by the elemts of order, then this order also must have been in the foreground of political, economic and religious activities of the culture. An extensive sense of order was undoubtedly a main precondition for the strong influences of the Minoan Crete on the Greek and European culture.

The Minoan Crete: Attempting a Historic Epitome

Wolf-Dietrich Niemeier

The advanced Minoan civilization of bronze age Crete was named after the mythic king of Knossos, Minos. Minoan Crete is a culture without accessible written sources (the Minoan systems of writing have not been deciphered yet). Our attempt to reconstruct the history of Crete in the bronze age thus depends nearly exclusively on the interpretation of archeological finds. This is a difficult process not always leading to hard evidence. For reasons of space, the following has to simplify and to exclude a discussion of methodic problems.

Crete's geographic position is one of the main preconditions for the development of the first advanced civilization west of the older advanced civilizations. The island situation was a natural barrier against invasion and gave Crete a good basis from wich to develop a continous, relatively undisturbed civilization. With the development of navigation the sea got an important communicative function, connecting Crete with the rest of the world (fig. 23). Luckily enough, Crete's distance to all three mediterranean continents, Africa, Asia und Europe, was about the same.

Thus Crete, third biggest mediterranean island, was populated by single groups of stone-using agriculturists and hunters in the Paleolithic Age. Then Crete could be reached easily from the Peloponnese on simple boats or rafts thanks to a much lower sea level. In the Neolithic Age, shortly after 7.000 BC, the first permanent settlement developed at the site of the later 'palace' of Knossos. These settlers came from Minor Asia with a ready to use knowledge in farming and cattle raising. They already imported obsidian (black, glass-like volcano stone) from the Cycladic Island of Melos to produce stone-tools.

In the beginning, the population of Neolithic Crete consisted of a few clans who lived far apart from each other in open clay house settlements and caves. The population grew very slowly and a considerable extension of the settlements can be distinguished not before the end of the Neolithic (about 4.300-3.300 BC). Then, the settlement of Knossos had an extension of about 4 ha, and we conclude more than 1.000 inhabitants. Ethnological parallels indicate the existence of an institutionalized, hierarchic social structure. The few exotic prestige items - stone bowls from Egypt and ivory from Syria - further prove this conclusion.

We only have very little information about the settlements of the early-Minoan era or pre-palace time (3.300-2.100 BC). The few excavated examples (Myrtos, Vasiliki) are small rural settlements. However the architectural ruins and ceramic finds of this time under the later palace centers of Knossos, Phaistos and Mallia prove relatively large settlement. The biggest settlement, Knossos, had an area of 5 ha and between 1.300-1.900 inhabitants in early Minoan times.

In addition of the extension of the settlements presupposing the existence of social strata there are more indications for that. We have knowlegde of a division of labour and specialized handicraft in pre-palace times. The pottery of the Vasiliki-style (so called in reference to the first place of find) (fig. 26) that have been found all over the island of the middle of the 3rd mill. BC are of such a high quality and their charming decorations base on specialized procedures (reduction, partial reoxydation), that they could have been produced only in specialized pottery centres. Similar developments are noticable in metallurgy and in production of stonevessels and sealstones.

The burial customs of this time clearly show a social hierarchy. Besides the constructed tombs of an economically privileged group - in Southern Crete circular tombs with rectangular annexes (fig. 27), in Northern and Eastern Crete mainly housetombs (fig. 28) - we find in the same necropoles simple earth-burials, modest burials in Pithoi (storage jars) or stone-cists. The constructed circular and house tombs clearly distinguish themselves by the wealth of their furnishings and gifts. Especially the elite tombs of Mochlos and Gournia in Eastern Crete concentrate on precious objects. Due to comtemporary parallels to the Near East, we are able to interpret some of them - such as golden diadems - as symbols of authority (fig. 29).

In front of wealthy graves there are mostly paved plazas and altars (fig. 28). The finds of cult objects on these altars indicate that these graves were also the center of ritual activities and that the elite buried here, also had a religious function. We can thus conclude the existence of chieftains - an ethnological term. Generally, theocracies (societies led by a religious hierarchy are characterized by the worship of the ancestral chiefs. The development of religious imagery is closely interrelated with this theocratic system. The famous Minoan cult symbols 'double axe' and 'horns of consecration' appear first during the pre-palace time. The first visualizations of goddesses are also from this time. (fig. 30).

During the pre-palace time, Crete developed trade with the other regions of the Aegean sea. We know about imports from the Cyclades and mainland Greece and vice versa. The first Cretan trade post abroad was Kastri on Kythera, a harbor for the trade route between Western Crete and Peloponnese, Kastri was founded around the middle of the 3rd millenium BC. Many finds prove these distant trade relations with Egypt, Cyprus and the Eastern Mediterranean Coast; Egyptian stone vases, Syro-palestinian roll-seals and exotic raw materials like ivory and ostrich eggs in pre-palace Crete; Cretan daggers in Cyprus graves. These objects certainly were mere by-products of a trade we mainly habe to speculate on.

A main goal of Cretan foreign trade must have been the acquisiton of those metals that did not or only insufficiently occur on the island. Scientific analyses have shown that lead and silver were imported from the Cycladic Island of Siphnos and from Laurion in Attica. The origin of the other metals is harder to determine. Copper possibly also came from Laurion, from Laconia - which would explain the Cretan 'colony' on Kythera - and from Cyprus. Gold came from Macedonia, North-West Anatolia (Troy) or Egypt. Tin surely had a non Aegean origin and was used for the production of bronze in pre-palace Crete. Tin-bronze was more resistant than the more common arsenic bronze. We know tin-bronze in Troy already around 3000 BC where it appears commonly around the mid 3rd millenium. Thus tin was possibly imported from North Western Anatolia. The origin of tin was almost already Afghanistan (cf. below).

The lack of metal and its resulting organization of a foreign trade to acquire these metals seem main cause to develop an executive organization and consequently, Crete's advanced civilization. The parallel to the older advanced civilizations Egypt and Mesopotamia wich were also poor in natural resources is at hand.

Due to strong disturbance in the relevant layers, we only have insufficient information on the last phases of development which led to the rise of urban centers and first ('old') palaces. Recent identifications of 'proto-palaces' from the late 3rd millenium under the palaces of Knossos and Mallia, prove the change in the beginning of the old palace era as less abrupt as it might first appear.

Why did the first advanced civilization west of the older advanced civilizations of Egypt and the Near East develop in Crete? Taking a look around the 3rd millenium Aegean Sea, we find three cultures, in their advance comparable to the Minoan. The so-called Early Helladic in Central Greece and the Peloponnese, the Early Cycladic of the central Aegean islands and the North West Aegean along the North Western coast of Minor Asia and its islands. These cultures were about to merge into being advanced civilizations around the mittle of the 3rd millenium because they had large settlements with designed street-nets (eg. Manika on Euboes with an area of 50 ha, Poliochni on Lemmos), palace-like central edifices (Lerna, Troy) and an outstanding art production (Cycladic figurines). In the second half of the 3rd millenium this development came to a violent end by intended destructions. Archeological finds have proved that newly immigrated peoples from Anatolia and the Balkan have caused these destructions. Apparently, Crete did not suffer from these migrations and in contrast to the other Aegean cultures did not experience any cultural break or decline. Crete was able to continue its development and further intensified the contacts with the advanced cultures of the Eastern Mediterranean. When Crete's social development had reached a certain level it incorporated in its own, independent way the decisive impulses received from these advanced civilizations.

Around 2000 BC, the first cities were founded on Crete. At this time, Knossos reached a size unsurpassed until the end of the Minoan culture. With an area of at least 45 ha, it had a population of at least 11.000 to 18.000. Mallia and Phaistos were not much smaller. These cities show a well organized design with paved streeets (fig. 31).

The center of these urban settlements was a monumental central edifice which we refer to as palace (fig. 32) – since Sir Arthur Evans believed to have found the palace of the mythic king Minos in Knossos. A number of design and construction techniques applied in these palaces were adapted from egyptian and/or Near Eastern models: nearly exact North-South orientation, orthostates (big, square limestone blocks as basis of the exterior facades), square stone constructions. All in all, this type of architecture represents a specifically Cretan development with its wings arranged around a large Central Court and an additional plaza in front of the West facade. When the old palaces were destroyed by an earthquake around 1700 BC, they were rebuilt relatively fast and were even more impressive as 'new palaces'.

When Evans excavated Knossos in the beginning of the century, Queen Victoria still ruled over England and the picture of the Minoan palaces' function was mainly shaped by contemporary attitudes. Finds prove that these monumental central edifices had a variety of functions:

1. An administration modeled after the ones of the old oriental cultures finds proof in the sealing or seal stones (fig. 33) different objects (door and box handles, bowls) and in the use of the newly introduced writing (Cretan Hieroglyphic Script, 'Linear A') for bureaucratic purposes (clay tablets) (fig. 34).

2. Religion and ritual become evident in numerous rooms with obvious religious-ritual function, cult objects and – in the 'new palace era', the religious ritual imagery of the wall paintings in the palace of Knossos (fig. 21).

3. The existence of extensive storage rooms (fig. 35) and large grain silos imbedded in the West Courts of the palaces of Knossos and Phaistos prove that storage far exceeded the needs of the 'palace' and its inhabitants.

Paul Halstead described this multi-functional central edifice of Knossos with British humor when he noted that under one roof the so-called palaces incorporated the equivalents of Buckingham Palace, Whitehall, Westminster Abbey and Wembley Stadium. The latter refers to the Minoan bull-leaping (fig. 12). This dangerous 'sport' was almost definitely connected with the religious rite of bull sacrifice.

Both, over-proportional palace storage and bureaucracy as manifested in sealing and clay tablets indicate an economic system called redistribution (an exchange mode were goods and services are delivered to a central administration which distributes these services and goods in a different apportionment). This economic system allowed for the specialization of artisans because the Minoan leadership supported them so that they did not have to physically produce their own food.

Redistribution allowed for a qualitative intensification of artisan production and led to the production of prestige objects of supreme quality. The Cretan expansion in the Aegean Sea depended mainly on their metallurgy which produced advanced weapons (longswords, blades) and the creation of their fleet which, at the time, did not have any serious competition. Precious vases and bowls were made from metals (bronze, silver, gold) and goldsmiths imported the Near Eastern techniques of filigree and granulation (fig. 17). Cretan metal bowls were export articles of high demand and are mentioned in the clay tablet archive of the Mari palace at the central Euphrat. Cretan silver vessels were found in the

Royal Tombs of Byblos in today's Lebanon. During the new palace era, Cretan precious metal bowls and weapons were also exported to mainland Greece. Finds give plenty of proof for Crete's fame in metal: the shaft graves at Mycenae, and also the graves of Egyptian administrators where Keftiu (Cretans) carrying these vessels are visualized (fig. 36).

During the old palace era the potter's wheel was introduced and helped to develop the socalled Kamares ware, named after the location of its first excavation, the Kamares cave at Mt. Ida (fig. 37). Some of these vases are very thin-walled ('egg-shell ware'). The Kamares-ware was also produced in the palace centers and belongs to the most beautiful ceramic ware ever. Along the Eastern Mediterranean Coast and Egypt they had the demand status of Chinese porcelain in 18th century Europe.

In the beginning of the Old Palace Period, the fresco technique (painting on freshly applied, still wet plaster) was first used in Crete. Later, in the beginning of the new palace era, this technique was exported to the Eastern Mediterranean Coast as is demonstrated by the fresco decorations on the walls and the floor of a ceremonial hall in the palaces of Canaanite rulers of Alalach and Tel Kabri (Rechob). We are able to pinpoint that the Cretans after having received stimuli from Near Eastern civilizations started to take over an active part in the exchange and developed to being an equal partner of those older advanced civilizations. Especially Crete's artware was of high value to these civilizations. The mythic texts of Ugarit where the Canaanites immortalized their idea of the God of Art being from Crete is one reflection of Crete's art trade.

The economically vital metal trade partly explains the close relationship between Minoan Crete and the Canaanite civilization of the Levantine Coast. Tin, necessary for the production of bronze, was rare. Clay tablets of the Mari palace archive inform us about a Cretan executive buying tin at Ugarit from Mari palace agents. The Cretan executive also had a personal interpreter for the negotiations. Another tablet notes how the tin was brought to the Mari palace: caravans brought the tin from nowadays Afghanistan to Mesopotamian intermediaries who sold it to Mari.

Coming back to Crete, we have to refer to the fact that in the beginning of the old palace era, the first political organizations which deserve the term 'states' were found west of the Near East and Egypt. In this context the aforementioned lack of written sources is especially obstructive. Nevertheless, we can reconstruct that each urban center had its own territory: peak sanctuaries were built at the same time as the first palaces to cover the entired island. A hierarchy among these peak sanctuaries becomes apparent: one is located close to the palace and urban center thus tightly connected with a respective main sanctuary and a number of smaller sanctuaries can be seen from the main sanctuary. Besides these indications, regional ceramic styles and the manufacture of certain products (seals of a certain palace shop) hint a territorial structure of Minoan Crete.

In the old and new palace era, Crete displays a settlement design of about six urban and palatial centers (fig. 38) which had a mean distance of 35–40 kilometers. These centers each had a territory of approximately 1.000-1.500 square kilometers. Thus the political structure of Minoan Crete apparently followed a model characteristic for many early state creation, so eg. for the Sumeric, Etruscan, Mayan but also for the Mycenaean culture of mainland Greece and the origin of the greek city-state, the polis. British archeologist Colin Renfrew defined this state model as "early state module". The examples represent a number of smaller, politically independent state organizations without political but with cultural and ethnic unity.

With the new palace era, the single territories display a clear settlement hierarchy with sub-centers (settlements, villas) subordinated to the respective palace. Archaeological finds cannot definitely clarify whether or not Minoan Crete was a political unit with a central administration. At least in the old palace era, Crete has to be considered as a community of cities, as we know it from the Old Orient (Sumer) and Etruria. During the new palace era (around 1700-1500 BC), Knossos seems to have had central executional power over the island. This point is supported by finds of clay seals of the Knossos administration at a number of Cretan locations and the Egyptian sources speaking of a bigger Cretan state (see below).

After having founded the colony Kastri on Kythera, already in the pre-palace era, the Minoans further expanded in the old palace era. More colonies were established on Eastern Aegean islands (Kasos, Karpathos, Rhodos, Samos) and along the coast of Minor Asia. They most probably were needed to secure the trade route. During the new palace era, more places in the Eastern Aegean belonged to the Cretan sphere of power: Telos, Kos, Milet and a number of Cyladic islands: Thera, Melos, Keos, Naxos, (fig. 39). This consideration finds proof in Egyptian sources of Tuthmosis III time about "Keftiu (Crete) and the islands in the middle of the Great, Green Sea", namely Crete as the center of an island empire. In historic times, Greek tradition still remembered the existence of such an island empire. The great Athenian historian of the 5th century, Thukydides, wrote (I. iv): "Minos was the first we know about to have built a fleet, ruled over the nowadays Hellenic Sea, conquered and mostly colonized the Cyclades fought the Carians and placed his own sons as governors."

The executive system in Minoan Crete still forms a problem. A typical old Oriental city is shaped by duality and sometimes rivalry between temple and palace. In contrast to this, Minoan cities only have one central edifice always designed for administrative and religious-ritual functions. Cretan palaces seemingly united central administration with urban, religious centers. They could be called 'palace temples' or 'temple-palaces'.

Another surprising element of Minoan culture also needs consideration: it is the lack of any representations of their rulers which are characteristic for Old Oriental and Egyptian art. Apparently it was not the intent of Minoan art to propagate rulers but to propagate cult and ritual which had a high status (fig. 19). Behavior scientist Karl Lorenz has shown that ritualization is able to reduce aggressions and to establish a feeling of social unity. A religiously motivated ideology as basis of power may also replace the stick with popular support for the ruling group. This seems to be the mystery behind this peculiarity in comparison to the cultures of the Near East: the lack of palace and city fortification. As palaces are located within these 'free' cities it is sometimes impossible to determine were the city ends and the palace begins. Crete thus had an inner, social peace based on the religious authority of the ruling class and the economic well-being of the population. External enemies did not represent a threat thanks to the island situation and the strong fleet.

In contrast to the advanced civilizations of Egypt and the Near East, new palace era Crete seems to have had identical religious and political leadership. This exception may be caused in the island situation and British archaeologist John Evans noted that "island societies tend to overemphasize one development of their culture which is often connected to the ritual sphere."

After the rise in the old palace era (2000-1700 BC), Minoan Crete of the new palace era was at the height of its economic and political power. The eruption of the Thera volcano, which was earlier considered as having caused the end of Minoan culture, did not constitute a considerable break. Scientific methods of dating have made clear that this eruption happened around 1625 BC, more than 100 years before the destructions on Crete. In Eastern Crete and the Eastern Aegean islands, where the tephra (volcanic ash) came down, people in the Minoan settlements cleaned up the ashes to immediately rebuild their homes.

Around 1500 BC, a number of destructions completely changed Crete's political system. All 'palaces' except Knossos and the palace administration's representations known as "mansions" of "villas" were destroyed and never resurrected. Finds indicate that a number of these destructions were caused by earthquakes. Yet, earthquakes are not the sole reason for the profound political changes reflected in the archaeological heritage. After the palaces were destroyed for the first time by an earthquake, they were resurrected. Why was it so much different this time?

That of the palaces only one, namely Knossos, survived the catastrophe, supports the thesis of inner Cretan conflicts. It is likely that the other palaces felt Knossos 'centralized administration had gone too far. This reason most probably caused a rebellion against Knossos which was successfully subdued. Facts like these seem to serve as basis for the mythologic tradition about Minos of Knossos' struggles with Sarpedon, ruler of Lyktos (Malia?) and Rhadamanthys, ruler over Phaistos. After these struggles, Minos is said to have expelled them and their followers from the island.

These interior difficulties decisively weakened Crete and consequently caused the decline of an independent Minoan culture. Around 1500 BC, the Mycenaeans from mainland Greece took over the Cycladic islands and a mere century later, they conquered the Minoan colonies in the Eastern Aegean and Crete itself. They rebuilt the partly destroyed palace of Knossos to centrally administer most of the island. For administrative purposes they developed, most likely supported by Minoan writers, their own writing for their language, called 'Linear B' which is derived from the Minoan 'Linear A'. British archaeologist Michael Ventris who deciphered 'Linear B' has demonstrated that their language already was Greek.

Crete's past Aegean hegemony lives in the legend. This legend tells us cruel tales, like the one about the Minotaur. Minos 'wife Pasiphae had sodomy with a bull to give birth to her monster son. Minotaur received sacrifices of Athenian boys and girls who were a tribute of Athens to Crete. The bull-human was fed with this human tribute until Theseus, supported by Ariadne, was able to kill the dreadful beast. But this legend belongs to the victors's tradition and losers usually do not get much credit in the winner's version. In this respect, the Etruscans and Carthago were equally dicriminated by the victorious Romans.

The archaeological discoveries of the beginning of our century, have established that Crete's civilization during the bronze age was home to a society highly sophisticated in all respects; the Mycenaeans Greeks owe much to the Minoan Cretans. Without Crete' model the development of Mycenaean culture would not have been possible. After Crete was conquered by the Mycenaeans, about 1400 BC, the manners of Minoan style court life were even intensified. The carriers of Mycenaean civilization were the direct ancestors of the Greeks, who have influenced European culture until today. The common term for Minoan Crete as Europe's first advanced civilization is truly anachronistic. Of course, the Minoans did not consider themselves Europeans but were youngest member of a community of advanced cultures with an Eastern extension as far as the Nile valley and the rivers Tigris and Euphrat. The Cretans' ability to create an independent culture from the stimuli and ideas received from these highly advanced culture is important precondition for all further 'European' development. Crete's importance for Europe is caused in precisely this achievement.

Minoan Archeology in Western Crete

Yannis Tzédakis

Crete, the largest of the Greek islands, lies on Greece's southernmost boundary at what has always been one of the most strategic points in the Mediterranean ever since the Neolithic period.

Western Crete contains the prefectures of Hania and Rethymni, which between them encompass nearly a half of the island. The natural boundary on the east is Mt Ida or Psiloritis, the highest mountain on Crete with an altitude of 2,456 m, while the prefecture of Hania is dominated by the White Mountains, whose height is 2,453 m. The formation of the terrain, the abundance of trees, which would certainly have existed in the past, and the springs, which still exist today, give us a clear picture of the climatic conditions, flora and environment in which the people of Neolithic and Minoan times lived, for it is now generally agreed that the climate and conditions of life would not have been very different then.

The first excavations at Knosos, Phaistos, Tylissos, Malia, Gournia, Palaikastro and elsewhere focussed the attention of archaeologists on East and Central Crete, where the richness and quality of the finds, as well as the importance of the sites, are truly remarkable. The result was that after the heroic age of Cretan archaeology, with such great figures as Evans, Hadzidakis and Pernier, all the Greek and foreign archaeologists who worked in Crete interested themselves almost exclusively in East and Central Crete, while the western part was only visited or surveyed by archaeologists incidentally (we refer here only to the prehistoric period).

This lack of archaeological interest in West Crete may be explained by its natural ruggedness and the mountainous mass of Ida, which fostered the theory of a total or nearly total absence of a Neolithic and Minoan presence before the final destruction of the Palace of Knosos in 1375 BC. The father of this theory was the English archaeologist Pendlebury, who believed that after the dissolution of the central authority of Knosos, the Minoans were driven by necessity to explore the region west of Mt Ida, where previously there had only existed isolated outposts. In his presentation of the archaeological material described in his book he tried to demonstrate this theory scientifically. He also refers in his other writings to attempts at settlement that were unsuccessful and to fishing villages.

During the course of World War II the Germans proceeded without permission to excavate in different parts of the island, chiefly in West Crete, the results of which were published in 1951. One may therefore say that German archaeologists were the first to work systematically in this part of the island. However, the presentation of this new material and the archaeological observations of the Germans had no effect on the attitude of the Cretological specialists towards this region or its role in the development of the Neolithic and Minoan cultures on the island. The English archaeologist S. Hood in his review of F. Matz's book about the German excavations in the War made a study of the Minoan site at Hania, but did not proceed to a wider survey of all of West Crete until many years afterwards, between 1962 and 1965.

In this same period Linear B was deciphered by Ventris and Chadwick: among the place-names we find ku-do-ni-ja and a-pa-ta-wa, which correspond to Kydonia and Aptara; there can therefore be no further doubt about the existence of these two cities in Minoan times, since the tablets contain administrative texts dating to before the final destruction of the Palace of Knosos. Nevertheless, in the course of the general upset of the historical chronology occasioned by the success of the British research into the origin and nature of the language of the tablets, as well as by the new perspectives opened up by this discovery. It seems that these details were forgotten.

Here we must mention the great contribution of Professor P. Faure. who visited the whole of Crete over a period of many years, exploring its caves and collecting important material. His dating of the vases and sherds he found may not always have been correct, and the author's theories may at times seem a little strange, but his books and articles are basic to the history of archaeology in West Crete; they are pioneering works and should be respected as such.

The establishment of an Ephoria of West Cretan Antiquities for the first time in 1964 made it possible to study the region, with the aid of the literary sources, and to carry out surface surveys and systematic excavations. The central idea behind this research was the conviction that it was not possible for a mountain or rugged terrain to have deterred the people of Neolithic and Minoan times from colonizing such a fertile region.

The last twenty-five years, then, have been for West Crete a "promising start to a brilliant future". Systematic excavations, some of which are still in progress, have yielded results that have radically altered our ideas about the Neolithic and Minoan presence on the island, and new sites are continuously being added to the archaeological map of the region.

The reports published in recent years, whether scholarly or popularizing, have led certain archaeologists, chiefly Greek, to claim that there is a conscious attempt to belittle the great archaeologists who have worked or are still working in Crete. I think the position is a mistaken one, only to be explained by an excessively sensitive attitude to the really great scholars of the past and the present, a sensitive attitude that we all possess towards scholarship itself and our colleagues. The finds that have come to light since 1964/65 are not locked away and inaccessible to study by fellow archaeologists: quite the reverse, because it is worth everyone's while to see them and, in the final count, such publicity only adds to the prestige of the excavators.

It is therefore difficult to understand why certain monographs and articles that were published at the end of the 70's base their references to Neolithic and Minoan Crete on bibliographies that are virtualy prewar. The archaeologists in the bibliographical references are, it is true, better known than the Greek and foreign excavators and scholars who were working at that time in West Crete. Scholarship, however, is not necessarily furthered by the name of the scholar, but rather by archaeological discovery; and when this happens to contradict a generally accepted theory, to persist in this theory indicates, at the very least, a want of scholarly enlightenment.

West Crete was open to all archaeologists and it has befallen the lot of everyone who has worked and is working here to have the opportunity and satisfaction of discovering important examples of the Neolithic and Minoan cultures, which show that culturally the island was always a unity, without natural or artificial boundaries.

What, then, is the importance of the excavations in West Crete for archaeological research, and how much do they assist in a more accurate and complete understanding of the Neolithic and Minoan cultures as a whole throughout the island?

The cave of Yerani at Rethymno has given us a pretty clear idea of the daily lives and occupations of one group of people throughout nearly the whole of the Neolithic period. The data from the excavation, a study of the stratigraphy and the finds (pottery, stone and bone artifacts, and animal bones) show us that habitation of the cave was not permanent but periodic and directly related to the seasonal occupations of the inhabitants - agriculture, fishing, animal husbandry and hunting. The periodic nature of the occupation is apparent from the kinds of pottery found - there are no large storage vessels, for example - as well as from all the other finds, such as figurines and tools. During the periods of occupation a workshop for making bone tools must certainly have been functioning. In addition to complete tools, many half-finished ones were found together with the raw material: animal bones, among which were those of wild deer.

The cave was abandoned in the Late Neolithic period, probably due to rockfalls that blocked the entrance. It is thus one of the very few caves that have produced a pure Neolithic stratigraphy uncontaminated by later occupation. The cave was discovered in the course of construction work on the new Hania - Rethymno national road in 1969.

On the other hand the caves at Akrotiri, Hania and especially in the foothills of Kerameia - the caves of Koumarospilio and Platyvola - have given us an abundance of Late Neolithic, transition and Early Minoan pottery, not clearly stratified but extremely interesting. Mention should be made in particular of the EM II workshop that made pots with incised decoration, and which seems to have been one of the most important in all the island. The pots were imitations of stone vases, and this fact, interesting in itself, when taken together with the presence of EH II imported or imitation sauceboats and the discovery at Nea Roumata of a cemetery with graves of an Early Cycladic type, clearly demonstrates the existence of contacts and connections between this part of Crete, the Greek mainland and the Cyclades. The graves at Nea Roumata, moreover, lead us to regard with some scepticism the well-known theory about the establishment of settlements and their cemeteries during the Early Cycladic period on or close to the sea-coast, since this cemetery lies over 16 km inland on the lower slopes of the White Mountains.

Important excavations covering the end of the Neolithic and the Early Minoan periods include the following:

1. The Greek-Italian excavation at Nerokourou
2. The Greek-British excavation at Debla
3. The Greek-Swedish excavation at Kastelli, Hania

One of the great problems in Aegean archaeology are the relations between and the origins of the inhabitants of Crete, Greece, the Islands and the Asia Minor coast in the Early Bronze Age; there are conflicting theories, each of which stress the importance of the region in which the particular archaeologist's own interest lies. I believe that the recent finds from West Crete may assist these endeavours of the specialists.

The coming and going between the cultural centres of the Eastern Mediterranean basin that is known to have existed since the Neolithic period continued without a break. In the case of Hania, the connections with Kythira are of considerable interest. The English excavations showed that the settlement at Kastri was established by Minoans at the turn of the Middle Bronze Age. Did these colonists start out from the Hania region? It seems very probable, since early Barbotine ware is commoner here than in other Minoan centres.

What did Hania represent, however, during the course of the Middle Minoan period? There was already an important settlement on the site of Kastelli above the harbour and dense habitation at Akrotiri, on the Kerameia plateau in the district of Drapania Kissamou. They used caves like those at Perivolia and peak sanctuaries like those at Sklopa and Drapano for religious ceremonies.

The Kastelli settlement, which was provincial in character, maintained contacts with the great centres, expanded rapidly and by the beginning of the second palaces had grown into an important centre which reached its peak of prosperity in the LM I phase. Kastelli had houses with a system of streets and squares in accordance with the new architectural ideas and organized bureaucracy, as they appear from the archive of Linear A tablets and seals, and it produced its own pottery in a workshop that, apart from other wares, exported the famous cups of the Alternative style.

These are some of the discoveries underlining the cultural importance of the town. Whether or not it was called Cydonia is not significant, I think, although it would of course be interesting if it could be proved.

The Suda plain became thickly populated at this time; this can be seen from the series of Minoan houses uncovered in the course of the Greek-Italian excavations (1977-1979) and the Greek rescue excavations later on.

At this point mention should be made of the Greek excavations at Monastiraki, where a large group of storerooms and workshops was discoverd. The monumental architecture, the evidence for the existence of a religious centre and the archives of seals all point to the palatial character of the site.

Chronologically contemporary is the site of Apodoulou, which was excavated by a Greek-

Italian mission; a great many utility and storage pots were found.

To return, however, to Hania and the settlement of Kastelli: the old theory, if it still survives, that the LM II phase occured only at Knosos is no longer acceptable, because we now have the remains of a building and finds from that phase at Kastelli; they are for the moment few, but they are very characteristic. It has taken us quite a time to persuade our colleagues of this, but I think it has been justified.

With the final destruction of the palace at Knosos Minoan Cydonia reached its peak, where it stayed until the LM IIIC phase. It had relations with Cyprus and Palestine, and it exported its pottery – the well-known products of the local workshop with the characteristic sub-white ground – all over the island and to Greece and Cyprus. Recent research has indeed shown that commercial stirrup jars with Linear B writing, which are known on the Greek mainland, came from Hania. Thus the wa-nax of Cydonia at least controlled the export trade of West Crete.

One important piece of evidence to emerge is that no destruction level was observed in LM IIIA at Kastelli, but there was one, though limited in extent, at the beginning of the LM IIIB phase. Finally, relations between Cydonia and centres in Sicily and Sardinia are beginning to seem very probable, on the basis of the handmade LM IIIB pottery.

A brief reference is here necessary to the Mycenean conquest and presence on the island. With the exception of the language, which existed, incised on tablets and vases, in more or less all the Postpalatial centres known to us at present on Crete, both the architecture and the pottery rather argue against such a presence. In the case of the pottery in particular only some 5% of the total are Mycenean imports or local imitations. The local pottery workshop continued the Minoan tradition in both the shapes and the decoration, and borrowings from the Mycenean repertoire are very few.

The imported ivory caskets and other elements interpreted as being Mycenean or in the Mycenean style, are certainly interesting, but there is a long road ahead before the full extent of the problem is cleared up and the truth so much desired by everyone is established.

I am therefore particularly careful in my use of the term "Mycenean Crete", or of the other expression in current use but without real content, the "Creto-Mycenean period". I prefer the simpler traditional "Late Minoan period".

Examples of the Linear B script on stirrup jars have also been found outside the settlement at Hania in somewhat unexpected places: in the Perivolia cave and at Armeni, Rethymni, in a chamber tomb.

The LM III cemetery near the village of Armeni consists of clusters of chamber tombs and a small tholos tomb (207 have been excavated so far).

It is the first time that an archaeologist's pick has had the opportunity to uncover an entire cemetery of this period; it has been possible because the cemetery lies outside any habitation zone. The evidence that has emerged is particularly interesting. The inhabitants of the at present unknown town chose the site and laid out the cemetery. This is evident from the preliminary work of preparation, which involved levelling parts of the natural rock, creating access pathways to the different clusters and separating the tombs into clusters of large and small ones.

The architecture of the tombs, which all face northeast, consists of a simple descending ramp, a passage, and a semicircular or four-sided chamber. Some of them have steps going down, a large four-sided chamber with a pillar in the centre or at the end and a bench. Two of these each produced a gravestone, which was not found in situ but whose function may be considered certain.

Apart from the larnakes, a number of which have religious representations on them, the finds consist of pottery, many bronze weapons and ornaments, seals made of semiprecious stones, a boar's tusk helmet, a straw basket and a stirrup jar with Linear B writing, bearing the name wi-na-jo; the latter is also known from a vase found at Knosos and from Linear B tablets; perhaps this is the first name of a dead person in the Minoan period.

But what could have been the reason for establishing a town in about 1375 BC, which existed for some six generations until 1200 BC, as we can tell from the finds in the tombs, and a town that was quite large, to judge from the 50 tombs excavated so far?

The final answer will be given when the town itself has been found and excavated. An initial tentative theory is suggested by the existence of so many bronze objects of excellent quality and the presence nearby of a copper mine, although its use during the LM III period has not yet been confirmed.

All this may indicate that an industrial town was functioning on the site, because we know that the importation of copper from Cyprus to Crete had already come to an end at this time. Future research will demonstrate the truth or otherwise of this theory.

La Crète. Le réveil de l'Europe – D'un point de vue archéologique

Wolfgang Schiering

Dans la légende, Zeus, métamorphosé en taureau, attira Europe, princesse Phénicienne, et, alors, qu'en toute confiance, elle s'était assise sur son dos, l'enleva, lui fit traverser la mer et la conduisit en Crète. Minos, Rhadamante et Sarpédon, trois fils issus de cette union avec le père des dieux, y virent le jour. Minos devint roi de Cnossos, Rhadamante régna sur Phaistos. Europe, elle, donna certes son nom à tout un continent, mais si la Crète se trouve au commencement de l'histoire européenne, la raison n'en est pas seulement cette légende qui inspira comme peu d'autres l'ont fait l'art antique et moderne (jusqu'à Max Beckmann), mais bien plus son archéologie et son histoire.

La Crète, c'est à dire dans ce contexte, ce qu'on nomme aujourd'hui la Crète minoenne d'après le fils de Zeus et d'Europe; cette Crète qui commença à s'épanouir dans la deuxième moitié du troisième millénaire, qui connut un premier apogée au dix neuvième siècle, un second aux dix-septième et seizième siècles avant Jésus-Christ. Il ne faut pas oublier que cette île fut également appelée à jouer un rôle culturel important plus tard, alors que, sous domination dorienne, selon la tradition, elle était couverte de cent villes florissantes. Au huitième et septième siècle av. JC. à l'époque de ce qu'on a coutume d'appeler l'époque orientalisante, la Crète n'eut pas seulement un rôle décisif d'intermédiaire entre l'orient et l'occident entre la Syrie du nord, la Phénicie et la Grèce, mais encore, elle assuma au septième siècle une position prédominante dans la naissance de la sculpture hellénique archaïque que la littérature rattache à un second, à un nouveau Dédale. Bien plus tard encore, à l'époque byzantine, jusqu'à celle du Crétois El Greco (Theotokopoulos), la Crète, si peu aimablement traitée par Saint-Paul, eut une dimension européenne.

Revenons au premier Dédale, ce magicien du Roi Minos. C'est lui, qui, d'après la légende construisit le Labyrinthe de Cnossos. Nous savons depuis longtemps que l'origine du domicile légendaire du Minotaure, engendré dans l'union contre-nature de l'épouse de Minos avec un taureau de Poseidon, remonte au palais du Roi de Cnossos qui fut dégagé et partiellement reconstruit par l'archéologue Anglais Sir Arthur Evans au début de ce siècle, près de la ville actuelle d'Heraklion. Ce que nous savons du taureau-Zeus et d'Europe, du taureau de Poseidon et de l'épouse du Roi Minos, du Minotaure, cet homme à la tête de taureau, indique déjà, en l'absence de toute pièce archéologique correspondante, une signification extraordinaire accordée au taureau dans l'imaginaire religieux crétois minoen.

Les objets provenant des fouilles confirment non seulement l'existence d'un culte du taureau par les nombreuses représentations de tauromachies crétoises, somme toute encore très mystérieuses (fig. 12), mais bien aussi par d'innombrables autres représentations de taureaux (fig. 13), d'hommes-taureaux, de cornes de taureaux exécutées de façon plus ou moins abstraite, ainsi que par des moulages et des représentations symboliques diverses, de petites ou de grandes dimensions, de la double hache avec laquelle le taureau était immolé.

La Crète minoenne développa la première culture évoluée européenne, qui, avec l'organisation hiérarchique et bureaucratique d'un système administratif et économique de plus en plus centralisé, des structures politiques et religieuses étroitement imbriquées les unes aux autres, est comparable à celles de l'Egypte et du Proche-Orient et à classifier à leurs côtés. La preuve archéologique de cette affirmation globale nous est donnée par les constructions mises au jour et par les nombreuses pièces provenant de fouilles archéologiques. En ce qui concerne les témoignages architecturaux, la plupart des renseignements nous sont fournis par les ruines de palais de Cnossos, de Phaistos, de Mallia et de Kato Zakros. Ce qu'il est convenu d'appeler les "villas" (domaines agricoles) et qui prend une place intermédiaire entre les palais et les sites urbains, Haghia Triada, Tylissos, Vathypetron, est aussi une source importante. Les villes qui entouraient les palais doivent encore être l'objet de recherches plus approfondies. Elles nous fournissent cependant, dès à présent, des points de repères essentiels et c'est ainsi que l'on peut, prudemment, se faire une idée des liens unissant villes et palais. Les résultats des fouilles effectuées en sites urbains où, jusqu'ici, n'ont été retrouvés ni palais ni centre équivalent, nous autorisent à nous prononcer sur la prospérité des villes, les performances techniques, les ateliers, les travaux administratifs, les équipements portuaires et le culte. S'ajoutent enfin de nombreuses installations, pour la plupart à caractère agricole. N'ometons pas non plus de citer les aires funéraires qui nous sont souvent parvenues en meilleur état que les sites d'habitat, mieux conservées et plus complètes, que ces derniers dont quelque fois nous ignorons encore tout. Parmi ces tombeaux, les installations familiales et les édifices circulaires du troisième et du début du deuxième millénaires ainsi que les imposants tombeaux "royaux" comme le "tombeau-temple" près de Cnossos dévoilent plus particulièrement les structures sociales de la Crète minoenne.

Le déroulement de la vie dans les palais (fig. 14), dans les "villas" et les maisons de la Crète minoenne nous est révélé par les édifices et par les installations, (cours, chemins, escaliers, halls, bassins destinés au culte, magasins, ateliers) ainsi que par des restes de décoration murales (fresques et bas-reliefs) et ce qui subsiste de mobilier (trônes et autres éléments, vase de terre cuite ou de pierre). Il est intéressant de noter que, en comparaison, des maisons relativement modestes peuvent présenter des installations (cour, hall, bassin, premier étage) qui, de fait, en termes de qualité, réduisent la différence qui les séparaient des "villas" et des palais et que donc la vie dans les unes et dans les autres ne différait que de façon graduelle et non pas fondamentalement. A Thera, près d'Akrotiri, ville construite sous influence minoenne, toutes les maisons étaient décorées de fresques. Les thèmes en partie sacrés utilisés pour cette décoration rappellent ceux des palais et "villas" crétois. Sacré ou domestique se retrouvent donc étroitement liés, au-delà des palais et des "villas", de façon saisissante, dans les sites d'habitat. Les domestique se reconnaissant toutefois plus facilement dans les maisons que dans les palais où il est même parfois difficile de distinguer ce qui constituait la cuisine.

Le quotidien profane, bureaucratique des palais et "villas", lui, nous est révélé d'une part par les constructions et installations telles que magasins, trésors, moulins à huile, pressoirs, pithoi et d'autre part par les témoignages écrits et les cachets et les sceaux qui, eux, fournissent un aperçu des formes administratives et bureaucratiques en usage. Dans les palais, "les villas", les maisons ainsi que les monuments funéraires de différent type, des pièces se révélant consacrées au culte soit par leur conception architecturale, soit par l'inventaire de ce qu'elles contiennent (matériel de culte, symboles, représentations) nous permettent d'aborder les activités rituelles. A l'extérieur, ce sont des sanctuaires situés au sommet des montagnes, ou dans des grottes.

Il semblerait que l'ordre économique, politique et religieux de la culture crétoise minoenne ne soit issu ni simplement du fait de la croissance et du développement des familles et des transformations sociales et politiques tels que ces deux facteurs apparaissent dans l'histoire de l'évolution des habitats à la deuxième moitié du troisième millénaire, ni uniquement d'influences venues d'Egypte ou du Proche Orient. L'expansion intérieure favorisée par l'insularité et la situation géographique a plutôt conduit à une expansion extérieure, dirigée aussi bien vers le nord, les Cyclades, que l'ouest, les îles Lipari; ceci fait des Crétois, peu portés sur les pratiques guerrières mais excellents marins, par nature doués pour le commerce, dans un premier temps des élèves avides et assidus de ces anciennes cultures avant d'en devenir des partenaires placés sur un pied d'égalité.

Au centre du système économique et commercial crétois se trouvait une économie basée sur la gestion des magasins, c'est-à dire avant tout sur une économie de troc portant sur les produits conservés et stockés dans les grands pithoi de terre cuite, dans des caisses de pierre enterrées ou dans des jarres appropriées (céréales, olives, miel, huile, vin). Parallèlement, le bois, indispensable à la construction des navires et á celle des bâtiments a dû jouer un rôle important. Les produits d'une industrie métallurgique locale (des outils les plus simples aux vases les plus travaillés en passant par les armes) relevaient, avec les matières premières nécessaires à leur fabrication, en général importées, de cette économie de gestion d'entrepôts, de même que la poterie, les ateliers de production d'objets de pierre, de vases ou de lampes, tels qu'ils se laissent localiser grâce aux fouilles des palais de Cnossos et de Kato Zakros, ainsi que les manufactures travaillant les métaux précieux (ivoire et métaux précieux) ou bien encore les matières premières tel le cuivre qui n'était entreposé que dans un but de négoce. Rappelons enfin tout le secteur textile jusqu'à celui de la mode et des vêtements domestiques ou sacrés de la Crétoise (fig. 15). Stockage de produits bruts ou de produits manufacturés sur place ou encore importés, production locale dans l'enceinte du palais et commerce semblent avoir été étroitement liés.

Les objets retirés des fouilles de même que les représentations diverses trouvées, illustrent fort bien les liens existant entre ce système économique si complexe, basé sur la gestion des magasins et les activités commerciales et les palais et les "villas" (domaines agricoles) et nous donnent un aperçu de ce que pouvait être la vie de la société minoenne. Ce que nous contemplons aujourd'hui dans des représentations comme le fragment de fresque provenant de Cnossos, appelé communément "La Parisienne" (fig. 16), est moins l'émanation d'un "art de cour" d'un art pour la cour, d'un art pour le culte, d'un art pour l'art, que celle pour ainsi dire naturelle, traduite en formes esthétiques et artistiques, de l'abondance, de l'opulence d'un système économique performant dont les retombées bénéfiques grâce à un maniement de bon aloi, de toute évidence, s'étendent à une large couche de la population. Le fait qu'une économie florissant produise de telles manifestations artistiques, inimaginables sans la prospérité d'un style de vie original ni la stimulation du commerce extérieur, s'était déjà rencontré à l'époque prépalatiale, à la deuxième moitié du troisième millénaire, alors que, par exemple, de riches habitants de Mochlos font édifier des maisons funéraires pour leurs morts et qu'ils les dotent de somptueuses offrandes tombales. Apogée de ce que l'on pourrait qualifier "d'art de cour", par contre, au dix-neuvième siècle av. JC, à l'époque des Premiers Palais, le pendentif en or représentant deux abeilles (fig. 17) dégagé de la nécropole de Mallia, par exemple, ou encore, au dix-septième, également retrouvée à Mallia, la partie supérieure d'un sceptre en stéatite dont la moitié représente un léopard et l'autre une hache (fig. 18) pour le seizième siècle, l'ère néopalatiale, une tête de taureau sculptée, elle-aussi en stéatite, qui servait de vase à offrandes dans le Palais de Cnossos (fig. 13).

Dans une culture où la vie et le culte étaient si étroitement liés, il n'est pas toujours facile, et le domaine artistique n'y fait pas exception, de différencier les utilisations originales des objets dégagés dans les fouilles, de déterminer leur appartenance primaire au sacré ou au profane. Cela se voit bien dans la glyptique. Les cachets comportant des représentations sacrées prennent de plus en plus d'importance (fig. 19). On aimerait être en mesure d'affirmer à propos des autres cachets comme à propos du pendentif aux abeilles de Mallia (fig. 17) qu'ils étaient d'abord utilisés pendant la vie de leurs propriétaires avant d'être déposés dans les sépulcres comme offrandes funéraires.

Nous venons de montrer que les ruines de palais mises au jour donnent des renseignements des plus importants sur la vie et le culte (fig. 20). Ces ruines ont beaucoup de points communs, entre autre, la cour centrale, le centre du palais. Comme dans nos châteaux et châteaux-forts, en partant de cette cour, on pouvait accéder à toutes les parties du palais. En sa qualité de cour, elle devait remplir beaucoup de fonctions dont au moins une n'a pas d'équivalent dans nos châteaux et châteaux-forts, celle relevant du culte. Pour les tauromachies, ces cours centrales ne semblent pas avoir été assez longues. On peut cependant penser que d'autres jeux sacrés, d'autres manifestations religieuses y avaient lieu, comme tendrait à nous le prouver une fresque, il est vrai fortement retaurée (fig. 21). La cour-Ouest, du côté de l'entrée principale du palais est celle où avaient lieu aussi bien des réunions à caractère religieux que profane. Venant de la ville, les gens y arrivaient pour prendre part à des manifestations pour lesquelles les palais de Cnossos et de Phaistos sont dotés d'une partie supplémentaire que l'on a appelé "théâtre" en raison de l'escalier monumental qu'on y a dégagé. Dans la cour-Ouest et dans l'aile-Ouest du palais, on apportait également les denrées destinées aux grands silos circulaires, aux pithoi et aux caisses de pierre des magasins, livraisons qui étaient autant de prétextes à célébrer des fêtes des récoltes à caractère sacré. Les façades du palais étaient conçues comme des façades principales, donnant sur la ville et intentionnellement prestigieuses et attrayantes. L'architecture des palais minoens n'était certainement pas, comme on a voulu le faire croire, le résultat laissé au hasard d'une technique de construction accolant des éléments les uns aux autres.

La façade-Nord de la cour centrale de Phaistos montre, plus nettement que les façades de l'aile-Ouest, en quoi l'agencement architectural des palais minoens ouvre la voie à la première architecture européene qui n'a rien à rien envier à celle du Proche-Orient que les architectes Crétois, par ailleurs, connaissaient (fig. 22). Elle anticipe l'architecture Mycénienne, c'est-à-dire les constructions comme celle de la façade monumentale du tombeau dit "d'Atrée" à Mycène, en accentuant la partie médiane percée d'une porte flanquée de colonnes et de niches et en imposant une légère asymétrie voulue, à toute la largeur. Comme nous allons le voir plus loin, il est facile de démontrer en relevant des exemples existant déjà au Minoen que l'ordre en tant que principe esthétique n'est pas apparu pour la première fois au Mycénien.

Tout d'abord énumérons les autres compétences léguées par la civilisation minoenne à la civilisation européenne par l'intermédiaire de la civilisation mycénienne. Dans le domaine des techniques, on citera en premier lieu celles concernant la voierie, la construction de ponts, le charronnage, la construction navale ainsi que finalement celle se rapportant au système de canalisation et d'égout (y compris WC) tel que nous pouvons l'observer dans les palais et les "villas". Si nous mettons en correlation d'impressionnantes représentations de navires comme celle que nous livre une très belle fresque murale d'Akrotiri à Thera (fig. 23) avec ces hangars à bateaux dont nous connaissons depuis peu au moins une réalisation monumentale à Kommos, en Crète, et toute les conditions et tous les prémisses requis, inconnus ou connus, cernant la technique et l'art de la navigation qui amèneront plus tard les historiens grecs (Thucydide) à chanter les louanges du Roi Minos, souverain des mers (Thalassocratie), nous appréhendons quel haut niveau, dans le domaine de la navigation, les Mycéniens ont hérité des Minoens.

Ce n'est pas un hasard si, plus tard, on vit dans le personnage mythologiquement idéalisé de Dédale non seulement l'artiste mais aussi, au moins autant, le technicien, l'ingénieur, l'inventeur, campant symboliquement tout l'esprit de découverte et d'invention de la Crète minoenne. En archéologie, nous pouvons prouver des inventions, respectivement des innovations dans les domaines suivants: technique de la peinture murale, de la poterie (température des fours, couleur blanche, à base de talc, des vases dits de Kamares) de la métallurgie, celle utilisée dans l'atelier du graveur de cachets (aiguille à rotation rapide), dans celui de l'orfèvre (filigranne et granulation). La presque totalité de ces inventions a été léguée aux Mycéniens. On peut également qualifier d'innovatrice la mode minoenne, c'est-à dire la mode féminine (fig. 15, 16) qu'elle avait créée avant qu'elle ne se répande dans la culture mycénienne. Cette haute-couture implique une maîtrise de certaines techniques de production, de teinture, de décoration des étoffes employées ainsi que des prémisses esthétiques qui lui confèrent son côté innovateur, créateur. Les tauromachies qui faisaient partie des jeux sacrés minoens et dont les Mycéniens eurent connaissance, se rangent également parmi ces inventions, ces innovations. L'acquisition de leur technique est si difficile que la tauromachie espagnole contemporaine ne sait comment l'aborder. Une épée d'apparat trouvée à Mallia aux côtés d'autres épées minoennes peut symboliser l'art de l'armurerie minoenne. Nous connaissons également les casques de bronze des guerriers Minoens. C'est pourquoi nous pouvons affirmer que la Crète minoenne, même dans ce domaine, ce qui semble peu compatible avec la conception que nous avons de la "paix minoenne", de ces villes sans fortifications, pouvait éveiller l'intérêt des Mycéniens connus, eux, pour leurs penchants guerriers.

L'expansion minoenne a répandu, en exportant son système administratif et économique structuré bureaucratiquement, sur d'autres îles de la Mer Egée (Thera, Melos, Chios) et dans certaines villes de la côte occidentale d'Asie Mineure mais surtout en Grèce continentale, non seulement des éléments architecturaux qui l'accompagnaient (salle de réception, magasins) mais elle y a introduit et imposé la pratique de son écriture et l'utilisation des sceaux. Les importantes archives en tablettes d'argile des services administratifs des palais mycéniens comme celui de Pylos peuvent être comparées à celles plus anciennes des Minoens mais aussi à celles de service comparables en Egypte ou au Proche-Orient. Dans la première moitié du deuxième millénaire, la Crète minoenne avait déjà crée un système de hiéroglyphes et d'autres systèmes d'écriture à graphie linéaire. Jusqu'à maintenant aucune de ces écritures n'a pu être déchiffrée. C'est cependant à partir de l'écriture minoenne de typ A que l'écriture linéaire de type B s'est développée, écriture d'une langue grecque archaïque de Mycène déchiffrée par M. Ventris et J. Chadwick. Le fait que la Crète soit le berceau de cette écriture syllabique que, d'ailleurs les Mycéniens ont utilisée dans le palais postminoen de Cnossos, est l'un des legs les plus importants de la Crète à l'Europe.

Le temple grec considéré comme référence de base en architecture sacrée européenne puise lui-même son origine dans le "megaron" mycénien. Là aussi, dans le domaine de l'architecture sacrée, la Crète a été source d'inspiration, à savoir, à partir de ses salles de dimensions variées consacrées au culte ou bien encore de ses "façades sacrées" qui ont été à la base d'une évolution vers d'autres formes. Nous avons mentionné plus haut le fait que les célébrations religieuses aient eu également lieu dans les cours, en plein-air, sur des montagnes, dans des grottes-sanctuaires. Tout comme le mégaron, appelé à devenir le fier centre des palais Mycéniens (Tiryns, Pylos) les imposants murs crétois construits d'énormes polygônes ne parvinrent jamais en Grèce continentale. Mais ces murs cyclopéens, au contraire du mégaron, n'ont eu aucune influence directe, dans leur forme typique en tout cas, sur l'évolution de l'architecture grecque ultérieure.

En conclusion, revenons une dernière fois au principe esthétique basé sur la notion d'ordre telle que nous l'avons observée en architecture dans les palais minoens (fig. 14). Prenons par exemple, le pendentif en or "aux abeilles" de Mallia (fig. 17), la fresque "aux fleurs de lys" d'Amnissos (fig. 24) et une vase de Palaikastro (fig. 25). Ces trois œuvres ont en commun la symétrie: deux abeilles, trois fleurs de lys, huit tentacules. En les observant de plus près on voit que les détails de la fresque (bourgeons, fleurs), eux, sont disposés de façon asymétrique, mais c'est dans le remarquable mouvement qui anime les tentacules que l'asymétrie s'observe le mieux, à première vue. Les corps et les ailes des abeilles se reflètent comme dans un miroir de façon absolument symétrique. Ici, c'est surtout le disque convexe placé entre les deux abeilles, orné d'une granulation concentrique qui est décalé, de façon évidente, vers la droite. De plus, la cage sphérique située au-dessus des têtes des abeilles et l'anneau qui la surmonte ne sont pas placés en position médiane équilibrée par rapport aux abeilles. Je doute enfin que les trois pendentifs en forme de disque aient jamais été suspendus verticalement de façon symétrique, ce qui pourtant aurait été possible. Donc ces trois motifs comme tant d'autres en art minoen sont simultanément ordonnés et libres, immobiles et animés. Des concepts du type "ordre libre", "liberté ordonnée", "animation dans l'immobilité", "immobilité dans l'animation", se pressent à notre pensée. Pour appréhender ce phénomène de façon plus concrète, sélectionnons parmi nos trois motifs, celui du vase de Palaikastro (fig. 25) dans lequel les principes de liberté et de mouvement semblent jouer un plus grand rôle que ceux d'ordre et d'immobilité.

Sur le vase, le poulpe est représenté deux fois, une fois sur une face, une fois sur l'autre. Pourtant il ne s'agit pas d'une représentation continue, que l'on pourrait intituler "image marine". Les nombreux coraux, les escargots marins, les oursins, disposés entre les tentacules, ne le sont pas pour donner une impression de la vie marine mais se trouvent là en pièces rapportées et s'intègrent, éléments plus formels que conceptuels, au sens de "horror vacui", aux espaces vides. L'observateur voit sur ce vase comportant deux faces donc deux éléments, chacune d'elle en tant que tout, et non pas deux faces formant un tout, image naturaliste avec deux poulpes et une myriade d'hôtes marins. Pour le peintre de ce vase minoen, la nature n'était pas un point de départ pour en représenter l'unité mais un stimulus pour réaliser une représentation artistique en partie non-figurative qui s'était développée dans la peinture sur vases à la première moitié du deuxième millénaire utilisant de compositions magnifiques en spirales etc. (style dit "de Kamares"). A la place d'éléments de décoration non-figuratifs ou du moins difficiles à identifier, les peintres ont choisi la poulpe, entre autre, parce qu'il était propre en tant que forme naturelle idéale à reprendre à son compte l'énoncé esthétique des motifs antérieurs. Une interprétation selon laquelle le poulpe serait peint comme bondissant rapidement sous les yeux de l'observateur ne tient plus face aux photographies sous-marines. Elle doit être aujourd'hui remplacée par l'idée que le peintre avait beaucoup plus observé de poulpes morts ou captifs que de poulpes évoluant dans leur mileu naturel, que c'est à son imagination d'artiste qu'il devait de savoir les intégrer dans les formes esthétiques adéquates. Ce n'est pas la nature qui domine, mais l'art, le mouvement naturel étant amené au repos et soumis au mouvement artistique, la liberté naturelle entre dans l'ordre esthétique. C'est ainsi que naquit un motif qui pouvait être dédoublé, voire multiplié à l'infini comme les lys d'Amnissos (fig. 24), les poissons volants d'une fresque de Melos, les coraux de notre vase ou les éléments architecturaux minoéns.

Ce qui préoccupait les artistes minoens, ce n'était pas le tout dans le sens contemporain du terme, mais la somme, le résultat de l'addition d'une série d'éléments conçus et pensés pour s'emboîter les uns aux autres. Le Minoen voyait, percevait le tout, uniquement en éléments ou en somme d'éléments ou de parties. Dans l'avant dernier cas le principe permettant l'assemblage était soumis à une règle esthétique, conçu comme une chaîne avec un nombre infini ou fini de maillons, adapté aux fonctions requises, employant la symétrie, le concentrisme etc. selon le cas. Agglutination, un terme que l'on appliquait autrefois (cf plus haut) à l'architecture minoenne, peut décrire cet enchaînement progressif, à condition que l'on s'imagine cette agglutination comme un acte conscient qui ordonne des éléments et non pas comme quelque chose d'arbitraire, de naturel, d'incontrôlé.

Il est d'autant plus évident qu'une culture dans laquelle le principe de l'énoncé artistique est soumis de façon fondamentale à celui de l'ordre, avait également placé ce même principe d'ordre au tout premier plan de sa vie politique, économique et religieuse. Ce sens prédominant de l'ordre était sans doute la prémisse nécessaire à la forte influence que la Crète minoenne exerça sur l'évolution de la culture grecque et de la culture européenne.

La culture minoenne crétoise – Tentative d'une esquisse historique

Wolf-Dietrich Niemeier

La culture de l'âge du Bronze appelée culture minoenne d'après le souverain mythique de Cnossos, Minos, appartient aux civilisations dont nous ne possédons aucun texte lisible, (les systèmes d'écriture minoens n'ont pas encore été déchiffrés.), et dont les seules sources écrites à notre disposition sont des sources indirectes originaires de cultures voisines.

C'est la raison pour laquelle une tentative de reconstruction de l'histoire de la Crète à l'âge du Bronze nous limite presque exclusivement à l'interprétation de ce qu'on a trouvé dans les fouilles et excavations archéologiques, entreprise jamais facile ni toujours couronnée de résultats tangibles. L'esquisse suivante se voit donc obligée, dans l'espace qui lui est imparti, de simplifier bien souvent et de laisser de côté, globalement, toute discussion de méthode.

La situation géographique de la Crète lui valut de jouir des conditions nécessaires et essentielles pour que s'y développât la première culture évoluée à l'ouest des anciennes cultures du Proche-Orient et de l'Egypte. Son insularité offrit des conditions favorables, la protègeant des invasions ennemies et lui garantissant une évolution continue, dans l'ensemble peu troublée, de sa culture. D'autre part, le développement de la navigation (fig. 23) fit de la mer un important moyen de communication avec l'extérieur.

Le fait que la Crète, (la troisième des grandes îles méditerranéennes) occupât cette position privilégiée à presque égale distance des continents africain, asiatique et européen en fit un tremplin intercontinental.

Après qu'au paléolithique, époque à laquelle le niveau de la mer étant extrêmement bas, atteindre la Crète à l'aide de barques ou de radeaux ne posait pas de problèmes majeurs et que, des hordes de chasseurs ou de populations vivant de cueillette y eurent effectué des incursions, les premiers habitants permanents y arrivèrent, au néolithique, juste après l'an 7000 av. JC.; ils s'établirent à l'emplacement de ce qui serait plus tard le "Palais" de Cnossos. Ces habitants étaient originaires d'Asie Mineure d'où ils apportèrent une agriculture mixte, travaux des champs et élevage, déjà bien développée. Ils importaient déjà pour la fabrication de leurs outils de pierre de l'obsidienne (une pierre volcanique noire et ayant l'aspect du verre) de Melos, une des îles des Cyclades.

Au début, la population de la Crète néolithique se compose de quelques tribus dispersées, habitant soit des huttes de torchis, soit des grottes. Ce n'est que peu à peu que la population croît et ce n'est qu'à la fin du néolithique que l'on peut noter une importante multiplication des sites d'habitat et leur plus grande répartition sur l'île (environ 4300 – 3300 av. JC). Le site de Cnossos s'étendait, à cette époque, sur environ 4 ha ce qui laisse conclure à une population de plus de 1000 personnes. Des parallèles ethnologiques indiquent que ce chiffre implique déjà l'existence d'une forme sociale institutionnellement structurée de façon hiérarchique, ce que confirment les quelques objets d'apparat qui arrivèrent à Cnossos à cette époque: vases de pierre d'Egypte et ivoire de Syrie.

Nous possédons extrêmement peu d'informations sur les sites d'habitat de l'époque minoenne ancien ou de l'époque pré-palatiale 3300 – 2100 av. JC). Les quelques exemples qui ont été dégagés (Myrtos, Vasilikis) se présentent comme de petites aglomérations rurales. Les restes architecturaux et les céramiques de cette époque trouvés sous les Palais de Cnossos, Phaistos, et Mallia, indiquent cependant qu'il s'agit déjà d'habitats de dimension respectables. Cnossos, le plus grand d'entre eux, occupait, dans la partie tardive de l'époque du minoen ancien, déjà presque 5 ha et comptait entre 1300 et 1900 habitants.

La nécessité de l'existence d'une forme structurée de société s'appuie sur toute une série d'indices autres que ceux se rapportant à l'importance des sites d'habitat. On peut retracer un partage différencié du travail, un artisanat spécialisé dans cette Crète pré-palatiale.

Jusqu'à la moitié du troisième millénaire avant notre ère, les poteries répandues sur toute l'île, désignées du nom de l'endroit où on les rencontra pour la première fois, les poteries dites de Vasiliki, ces poteries sont d'une telle perfection et leurs décorations reposent sur des procédés de production si élaborés (réduction-réoxydation partielle à la cuisson) qu'elles ne peuvent avoir été produites ailleurs que dans des centres spécialisés (fig. 26). Un développement semblable se retrouve pour la métallurgie, la production des vases de pierre et celle des sceaux.

Les coutumes funéraires de cette époque montrent clairement une hiérarchie sociale. C'est ainsi que l'on trouve à côté de tombeaux édifiés pour un groupe social économiquement privilégié-dans le sud, ce sont des édifices funéraires circulaires avec des annexes rectangulaires (fig. 27), dans le nord et l'est, principalement des "maisons des morts" (fig. 28), dans les mêmes nécropoles, de simples tombes creusées, ou de modestes pithoi utilisés pour les obsèques ou encore des caisses de pierre. Les édifices funéraires, eux, circulaires ou non, se distinguent également par la richesse des offrandes tombales qu'ils renferment.

On constate, en particulier dans les tombeaux de l'élite à Mochlos et Gournia, une concentration d'objets précieux. On peut voir dans certains de ces objets, comme par exemple les diadèmes dorés, en raison de la présence d'objets comparables de la même époque au Proche Orient, des symboles d'autorité (fig. 29).

On trouve des emplacements pavés et des autels devant ces tombeaux (fig.28). Ceux-ci, tout comme les objets de culte, indiquent que ces sortes de tombeaux étaient également le lieu de cérémonies rituelles, c'est-à dire que l'élite qui y fut enterrée avait aussi une fonction religieuse. Ces faits parlent pour l'existence de ce qu'on désigne en ethnologie sous le terme de "chefferies". Ces dernières sont en règle générale des théocraties (des gouvernements de dieu, c'est-à-dire des formes de souveraineté dans lesquelles la hiérarchie religieuse se trouve à la tête de la société), dans lesquelles un culte des ancêtres des "chefs" jouait un rôle capital. Etroitement liée à ce système théocratique, nous trouvons toute une imagerie religieuse. C'est dans la période pré-palatiale que l'on voit apparaître pour la première fois les symboles du culte que sont les doubles haches et les "cornes de consécration", les premières représentations de divinités en notre possession datent, elles-aussi, de cette même époque (fig. 30).

C'est également à cette époque pré-palatiale que se développent les premiers échanges commerciaux entre la Crète et les autres régions du monde égéen. Nous connaissons des matières importées des Cyclades et de Grèce continentale, en Crète et vice versa. Vers le milieu du troisième millénaire, le premier comptoir crétois fut fondé, à l'extérieur de l'île, à Kastri, sur Cythère, escale sur la route commerciale entre la Crète occidentale et le Péloponnèse. Ce qui à été trouvé dans les fouilles, en vases de pierre égyptiens, en sceaux syro-palestiniens, en matières premières exotiques comme l'ivoire et les oeufs d'autruche, et les poignards crétois des tombeaux cypriotes, fournit autant de preuves de l'existence de relations commerciales entre la Crète pré-palatiale, Chypre et le Levant. Ces objets n'étaient d'ailleurs que les sous-produits d'un commerce d'autres marchandises, selon toute vraissemblance, mais nous ne pouvons que spéculer sur la nature de ces marchandises.

L'un des buts principaux du commerce crétois doit en tout cas avoir été d'acquérir des métaux dont les gisements de minerai étaient pour ainsi dire inexistants ou insignifiants sur l'île. Il a été prouvé, sur le fondement d'analyses scientifiques, que le plomb et l'argent étaient importés de l'île de Siphnos dans les Cyclades et de Laurion, en Attique. L'origine des autres métaux n'est pas aussi facilement définissable. Le cuivre serait venu également de Laurion, de Laconie (ce qui expliquerait peut-être la "colonie"crétoise sur Cythère) et de Chypre, l'or de Macédoine, de l'Anatolie du nord-ouest (Troie) ou de l'Egypte. Ce qui est sûr c'est que l'étain venait d'une région n'appartenant pas au monde égéen, étain, qui, à l'époque pré-palatiale était déjà utilisé en alliage avec le cuivre dans la production d'un bronze plus résistant que celui fourni par alliage du cuivre à l'arsenic. Il semblerait qu'il ait été importé à partir du Nord-Ouest de l'Anatolie. En effet, à Troie, en l'an 3000 av. JC, on connaissait déjà ce bronze, alliage de cuivre et d'étain, et vers le milieu du troisième millénaire, il y semble d'usage courant. Selon toute vraissemblance, l'origine de l'étain utilisé serait, déjà à cette époque, l'actuel Afghanistan (voir ci-dessous).

La rareté de ces métaux recherchés aurait rendu nécessaire l'organisation d'un commerce extérieur dans le but d'en acquérir; cette nécessité serait donc le stimulus engendrant la création d'organisations étatiques et ainsi, celui donnant également naissance au développement d'une culture de type "évolué", phénomène parallèle à ce qui s'était passé dans les cultures égyptiennes et mésopotamiennes qui, elles-aussi, se dont développées dans des contrées pauvres en minerai.

Les couches de terrain concernées ayant été profondément bouleversées par la construction des "Premiers Palais", nous n'avons que peu d'informations concernant les dernières phases de ce développement qui entraîne finalement la création de centres urbaines, au début de ce que l'on appelle "l'époque des Premiers Palais" (vers 2000 av. JC) en Crète. L'identification récente de proto-palais de la fin du troisième millénaire sous le Palais de Cnossos et de Mallia révèle que les changements au début de cette période des "Premiers Palais" n'ont pas été aussi radicaux qu'on le croyait à première vue.

Pourquoi est-ce en Crète que la première culture "évoluée" s'est développé, à l'Ouest des anciennes culture égyptienne et de celles du Proche-Orient? Si nous considérons le monde égéen au troisième millénaire, nous y trouvons trois communautés culturelles qui ont atteint au moins le même niveau que celui de la Crète minoéenne: le helladique primitif en Grèce centrale et sur le Péloponèse, le cycladique primitif sur les îles de la mer Egée centrale et l'égéen du nord-ouest, sur la côte nord-ouest de l'Asie Mineure et les îles adjacentes. Vers la moitié du troisième millénaire, ces communautés culturelles se trouvaient pour ainsi dire à la veille de développer, elles-aussi, une culture évoluée; elles possédaient des centres urbains parcourus d'un réseau de voies de communication (ex: Manika sur Eubée, d'une superficie de 50 ha, Poliochni sur Lemnos), des bâtiments centraux presque comparables aux "palais" (ex: Lerna et Troie) et une production artistique de haut niveau (ex: l'idole des Cyclades). A la deuxième moitié du troisième millénaire, ce développement prit fin de façon brutale et l'on constate de violentes destructions. Les témoignages archéologiques se réfèrent à l'arrivée de nouveaux groupes de populations venant d'Anatolie et des Balkans. La Crète semble avoir été épargnée par cette invasion et au contraire des autres régions du monde égéen, elle ne connut pas de rupture culturelle ni de déclin. De cette façon, elle put continuer à se développer, à intensifier ses contacts avec les hautes cultures de la méditerrannée orientale er lorsque le moment, grâce au développement social sur l'île, le permit, à en recevoir puis à en assimiler d'une façon originale qui lui est propre, les éléments principaux.

C'est donc vers 2000 av. JC que les premières villes furent construites en Crète. A cette époque Cnossos atteint déjà de telles dimensions qu'elles ne seront pour ainsi dire plus jamais dépassées jusqu'à la fin de la culture minoenne. Elle recouvrait une superficie d'au moins 45 ha et comptait au minimum entre 11000 et 18000 habitants. Mallia et Phaistos n'étaient guère plus petites. Ces villes furent construites selon des plans bien organisés et le long de rues pavées (fig. 31).

Au centre de ces aglomérations urbaines, toujours un bâtiment central que nous avons coutume de désigner sous le terme de "Palais" depuis que Sir A. Evans crut avoir découvert à Cnossos le palais du souverain mythique Minos (fig. 32). Toute une série de conceptions et de techniques de construction de ces "palais" sont copiées de précédents égyptiens ou d'Asie Mineure: une orientation presque exactement nord-sud, des orthostates (d e grands blocs de grès verticaux) pour les soubassements des façades, une construction rectangulaire. Ce type d'architecture révèle, cependant dans son ensemble, une évolution particulière de type crétois par la présence d'une cour centrale flanquée d'ailes, d'une autre grande cour toujours située devant la façade-ouest. Les "Premiers Palais" ont été détruits ves 1700 av. JC par un tremblement de terre mais vite reconstruits et quelques fois de façon encore plus somptueuse: c'est ce qu'on appelle les "Seconds Palais".

Quand Evans dégagea, au début de ce siècle, le Palais de Cnossos, la Reine Victoria règnait sur la Grande Bretagne et ce sont les idées de l'époque qui influencèrent alors l'image qu'on se fit de la fonction des palais minoens. Les fouilles archéologiques permettent cependant de reconnaître toute une série de fonctions à ces bâtiments centraux monumentaux.

1. Une administration mise en place selon le modèle des anciennes cultures orientales qui ne se limite pas à l'application de sceaux sur des cachets d'argile (fig. 33) de divers objets (poignée de porte/de caisse/de jarre) mais également utilise l'écriture alors nouvellement introduite (hieroglyphes-écriture linéaire de type A) à des fins bureaucratiques (tablettes d'argile (fig. 34)).

2. Religion et rites-de nombreuses salles destinées à des manifestations religieuses rituelles-de nombreux objets de culte-à l'époque des "Seconds Palais" des peintures murales, programmes religieux et rituels, à Cnossos (fig. 21).

3. Stockage de provisions-L'étendue des bâtiments réservés aux magasins et les grands silos à céréales semi-enterrés commes ceux des cours-ouest des Palais de Cnossos et Phaistos dont les capacités surpassent largement les besoins du palais et de ses habitants (fig. 35).

Cette multi-fonctionalité des palais a été rendue par l'humour tout britannique de Paul Halstead dans sa formule, le palais minoen réunissait sous un seul toit les équivalents du Palais de Buckingham, de Whitehall, de l'Abbaye de Westminster et probablement celui du stade de Wembley. En mentionnant ce dernier, il voulait bien sûr faire allusion aux tauromachies (fig. 12). "Ce sport", dont la pratique ne semble pas sans danger, est d'ailleurs plus vraissemblablement un rite religieux lié au sacrifice du taureau.

Les capacités disproportionnées de stockage des palais tout comme les sceaux et les tablettes d'argile, manifestations d'une bureaucratie bien établie, indiquent une forme de système économique basée sur la redistribution (on entend par redistribution un mode d'échanges dans lequel biens et services sont fournis à une administration centrale qui se charge de les redistribuer). Ce système économique permet la spécialisation des artisans puisque par la redistribution leur société ou son gouvernement les entretiendra et qu'ils n'auront plus à produire leur propre nourriture.

Le système de redistribution permet également une amélioration de la qualité de la production artisanale et entraîne la production d'objets d'apparat d'une extrême haute qualité. On se doit de mentionner en métallurgie les performances technologiques de l'armurerie (râpières, fers de lance perfectionnés) ce qui allant de paire avec la création d'une flotte sans égale en mer Egée, à cette époque, fournit les conditions nécessaires à l'expansion crétoise dans le monde égéen. Des récipients précieux, en métal, (bronze, argent, or) appartenaient également à cette production. Les orfèvres introduirent du Proche-Orient les techniques du filigranne et de la granulation (fig. 17). Les vases de métal et les armes crétois étaient des objets recherchés destinés à l'exportation. On les trouve mentionnés dans les archives de tablettes d'argile du Palais de Mari, sur le Moyen-Euphrate au 18 ème siècle av. JC. On a trouvé des vases d'argent crétois dans les tombeaux royaux, datant de la même époque, à Byblos, au Liban. A l'époque des "Seconds Palais", des récipients en metal précieux et les armes furent exportés en Grèce continentale comme le prouvent les résultats des fouilles des tombes en tranchées de Mycène ainsi qu'en Egypte où on trouve représentés dans des tombeaux de fonctionnaires de Thèbes des "Keftiu" (des Crétois) portant ces objets (fig. 36).

Au début de l'époque des "Premiers Palais", le tour rotatif du potier fut introduit et c'est grâce à lui qu'on pût mettre au point la technique permettant de produire ce qu'on appelle "les vases de Kamares" d'après l'endroit où on les a dégagés pour le première fois (fig. 37). Les vases de cette sorte, produits dans des centres palatieux, sont parfois d'une extrême finesse de parois (coquille d'oeuf) et appartiennent en tout cas à ce que la poterie artisanale a jamais produit de plus beau. Ils étaient presque autant recherchés au Levant et en Egypte que la porcelaine chinoise en Europe au 18 ème siècle de notre ère.

C'est aussi en Crète, au début de l'époque des "Premiers Palais que fut mise au point la technique de peinture de fresques (peinture appliquée sur un enduit de chaux encore humide) et au début de l'époque des "Seconds Palais" cette technique fut exportée également vers le Levant. Dans les palais des souverains de Kanaan, Alalach et Tel Kabri (Rechob), on a retrouvé, sur les murs et le sol, des fresques exécutées sous l'autorité d'artistes crétois.

Donc, si au début, les Crétois ont repris des idées venant de cultures du Proche-Orient et d'Egypte, bientôt ils ne se contentèrent plus de n'être que partie prenante mais se hissèrent vite à un rang d'égalité et devinrent de véritables partenaires à part entière de ces cultures. Ce sont en particulier leurs productions artistiques qui attirèrent l'attention et l'admiration, ceci se voit bien par le fait que dans l'imagination des Kanaanites, le dieu des arts, d'après un texte mythique, est originaire de Ugarit en Kaphtor (Crète).

Les relations étroites entre la Crète minoenne et la culture Kanaanite de la côte levantine s'expliquent en partie par le commerce des métaux, commerce d'une importance prédominante. L'étain nécessaire à la production du bronze était une matière première rare. Nous pouvons lire sur une tablette d'argile provenant des archives du Palais de Mari comment un commerçant Crétois achète de l'étain à l'agent du Palais, à Ugarit. Le Crétois a à sa disposition un interprete pour mener à bien les négociations. Une autre tablette raconte comment l'étain provenant de la région de l'actuel Afghanistan était transporté par les caravanes et après être passé entre les mains d'intermédiaires mésopotamiens, livré au Palais de Mari.

Retournons en Crète où il nous faut encore souligner qu'au début de l'époque des "Premiers Palais" se mit en place la première organisation politique que l'on peut décrire par le terme d' "état". C'est dans ce contexte que l'absence de sources écrites mentionnée plus haut se fait ressentir le plus fortement. Cependant, on peut retracer le fait que chaque centre urbain disposait d'un arrière pays, d'un territoire. Nous en trouvons la preuve, entre autre, dans la présence de sanctuaires construits au sommet des montagnes et dont l'île est parsemée. Une hiérarchie régit cet ensemble de sanctuaires; près du palais ou du centre urbain, nous trouvons un sanctuaire, lié à ce dernier, un sanctuaire principal et une série de sanctuaires de moindre importance qui sont tous situés à portée du regard de leur sanctuaire principal. A côté de ces indices, les styles régionaux de céramique et la présence de certains artefacts (cachets de l'atelier d'un certain palais etc ...) sont autant d'indications tendant à démontrer l'existence d'une structure territoriale en Crète minoenne.

On peut ainsi distinguer un ensemble de 6 centres urbains et "palatiaux" (fig. 38) pour la période des Premiers et Seconds Palais en Crète, éloignés les uns des autres de 35 à 40 km et ayant respectivement un territoire de 1000 à 1500 km². L'organisation politique de la Crète minoenne semble donc correspondre au modèle définit par l'archéologue britanique Colin Renfrew sous le nom de "early state module" et qui est caractéristique des formes étatiques primitives comme par exemple celle des Sumériens, des Etrusques ou des Mayas mais aussi de la culture mycénienne de la Grèce continentale et de la Grèce des Cités, des Poleis. Tous ces exemples ont en commun une série de petites entités politiques indépendantes qui ne forment pas d'unité politique mais une unité culturelle et ethnique.

On distingue, au plus tard pendant la période des Seconds Palais, une hiérarchie nette entre les palais et les sous-centres qui en dépendent (villages, villas). La question de savoir si la Crète minoenne était une entité politique administrée de façon centraliste ne peut se résoudre de façon satisfaisante par de seules recherches archéologiques. Du moins, à l'époque des Premiers Palais, elle était constituée d'une sorte d'alliance de villes, d'une sorte de fédération comme nous en connaissons à Sumère et en Etrurie. Il semblerait que ce soit seulement à l'époque des Seconds Palais (1700 - 1500) que Cnossos exerçât une domination centraliste sur l'ensemble de l'île. C'est ainsi que nous interprétons les empreintes des sceaux de l'administration de Cnossos trouvés dans toute une série de fouilles ainsi que les témoignages égyptiens mentionnant l'"état crétois" comme un "état" assez grand.

Après avoir fondé la "colonie" minoenne de Kastri sur Cythère, à l'époque des protopalais, les Crétois étendirent leur territoire au-de-là de leur île, à l'époque des Premiers Palais. D'autres "colonies" furent fondées sur les îles de la mer Egée orientale (Kasos, Karpathos, Rhodes, Samos) et sur les île du littoral d'Asie Mineure (Knidos, Iasos). Elles avaient la fonction, selon toute évidence, d'assurer le libre passage et de maintenir la route commerciale ouverte. A l'époque des Seconds Palais, la zone d'influence de la Crète minoenne s'adjoint d'autres points en mer Egée orientale (Milet, Telos, Keos) ainsi que toute une série d'îles des Cyclades (Thera, Melos, Keos, Naxos) (fig. 39). On en trouve trace dans des sources égyptiennes de l'époque de Tuthmosis II, dans lesquelles il est question de "Keftiu (la Crète) et des îles du milieu de la grande mer verte", ce qui implique que la Crète est perçue comme le centre d'un empire insulaire. A l'époque historique, la tradition grecque rapporte l'existence de cet "empire insulaire". C'est ainsi que Thucydide, le grand historien athénien du 5ème siècle av. JC (I. IV) écrit: "Minos fut le premier dont nous savons qu'il fît construire une flotte qui dominait ce que nous appelons aujourd'hui la mer hellénique, qui conquit les Cyclades qu'il peupla en repoussant les Cariens et en y mettant ses propres fils comme gouverneurs."

La forme de gouvernement de la Crète minoenne nous pose un problème. La cité orientale est caractérisée par la dualité entre le Palais et le Temple, voire par la rivalité entre le Palais et le Temple. Dans les cités crétoises, au contraire, un seul bâtiment central, monumental, le Palais, qui comme nous l'avons déjà dit, remplit, parallèlement à ses fonctions économiques et administratives, des fonctions religieuses et rituelles. Le palais crétois selon toute évidence serait le siège de l'administration centrale, et celui d'une institution centrale religieuse. Il unit en lui-même ces deux fonctions. On pourrait donc le définir comme palais-temple ou encore temple-palais.

A ceci s'ajoute une caractéristique encore plus surprenante de la culture minoenne. L'absence totale de représentation d'un souverain, qui, dans l'art égyptien et dans l'art du vieil orient est une manifestation caractéristique. La fonction politique de l'art figuratif en Crète ne semble pas être celle de faire de la propagande pour un souverain mais de propager un culte et un rituel qui, d'après les preuves fournies par les images que nous avons à notre disposition (fig. 19), sont fortement valorisés. Le spécialiste du comportement, Konrad Lorenz, a montré que la ritualisation peut contenir les agressions et réenforcer les liens sociaux. Un pouvoir reposant sur une religion fondée sur une idéologie peut aussi avoir la fonction d'assurer le soutien populaire au groupe qui exerce le pouvoir au lieu que ce dernier ne doive utiliser le bâton de la force. C'est là, semble-t-il, que réside le secret de ce qui se cache derrière cette comparaison avec les cultures du Proche-Orient, ce fait remarquable de palais non fortifiés dans des cités également non fortifiées au point de nous rendre difficile la délimitation entre ville et palais. Il y règne donc une paix sociale reposant sur l'autorité religieuse ainsi que certainement sur le niveau de vie de la population. Des ennemis extérieurs ne sont pas à craindre, l'insularité et une flotte puissante la protégeant.

Dans la Crète des palais, c'était déjà le cas dans la Crète pré-palatiale, au contraire des cultures égyptiennes et du Proche-Orient, la couche dirigeante politique et la couche dirigeante religieuse semblent donc avoir été identiques. Ce fait exceptionnel tient peut-être de l'insularité car ainsi que l'a fait remarquer l'archéologue J. Evans, les communautés insulaires tendent à développer exagérément un aspect de leur culture, souvent lié au domaine du cérémoniel.

Après son ascension à l'époque des Premiers Palais (2000 - 1700), la Crète minoenne atteint son apogée économique et politique à l'époque des Seconds Palais. Même l'éruption du Thera, qui, autrefois était tenue comme responsable de la disparition de la culture minoenne, en semble pas avoir entraîné d'interruption significative. Des méthodes scientifiques de datation nous permettent de fixer cette éruption vers 1625 av. JC; c'est-à-dire plus de cent ans avant les destructions. En Crète orientale, là où il y eut de fortes retombées de cendres, les sites d'habitat furent vite déblayés et reconstruits.

Mais vers 1500 av. JC, eurent lieu en Crète toute une série de destructions après lesquelles il y eut un changement total de système politique. Tous les palais à l'exception de celui de Cnossos furent détruits et ne furent pas reconstruits; il en fut de même pour les "villas", ces filiales de l'administration. Il existe certainement un rapport entre les destructions en question et des séismes, du moins en ce qui concerne certaines d'entr'elles. Des séismes et uniquement des séismes ne peuvent avoir été la seule cause de ce bouleversement politique, tel qu'il se reflète dans l'héritage archéologique. Après la première destruction des palais par une catastrophe sismique, ne les avait-on pas reconstruits immédiatement? Pourquoi, cette fois, en fut-il autrement?

Le fait que seul le Palais de Cnossos ait survécu tendrait plutôt à indiquer un conflit intérieur. Il se peut que la centralisation de l'administration et le monopole commercial des dirigeants de Cnossos soient allés trop loin et n'aient plus été supportés des autres palais, aient donc conduit à une rebellion contre Cnossos, qui, cependant aurait été contenue avec succès. C'est peut-être ce type d'événement qui est à l'origine de la tradition mythologique selon laquelle Minos de Cnossos eut un conflit armé avec Sarpédon, souverain de Lyktos (Mallia) qu'il s'opposa ensuite également à Rhadamante, souverain de Phaistos, en une violente dispute, au terme de laquelle il les expulsa tous deux et leurs suites, hors de l'île.

Ces conflits intérieurs affaibliront considérablement la Crète et cette faiblesse entraîna le déclin de la civilisation minoenne originale. Vers 1500, des Mycéniens de Grèce continentale s'emparèrent des colonies minoennes des Cyclades, un peu moins d'un siècle plus tard, ils envahirent les comptoirs minoens situés en mer Egée orientale et finalement, la Crète elle-même. Ils reconstruisirent en partie le Palais de Cnossos pour régner à partir de ce point central sur la plus grande partie de l'île. Ils mirent au point, certainement avec l'aide de scribes minoens, à partir de l'écriture crétoise linéaire de type A, une écriture propre de type B, adaptée à leur langue, à des fins administratives. Il ressort du déchiffrement de l'écriture de type B effectué par le chercheur Britanique M. Ventris qu'il s'agissait déjà d'une langue grecque.

De la domination crétoise, il ne resta bientôt plus que la légende. Et cette légende nous rapporte des histoires cruelles comme celle du Minotaure, ce monstre enfanté par Pasiphae et un taureau à qui l'on jetait en pâture de jeunes vierges et des adolescents athéniens, sorte de tribut qu'il dévorait jusqu'à ce que Thésée sût, aidé par Ariadne, fille de Minos, tuer ce monstre assoiffé de sang. Cette légende, nous la tenons des vainqueurs, et les vaincus se tirent toujours mal d'affaire dans les contes des vainqueurs. Les Etrusques, les Cathagénois, subirent le même sort, à cet égard, de la part de leurs vainqueurs, les Romains.

Grâce aux découvertes archéologiques faites en Crète au début de notre siècle, il devint cependant évident que cette île avait été, à l'âge du Bronze, le foyer d'une société hautement cultivée à qui les Mycéniens devaient beaucoup. Sans cet exemple, sans ce précédent, la culture mycénienne du 17ème siècle av. JC est inimaginable; après la prise de la Crète par les Mycéniens en 1400 av. JC la culture de cour qui règnait dans les forteresses et dans les résidences en est encore plus marquée.

Ces Mycéniens-là étaient les ancêtres de ces Grecs qui ont influencé notre culture européenne de façon si marquante jusqu'à aujourd'hui. En fait, la formule courante qualifiant la culture minoenne de première culture avancée de l'Europe est un anachronisme. Les Minoens ne se voyaient pas en tant qu'Européens mais ils formèrent un maillon, l'élément le plus récent d'une communauté de civilisations qui s'étendaient de l'Orient à la Vallée du Nil, à celles du Tigre et de l'Euphrate. C'est en créant à partir de modèles qui les avaient stimulés, une civilisation propre, originale et en en transmettant les progrès culturels à la Grèce continentale que les Crétois ont fourni les conditions nécessaires à tout développement ultérieur. Et c'est là que réside la signification européenne de la culture minoenne.

Archéologie minoen dans la Crète occidental

Yannis Tzédakis

La Crète, la plus grande île grecque, se trouve à l'extrémité sud de l'aire de domination grecque, à l'un des endroits les plus importantes du monde au plan stratégique, et ce déjà à la période néolithique.

La Crète occidentale comprend les nomes de La Canée et de Réthymnes, c'est à dire presque la moitié de l'île. La limite naturelle Est en est le mont Ida, ou Psiloreites, la plus haute montagne de Crète, qui culmine à 2.456 m. Le nome de La Canée comprend les Lefka Ori, dont le sommet est à 2.453 m. La morphologie du sol, l'abondance d'arbres qui était sans doute la même dans le passé, les sources que nous voyons encore aujourd'hui, nous donnent une image assez claire des composantes climatiques, de la flore et de l'environnement dans lequel vivaient les hommes des époques néolithique et minoene: il est aujourd'hui généralement admis que le climat et les conditions de vie étaient assez semblables à ces époques-là.

Les premières fouilles à Cnossos, Phaestos, Tylissos, Mallia, Gournia, Palaiokastro et ailleurs ont concentré l'intérêt des archéologues sur la Crète orientale et centrale, où la richesse et la qualité des trouvailles, de même que l'importance des sites, sont vraiment surprenantes. Ainsi, après la période héroïque de l'archéologie crétoise avec Evans, Hatzidakis et Pernier, tous les archéologues, grecs comme étrangers, qui travaillaient en Crète, ont montré un intérêt presque exclusif pour la Crète orientale et centrale, tandis que la partie occidentale accueillait par hasard la visite de chercheurs ou des recherches archéologiques (nous nous limitons à la période préhistorique).

Ce manque d'intérêt scientifique pour la Crète occidentale pourrait être expliqué par la sauvagerie de la nature et la masse montagneuse du mont Ida, qui ont appuyé la théorie d'une absence complète ou presque complète du Néolithique et du Minoen jusqu'à la catastrophe finale du palais de Cnossos en 1375 av. J. C. Le père de cette théorie est l'archéologue anglais Pendlebury qui croit qu'après la chute du pouvoir central de Cnossos, les Minoens se sont trouvés dans la nécessité d'explorer la contrées à l'ouest de l'Ida, où il n'y avait auparavant que des postes isolés. La présence du matérial archéologique qu'il décrit dans son livre démontre "de façon scientifique" l'opinion ci-dessus. Finalement, dans ses autres textes, il y voit des tentatives d'installations avortées et des villages de pêcheurs.

Pendant la deuxième guerre mondiale, les allemands, sans aucune autorisation, ont mené des fouilles dans différents endroits de l'île, surtout en Crète occidentale, dont les résultate ont été publiés en 1951. Nous pouvons donc dire que les archéologues allemands ont été les premiers à travailler systématiquement dans cette partie de l'île. De toute manière, la présence d'un nouveau matériel et les remarques archéologiques des allemands n'ont pas influencé la position des spécialistes "crétologues" sur cette région et son rôle dans l'évolution des civilisations néolithique et minoenne de l'île. L'archéologue anglais S. Hood, dans sa critique du livre de Fr. Matz sur les fouilles allemandes durant la guerre, a étudié le site minoen de La Canée, mais n'a pas poussé les recherches plus loin on ce qui concerne la Crète occidentale, si ce n'est beaucoup plus tard, entre 1962 et 1965.

A la même période l'ecriture linéaire B a été déchiffrée par Ventris et Chadwick: parmi les toponymes nous trouvons KU-DO-NI-JA et A-PA-TA-WA qui correspondent à Kydonia et Aptara; après cela il ne peut plus y avoir de doute sur la coexistence de ces deux villes à l'époque minoenne, puisque les tabletts contiennent des textes administratifs que l'on date d'avant la catastrophe définitive du palais de Cnossos. Il semble, cependant, que dans le bouleversement général des données historiques, provoqué par la réussite des recherches anglaises sur l'origine et la nature de la langue des tablettes, aussi bien que par les nouvelles perspectives qu'ouvrait cette découverte, ces détails furent oubliés.

Il nous faut faire référence ici à la grande contribution du prof. P. Faure, qui parcourut toute la Crète en explorant les grottes des années durant, rassemblant un matériel important. La chronologie des vases et des tessons trouvés peut ne pas être toujours parfaitement exacte, et les théories de l'auteur peuvent être parfois étranges, pourtant ses livres et articles sont fondamentaux pour l'histoire de l'archéologie dans la Crète occidentale. Ce sont des œuvres d'avant, et elles doivent être considérées comme telles.

La création d'une Ephorie des Antiquités de Crète occidentale en 1964, pour la première fois dans l'histoire du Service des Antiquités de la Grèce, et la définition de ses cadres de fonctionnement, ont rendu possible l'étude de la région, avec l'aide des sources philologiques, de la prospection et des fouilles systématiques. L'idée centrale, présente dans toute cette recherche, était la conviction qu'une montagne ou la sauvagerie de la nature n'avait pas pu empêcher les hommes du Néolithique et du Minoen de se répandre dans la Crète occidentale, région très fertile.

Les 25 années qui viennent de passer sont pour la Crète occidentale "un début impressionnant pour un futur brillant". Les fouilles systématiques, dont certaines sont encore en cours, ont donné un matériel en mesure de changer radicalement l'idée de la présence dans l'île du Néolithique et du Minoen, et d'enrichir la carte archéologique de la région de nouveaux sites.

Les communications publiées ces dernières années – scientifiques ou non – ont donné l'occasion à certains archéologues, surtout grecs, de soutenir que l'on assiste à une tentative consciente d'amoindrissement de grande savants qui ont travaillé ou continuent à travailler en Crète. Je pense que c'est un fausse position, justifiée par une sensibilité excessive envers des chercheurs vraiment éminents, du passé et du présent, une sensibilité que nous possédons tous, aussi bien envers la science qu'envers nos confréres. Les trouvailles des années 1964/65 n'ont pas été mises sous clé de façon que leur approche et leur étude par d'autres chercheurs soit impossible, c'est le contraire qui s'est produit; car il valait la peine que tous voient ces objets, et cette publicité, finalement, a augmenté le prestige des fouilles.

On doit donc se demander comment quelques monographies et articles publiés à la fin des années 70 s'appuient sur une bibliographie, dans les références à la Crète néolithique et minoenne, datant presque d'avant-guerre. Bien sûr, les archéologues de ces notes bibliographiques étaient plus connus que les fouilleurs et chercheurs d'alors, grecs ou étrangers, en Crète occidentale. Pourtant lorsque la science va de l'avant, sa boussole n'est pas nécessairement le nom des chercheurs, mais la recherche elle-même. Et lorsque celle-ci vient renverser une théorie généralement reconnue, le fait de persister dans la voie précédente montre un manque d'information scientifique.

La Crète occidentale était ouverte à tous les chercheurs. Tous ceux qui y travaillaient et y travaillent ont au la chance de faire des découvertes d'importance datant des civilisations néolithiques et minoennes, découvertes qui montrent que l'île était une entité culturelle, sans frontières ni artificielles.

Quelle est donc l'importance pour la recherche scientifique des découvertes des fouilles de la Crète occidentale, et quelle aide ont-elles apportée dans l'approfondissement et le renouvellement de la connaissance de la culture néolithique et minoenne dans leur ensemble sur l'île entière?

La grotte de Gérani à Réthymno nous a donné une image assez claire de la vie quotidienne et des occupations d'un groupe d'hommes, durant presque tout le Néolithique. Les données des fouilles, l'étude de la stratigraphie et des trouvailles (céramique, objets en pierre, en os, ossements d'animaux) nous montre que l'habitat n'était pas permanent, mais périodique, en liaison immédiate avec les occupations saisonnières des habitants (agriculture, pêche, èlevage, chasse); l'habitat permanent se trouvait ailleurs, et n'a pas encore ete localise. Cette occupation periodique est évidente d'après la céramique - il n'y a pas de grands vases destinés à la conservation -, aussi bien que d'après les autres trouvailles, statuettes et outils. Parallèlement aux périodes d'occupations, un atelier de confection d'outils en os devait fonctionner. Outre les outils intacts, on en a trouvé beaucoup à demi terminées, ainsi que bien sûr la matière première: des os d'animaux, dont le cerf sauvage.

Cette grotte a été abandonnée durant la dernière phase du Néolithique, peut-être après un éboulement ayant fermé l'entrée. Elle fait ainsi partie du peu de grottes qui ont donné des couches clairement néolithiques, sans occupation ultérieure. On sait qu'elle a été localisée au cours des travaux pour la nouvelle route La Canée-Réthymno, en 1969.

Au contraire, les grottes d'Akrotiri Hanion et surtout - sur le plateau de Kérameia - celle de Koumaro et Platyvola, nous ont donné une riche céramique du Néolithique récent, et de la transition du Néolithique au Minoen ancien, sans stratigraphie claire, mais très intéressante. Je m'arrêterai surtout à l'atelier de céramique MA II au décor incisé, atelier qui semble être l'un des plus importants de l'île, et imite des récipients en pierre, fait très intéressant. Si on le relie à la présence de céramique HA II importée ou d'imitations du type "saucière", et à la découverte d'une nécropole à tombes de type protocycladique à Néa Roumata, on voit clairement l'existence de contacts et de liens entre cette partie de la Crète, le monde helladique et les Cyclades. La tombe, précisément à Néa Roumata, nous oblige à voir avec quelque scepticisme la théorie connue sur l'établissement des habitats et de leurs nécropoles, durant la période protocycladique, près ou tour près de la mer, car cette nécropole se trouve à plus de 16 km à l'intérieur des terres, au pied des Lefka Ori.

Les fouilles suivantes, qui couvrent la fin du Néolithique et la période du Minoen Ancien, sont très importantes:
1. La fouille gréco-italienne de Nérokourou
2. La fouille gréco-anglaise de Débla
3. La fouille gréco-suédoise de Kastelli, Khania.

Il est connu que les liens entre les habitants de la Crète, de la Grèce , des îles et de la côte d'Asie Mineure à l'époque du Bronze Ancien, aussi bien que leur origine, constituent l'un des plus grands problèmes de l'archéologie égéenne, avec des théories qui se heurtent les unes aux autres, chacune accordant plus de poids au champ d'intérêt scientifique du chercheur. Je crois que les dernières trouvailles de Créte occidentale peuvent aider cette tentative des spécialistes.

Cependant, les allées et venues dans les centres culturela du bassin oriental de la Méditerranée, qui nous sont connues depuis l'époque néolithique, continuent sans interruption. Il est intéressant de noter les contacts de La Canée avec Cythère. Les fouilles anglaises y ont montré que l'habitat de Kastri a été établi par des Minoens au tournant du Bronze Moyen. Ces colons sont-ils donc partis de la région de La Canée? C'est vraisemblable, puisque par exemple le type de ceramique du premier style Barbotine ware est plus commun ici que dans aucun autre centre minoen.

Mais que représente La Canée au Minoen Moyen? Il existe un habitat déjà organisé à Kastelli, au-dessus du port, et des habitations groupées à Akrotiri, sur le plateau de Kérameia dans la région de Drapania Kissamou. On utilise des grottes, commes celles de Périvolia et de Iéro Koryphes, comme à Sklopa et Drapano pour les cérémonies religieuses.

L'habitat de Kastelli qui a pour sûr un caractère provincial, entretient des liens avec les grands centres, so développe rapidement, et au début de l'époque des deuxièmes palais, se transforme en centre important qui arrive à son apogée au MR I. Cette civilisation a construit des maisons dotées d'un système de rues et de places, selon la nouvelle conception architecturale. Elle était organisée de façon bureaucratique, comme cela apparaît dans les archives (sceaux ou tablettes en linéaire A), elle avait sa propre production de céramique, dans un atelier qui, entre autres, expertes les coupes bien connues (Alternative style).

Voilà quelques-uns des éléments qui définissent l'importance culturelle de la ville. Que son nom ait été Kydonia ou non, je ne pense pas que ce soit significatif, bien qu'une réponse à cette question soit intéressante.

Durant cette période, la plaine de Souda est assez densément peuplée, cela apparaît d'après la série de maisons minoennes découvertes pendant les fouilles gréco-italiennes (1977-

1979) et plus tard les fouilles de sauvetages grecques.

Parvenus à ce point, nous devons rappeler les fouilles grecques de Monastiraki, où un grand groupe de magasins et d'ateliers a été trouvé. L'architecture monumentale, les éléments faisant supposer l'existence d'un centre religieux et les archives de sceaux plaident pour le caractère palatial des bâtiments.

Le site d'Apodoulo date de la même époque, il est fouillé par une mission gréco-italienne; un grand nombre de vases d'usage domestique ou funéraire ont été découverts.

Mais retournons à La Canée et à l'habitat de Kastelli: la théorie (si elle existe encore) que le MR II est circonscrit à Cnossos devient obsolète. Ici encore nous avons des restes d'un bâtiment et des trouvailles, encore peu nombreuses mais assez caractéristiques. Cela nous a pris du temps d'essayer de persuader nos confrères, mais je pense que cela valait la peine.

Aprés la catastrophe finale du palais de Cnossos, la ville minoenne de Kydonia arrive à son apogée, qui dure jusqu'au MR III C. Elle a des liens avec Chypre et la Palestine. Elle exporte de la céramique - les vases bien connus de l'atelier local, au fond caractéristique blanchâtre - dans toute l'île, la Gréce et Chypre. Les dernières recherches ont montré que des vases à étrier portant du linéaire B, très connus dans le monde helladique, venaient de Kydonia. Ainsi, le WA-NAX de Kydonia contrôle le commerce d'exportation au moins de la Crète occidentale.

Un élément important est qu'ici il n'a pas été trouvé de couche de destruction au MR III A, mais une extension limitée au MR III B. Sur la base de la céramique faite à la main du MR III B, l'existence d'un lien entre Kydonia et des centres de Sicile et de Sardaigne commence à paraître très probable.

Il est nécessaire de faire ici une petite allusion à la conquête mycénienne ou à la présence mycénienne dans l'île. Si nous exceptons la langue - que nous trouvons sur les vases et les tablettes - présente dans plus ou moins tous les centres de la Crète post-palatiale découverts jusqu'à maintenant, l'architecture aussi bien que la céramique sont des éléments contraires à cette hypothèse. La céramique, particulièrement, n'est qu'à 5% d'importation mycénienne ou une imitation locale. L'atelier local continue la tradition minoenne aussi bien dans les formes que dans les décors, alors que les emprunts au répertoire mycénien sont très rares.

Les boîtes en ivoire importées et d'autres éléments considérés comme mycéniens ou de style mycénien ont de l'intérêt; il y a encore beaucoup de chemin à faire pour résoudre le problème dans toute son ampleur, et trouver la vérité objective que nous désirons tous.

Je suis donc particulièrement prudent dans l'usage du terme "Crète mycénienne", ou de l'estimé, quoique sans substance, "periode crétomycénienne", pour leur préférer tout simplement le terme traditionnel "période postminoenne".

Des écrits en linéaire B ont été trouvées sur des vases à étrier, ailleurs qu'a La Canée, dans des lieux inattendus: dans la grotte de Périvolia et le site d'Arménoi Réthymnes, dans une tombe à chambre.

La nécropole MR III près du village d'Arménoi est composée de groupes de tombes à chambre et une petite tombe à tholos (207 tombes ont déjà été fouillées).

C'est la première fois que la pioche de l'archéologue a la possibilité de travailler à dégager une nécropole de cette période, puisqu'elle se trouve en dehors des zones habitées. Les éléments ainsi collectés sont particulièrement intéressants. Les habitants de cette ville encore inconnue ont choisi et "dessiné" cette nécropole. C'est ce que montrent les travaux de terrassement - l'aplanissement des endroits rocheux, l'accés aux différents groupes de tombes (calderimi), l'organisation des tombes en grands et petits groupes.

L'architecture des tombes, qui toutes sont tournées vers le NE, se compose d'une simple rampe de descente, un couloir, une chambre semi-circulaire ou carrée. Quelques-unes ont un escalier d'accès, une grande chambre carrée, de la mosaïque au milieu ou au fond et un banc. Deux d'entre elles nous ont donné une stèle funéraire, qui n'a pas été trouvée in situ bien sûr, mais dont l'usage doit être considéré comme une donnée.

Les trouvailles, à part les larnakes dont beaucoup portent des représentations religieuses, sont de la céramique, des armes et des bijoux en bronze, des sceaux de pierre semi-précieuses, un casque de défenses de sanglier, un panier tressé en fibre végétale, et un vase à étrier portant le nom WI-NA-JO en linéaire B, connu par un vase semblable trouvé à Cnossos et des tablettes en linéaire B: c'est peut-être le premier nom d'un mort de la période minoenne.

Mais pour quelle raison fonder une ville vers 1375 av. J. C.? Une ville qui a duré environ six générations (jusqu'en 1200), comme le montrent les trouvailles des tombes d'une ville assez grande, si nous comptons que les tombes à fouiller sont encore plus de 50.

La réponse finale sera donnée par la découverte de cette ville, et la recherche avance. Une première théorie vient de la présence de nombreux objets en bronze, de très bonne qualité, et l'existence relativement proche d'une mine de cuivre dont l'exploitation durant le MR III n'est pas sûre.

Dans ce cas, nous serions en présence d'une ville fondée et habitée pour cette industrie, puisque nous savons qu'à cette époque l'importation en Crète de bronze de Chypre a déjà cessé. La recherche à venir confirmera ou infirmera cette théorie.

Katalog

Die Paläste   (Nr.   1 - 16)

Die minoische Gesellschaft   (Nr. 17 - 120)

Religion und Kult   (Nr. 121 - 145)

Grab und Tod   (Nr. 146 - 180)

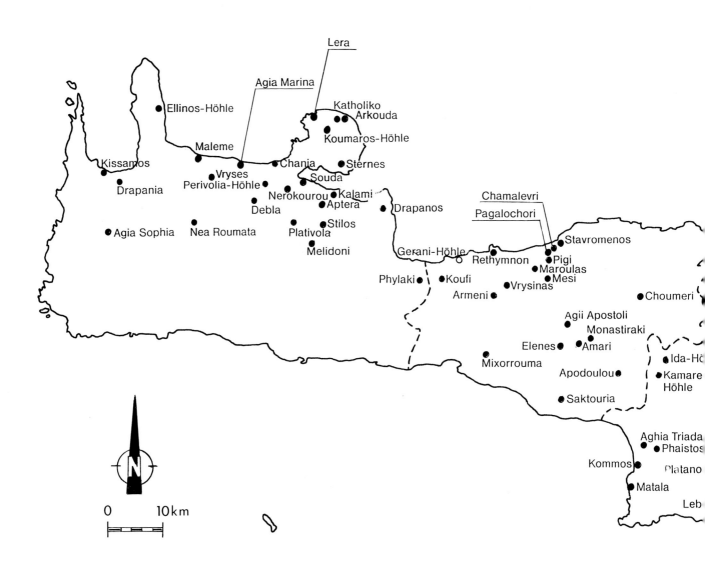

Minoische Fundstätten auf Kreta

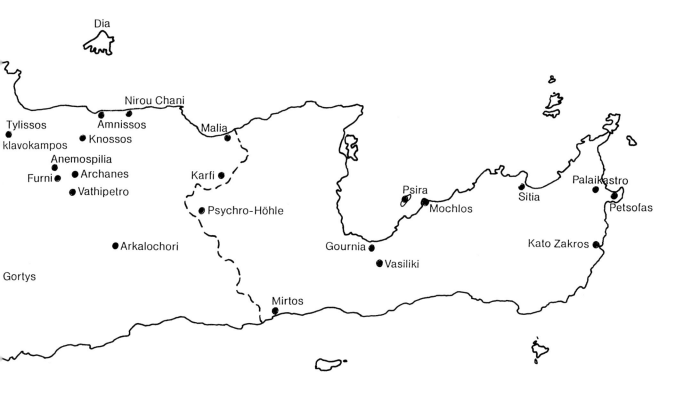

Abkürzungen im Katalogteil

(deutsch - englisch - französisch)

FM Frühminoisch	EM Early Minoan	MA Minoen ancien
MM Mittelminoisch	MM Middle Minoan	MM Minoen moyen
SM Spätminoisch	LM Late Minoan	MR Minoen retard
Dm Durchmesser	d diameter	diam. diamètre
B Breite	w width	larg. largeur
H Höhe	h height	haut. hauteur
L Länge	l length	long. longueur
T Tiefe (Dicke)	th thickness	épaiss. épaisseur

1 **Siegelabdruck**
SM I B (Mitte des 15. Jhs. v. Chr.)
Ton
Aus Kastelli, Kissamos
Dm 0,032 m, D 0,0063 - 0,018 m
Chania, Archäologisches Museum
Rundes Tonstück mit starken Brandspuren. Die Schnurabdrücke auf der Rückseite weisen darauf hin, daß hiermit wahrscheinlich ein Schriftstück versiegelt war. Auf der Hauptseite ist das Bild eines Siegelringes mit ovaler Siegelplatte abgedruckt: dargestellt ist ein symmetrisch angeordneter Baukomplex in einer felsigen Küstenlandschaft. In der Mitte erhebt sich ein großer Fels, dessen Fuß von stillisierten Meereswellen umspült ist. Der Gebäudekomplex ist von einer Mauer mit zwei Toren eingefaßt, deren Türflügel aus Holz bestehen und deren Türsturz mit zwei gegenständigen Halbrosetten geschmückt ist. Die bis zu drei Stockwerke hohen Gebäude sind mit Kulthörnern bekrönt. Auf dem mittleren Gebäude steht eine herrscherliche männliche Gestalt, in minoischem Schurz und mit reicher Haartracht, in der ausgestreckten Rechten ein Szepter haltend.
Dieser Siegelabdruck ist ein besonders bedeutender Fund. Der Gebäudekomplex wird als Stadt, Palast oder Heiligtum gedeutet und die männliche Gestalt als erscheinende Gottheit oder als Herrscher. Bemerkenswert ist, daß in diesem Siegelbild minoische und mykenische Merkmale zusammen auftreten. Das Stück gibt uns die Möglichkeit, die Architektur dieser beiden Kulturen besser zu verstehen.

2 **Siegelabdruck**
SM I B (Mitte des 15. Jhs. v. Chr.)
Ton
Aus der Stadt Chania
L 0,023 m, B 0,014 m
Chania, Archäologisches Museum
Unversehrt erhaltenes Tonstück mit dem Abdruck der ovalen Platte eines Siegelrings. Die Schnurreste auf der Rück- und den Schmalseiten lassen erkennen, wie das Stück auf dem versiegelten Gegenstand befestigt war. Dargestellt ist eine Göttin auf einem gestuften Sitz oder Sockel. Sie trägt die typisch minoische Tracht und füttert ein gehörntes Tier.
Die „Herrin der Tiere", eine der Erscheinungsformen der minoischen weiblichen Gottheit, ist ein besonders beliebtes Thema der minoischen Kleinkunst.

3 **Siegelabdruck**
SM I B (Mitte des 15. Jhs. v. Chr.)
Ton
Aus der Stadt Chania
H 0,013 m, B 0,017 m
Chania, Archäologisches Museum
Linsenförmiges Tonstück mit mandelförmigem Siegelabdruck. Durchbohrung in der Querachse. Abgebildet ist ein symmetrisches pflanzliches Motiv amulettartigen Charakters, das „Löwenmaske" genannt wird.
Die Kategorie der sogenannten amulettartigen Siegelsteine scheint in der Periode MM III aufgekommen zu sein. Ein ähnliches Stück ist aus Palaikastro bekannt.

4 **Kriegerkopf**
SM III A-B (14.-13. Jh. v. Chr.)
Elfenbein
Aus Phylaki, Apokoronou (Kuppelgrab)
H 0,06 m, max. B 0,04 m, max. T 0,012 m
Chania, Archäologisches Museum
Relief eines Kriegerkopfes nach rechts. Gesichtszüge ohne Ausführung von Details: breite Stirn, mandelförmiges Auge, schneckenförmige Ohrmuschel, schmale, leicht lächelnde Lippen und zweifach gestufter Haarschnitt. Er trägt den typisch mykenischen Eberzahnhelm aus zwei gegenständigen Reihen von Hauern und einem Knauf als oberem Abschluß. Auf der flachen Rückseite befinden sich zwei kleine Dübel übereinander zur Befestigung an einer wahrscheinlich hölzernen Fläche.
Entsprechende Darstellungen dieses Themas stammen aus Kreta und vom griechischem Festland.

Vergl. Kat.-Nr. 125

5 Sphinx
SM III A-B (14.-13. Jh. v. Chr.)
Elfenbein
Aus Phylaki, Apokoronou (Kuppelgrab)
H 0,07 m, B 0,0435 m
Chania, Archäologisches Museum
Rechteckiges Plättchen mit gravierter Darstellung einer Sphinx in Seitenansicht mit erhobenem Oberkörper. Das Gesicht hat eine lange Nase, ein mandelförmiges Auge und fleischliche Lippen. Auf dem Kopf trägt sie ein Diadem mit einer Quaste und um den Hals eine Kette. Der Körper mit den vollen Brüsten ist schwer, die Flügel mit vielfältig gestaltetem Gefieder sind nach hinten ausgestreckt.
Die aus dem Osten stammende mythische Gestalt der Sphinx mit Löwenkörper, weiblichem Kopf und Greifenflügeln war in der mykenischen Kunst ein besonders beliebtes Thema. Die Minoer haben sie dagegen viel seltener dargestellt.

6 Miniaturschild
SM III A-B (14.-13. Jh. v. Chr.)
Elfenbein
Aus Phylaki, Apokoronou (Kuppelgrab)
L 0,076 m, B 0,045 m, erhalt. D 0,026 m
Chania, Archäologisches Museum
Bis auf einige Stoßstellen unversehrte Nachbildung eines achtförmigen Schildes mit breitem Rand. Die Oberfläche der Vorderseite ist durch eine umlaufende Profilleiste in zwei Ebenen unterteilt. In den oberen Teil sind sechs Gruppen von je drei runden Vertiefungen eingearbeitet, in die Zierteile aus anderem Material eingelassen waren.
Der achtförmige Schild war ein typisch mykenisches Kultsymbol und ein sehr beliebtes Motiv im Dekor der Kleinkunst, der Wand- und der Gefäßmalerei. Die Bauform des Grabes, aus dem der Schild stammt, und die zusammen damit gefundenen Gegenstände lassen darauf schließen, daß sich mykenischer Einfluß an diesem Ort geltend gemacht hat.

7 Zwei Miniaturschilde
SM III A-B (14.-13. Jh. v. Chr.)
Elfenbein
Aus Phylaki Apokoronou (Kuppelgrab)
L 0,028 - 0,029 m, B 0,017 - 0,019 m, D 0,011 - 0,012 m
Chania, Archäologisches Museum
Stellenweise bestoßene, sonst unversehrte achtförmige Miniaturschilde mit glänzender, unverzierter Vorderseite. Auf der Rückseite ein tiefes Stiftloch zur Befestigung an einem hölzernen Gegenstand.

8 Schrifttäfelchen
SM I B (Mitte des 15. Jhs. v. Chr.)
Ton
Aus Kastelli, Chania
H 0,11 m, B 0,082 m
Chania, Archäologisches Museum
Rechteckiges Täfelchen, aus zwei Bruchstücken zusammengesetzt. Der Text ist in Linear A-Schrift verfaßt und in waagerechten Reihen geschrieben. Es handelt sich um eine Aufzählung landwirtschaftlicher Produkte und von Haustieren. Das geht aus den folgenden Ideogrammen hervor, die von Zahlzeichen begleitet sind

 Getreide

Wein

Feigen

weibliches Schaf

Im oberen Teil des Täfelchens sind fünf kleine Löcher vorhanden.
Die aus rötlichem Ton bestehende Schrifttafel ist erhalten, weil sie wie die entsprechenden Stücke im Feuer gehärtet wurde, als das Gebäude, in dem es sich befand, verbrannte. Die minoische Siedlung in Kastelli im Verwaltungsbezirk Chania ist bis jetzt außer Knossos die einzige, in der sowohl Linear A- als auch Linear B-Texte gefunden wurden.

9   Schrifttäfelchen
SM III A-B (14.-13. Jh. v. Chr.)
Ton
Aus Knossos
H 0,028 m, L 0,14 m
Heraklion, Archäologisches Museum
Blattförmiges Tontäfelchen, aus drei Fragmenten zusammengesetzt, mit starken Brandspuren auf der Oberfläche. In den Ton sind Silbenschriftzeichen und Ideogramme der Linear B-Schrift geritzt. Der Text bezieht sich auf ein spezielles purpurfarbenes (po-pu-re-ja) Kleidungsstück (pu-ka-ta-ri-ja), das möglicherweise Klagefrauen trugen.
Ein entsprechendes Gewand wird bei Homer erwähnt („φάρος πορφύρεον"). Das zeigt, daß mit dieser mykenischen Linear B-Schrift die griechische Sprache aufgezeichnet wurde.

10 Kanne
MM I A (Ende des 3. Jts. v. Chr.)
Ton
Aus Phaistos
Erhalt. H 0,165 m, max. DM 0,145 m
Heraklion, Archäologisches Museum
Das eindrucksvolle Gefäß ist ein repräsentatives Exemplar des Barbotine-Stils. Der Ausguß fehlt. Kugelig-doppelkonischer Körper, flacher Boden, senkrechter Henkel, enger Hals mit einer Knubbe auf beiden Seiten, gezahnte Lippe. Die ungleichmäßige schwarzbraune bis rötliche Färbung des Überzugs ist durch die Brennung hervorgerufen. Weiße Streifen umziehen den unteren Teil des Köpers, während der obere mit plastischem Dekor, weißen Flecken und ineinandergestreckten Bögen verziert ist.
Gefäße dieses besonders um 2000 v. Chr. beliebten Stils kommen hauptsächlich in Mittelkreta vor, im Osten und Westen der Insel dagegen nur vereinzelt. Eine große Anzahl stammt aus Phaistos, das wahrscheinlich ein bedeutendes Produktionszentrum dieser Ware war.

11 Knickwandschale
MM II A (19. Jh. v. Chr.)
Ton
Aus Chalara, Phaistos
H 0,062 m, Mündungs-Dm 0,091 – 0,097 m
Heraklion, Archäologisches Museum
Hervorragend gearbeitete und erhaltene Knickwandschale des Kamares-Stil mit senkrechtem Bandhenkel, einem größeren und vielen kleineren Ausgüssen. Das Gefäß ist innen und außen mit schwarzbraunem Firnis überzogen. Der vielfarbige Dekor darauf besteht aus Streifen, einer Zone mit hängenden und stehenden Bögen und aus paarweise gegenläufigen Spiralen mit gemeinsamem Stiel. Diese Kamares-Gefäße werden wegen ihrer äußerst dünnen Wandung Eierschalengefäße genannt und bilden eine Sondergruppe der Kamares-Gattung.

12 Kanne
MM II A (19. Jh. v. Chr.)
Ton
Aus Phaistos
H 0,17 m, max. Dm 0,14 m
Heraklion, Archäologisches Museum
Schönes, für den vielfarbigen Kamares-Stil repräsentatives Gefäß mit eiförmigem Körper, flachem Boden, weitem, niedrigen Hals, Tülle und drei senkrechten Henkeln, die metallischen Vorbildern nachgestaltet sind. Schwarzbrauner bis rötlicher Überzug bedeckt die ganze Oberfläche. In weißer Farbe ist auf beiden Seiten je ein große Rosette gemalt.
In erstaunlicher Weise sind die vielfältigen, bunten Ornamente der Kamares-Ware auf die kunstvollen, dynamischen Gefäßformen abgestimmt. Mit dem Kamares-Stil, in seinem ganzen Charakter ein Palaststil, erreicht die minoische Keramik ein Niveau der Vollendung.

13 Kanne
MM III (16. Jh. v. Chr.)
Ton
Aus Phaistos
H 0,14 m, max. Dm 0,083 m
Heraklion, Archäologisches Museum.
Unversehrtes Exemplar des Flora-Stils, grob gearbeitet. Konischer Körper, flacher Boden und niedriger Hals mit überrandständigem Ausguß. Zwei waagerechte Henkel auf dem Bauch und ein senkrechter, der an der Lippe ansetzt. Auf beiden Seiten des Ausgusses je eine Knubbe. Der Körper des Gefäßes ist mit schilfartigen, senkrecht stehenden Pflanzen aus braunrotem Firnis geschmückt.

14 Becher
SM I (Ende des 16. Jhs. v. Chr.)
Ton
Aus Knossos, Königliche Straße
H 0,068 m, Mündungs-Dm 0,101 m, Boden-Dm 0,03 m
Heraklion, Archäologisches Museum.
Sorgfältig gearbeitetes Gefäß im Flora-Stil mit konischem Körper, leicht gewölbter Wandung und flachem Boden. Natürlich wiedergegebenes Schilf in braunrotem Firnis bedeckt die Außenwandung. Innen ist das Gefäß gänzlich mit Firnis überzogen.
In der Themenwahl ist der Flora-Stil stark von der Wandmalerei beeinflußt. Das bezeugen unter anderem auch einige Gefäße aus Knossos.

15 Alabastron mit Deckel
SM I B (Ende des 16. Jhs. v. Chr.)
Ton
Aus Kastelli, Chania
H 0,185 - 0,190 m, max. Dm 0,181 m,
Mündungs-Dm 0,119 m, Körper-H 0,057 m,
Körper-Dm 0,153 m
Chania, Archäologisches Museum
Körper kugelig-eiförmig, flacher Boden, niedriger, zylindrischer Hals und vier horizontale Bandhenkel. Gruppen von orangefarbenen Streifen umlaufen den unteren Teil des Körpers, während der obere in zwei Zonen gegliedert ist, die mit laufenden Spiralen und stilisierten Schwertlilien verziert sind. Der konische Deckel endet mit einem flachen Knauf und hat einen waagerechten Rundhenkel. Der Dekor besteht aus Linien.
Das Gefäß ist ein repräsentatives Exemplar der Keramik von Chania. Daß bei der Auffindung verkohlte Oliven darin gefunden wurden, spricht dafür, das es sich um ein Vorratsgefäß handelte.

16 Ephyräischer Becher
SM II (2. Hälfte des 15. Jhs. v. Chr.)
Ton
Aus Knossos (Wohnhaus, noch unerforscht)
H 0,113 m, Mündungs-Dm 0,132 m,
Boden-Dm 0,06 m
Heraklion, Archäologisches Museum
Ephyräischer Becher, zusammengesetzt und ergänzt. Hoher, trichterförmiger Körper mit ausladender Lippe, zwei senkrechten Bandhenkeln und niedrigem Fuß auf Standplatte. Der braunschwarze Dekor entfaltet sich auf beiden Seiten des Gefäßes und besteht aus je einer Palmette mit zweifacher Umrißlinie und einem Punkt auf dem Boden, und aus konzentrischen Bögen als Begleitmotiven. Der Gefäßboden ist vollständig gefirnißt.
Dieser Stil ist helladischen Ursprungs und für die Phase SH II B charakteristisch. Gekennzeichnet ist er durch den einfachen und klaren Dekor, der sich auf eine einzelne pflanzliche Figur oder ein Meeresmotiv beschränkt.

17 Halskette
SM III A-B (14.-13. Jh. v. Chr.)
Sardonyx
Aus Armeni (Nekropole), Rethymnon
Dm 0,003 - 0,025 m
Rethymnon, Archäologisches Museum
Kette aus 49 Gliedern, die fünf mittleren sind linsenförmig bikonvex, die übrigen kugelig und unterschiedlich groß.
Der Halbedelstein Sardonyx war in der kretisch-mykenischen Welt sehr beliebt, wie aus den zahlreichen daraus hergestellten Perlen und Siegelsteinen hervorgeht, die bislang gefunden wurden. Sardonyx wurde in großen Mengen, meist unbearbeitet, aus dem Osten eingeführt.

18 Halskette
SM III A-B (14.-13. Jh. v. Chr.)
Glaspaste
Aus Armeni (Nekropole), Rethymnon
L 0,027 m, B 0,01 mm
Rethymnon, Archäologisches Museum
17 Kettenglieder in Form von länglichen Blättchen, deren Ansichtsseite mit je drei reliefierten, senkrecht angeordneten Schneckenspiralen geschmückt ist.
Glaspaste wurde in Mesopotamien bereits im 4. Jt. v. Chr. erzeugt. Nach Kreta kam die Kenntnis der Herstellung im 16. Jh. v. Chr. Die grauweißen oder blauen Kettenglieder dieser Art wurden in steinernen Gußformen gefertigt.

19 Halskette
SM III A-B (14.-13. Jh. v. Chr.)
Bergkristall
Aus Armeni (Nekropole), Rethymnon
L 0,027 m, B 0,01 m
Rethymnon, Archäologisches Museum
Die Kette besteht aus 19 verschieden großen, runden, ellipsoiden und zylindrischen Gliedern.
Bergkristall wurde schon seit der mittelminoischen Epoche sehr viel zur Herstellung von Schmuck und Gefäßen benutzt.

20 Halskette
SM III A-B (14.-13. Jh.)
Fayence
Aus Armeni (Nekropole), Rethymnon
L 0,016 m
Rethymnon, Archäologisches Museum
Die Kette besteht aus 20 Gliedern, 12 davon sind doppelkonisch und acht haben die Form eines Weizenkorns.
Fayence wurde in Mesopotanien schon seit dem 5. Jt. v. Chr. erzeugt, in Kreta wurden seit der 1. Hälfte des 3. Jts. Perlen und Gefäße daraus hergestellt.

21 Pyxis mit Deckel
SM III (14. Jh. v. Chr.)
Ton
Aus Vigla, Stavroumenou (Kammergrab), Rethymnon
H (mit Deckel) 0,01 m,
Mündungs-Dm 0,085 m, Boden-Dm 0,093 m
Rethymnon, Archäologisches Museum
Vollständig erhalten. Boden flach, Körper zylindrisch, vier Löcher in der Schulter. Deckel von derselben Form mit einem Loch in der Mitte. Der schwarze, glänzende Dekor besteht auf dem Körper aus parallelen Linien und stilisierten „papyrusartigen" Motiven und auf dem Deckel aus konzentrischen Kreisen.
Die zylindrischen und ellipsenförmigen Pyxiden, die eine häufige Grabbeigabe darstellen, erscheinen in Kreta in der FM Periode und sind unter kykladischem Einfluß entstanden. Mit großer Wahrscheinlichkeit wurden in diesen Gefäßen persönliche Toilettenartikel aufbewahrt. Für diese Ansicht sprechen auch die Löcher, durch die ein Band zur Befestigung des Deckels gezogen wurde.

22 Armreif
SM III A-B (14.-13. Jh. v. Chr.)
Bronze
Aus Armeni (Kammergrab 140), Rethymnon
Dm 0,053 - 0,055 m
Rethymnon, Archäologisches Museum
Sehr gut erhaltener Armreif aus dickem Bronzedraht mit dünnen Enden, die spiralförmig umeinander gewunden sind. Dieser Verschluß erlaubt es, den Reif zu erweitern oder zu verengen.

23 Armreif
SM III A-B (14.-13. Jh. v. Chr.)
Bronze
Aus Armeni (Kammergrab 140), Rethymnon
Dm 0,071 m
Rethymnon, Archäologisches Museum
Unversehrter Armreif aus dickem Bronzedraht, der sich an den Enden stark verdünnt. Die beiden Enden sind spiralförmig umeinandergedreht. Die Typusvariante, zu der dieser Armreif gehört, stammt aus Mesopotanien und verbreitete sich seit dem Beginn des 3. Jt. v. Chr. von dort nach Westeuropa.

24 Armreif
SM III A-B (14.-13. Jh. v. Chr.)
Bronze
Aus Armeni (Kammergrab 124), Rethymnon
Dm 0,08 m
Rethymnon, Archäologisches Museum
Allgemein übliches Schmuckstück. Der Reif ist von rundem Durchschnitt, und seine Enden überlappen sich, ohne aneinander befestigt zu sein; die Enden haben dreieckige Form.

25 Ring
SM III A-B (14.-13. Jh. v. Chr.)
Bronze
Aus Armeni (Kammergrab 86) Rethymnon
Dm 0,0145 m
Rethymnon, Archäologisches Museum
Spiralförmiger Ring mit drei Windungen aus Bronzedraht. Das eine Drahtende ist frei, das andere an der Spirale befestigt.

26 Ring
SM III A-B (14.-13. Jh. v. Chr.)
Bronze
Aus Armeni (Kammergrab 108), Rethymnon
Dm 0,119 m
Rethymnon, Archäologisches Museum
Unversehrtes Schmuckstück aus einem Blechstreifen, der so zu einem Ring gebogen ist, daß beide Enden sich frei überlappen.

27 Pinzette
SM III A-B (14.-13. Jh. v. Chr.)
Bronze
Aus Armeni (Kammergrab 100), Rethymnon
L 0,08 m
Rethymnon, Archäologisches Museum
Kosmetikgeräte dieser Art gibt es im ägäischen Raum seit dem 3. Jt. v. Chr. bis heute in unveränderter Form. Dieses Exemplar besteht aus einem Bronzeblechstreifen, der in der Mitte zu einem offenen Ring gebogen ist. Die unteren Enden der Schenkel sind nach innen gebogen. Eine gravierte Linie läuft die Ränder des Bleches entlang.

28 Spiegel
SM II (15. Jh. v. Ch.)
Bronze
Aus Knossos, Friedhof Zafer Papouras
Dm 0,12 m
Heraklion, Archäologisches Museum
Unversehrte Spiegelscheibe mit zwei Löchern am Rand zur Befestigung des Griffes, der aus organischem Material, Holz oder Bein, bestand. Auf der glatten Spiegelfläche lassen sich Schleifspuren erkennen.
Dieser Typus von Spiegeln, die ausreichend Licht reflektierten, ist unter ägyptischem Einfluß entstanden und bleibt während der ganzen Bronzezeit unverändert.

29 Fibel
SM III A-B (14.-13. Jh. v. Chr.)
Bronze
Aus Armeni (Kammergrab 67), Rethymnon
L 0,135 m
Rethymnon, Archäologisches Museum
Spiralfibel, zusammengesetzt. Dünner, langer Bügel von quadratischem Querschnitt, der am einen Ende spitz ausläuft und am anderen zu einer bandförmigen Spirale aufgewickelt ist. Kleine Toilettenartikel dieser Form finden sich im ägäischen Raum schon seit dem 3. Jt. v. Chr. und dienten höchstwahrscheinlich als Haarnadeln von Frauen und nicht zum Feststecken von Gewändern.

30 Siegelzylinder (Abdruck)
SM III A-B (14.-13. Jh. v. Chr.)
Fayence
Aus Armeni (Kammergrab 108), Rethymnon
H 0,019 m, Dm 0,010 m
Rethymnon, Archäologisches Museum
Die in den Mantel des Zylinders geschnittene Darstellung zeigt zwei hintereinanderstehende Tiere: einen stilisierten Vogel mit länglichem Körper, Strichflügeln und -beinen und eine Gestalt, die vielleicht eine Wildziege darstellt und stilistisch in derselben Weise wiedergegeben ist.
Die Rollsiegel stammen ursprünglich aus Südmesopotanien, wo sie um die Mitte des 4. Jahrtausends zum ersten Mal benutzt werden.

31 Siegelstein
SM III A-B (14.-13. Jh. v. Chr.)
Steatit
Aus Armeni (Kammergrab 104), Rethymnon
Dm 0,018 m
Rethymnon, Archäologisches Museum
Linsenförmiger Siegelstein mit kleinen Stoßstellen auf beiden Seiten. Bemerkenswert ist das unvollendete Siegelbild mit Gruppen von Kreislinien, die eine Figur, wahrscheinlich ein Tierbein, umgeben.

32 Siegelzylinder
SM III A-B (14.-13. Jh. v. Chr.)
Chlorit
Aus Armeni (Kammergrab 80), Rethymnon
H 0,015 m, Dm 0,010 m
Rethymnon, Archäologisches Museum
Unversehrtes Rollsiegel. Zwei tiefe Längsstreifen unterteilen den Mantel des Zylinders in zwei verschieden große Siegelfelder mit gleichem Dekor: einer diagonalen Kerbe, zu deren Seiten sich je ein kleiner Kreis mit punktförmigem Kern befindet.

33 Siegelstein
SM III A-B (14.-13. Jh. v. Chr.)
Bergkristall
Aus Armeni (Kammergrab 85), Rethymnon
Dm 0,0195 - 0,0210 m
Rethymnon, Archäologisches Museum
Linsenförmiger Siegelstein mit kleinen Abnutzungsspuren auf beiden Seiten. Der Dekor der Siegelfläche besteht aus senk- und waagerechten Streifen, die sich schneiden, und aus parallelen Strichen, die die Zwischenräume ausfüllen.

34 Siegelstein
SM III A-B (14.13. Jh. v. Chr.)
Bergkristall
Aus Armeni (Kammergrab 108), Rethymnon
Dm 0,015 m
Rethymnon, Archäologisches Museum
Linsenförmiger Siegelstein mit kleinen Stoßstellen am Rand. Die Hauptseite ist mit Paaren von senk- und waagerechten Linien verziert, die sich schneiden. Dazwischen Gitterwerk als Füllsel.

35 Siegelstein
SM III A-B (14.-13. Jh. v. Chr.)
Bergkristall
Aus Armeni (Kammergrab 79), Rethymnon
Maße: 0,013 x 0.015 m
Rethymnon, Archäologisches Museum
Unversehrter, mandelförmiger Siegelstein mit Durchbohrung in der Querachse. Die Bildfläche ist mit einem einfachen Linienmuster verziert: zwei sich überkreuzende Linien teilen das Bildfeld in vier Dreiecke. Zwei davon sind mit Strichen ausgefüllt und zwei mit Winkelgruppen.

36 Siegelstein
SM III A-B (14.-13. Jh. v. Chr.)
Chlorit
Aus Armeni (Kammergrab 115), Rethymnon
Dm 0,017 m
Rethymnon, Archäologisches Museum
Vollständig erhalten, linsenförmig. In die Siegelfläche ist ein breiter, diagonaler Streifen geschnitten, von dessen Mitte Linien schräg zu den Rändern hin führen und schraffierte Dreiecke bilden.

37 Siegelstein
SM III A-B (14.-13. Jh. v. Chr.)
Chlorit
Aus Armeni (Kammergrab 138), Rethymnon
Dm 0,019 m
Rethymnon, Archäologisches Museum
Linsenförmig mit kleiner Stoßstelle. Durchbohrung in der Längsachse. Die Siegelfläche ist fast ganz mit dem Bild eines von vorn dargestellten Vogels ausgefüllt. Bemerkenswert ist, daß hier minoische und mykenische Stilelemente zusammen auftreten: die schematische Darstellungsweise der Gestalt im Gegensatz zur Genauigkeit in der Wiedergabe der Details (Augen, Gefieder). Die Linie unter den Beinen des Vogels deutet möglicherweise den Boden an. Sichelförmiges Motiv mit Punkt in der Mitte als Füllornament.

39 Siegelstein
SM III A-B (14.-13. Jh. v. Chr.)
Ophit
Aus Armeni (Kammergrab 114), Rethymnon
Dm 0,014 m
Rethymnon, Archäologisches Museum
Unversehrter, linsenförmiger Siegelstein. In die Hauptseite ist ein lineares Ornament aus einer doppelten Raute schnitten mit je einem Punkt in der Mitte und an den vier Rändern.

40 Siegelstein
SM III A-B (14.-13. Jh. v. Chr.)
Bergkristall
Aus Armeni (Kammergrab 123), Rethymnon
Dm 0,013 - 0,012 m
Rethymnon, Archäologisches Museum
Unversehrt, linsenförmig, Durchbohrung in der Längsachse. Dargestellt ist ein stilisierter Baum mit dickem Stamm, unsymmetrisch entspringenden Ästen und gestrichelten Blättern. Rechts des Baumes sind zwei sichelförmige Motive zu erkennen.
Die Darstellung eines Baumes als Hauptgestalt ist ein ureigenes minoisches Thema auf Siegelsteinen und hat unmittelbar religiösen Bezug. Im Gegensatz dazu ist der Baum auf mykenischen Darstellungen ein Nebenmotiv

38 Siegelstein
SM III A-B (14.-13. Jh. v. Chr.)
Grünlicher Stein
Aus Armeni (Kammergrab 24), Rethymnon
D 0,016 m
Rethymnon, Archäologisches Museum
Unversehrter, linsenförmiger Siegelstein. Dargestellt ist eines der beliebtesten Themen der minoischen Kunst: ein galoppierender Stier. Das wegen der Form des Siegelsteines komprimiert dargestellte Tier hat seinen Kopf heftig rückwärts gewandt, so daß sich die Hörner mit seinem stämmigen Körper überschneiden. Der frontal wiedergegebene Kopf eines zweiten Stieres ist als Füllornament über dem Körper des ersten zu sehen.

41 Siegelstein
SM III A-B (14.-13. Jh. v. Chr.)
Karneol
Aus Armeni (Kammergrab 115), Rethymnon
Erhalt. L 0,015 m, B 0,014 m
Rethymnon, Archäologisches Museum
Sehr flache zylindrische Form. Ein Stück vom einen Ende fehlt. Dargestellt ist eine Wildziege in Seitenansicht mit stämmigem Körper, großen gebogenen Hörnern und Bart. Eine buschige Pflanze mit lanzettenförmigen Blättern füllt den Raum vor dem Tier.

42 Siegelstein
SM III A-B (14.-13. Jh. v. Chr.)
Chlorit
Aus Armeni (Kammergrab 83), Rethymnon
L 0,023 m, B 0,011 m, T 0,007 m
Rethymnon, Archäologisches Museum
Siegelstein mit vier Siegelflächen, am einen Ende etwas abgeflacht. Durchbohrung in der Längsachse. Die vier Siegelflächen sind mit parallelen Punktreihen versehen, die von ganzen oder unvollständigen kleinen Kreisen umschlossen sind.

43 Siegelstein
SM III A-B (14.-13. Jh. v. Chr.)
Hämatit
Aus Armeni (Kammergrab 115), Rethymnon
Dm 0,016 m
Rethymnon, Archäologisches Museum
Schöner, unversehrter linsenförmiger Siegelstein mit Durchbohrung in der Querachse. Die Hauptseite zeigt einen galoppierenden Stier mit heftig zurückgewandtem Kopf. Bemerkenswert ist die besonders detaillierte Wiedergabe.

44 Zweihenkeliger Stamnos
Wende Neolithikum/FM I
(Anfang des 3. Jts. v. Chr.)
Ton
Aus Elenes, Amari
H 0,156 m, max. Dm 0,158 m,
Mündungs-Dm 0,138 m
Rethymnon, Archäologisches Museum
Gebrauchsgefäß, mit Gips ergänzt, konischer Körper, flacher Boden, weiter, zylindrischer Hals und zwei senkrechte Henkel auf der Schulter.

45 Kelch
FM I (1. Hälfte des 3. Jt. v. Chr.)
Ton
Aus Elenes, Amari
H 0,148 m
Rethymnon, Archäologisches Museum
Hochfüßiger Kelch, ergänzt, repräsentatives Exemplar des Pyrgos-Stils. Hoher konischer Körper mit dreieckiger durchlöcherter Knubbe. Wulst am Ansatz des hohen Fußes, dessen Standfläche konkav ist. Der Fuß ist mit eingeriebenem Politurmuster aus umlaufenden, schwarz-braun gefüllten Ritzlinien verziert. Dieser Stil, der nach dem Ort Pyrgos im Verwaltungsbezirk Heraklion benannt ist, zeichnet sich durch die stark ausgeprägten, aus dem späten Neolithikum übernommenen Merkmale aus.

46 Skyphos
Wende Neolithikum/FM I
(Beginn des 3. Jts. v. Chr.)
Ton
Aus Elenes, Amari
H 0,114 m, Mündungs-Dm 0,147 m
Rethymnon, Archäologisches Museum
Zusammengesetzt und ergänzt. Hoher Körper mit steiler, schwach eingebogener Wandung und konvexem Boden. Vier Knubben an der Kante, zwei davon mit Loch. Die Oberfläche ist sorgfältig geglättet und mit schwarzbraunem Überzug bedeckt. Politurmuster aus Gruppen von je drei senkrechten Linien von den Knubben bis zur Lippe.

47 Löffel
Wende Neolithikum/FM I
(Beginn des 3 Jts. v. Chr.)
Ton
Aus Elenes, Amari
Erhalt. L 0,08 m
Rethymnon, Archäologisches Museum
Kleines Gebrauchsgerät, am Stil ergänzt. Ellipsenförmiger Schöpfteil mit Brandspuren auf der Oberfläche.
Aus Knossos und Mochlos sind entsprechende Exemplare bekannt.

48 Kelch
FM II B (2. Hälfte des 3. Jts. v. Chr.)
Ton
Aus der Höhle von Platyvola
H 0,078, Mündungs-Dm 0,083,
Boden-Dm 0,048 m
Chania, Archäologisches Museum
Zusammengesetztes und ergänztes Gefäß im Vasiliki-Stil mit halbkugeligem Körper und konischem, niedrigen Fuß. Die ganze Gefäßoberfläche ist mit rotbraunen und schwarzbraunen Flecken verziert.
Dieser für den Vasiliki-Stil charakteristische Dekor ist durch die absichtlich ungleichmäßige Brennung entstanden.

49 Lekanis
FM I/II (Mitte des 3. Jts. v. Chr.)
Ton
Aus der Höhle von Platyvola
H 0,08 m, Mündungs-Dm 0,207 m
Chania, Archäologisches Museum
Gebrauchsgefäß, aus vielen Fragmenten zusammengesetzt. Weite Mündung, ein Horizontalhenkel auf halber Höhe des Körpers und gewölbter Boden mit drei Knubben.

50 Kanne
MM I (Beginn des 2. Jts. v. Chr.)
Ton
Aus Apodoulou, Amari
H 0,16 m, max. Dm 0,16 m
Rethymnon, Archäologisches Museum
Zusammengesetztes und ergänztes Gefäß mit eiförmigen Körper, flachem Boden, senkrechtem Rundhenkel und schnabelförmigem Ausguß. Der auf die Bauch- und Schulterzone beschränkte Dekor besteht aus Erhebungen, die sich netzartig über die Fläche breiten. Die Dekoration wurde geschaffen, solange der Ton noch feucht war.
Die Art dieser eigenartigen Verzierung stellt eine Variante des Barbotine-Stils dar und wird Barnacle-Stil genannt.

51 Schnabelkanne
MM II (19.-18. Jh. v. Chr.)
Ton
Aus Monastiraki, Amari
H 0,30 m, Boden-Dm 0,08 m
Rethymnon, Archäologisches Museum
Schnabelkanne mit zwei Knubben am Hals. Zusammengesetzt. Ton braungelb mit Brandspuren und schwarzem Firnis. Der Dekor ist nicht farbecht und besteht aus weißen Punkten mit rauher Oberfläche.

52 Tüllenkanne
MM II (19.-18. Jh. v. Chr.)
Ton
Aus Monastiraki, Amari
H 0,126 m, Mündungs-Dm 0,078 m, Boden-Dm 0,06 m
Rethymnon, Archäologisches Museum
Kanne mit zwei waagerechten Henkeln und einer Tülle, die durch einen Steg mit der Lippe verbunden ist. Zusammengesetzt. Ton bräunlich aschgrau, Firnis rotbraun.

53 Kleeblattkanne
MM II (19.-18. Jh. v. Chr.)
Ton
Aus Monastiraki, Amari
H 0,15 m, Boden-Dm 0,072 m
Rethymnon, Archäologisches Museum
Zusammengesetztes und ergänztes Gefäß aus orangebraunem Ton mit Brandspuren auf der Oberfläche, kleeblattförmiger Mündung und senkrechtem Henkel. Gefäße dieser Form werden von den Forschern auch „Milchkannen" genannt.

54 Kanne
MM II (19.-18. Jh. v. Chr.)
Ton
Aus Monastiraki, Amari
H 0,14 m, Boden-Dm 0,004 m
Rethymnon, Archäologisches Museum
An Körper und Mündung ergänztes Gefäß aus bräunlich aschgrauem Ton mit rauher Oberfläche und Brandspuren.

55 Kanne
MM II (19.-18. Jh. v. Chr.)
Ton
Aus Monastiraki, Amari
H 0,09 m, Boden-Dm 0,049 m
Rethymnon, Archäologisches Museum
Einhenkelige Kanne, an einer kleinen Stelle ergänzt. Ton hellorange, Oberfläche rauh mit verstreuten Blattabdrücken.

56 Becher
MM II (19.-18. Jh. v. Chr.)
Ton
Aus Monastiraki, Amari
H 0,04 m, Mündungs-Dm 0,067 m
Rethymnon, Archäologisches Museum
Unversehrter Becher von einem Drillingsgefäß, einem Kultgefäß aus drei Bechern, von denen die anderen beiden verloren sind. Ton braunrosa. In der rauhen Oberfläche sind Finger- und Blattabdrücke zu erkennen.

57 Knickwandtasse
MM II (19.-18. Jh. v. Chr.)
Ton
Aus Monastiraki, Amari
H 0,05 m, Mündungs-Dm 0,075 m, Boden-Dm 0,032 m
Rethymnon, Archäologisches Museum
Knickwandtasse, zusammengesetzt. Ton von guter Qualität. Der Überzug, der das Gefäß innen und außen bedeckt, ist nicht farbecht. Der Fundort des Gefäßes hat Anhaltspunkte zur Organisation der Verwaltung und zu kultischen Veranstaltungen geliefert.

58 Becher
MM II (19.-18. Jh. v. Chr.)
Ton
Aus Apodoulou, Amari
H 0,0942 m, Mündungs-Dm 0,065 - 0,069 m, Boden-Dm 0,03 m
Rethymnon, Archäologisches Museum
Kleines, grob gearbeitetes Gefäß, zusammengesetzt, mit konischem Körper und flachem Boden.

59 Becher
MM II 19.-18. Jh. v. Chr.)
Ton
Aus Apodoulou, Amari
H 0,078 m, Mündungs-Dm 0,076 - 0,082 m, Boden-Dm 0,04 m
Rethymnon, Archäologisches Museum
Gebrauchsgefäß, zusammengesetzt. Hoher, ellipsoider Körper mit Ausguß an der Lippe und zwei einander gegenüber angebrachten Knubben. Der Dekor besteht aus rotbraunem Firnis, der in kleinen Rinnsalen über die Gefäßwandung herabgeflossen ist.

60 Zwillingsgefäß
MM II (19.-18. Jh. v. Chr.)
Ton
Aus Monastiraki, Amari
H 0,026 m, Gesamt-Dm 0,125 m
Rethymnon, Archäologisches Museum
Zusammengesetztes und ergänztes Gefäß aus braungelbem Ton. Es besteht aus zwei konischen, an einer Seite miteinander verbundenen Bechern mit rauher Oberfläche und Brandspuren im Innern.
Gefäße dieser Form werden auch „Salz- und Pfeffernäpfchen" genannt.

61 Vier Siegelabdrücke
MM II (19.-18. Jh. v. Chr.)
Ton
Aus Monastiraki, Amari
L 0,03 - 0,09 m, B 0,038 - 0,12 m,
D 0,014 - 0,03 m
Rethymnon, Archäologisches Museum
Vier unregelmäßig geformte Stücke aus braunem oder orangefarbenen Ton mit Siegelabdrücken. Von dem jeweiligen Gegenstand, der damit versiegelt wurde, sind auf der Rückseite noch Schnurabdrücke zu sehen. Die Hauptseite der Stücke trägt je vier bis elf Siegelabdrücke, größtenteils mit linearen Motiven, acht- und S-förmigen Ornamenten sowie Hakenkreuzen, die von Nebenmotiven umrahmt sind.
Im Gebäudekomplex von Monastiraki wurden zwei Siegelarchive freigelegt, eines in einem Raum, den man dann danach benannt hat, und eines in den Magazinen. Wir können daraus schließen, daß es ein strenges Verwaltungs- und Kontrollsystem gegeben haben muß.

62   Webgewicht
MM II (19.-18. Jh. v. Chr.)
Ton
Aus Monastiraki, Amari
L 0,075 m, Loch-Dm 0,01 m
Rethymnon, Archäologisches Museum
Zylindrisches Webgewicht aus braunem Ton mit Einschlüssen, Loch in der Querachse, Brandspuren auf der Oberfläche.

63   Deckel mit Henkel
MM II (19.-18. Jh. v. Chr.)
Ton
Aus Monastiraki, Amari
H (mit Henkel) 0,06 m, Dm 0,15 m
Rethymnon, Archäologisches Museum
Zusammengesetzt. Ton hellorange, Firnis braunrosa. Auf der Oberfläche haben sich Spuren von glänzendem Überzug erhalten. Einfache Streifen verzieren Deckel und Henkel.

64   Miniatur-„Teekanne"
MM II (19.-18. Jh. v. Chr.)
Ton
Aus Apodoulou, Amari
H 0,026 m, max. 0,047 m,
Mündungs-Dm 0,034 m
Rethymnon, Archäologisches Museum
Ergänztes Gefäß in Miniaturform mit doppelkonischem Körper und zwei einander gegenüber angebrachten Knubben, flachem Boden und zylindrischer, überrandständiger Tülle. Gefäße dieser Formen wurden auch in Phaistos gefunden. Sie werden als Öllämpchen gedeutet.

65   Reibe
MM II (19.-18. Jh. v. Chr.)
Ton
Aus Monastiraki, Amari
H 0,07 m, max. L 0,15 m
Rethymnon, Archäologisches Museum
Schale mit zwei Horizontalhenkeln an der Mündung. Der Boden im Innern der Schale hat eine flache Erhebung, die mit Kerben reliefiert ist. Von dieser Reibe hat sich nur etwa ein Drittel erhalten, das uns jedoch erlaubt, ihre Form mit Sicherheit zu rekonstruieren. Hellgrauer Ton und Spuren von schwarzem Firnis im Innern des Gefäßes.
Dies ist ein hervorragendes Beispiel eines Gebrauchsgefäßes, dessen Form sich bis heute fast unverändert erhalten hat. Ein entsprechendes Exemplar ist im alten Palast von Phaistos gefunden worden.

66   Pithos
MM II (19.-18. Jh. v. Chr.)
Ton
Aus Monastiraki, Amari
H 0,315, Mündungs-Dm 0,0145,
Boden-Dm 0,11 m
Rethymnon, Archäologisches Museum
Zweihenkliger Pithos mit Knubben, zusammengesetzt. Ton bräunlich aschgrau, Firnis schwarz. Der untere Teil des Körpers und der Hals sind mit Streifen verziert, die Schulter mit hängenden Bögen.

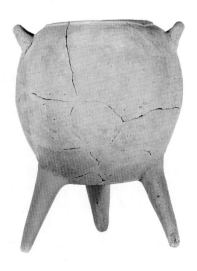

67 Dreibeiniger Topf
MM II (19.-18. Jh. v. Chr.)
Ton
Aus Monastiraki, Amari
H 0,32 m, Mündungs-Dm 0,17 m,
Boden-Dm 0,13 m
Rethymnon, Archäologisches Museum
Kochtopf, zusammengesetzt und ergänzt. Ton rotbraun, Oberfläche rauh.

68 Pithosförmiges Gefäß
MM II (19.-18. Jh. v. Chr.)
Ton
Aus Monastiraki, Amari
H 0,18 m, Mündungs-Dm 0,12 m,
Boden-Dm 0,08 m
Rethymnon, Archäologisches Museum
Unversehrtes kleines, henkelloses Gefäß von der Form eines Pithos. Ton hellorange, Oberfläche rauh mit Blattabdrücken.

69 Amphora
MM II (19.-18. Jh. v. Chr.)
Ton
Aus Monastiraki, Amari
H 0,32 m, Mündungs-Dm 0,097 m,
Boden-Dm 0,10 m
Rethymnon, Archäologisches Museum
Unversehrt. Ton braungelb. Das ganze Gefäß war mit braunschwarzem Firnis überzogen, wovon sich Spuren an der Lippe und der Außenwandung des Halses erhalten haben.

70 Lampe
MM II (19.-18. Jh. v. Chr.)
Ton
Aus Monastiraki, Amari
Erhalt, H 0,08 m, Außen-Dm 0,313 m
Rethymnon, Archäologisches Museum
Zusammengesetzt und ergänzt. Der Fuß ist verloren. Braungelber Ton mit glänzendem Überzug und starken Brandspuren im Becken.

71 Pithos
MM II (19.-18. Jh. v. Chr.)
Ton
Aus Monastiraki, Amari
H 0,44 m, Mündungs-Dm 0,25 m,
Boden-Dm 0,135 m
Rethymnon, Archäologisches Museum
Pithos zusammengesetzt, mit Ausguß und vier Henkeln (zwei waag- und zwei senkrechten), Braungelber Ton mit Brandspuren, Obefläche rauh.

72 Pithos
MM II (19.-18. Jh. v. Chr.)
Ton
Aus Monastiraki, Amari
H 0,69, max. Dm 0,50, Mündungs-Dm 0,39 m
Rethymnon, Archäologisches Museum
Aus vielen Fragmenten zusammengesetzt. Ton braungelb, Firnis braun. Körper eiförmig mit vier senkrechten Henkeln am Hals. Der Firnis ist in kleinen Rinnsalen über die Innen- und Außenfläche des Gefäßes geflossen.

73 Lampe
SM I (16. Jh. v. Chr.)
Ophit
Fundort unbekannt
H 0,045 m, max. Dm 0,12 m,
Rethymnon, Archäologisches Museum
Steinlampe, Henkel unvollständig, Stoßstellen an der Oberfläche. Hohe Basis mit flachem Boden, konischer Körper mit ellipsoider Vertiefung für das Öl; der horizontale Henkel ist mit der Lampe aus demselben Stück gearbeitet. Dieser Typus ist tönernen Vorbildern der Periode MM nachgebildet und kommt in der Zeit MM I bis SM I vor.

74 Kanne
SM IB (Ende des 16. Jhs. v. Chr.)
Ton
Aus der Stadt Chania
H 0,137 m, Mündungs-Dm 0,117 - 0,122 m, Boden-Dm 0,051 m
Chania, Archäologisches Museum
Wenig sorgfältig gearbeitetes Gefäß, zusammengesetzt. Konischer Körper auf Standplatte, kurzer weiter Hals, mit rinnenförmiger Tülle und einem senkrechten Henkel, dessen Ansatz an Metallgefäße erinnert. Umlaufende Streifen verzieren Körper und Hals und laufende Spiralen mit gewundenen Stielen die Schulterzone.

75 Tüllenbecher
SM I B (Ende des 16. Jhs. v. Chr.)
Ton
Aus Kastelli, Chania
H 0,082 m, max. Dm 0,098 m
Chania, Archäologisches Museum
Bis auf einige abgenutzte Stellen auf der Oberfläche unversehrtes Gefäß mit abgeplattet-kugeligem Körper, weitem Hals, Röhrenausguß, einem senkrechten Henkel und zwei Wülsten auf der Schulter. Der braunrosa Dekor zeigt hängende und laufende Spiralen.

76 Hydria
SM II (15. Jh. v. Chr.)
Bronze
Aus Koufi, Rethymnon
H, 0,48 m, Mündungs-Dm 0,15 m,
max. DM 0,38 m, Boden-Dm 0,163 m
Rethymnon, Archäologisches Museum
Hydria, auf der Schulter bestoßen. Der birnenförmige Körper besteht aus drei horizontalen Blechstreifen, die mit Nieten verbunden sind. Das Gefäß hat zwei Henkel, einen senkrechten, der von der Lippe zur Schulter führt und einen horizontalen an der unteren Hälfte des Körpers. Der unter Abschluß des Gefäßes ist scheibenförmig.
Bronzehydrien treten im kretisch-mykenischen Raum in der 2. Hälfte des Jhs. v. Chr. auf.

77 Kanne
SM III A (14. Jh. v. Chr.)
Ton
Fundort unbekannt
H, 0,28 m, max. Dm 0,185 m
Rethymnon, Archäologisches Museum
Das schlanke, sorgfältig gearbeitete und gut erhaltene Gefäß ist Metallvorbildern nachgestaltet. Konisch-birnenförmiger Körper, fast scheibenförmiger Boden, Röhrenhals, Schnabelausguß und senkrechter Bandhenkel mit Druckspur am Ansatz auf der Schulter des Gefäßes. Der kräftig orangefarbene Dekor beschränkt sich auf einfache, umlaufende Streifen und eine Reihe von S-förmigen Motiven in der Schulterzone.

78 Zweihenkeliger Stamniskos
SM III A (14. Jh. v. Chr.)
Ton
Aus Armeni (Kammergrab 95), Rethymnon
H 0,133m, Mündungs-Dm 0,09 m,
Boden-Dm 0,42 m
Rethymnon, Archäologisches Museum
Unversehrtes Gefäß mit hohem Boden, birnenförmigem Körper, Standplatte, weitem Hals und zwei Bandhenkeln. Unregelmäßiger Farbauftrag. Der Hauptdekor beschränkt sich auf konzentrische Bögen in der Schulterzone. Gefäße dieses Typus sind im 14. und 13. Jh. v. Chr. im östlichen Mittelmeerraum sehr weit verbreitet.

79 Alabastronförmiges Gefäß
SM III (14. Jh. v. Chr.)
Ton
Aus Armeni (Kammergrab 35), Rethymnon
H 0,15 m, max. Dm 0,17 m
Rethymnon, Archäologisches Museum
Alabastronförmiges Gefäß, an der Oberfläche stellenweise bestoßen und beschädigt. Der Körper hat die Form einer abgeplatteten Kugel, der Hals ist zylindrisch und hat einen Wulst am Ansatz und horizontalen Mündungsrand. Auf der Schulter sitzen zwei Bogenhenkel und zwei Knubben. Der Dekor besteht aus einer Reihe stilisierter Muscheln auf der Schulter sowie Punkten, Winkelgruppen und gegenständigen Bögen als Nebenmotiven.

80 Kleine Kanne
SM III A (14. Jh. v. Chr.)
Ton
Aus Armeni (Kammergrab 89), Rethymnon
H 0,065 m, max. Dm 0,067 m
Rethymnon, Archäologisches Museum
Unversehrte, einfarbige kleine Kanne mit kugeligem Körper, fast ringförmigem Fuß, schnabelförmigem Ausguß und einem Bandhenkel.

81 Dreihenkeliges Alabastron
SM III A (14. Jh. v. Chr.)
Ton
Aus Armeni (Kammergrab 78), Rethymnon
H 0,153 m, Mündungs-DM 0,088 m,
Boden-Dm 0,112 m
Rethymnon, Archäologisches Museum
Unversehrtes, nur stellenweise abgenutztes Gefäß mit zylindrischem Körper, flachem Boden, senkrechtem Hals, breitem Mündungsrand und drei Bogenhenkeln. Der braunrosa Dekor auf dem Körper des Gefäßes zeigt gereihte papyrusartige Blüten; die Zwischenräume der Henkel sind mit konzentrischen Halbkreisen verziert.

82 Zweihenkeliger kleiner Stamnos
SM III A1 (Beginn des 14. Jhs. v. Chr.)
Ton
Aus Armeni (Kammergrab 94), Rethymnon
H 0,103 m, max. DM 0,11 m,
Mündungs-Dm 0,082 m
Rethymnon, Archäologisches Museum
Kleines, gut erhaltenes Gefäß mit kugelig-konischem Körper, flachem Boden und weitem Hals. Eindrucksvoll ist der „metallische" Glanz der gänzlich schwarz gefirnißten Oberfläche.

83 Alabastron
SM III A (14. Jh. v. Chr.)
Ton
Aus Armeni (Kammergrab 67), Rethymnon
H 0,10m, Mündungs-Dm 0,093 m,
Boden-Dm 0,15 m
Rethymnon, Archäologisches Museum
Unversehrt, lediglich an der Lippe geringe Ergänzungen. Zylindrischer Körper und drei Bogenhenkel. Der Hauptdekor entfaltet sich in der Schulterzone und besteht aus einem stilisierten Blattband.
Die linsenförmig plankonvexen und zylindrischen Alabaster, die vermutlich minoischen Ursprungs sind und vielleicht weit entfernte Vorläufer in Ägypten haben, treten besonders häufig in der Periode SM III auf und dienten als Duftölgefäße.

84 Kylix
SM III A2/B (Ende des 14. Jhs. v. Chr.)
Ton
Aus Stavromenos, Rethymnon
H (mit Henkeln) 0,20 m,
Mündungs-Dm 0,174 m, Boden-Dm 0,094 m
Rethymnon, Archäologisches Museum
Zusammengesetzte Kylix mit hohem, konischem Körper und zwei überrandständigen, senkrechten Henkeln auf hohem Fuß mit breiter, gewölbter Standfläche. Die Henkelzone ist in rotbraunem Firnis mit gegabelten „minoischen Blüten" bemalt. Parallele Streifen zieren den Fuß und die Standfläche. Innen ist das Gefäß gänzlich mit Firnis überzogen.

85 Bügelkanne
SM III A 2 (Ende des 14. Jhs. v. Chr.)
Ton
Aus Armeni (Kammergrab 20), Rethymnon
H 0,17 m, max. Dm 0,163 m,
Boden-Dm 0,062 m
Rethymnon, Archäologisches Museum
Schlankes, gut erhaltenes Gefäß mit birnenförmigem Körper, Standring mit zwei Bandhenkeln. Der Hauptdekor entfaltet sich auf der Schulter und ist in zwei halbkreisförmige Felder unterteilt. Er besteht a) aus verschieden verzierten Dreiecken und beiden Seiten des Ausgusses und b) aus gereihten gegabelten "minoischen Blüten".

86 Einhenkeliger Becher
SM III A2/B1 (Ende des 14, Jhs. v. Chr.)
Ton
Aus Agii Apostoli (Kammergrab), Amari
H 0,078 m, Mündungs-Dm 0,105 - 0,115 m,
Boden-Dm 0,057 m
Rethymnon, Archäologisches Museum
Becher, vollständig mit Firnis überzogen, sehr gut erhalten. Bemerkenswert ist, daß der Becher Merkmale der beiden Perioden aufweist, wodurch er als Erzeugnis der Übergangsphase gekennzeichnet ist: im Gegensatz zum bauchigen Körper und der senkrechten Lippe sind der Bandhenkel, der konische Fuß und der eckige Umriß des Körpers Charakteristik der frühen Periode.

87 Niedriger Becher
SM III B (13. Jh. n. Chr.)
Ton
Aus Agii Apostoli (Kammergrab), Amari
H 0,55 m, Mündungs-Dm 0,164 m,
Boden-Dm 0,045 m
Rethymnon, Archäologisches Museum
Vollständig erhaltenes Gefäß, gänzlich mit Firnis bemalt, mit flachem Boden, konischem Körper und zwei horizontalen Henkeln. Gebrauchsgefäße diese Typus finden sich bereits seit der Periode SM III A häufig in Siedlungen und Gräbern.

88 Kleine Kanne
SM III B (13. Jh. v. Chr.)
Ton
Aus Armeni (Kammergrab 140), Rethymnon
H 0,64 m, max. Dm 0,067 m
Rethymnon, Archäologisches Museum
Zierliches Gefäß mit kleinen Ergänzungen. Kugeliger, gedrungener Körper, kleine Standfläche, aufwärts geneigter Ausguß von halbkreisförmigem Querschnitt und ein senkrechter Henkel. Der Hauptdekor entfaltet sich in der Schulterzone und besteht aus einem Flechtornament.

89 Kleine Kanne
SM III A (14. Jh. v. Chr.)
Ton
Aus Armeni (Kammergrab 98), Rethymnon
H 0,064 m, max. Dm 0,067 m
Rethymnon, Archäologisches Museum
Fein gearbeitetes, einfarbiges Gefäß in gutem Erhaltungszustand. Es hat einen kugeligen, gedrungenen Körper, zylindrischen Hals, schnabelförmigen Ausguß und senkrechten Henkel.

90 Becher
SM III B (13. Jh. v. Chr.)
Ton
Aus Agii Apostoli (Kammergrab), Amari
H 0,06 m, Mündungs-Dm 0,10 m, Boden-Dm 0,037 m
Retyhmnon, Archäologisches Museum
Vorzüglich erhaltenes Gefäß mit flachem Boden, halbkugeligem Körper und senkrechtem Henkel. Der glänzende, schwarze Dekor entfaltet sich auf dem oberen Bereich des Körpers und beschränkt sich auf hängende spiralförmige Ranken. Das Gefäßinnere ist gänzlich mit Firnis überzogen.

91 Kylix mit niedrigem Fuß
SM IIIB (13. Jh. v. Chr.)
Ton
Aus der Stadt Chania (Kammergrab 1)
H 0,11 m, Mündungs-Dm 0,125, Boden-Dm 0,065 m
Chania, Archäologisches Museum
Schönes Exemplar aus der Werkstatt von Chania (Kydonia); zusammengesetzt und ergänzt. Körper konisch und leicht kantig mit zwei senkrechten Henkeln; niedriger Fuß mit breiter Standfläche. Der orange Dekor entfaltet sich hauptsächlich in der Henkelzone und zeigt je zwei einzelne Papyrusblüten auf beiden Seiten des Gefäßes. Der Boden ist mit einem Spiralband verziert.

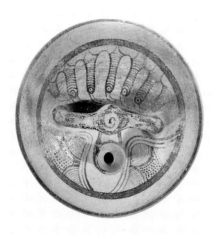

92 Bügelkanne
SM III B (13. Jh. v. Chr.)
Ton
Aus Armeni (Kammergrab 139), Rethymnon
H 0,12 m, max. Dm 0,156 m
Rethymnon, Archäologisches Museum
An einer kleinen Stelle der Mündung ergänzt, sonst unversehrtes Gefäß mit konischem Körper auf Standring und mit senkrechtem Ausguß. Der Hauptdekor entfaltet sich in der Schulterzone, die in zwei halbkreisförmige Felder unterteilt ist, und umfaßt a) gereihte Vogelköpfe und b) unterschiedlich verzierte Dreiecke.
Die Darstellung von Vögeln ist in der minoischen Kunst ein beliebtes Thema und erscheint zuerst in der Periode MM III in der Wandmalerei.

93 Dreibeiniges Gefäß
SM III B (13. Jh. v. Chr.)
Ton
Aus Armeni (Kammergrab 158), Rethymnon
H 0,204m, max. Dm 0,192 m,
Mündungs-Dm 0,082 m
Rethymnon, Archäologisches Museum
Oberfläche stellenweise abgenutzt, sonst unversehrtes Gefäß mit kugeligem Körper, flachem Boden, drei Beinen, vier Henkeln auf der Schulter (zwei senkrechte und zwei Bogenhenkel) und breitem zylindrischen Hals. Rotbrauner Firnis. Der Hauptdekor besteht a) aus ein- oder zweifachen Spiralen in den Zwischenräumen der Henkel und b) aus gegenläufigen spiralförmigen Ranken auf dem unteren Teil der Gefäßwandung.

94 Dreihenkelige kleine Amphora
SM III A2 (Ende des 14. Jhs. v. Chr.)
Ton
Aus Armeni (Kammergrab 67), Rethymnon
H 0,16 m, max. Dm 0,145 m,
Mündungs-Dm 0,097 m
Rethymnon, Archäologisches Museum
Bis auf kleine Stoßstellen unversehrtes Gefäß mit birnenförmigem Körper, zylindrischem Hals, Ringboden und Bogenhenkeln. Der nicht ganz farbechte braunrosa Dekor entfaltet sich hauptsächlich in der Schulterzone und ist in metopenartige Bildfelder unterteilt, die mit gegenständigen Bögen gefüllt sind.

95 Becher
SM III A2/B (Ende des 14. Jhs. v. Chr.)
Ton
Aus Agii Apostoli (Kammergrab), Amari
H 0,04 m, Mündungs-Dm 0,106 m
Rethymnon, Archäologisches Museum
Unversehrter, henkelloser, konischer Becher ohne Dekor. Becher dieses Typus treten in Kreta seit der Periode FM auf und sind immer Gebrauchsgefäße.

96 Miniaturkanne
SM III B (Beginn des 13. Jhs. v. Chr.)
Ton
Aus Armeni (Kammergrab 100), Rethymnon
H 0,055 m, max. Dm 0,059 m
Rethymnon, Archäologisches Museum
Zierliches Miniaturgefäß mit abgeplattet kugeligem Körper, Standring, weiter Mündung und senkrechtem Henkel. Die Schulterzone ist mit einem braunschwarzen durchbrochenen Flechtband verziert. Das Kännchen diente vielleicht als Spielzeug oder als Duftölgefäß.

97 Amphoroider Krater
SM III B (13. Jh. v. Chr.)
Ton
Aus der Stadt Rethymnon (Kammergrab)
H 0,45 m, Mündungs-Dm 0,38 m,
max. DM 0,34 m
Rethymnon, Archäologisches Museum
Eindrucksvoller Krater, an der Lippe zusammengesetzt, mit birnenförmigem Körper, konischem Fuß, hohem, zylindrischen Hals, horizontalem Mündungsrand und zwei senkrechten Bandhenkeln. Der orangebraune Dekor entfaltet sich auf beiden Seiten des Gefäßkörpers und besteht aus je einem stilisiertem Oktopus mit schlangenartigen Fangarmen. Diese Exemplar ist eine besonders charakteristische minoische Schöpfung, da sowohl die Form als auch das Thema des Dekors in Kreta entwickelt wurden und sich dann von hieraus im ägäischen Raum verbreiteten.

98 Messer
SM III A-B (14.-13. Jh. v. Chr.)
Bronze
Aus Armeni (Kammergrab 16), Rethymnon
L 0,18 m, max. B 0,017 m
Rethymnon, Archäologisches Museum
Einschneidiges Messer. Klinge und Angel, von der ein Stück abgebrochen ist, aus einem Stück. Klinge länglich und dreieckig mit abgerundeter Spitze. In der Angel stecken zwei Niete zur Befestigung des Holzgriffes, von dem noch ein Fragment vorhanden ist. An der einen Klingenseite hat sich ein Rest eines Stoffes erhalten, in den das Messer wohl eingewickelt war.

99 Messer
SM III A-B (14.-13. Jh. v. Chr.)
Bronze
Aus Armeni (Kammergrab 25), Rethymnon
L 0,195 m
Rethymnon, Archäologisches Museum
Unversehrtes einschneidiges Messer. Dreieckige Klinge mit geradem Rücken und viereckiger Angel, in der zwei Löcher und eine Niete zur Befestigung des Griffes aus organischem Stoff erhalten sind.
Dieser Typus des Gebrauchmessers ist in der Periode SH weit verbreitet und gelangt vom griechischem Festland um die Mitte des 14. Jhs. v. Chr. (SM III) nach Kreta.

100 Messer
SM III A-B (14.-13. Jh. v. Chr.)
Bronze
Aus Armeni (Kammergrab 95), Rethymnon
L 0,128 m, max. B 0,035 m
Rethymnon, Archäologisches Museum
Blattförmige, zweischneidige Klinge mit Schlagspuren an Spitze und Angel. Zwei Nieten zur Befestigung des Holzgriffes haben sich erhalten.
Welchem Zweck diese Geräte dienten, ist für die Forscher schwer zu bestimmen; so wurden sie auch als eine frühe Art Rasiermesser gedeutet.

101 Messer
SM III A-B (14.-13. Jh. v. Chr.)
Bronze
Aus Armeni (Kammergrab 71), Rethymnon
L 0,142 m, max. B 0,014 m
Rethymnon, Archäologisches Museum
Kleines einschneidiges Messer mit einer Schlagspur an der Angel; zwei Nieten zur Befestigung des Holzgriffes haben sich erhalten. Die dreieckige Klinge hat einen geraden Rükken und eine leicht abgerundete Spitze.

102 Hackmesser
SM III A-B (14.-13. Jh. v. Chr.)
Bronze
Aus Armeni (Kammergrab 55), Rethymnon
L 0,215 m, max. B. 0,07 m
Rethymnon, Archäologisches Museum
Unversehrtes Handwerksgerät mit kleinen Schlagspuren an der Schneide. Trapezförmige Klinge mit eingebogenem Rücken und geschweifter Angel, in der sich zwei Löcher und eine Niete zur Befestigung des hölzernen Griffes befinden. In den Klingenrücken sind drei parallele Linien graviert.
Dieser Werkzeugtyp ist in der ganzen Periode SM III in Gebrauch, tritt jedoch in der Folgezeit überhaupt nicht mehr auf.

104 Doppelaxt
SM II (15. Jh. v. Chr.)
Bronze
Fundort unbekannt
L 0,185 m, max. B 0,063 m
Rethymnon, Archäologisches Museum
Doppelaxt mit Schlagspuren an den Schneiden und rundem Loch zur Befestigung des Holzschaftes.
Diese Werkzeugform wurde in der Bronzezeit im ägäischen Raum erfunden und weiterentwickelt. Die Doppelaxt dient nicht nur als Gebrauchsgegenstand, sondern stellte auch das charakteristischste minoische Kultsymbol dar. Man unterscheidet zwei Typen, einen mit rundem und einen mit ellipsiodem Schaftloch.

105 Säge
SM III A-B (14.-13. Jh. v. Chr.)
Bronze
Aus Armeni (Kammergrab 115), Rethymnon
L 0,42 m, max. B 0,055 m
Rethymnon, Archäologisches Museum
Unversehrte Holzsäge. Das länglich dreieckige Blatt hat einen geraden Rücken, eine gezahnte Schneide und drei Löcher zur Befestigung des Holzgriffes. Die Angel ist viereckig und die Spitze abgerundet.
Dieser Typus ist rein kretischen Ursprungs und tritt in zwei Varianten auf, einer mit und einer ohne Löcher. Beispiele davon haben sich auch auf dem griechischen Festland gefunden.

103 Rasiermesser
SM III A-B (14.-13. Jh. v. Chr.)
Bronze
Aus Armeni (Kammergrab 127), Rethymnon
L 0,155 m, max. B 0,035 m
Rethymnon, Archäologisches Museum
Unversehrt, korrodiert. Fast trapezförmige Klinge mit leicht eingebogenem Rücken und geschweifter Angel, in der noch vier Nieten zur Befestigung des Holzgriffes erhalten sind.
Welchem Zweck Gegenstände von diesem Typus mit all seinen Varianten dienten, ist für die Forscher oft schwer zu bestimmem (vgl. Kat.-Nr. 179). Die kleine Größe dieses Exemplares spricht jedoch, wie wir annehmen, für seinen Gebrauch als Toilettenartikel.

106 Lanzenspitze
SM III A-B (14.-13. Jh. v. Chr.)
Bronze
Aus Armeni (Kammergrab 35), Rethymnon
L 0,255 m
Rethymnon, Archäologisches Museum
Unversehrt, flammenförmig. Die Tülle hat achteckigen Querschnitt und zwei Löcher zur Befestigung des Holzschaftes, von dem ein Stück in der Tülle erhalten ist. Die Spitze ist mit einer kräftigen Mittelrippe verstärkt.

107 Lanzenspitze
SM III A-B (14.-13. Jh. v. Chr.)
Bronze
Aus Armeni (Kammergrab 43), Rethymnon
L 0,283 m
Rethymnon, Archäologisches Museum
Es fehlt ein Teil der konischen Tülle, die mit zwei Stiftlöchern zur Befestigung des Holzschaftes und mit einem flachen Verstärkungsring am Tüllenmund versehen ist. Die flammenförmige Spitze hat eine breite Mittelrippe.

108 Kurzschwert
SM III A-B (14.-13. Jh. v. Chr.)
Bronze
Aus Armeni (Kammergrab 35), Rethymnon
L 0,375 m, Schulter-B 0,062 m
Rethymnon, Archäologisches Museum
Schwert aus zwei Teilen zusammengefügt. Klinge und Heft aus einem Stück gearbeitet. Das T-förmige Heft hat einen halbmondförmigen Knauf. Sein bis zum Klingenansatz aufgebogener Rand und die fünf erhaltenen Nieten dienten zur Befestigung der Griffschalen, die aus organischem Stoff bestanden. Klinge flach und zungenförmig, Schultern abgerundet.
Die meisten Exemplare dieses Typus stammen aus der ersten Hälfte des 14. Jhs. v. Chr.

109 Messer
SM III A-B (14.-13. Jh. v. Chr.)
Bronze
Aus Armeni (Kammergrab 115), Rethymnon
L 0,345 m
Rethymnon, Archäologisches Museum
Unversehrtes einschneidiges Messer, Klinge und Angel aus einem Stück, mit sichelförmigem Knauf und vier Nieten. In die aufgebogenen Ränder des Griffes waren die hölzernen Griffschalen eingebettet, wovon noch ein Stück erhalten ist. Der Rücken der dreieckigen Klinge ist gerade, die Spitze abgerundet. Auf beiden Seiten der Klinge ist je ein Linienpaar den Rücken entlang graviert.
Angeln mit aufgebogenem Rand treten am Ende der Periode SM II auf und sind ein charakteristisches Merkmal der Waffen in der letzten Phase der späten Bronzezeit.

110 Talent
SM I–II (16.–15. Jh. v. Chr.)
Kupfer
Aus Tylissos
L 0,345 m, B 0,25 m, T 0,06 m
Heraklion, Archäologisches Museum
Quaderförmiger Kupferbarren mit leicht eingebogenen Schmalseiten. Auf der einen Breitseite je eine unregelmäßige Eintiefung in die Ecken; in einer Ecke ein graviertes X-förmiges Zeichen.
Die Talente waren höchstwahrscheinlich die übliche Form, in der reines Kupfer als Rohrmaterial in den Handel kam, und bildeten folglich eine feste Rechnungs- und Zahlungseinheit im Handelsaustausch. Viele Talente stammen aus verschiedenen Orten Kretas, wogegen die Anzahl mykenischer Exemplare beschränkt ist.

111 Bügelkanne
SM III B (13. Jh. v. Chr.)
Ton
Aus Armeni (Kammergrab 8), Rethymnon
H 0,132 m, max. Dm 0,11 m,
Boden-Dm 0,047 m
Rethymnon, Archäologisches Museum
Schönes Exemplar aus der Werkstatt von Chania (Kydonia) (vgl. Kat.-Nr. 115), das sich durch die Feinheit von Form und Dekor auszeichnet. Der kugelige Körper ruht auf einer Standplatte. Drei vierblättrige Rosetten mit Punkten zwischen den Blättern und mehrfachem, wellenförmigen Stiel breiten sich über die Gefäßwandung aus.

112 Bügelkanne
SM III B1 (Beginn des 13. Jhs. v. Chr.)
Ton
Aus Armeni (Kammergrab 132), Rethymnon
H 0,122 m, max. Dm 0,138 m
Rethymnon, Archäologisches Museum.
Das sorgfältig gearbeitete Gefäß ist ein repräsentatives Exemplar der Keramik von Chania (Kydonia). Der konische Körper ruht auf einem Standring. Gleichbreite, schwarze, glänzende Firnisstreifen umziehen den Körper. Die Schulterzone ist mit gegabelten „minoischen Blüten" verziert.
Gefäße dieser Art wurden zum Transport kostbarer Flüssigkeiten benutzt. Das dieses Exemplar in der Nekropole von Armeni gefunden wurde, zeigt, daß der Außenhandel von Kydonia ziemlich ausgedehnt war.

113 Bügelkanne
SM III A (14. Jh. v. Chr.)
Ton
Aus Armeni (Kammergrab 79), Rethymnon
H 0,20 m, max. Dm 0,154 m
Rethymnon, Archäologisches Museum
Schlankes Gefäß, Oberfläche stellenweise bestoßen und abgenutzt. Es hat einen birnenförmigen Körper auf hohem konischen Fuß. Eine stilisierte doppelte Purpurschnecke in braunrosa Firnis bedeckt den Bauch des Gefäßes; die Schulterzone ist mit unterschiedlich verzierten, gegenständigen Dreiecken versehen.

114 Bügelkanne
SM III B (13. Jh. v. Chr.)
Ton
Aus Armeni (Kammergrab 143), Rethymnon
H 0,077 m, max. Dm 0,123 m,
Boden-Dm 0,045 m
Rethymnon, Archäologisches Museum
Kleine, gut erhaltene Kanne mit ausladendem konischen Körper auf Standring Die Verzierung der Schulterzone besteht a) aus je einer gegabelten „minoischen Blüte" auf beiden Seiten des Ausgusses und einer weiteren mit gewundenem Stiel auf der dritten Seite und b) aus einer Kette von Rauten, die in ihrer Mitte einen Punkt haben; die Rautenkette ist von je einer Wellenlinie gerahmt.

115 Askos
SM III A2/B (Ende des 14. Jhs. v. Chr.)
Ton
Aus Armeni (Kammergrab 108), Rethymnon
H 0,08 m, max. Dm 0,095 m
Rethymnon, Archäologisches Museum
Zusammengesetzt und mit Gips ergänzt. Gedrungener, kugeliger Körper, Bogenhenkel und senkrechter, zylindrischer Ausguß. Der orangebraune Dekor beschränkt sich auf parallele Bänder um den Bauch und konzentrische Halbkreise in der Schulterzone. Dieses Gefäß ist ein repräsentatives Exemplar der Werkstatt von Chania (Kydonia) der Nachpalastzeit. Daß Erzeugnisse dieser Werkstatt auch an anderen Orten Kretas, auf dem griechischem Festland und Zypern gefunden wurden, bezeugt, welche Bedeutung der Außenhandel dieses Gebietes in der kretisch-mykenischen Zeit hatte.

116 Ephyräischer Becher
SM II (2. Hälfte des 15. Jhs. v. Chr.)
Ton
Aus Knossos (Sog. Unerforschtes Haus)
H 0,096 m, Mündungs-Dm 0,111 m,
Boden-Dm 0,053 m
Heraklion, Archäologisches Museum
Kleiner Becher des ephyräischen Stils (vgl. Kat.-Nr. 16), zusammengesetzt und ergänzt. Halbkugeliger Körper, ausladende Lippe, niedriger, zylindrischer Fuß auf breiter, runder Standplatte, zwei Bandhenkel. Je ein Kreuz mit Winkelgruppen zwischen den Armen verziert die beiden Gefäßseiten. Innen ist der Becher gänzlich mit Firnis überzogen.
Das Gefäß ist in Form und Dekor getreu mykenischen Vorbildern nachgestaltet.

117 Lekythos in der Form eines Alabastron
SM III A1 (Beginn des 14. Jhs. v. Chr.)
Ton
Aus Armeni (Kammergrab 206), Rethymnon
H 0,123 m, max. Dm 0,15 m,
Mündungs-Dm 0,061 m
Rethymnon, Archäologisches Museum
Einhenkeliges Gefäß mit kleinen Stoßspuren, sonst unversehrt. Kugelig-konischer Körper, flacher Boden und trichterförmige Mündung. Die in braunem Firnis wahrscheinlich mit dem Pinsel aufgetragene Punktverzierung bedeckt die ganze Außenfläche des Gefäßes.
Dieses Muster ahmt die Oberfläche eines Straußeneis nach oder nach anderer Meinung einen Wanddekor, und erscheint zum ersten Mal in der Periode SM IB auf Kreta.

118 Dreihenkeliger Amphoriskos
SM III A2 (2. Hälfte des 14. Jhs. v. Chr.)
Ton
Aus Armeni (Kammergrab 198), Rethymnon
H 0,174 m, max. Dm 0,14 m
Rethymnon, Achäologisches Museum
Schönes Beispiel eines importierten mykenischen Amphoriskos. Bis auf kleine Stoßstellen unversehrt. Konisch-birnenförmiger Körper auf Standring, weiter, zylindrischer Hals und drei Bogenhenkel auf der Schulter, Bänder aus braunem, glänzenden Firnis umlaufen den Körper und Gruppen senkrechter Linien verzieren die Henkelzone.

119 Kelch
MM III/SM I (Mitte des 16. Jhs. c. Chr.)
Ophit
Aus der Stadt von Chania
H 0,097 m, max. Dm 0,155 m
Chania, Archäologisches Museum
Ergänztes Gefäß aus grauweißem Stein mit konischer Außenwandung und zylindrischer Innenwandung. Sechs senkrechte, reliefierte Blätter mit einem Rillenpaar in der Mitte verzieren das Gefäß außen.
Aus ganz Kreta ist eine große Anzahl von Gefäßen dieser Art bekannt. Welchem Zweck sie dienten, ist schwer zu bestimmen, einige wurden jedoch höchstwahrscheinlich als Schmink- oder Parfumgefäß benutzt.

120 Bügelkanne
SM III B (13. Jh. v. Chr.)
Ton
Aus Angeliana (Kammergrab), Mylopotamos
H 0,32 m, max. Dm 0,23 m
Rethymnon, Archäologisches Museum
Große, gut erhaltene Bügelkanne, grob gearbeitet. Körper kugelig-eiförmig, Fuß konisch mit flachem Boden. Ungleichmäßiger schwarzer bis roter Überzug bedeckt die ganze Oberfläche des Gefäßes. Der weißliche Dekor besteht aus einem schlangenförmigen Band auf dem Körper und Gruppen von Wellenlinien auf der Schulter.
Kannen dieser Art wurden als Transportgefäße für die Ausfuhr von Wein oder Duftöl benutzt.

121 Stierstatuette
MM II (19.-18. Jh. v. Chr.)
Ton
Vom Vrysinas-Berg (Gipfelheiligtum), Rethymnon
Erhalt. H 0,145 m, max. L 0,215 m
Rethymnon, Archäologisches Museum
Zusammengesetzt. Stämmiger Körper mit einer Einbuchtung an der Unterseite, zylindrische Beine, dreieckiger Kopf. Der Schwanz ist umgeschlagen. Interessant ist die stilisierte Wiedergabe der Details: flache Ritzlinien und eingerückte Vertiefungen stellen die Einzelheit am Kopf, die Hufe und Quaste des Schwanzes dar.

122 Stierstatuette
MM II (19.-18. Jh. v. Chr.)
Ton
Vom Vrysinas-Berg (Gipfelheiligtum), Rethymnon
Erhalt. H 0,08 m, max. L 0,14 m
Rethymnon, Archäologisches Museum
Nicht vollständig, Spuren von rotbraunem Firnis. Zylindrischer Körper mit deutlicher Wiedergabe der Genitalien. Die Einzelheiten des Kopfes sind nur angedeutet.

123 Stierstatuette
MM II (19.-18. Jh. v. Chr.)
Ton
Vom Vrysinas-Berg (Gipfelheiligtum), Retymnon
H 0,12 m, L 0,18 m
Rethymnon, Archäologisches Museum
Rinderstatuette, zusammengesetzt, mit Spuren von braunem Firnis. Der zylindrische längliche Körper ruht auf vier konischen Beinen. Mit Ritzlinien und eingedrückten Vertiefungen sind die Details des Kopfes dargestellt, die Ohren und Hörner sind plastisch wiedergegeben. Der Schwanz ist umgeschlagen und liegt über dem Rücken des Tieres.

124 Vogelstatuette
MM II (19.-18. Jh. v. Chr.)
Vom Vrysinas-Berg (Gipfelheiligtum), Rethymnon
H 0,028 m, L 0,07 m
Rethymnon, Archäologisches Museum
Stellenweise bestoßene, aus der Hand geformte Vogelfigur mit schlankem Körper und länglichen, schmalen Flügeln; auf dem erhobenen Hals sitzt ein kleiner Kopf mit offenem Schnabel und zwei Eintiefungen, die die Augen wiedergeben.
Der Vogel ist ein beliebtes Thema der minoischen Ikonographie. Im kultischen Bereich, z.B. als Weihgabe an die Gottheit, im täglichen Leben als Spielzeug und als Verzierung verschiedener Gegenstände sind Vogeldarstellungen außerordentlich verbreitet.

125 Weibliches Idol
MM II (19.-18. Jh. v. Chr.)
Ton
Vom Vrysinas-Berg (Gipfelheiligtum), Rethymnon
Erhalt. H 0,094 m
Rethymnon, Archäologisches Museum
Bis zur Taille erhaltener Oberkörper einer stehenden weiblichen Gestalt. Die Arme sind vor der unbekleideten Brust verschränkt. Kegelförmige Erhebungen geben die Brüste wieder, und senkrechte Rillen anatomische Einzelheiten des Rückens. Die Frau trägt eine vielfältig verzierte Kopfbedeckung (Polos) und eine Halskette aus hängenden Scheiben. Die Gesichtszüge sind stilisiert wiedergegeben.

126 Weibliches Idol
MM II (19.-18. Jh. v. Chr.)
Ton
Vom Vrysinas-Berg (Gipfelheiligtum), Rethymnon
H 0,09 m
Rethymnon, Archäologisches Museum.
Aus der Hand gefertigte, unvollständige Figur einer unbekleideten Frau mit Polos auf dem Kopf und gegürteter Taille. Augen, Ohren und Brüste sind plastisch aufgesetzt, während Mund und Nasenlöcher eingeritzt sind.

127 Weibliches Idol
MM II (19.-18. Jh. v. Chr.)
Ton
Vom Vrysinas-Berg (Gipfelheiligtum), Rethymnon
Erhalt. H 0,086 m
Rethymnon, Archäologisches Museum
Sehr unsorgfältig aus der Hand geformte Figur einer bis zur Taille unbekleideten Frau. Der Unterkörper mit dem Rock fehlt. Nur ein Arm ist erhalten. Die Brüste sind durch konische Erhebungen wiedergegeben, die Gesichtszüge nur schwach angedeutet. Auf dem Kopf trägt sie einen Polos.

128 Weibliches Idol
MM II (19.-18. Jh. v. Chr.)
Ton
Vom Vrysinas-Berg (Gipfelheiligtum), Rethymnon
Erhalt. H 0,10 m
Rethymnon, Archäologisches Museum
Zusammengesetzter, bis zur Taille erhaltener nackter Oberkörper einer stehenden Frau mit breitem Rumpf und konischen Erhebungen, die die Brüste wiedergeben. Der Kopf mit dem eigenartigen gewundenen Polos ist nach hinten gebogen und hat eine dreieckige Nase, runde Augen und plastisch gebildete Ohren.

129 Weibliches Idol
MM II (19.-18. Jh. v. Chr.)
Ton
Vom Vrysinas-Berg (Gipfelheiligtum), Rethymnon
Erhalt. H 0,098 m
Rethymnon, Archäologisches Museum
Fragmentarisch erhaltene, stark bestoßene Statuette einer Frau mit schlankem, nacktem Oberkörper und plastischer Wiedergabe der Brüste. Der mit einem Rock bekleidete Unterkörper und die Arme fehlen. Die Hände liegen auf dem Oberkörper. Auf dem Kopf trägt sie einen niedrigen Polos. Die Gesichtszüge sind stilisiert wiedergegeben.

130 Männliches Idol
MM II (19.-18. Jh. v. Chr.)
Ton
Vom Vrysinas-Berg (Gipfelheiligtum), Rethymnon
H 0,125 m
Rethymnon, Archäologisches Museum
Gänzlich mit Überzug bedeckte stehende Figur eines unbekleideten Mannes mit zurückgebogenem Kopf. Die Hände sind zur Brust geführt. Gesichtszüge und Genital sind nur schwach angedeutet.
Der Gestus der zur Brust geführten Hände kommt seit der Periode FM bei Statuetten vor, die wohl Adoranten darstellen.

131 Männliches Idol
MM II (19.-18. Jh. v. Chr.)
Ton
Vom Vrysinas-Berg (Gipfelheiligtum), Rethymnon
H 0,14 m
Rethymnon, Archäologisches Museum
Fragmentarisch erhaltene Figur eines unbekleideten Mannes. Augen, Nase und Genital sind plastisch gebildet. Die Haare sind teils geflochten, teils durch Querlinien wiedergegeben.

132 Weibliches Idol
MM II (19.-18. Jh. v. Chr.)
Ton
Vom Vrysinas-Berg (Gipfelheiligtum), Rethymnon
Erhalt. H 0,11 m
Rethymnon, Archäologisches Museum
Weibliche Gestalt mit Spuren von schwarzem Firnis, der ehemals die ganze Oberfläche bedeckte. Der Oberkörper ist nackt, während der verlorene Unterkörper mit einem Rock bekleidet war. Die Hände sind nach vorn geführt, vielleicht sollten sie darstellen, daß sie die Brüste drücken. Diese Haltung hat auch ein Rhyton in Form eines weiblichen Idols aus Mochlos. Die Gesichtszüge sind grob ausgeführt. Auf dem Kopf trägt die Frau einen fast runden Polos.

133 Köpfe von männlichen Idolen
MM II (19.-18. Jh. v. Chr.)
Ton
Vom Vrysinas-Berg (Gipfelheiligtum), Rethymnon
H 0,032 m - 0,045 m
Rethymnon, Archäologisches Museum
Zwei Statuettenköpfe mit erhabenen runden Augen und länglicher Nase. Bemerkenswert sind die Löcher in den nur andeutungsweise angegebene Ohren. Die Haare sind teils geflochten, teils durch Querlinien wiedergegeben.

134 Männliches Idol
MM II (19.-18. Jh. v. Chr.)
Ton
Vom Vrysinas-Berg (Gipfelheiligtum), Rethymnon
Erhalt. H 0,102 m
Rethymnon, Archäologisches Museum
Aus der Hand geformtes Idol mit runden Augen, offenem Mund, langer Nase, plastisch gebildeten Ohren und langen, geflochtenen Haaren. Die Hände sind zur Brust geführt. Der Mann trägt einen charakteristisch minoischen Schurz mit einem Dolch im Gürtel.
Eine entsprechende Kriegerstatuette stammt aus dem Petsofas-Gipfelheiligtum.

135 Nachbildung eines Opfertisches
MM II (19.-18. Jh. v. Chr.)
Ophit
Vom Vrysinas-Berg (Gipfelheiligtum), Rethymnon
H 0,068 m, erhalt. L 0,07 m
Rethymnon, Archäologisches Museum
Zur Hälfte erhaltene Nachbildung eines viereckigen Opfertisches aus grauem Stein. In die Tischplatte sind an den Rändern entlanglaufende Zeichen der Linear A-Schrift eingeritzt. Solche Inschriften in Linear-A sind vielleicht Weihinschriften oder geben Anliegen an die weibliche Gottheit oder Namen wieder.

136 Kleine Kultlekanis
MM III (17.-16. Jh. v. Chr.)
Ton
Aus der Mameloukos-Höhle bei Perivolia
H 0,08 m, Mündungs-Dm 0,20 m
Chania, Archäologisches Museum
Zusammengesetztes Gefäß mit konischem, weiten Körper und flachem Boden. Im Gefäßinnern sind unterhalb der Lippe sieben winzig kleine Nachbildungen von konischen Bechern angebracht, die sich gegenseitig teilweise überlagern.
Es handelt sich um ein kultisches Gefäß, einen "Kernos", in dem der Gottheit Feldfrüchte gespendet wurden.

137 Doppelaxt
SM I (Beginn des 15. Jhs. v. Chr.)
Bronze
Aus Malia (Haus E)
L 0,19 m, max. B 0,067 m
Heraklion, Archäologisches Museum
Unversehrte Doppelaxt mit ausgebogenen Schneiden und ellipsiodem Schaftloch. Die an den Schmalseiten erkennbaren Rillen sind beim Guß in der Form entstanden.
Diese Variante des Typus mit ellipsenförmigem Schaftloch, zu der dieses Exemplar gehört, ist ureigentlich mykenisch und war im helladischen Raum verbreitet.

138 Lekanis
SM III B (13. Jh. v. Chr.)
Ton
Aus Armeni (Kammergrab 24), Rethymnon
H (mit Henkel) 0,13 m,
Mündungs-Dm 0,16 m, Boden-Dm 0,09 m
Rethymnon, Achäologisches Museum
Gut erhaltenes Gefäß mit weiter Mündung. Es hat einen hohen konischen Körper mit flachem Boden und einem Doppelhenkel. Am Mündungsrand ist ein kleiner, trichterförmiger Becher angebracht. Parallele, gleichbreite Bänder umlaufen den Gefäßkörper. Die Lippe und der Becher daran sind gänzlich gefirnißt.
(Vgl. Kat. Nr. 139)

139 Lekanis
SM III B (13. Jh. v. Chr.)
Ton
Aus Armeni (Kammergrab), Rethymnon
H (mit Henkel) 0,105 m, Boden-Dm 0,11 m
Rethymnon, Archäologisches Museum
Gefäß mit weiter Mündung. Bis auf kleine Stoßstellen unversehrt. Konischer Körper, flacher Boden, doppelter Bogenhenkel und trichterförmiger Becher, der an der Lippe angebracht ist. Der rotbraune Dekor beschränkt sich auf Bänder und konzentrische Kreise.
Es wird angenommen, daß die Lekanen dieses Typus eine Art Kernos darstellen, ein Gefäß für Grabzeremonien.

  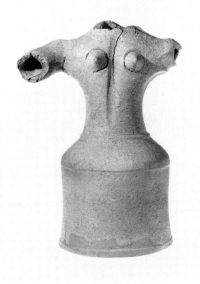

140 Zweihenkeliges Alabastron
SM III B (13. Jh. v. Chr.)
Ton
Aus Armeni (Kammergrab 119), Rethymnon
H 0,068 m, Mündungs-Dm 0,073 m,
Boden-Dm 0,033 m
Rethymnon, Archäologisches Museum
Kleines unversehrtes Alabastron mit doppelkonischem Körper, flachem Boden und weiter Mündung. Schraffierte Doppeläxte in braunem Firnis sind in der Henkelzone aufgereiht.
Dieses minoische religiöse Symbol erscheint als Motiv im Gefäßdekor zum ersten Mal in der Wende von der Periode MM III zu SM I A.

141 Ringförmiges Gefäß
Sm III A2 (2. Hälfte des 14. Jhs. v. Chr.)
Ton
Aus Armeni (Kammergrab 206), Retymnon
H 0,053 m, max. Dm 0,075 m
Rethymnon, Archäologisches Museum
Unversehrtes Duftölgefäß. Der Körper besteht aus einem Ring mit ellipsoidem Querschnitt. Ein Bogenhenkel setzt an der Innenseite des Ringes und überbrückt den Zwischenraum. Das Gefäß hat einen schrägen, zylindrischen Ausguß. Ein stilisiertes braunrosa Blattband verziert die Oberfläche des Körpers.

142 Idol einer Göttin
SM III B (13. Jh. v. Chr.)
Ton
Aus Kannia, Gortys
Erhalt. H 0,338 m, Boden-Dm 0,17 m
Heraklion, Archäologisches Museum
Auf der Drehscheibe gefertigtes Idol vom Typus der weiblichen Gottheit mit erhobenen Händen. Der Kopf und der größte Teil der Arme sind verloren. Die Figur ist bis Taille nackt und mit einem sehr vereinfacht wiedergegebenen Rock bekleidet. Charakteristisch ist der Versuch; den Körper plastisch darzustellen: kleine kegelförmige aufgesetzte Gebilde sollen die Brüste sein, und senkrechte Rillen auf Brust und Rücken geben die anatomischen Einzelheiten an.
Dieser Idoltypus ist in der mesopotamischen Ikonographie bekannt und wird in der Periode Mm I-II auf Kreta eingeführt, wo er in der ausgehenden Bronzezeit beliebt wird. Die erhobenen Arme sollen vermutlich darstellen, daß die Göttin die Gläubigen empfängt, grüßt oder segnet.

143 Kultisches Zwillingsgefäß
SM III A 2 (2. Hälfte des 14. Jhs. v. Chr.)
Ton
Aus der Stadt Chania (Kammergrab 11)
Max. H 0,205 m, Dm der Kanne mit Sieb 0,117 m, Dm der geschlossenen Kanne 0,122 m
Chania, Archäologisches Museum
Eigentümliches Gefäß aus der Werkstatt von Kydonia, hervorragend gearbeitet und erhalten. Es besteht aus zwei birnenförmigen Kannen mit flachen Böden, die miteinander verbunden sind a) durch eine kleine, an beiden Enden verstärkte Röhre in Bauchhöhe und b) durch einen überrandständigen Bandhenkel an der Lippe. Eindrucksvoll sind der Hals der geschlossenen Kanne, der als Tierprotome in Gestalt eines Hasen gebildet ist, und die stilisierte Figur eines trinkenden Vogels auf dem Sieb der zweiten Kanne. Bemalt ist die Siebkanne ebenfalls mit einem Vogel mit vielfältig verziertem Gefieder und buschigem Schwanz in einer Landschaft mit Papyruspflanzen. Die geschlossene Kanne ist mit Papyrusblüten in verschiedener Anordnung dekoriert.
Die außerordentlich sorgfältige Verzierung dieses Gefäßes, die wiederholte Darstellung des Vogels, der eine Erscheinungsform der Gottheit war, und seine zum praktischen Gebrauch unzweckmäßige Form sprechen dafür, daß es sich um ein Kultgefäß handelt.

144 Räuchergefäß
SM III B (13. Jh. v. Chr.)
Ton
Aus Armeni (Kammergrab 94), Rethymnon
Körper-H 0,065 m, Boden-Dm 0,13 m, Deckel-H 0,135 m
Rethymnon, Archäologisches Museum
Unversehrtes, grob gearbeitetes Gefäß. Es besteht a) aus einem Behälter für die Feuerung mit zylindrischem Körper, Vertikalhenkel und Standplatte und b) aus einem Deckel, der unten zylindrisch ist und oben konisch. Der konische Teil hat vier übereinanderliegende Reihen von Löchern und schließt mit einer ringförmigen Einfassung um ein Mittelloch ab.
Der Hauptdekor entfaltet sich auf dem zylindrischen Teil des Deckels. Er ist in metopenartige Bildfelder unterteilt. Diese sind mit senkrechten Wellenlinien und Kolumnen von gegenständigen konzentrischen Halbkreisen gefüllt, die schraffiert sind oder einen Punkt im Zentrum haben.

145 Räuchergefäß
SM IIIB (13. Jh. v. Chr.)
Ton
Aus Armeni (Kammergrab 25), Rethymnon
Körper-H 0,06 m, Boden-Dm 0,115 m, Deckel-H 0,112 m
Rethymnon, Archäologisches Museum
Kultgefäß, zusammengesetzt. Es besteht a) aus einem Behälter mit zylindrischem Körper und senkrechtem Henkel und b) aus einem ebenfalls zylindrischen Deckel mit gewölbtem oberem Abschluß und einer Öffnung als Rauchabzug. Der zylindrische Teil des Deckels ist mit einer Reihe stilisierter Muscheln verziert, die von Bogenreihen gerahmt ist.

146 Amphoriskos
SM III A1 (Ende des 14. Jhs. v. Chr.)
Ton
Aus Armeni (Kammergrab 167) Rethymnon
H 0,191 m, Mündungs-Dm 0,12 m,
Boden-Dm 0,065 m
Rethymnon, Archäologisches Museum
Schönes Beispiel einer kleinen Amphora, die einem mykenischen Vorbild nachgestaltet ist. Sie hat einen birnenförmigen Körper, flachen Boden, einen weiten, zylindrischen Hals mit ausgebogenem Rand und drei Bandhenkeln. Der schwarze, nicht ganz farbechte Dekor füllt die Flächen zwischen den Henkeln und besteht aus verschiedenen flaumfederartigen Formen.

147 Bügelkanne
SM III B (13. Jh. v. Chr.)
Ton
Aus Armeni (Kammergrab 140), Rethymnon
H 0,133 m, max. Dm 0,182 m
Rethymnon, Archäologisches Museum
Das unversehrte Gefäß ist ein charakteristisches Exemplar aus der Werkstatt von Chania (Kydonia) in der Nachpalastzeit. Der konische Körper ruht auf einem Standring. Über die beiden Seiten des Gefäßes breitet sich je ein stilisierter Oktopus aus. Die Schulterzone ist mit unterschiedlich verzierten Dreiecken beidseitig des Ausgusses und mit schraffierten Rhomben geschmückt. Gegenständige Bögen treten als Füllmotiv auf.

148 Hydria
SM III B (13. Jh. v. Chr.)
Ton
Aus Pigi (Kammergrab), Rethymnon
H 0,185 m, max. Dm 0,15 m,
Boden-Dm 0,058 m,
Rethymnon, Archäologisches Museum
Vollständig erhaltenes Gefäß mit flachem Boden, doppelkonischem Körper, trichterförmiger Mündung, einem senkrechten Henkel und zwei Bogenhenkeln. Der rosa Dekor beschränkt sich auf die Schulterzone und besteht aus stehenden Winkelgruppen. Tonhydrien dieser Form tauchen in der Periode SM III B1 auf Kreta und dem griechischen Festland gleichzeitig auf.

149 Bügelkanne
SM III B (13. Jh. v. Chr.)
Ton
Aus Armeni (Kammergrab 149), Retyhmnon
H 0,15 m, max. DM 0,145 m
Rethymnon, Archäologisches Museum
Sorgfältig gefertigtes Gefäß, stellenweise bestoßen. Der kugelige Körper ruht auf einem fast ringförmigen Boden. Eindrucksvoll ist der metallische Glanz des schwarzen Firnisses, mit dem auf jeder Seite des Gefäßes ein Oktopus gemalt ist.

150 Flasche
SM III A (14. Jh. v. Chr.)
Ton
Aus Armeni (Kammergrab 13), Rethymnon
H 0,225 m, max. Dm 0,165 m
Rethymnon, Archäologisches Museum
Vollständig erhaltenes Gefäß mit stark beschädigter Oberfläche, linsenförmig bikonvexem Körper, Röhrenausguß und zwei senkrechten Henkeln. Konzentrische, verschieden breite Ringe, in orangebraunem Firnis aufgetragen, breiten sich auf beiden Seiten über die Oberfläche des Körpers aus.
Die seltenen Gefäße dieses Typus wurden mit Duftöl oder Wein gefüllt.

151 Dreihenkeliges Alabastron
SM III A2/B1 (Ende des 14. Jhs. v. Chr.)
Ton
Aus Armeni (Kammergrab 74), Rethymnon
H 0,10 m, max. Dm 0,141 m,
Boden-Dm 0,121 m
Rethymnon, Archäologisches Museum
Stellenweise bestoßen, sonst unversehrtes Gefäß mit zylindrischem Körper, flachem Boden, Bogenhenkeln auf der Schulter und niedrigem Hals mit weiter Mündung. Doppelt gestielte, in Reihen geordnete Spiralen verzieren Schulter und Bauch des Gefäßes.

152   Vierhenkliger Stamnos
SM III B (13. Jh. v. Chr.)
Ton
Aus Armeni (Kammergrab 138), Rethymnon
H 0,157 m, max. Dm 0,181 m,
Mündungs-Dm 0,119 m
Rethymnon, Archäologisches Museum
Mit Gips zusammengesetzt und ergänzt. Kugeliger Körper, flacher Boden, weiter Hals mit Wulst am Ansatz und senkrechter Henkel. Die Zwischenräume der Henkel sind mit Gruppen von Bögen verziert, die mit Zickzacklinien gefüllt sind.

153   Hohes Alabastron
SM III A (14. Jh. v. Chr.)
Ton
Aus Armeni (Kammergrab), Rethymnon
H 0,22 m, Mündungs-Dm 0,13 m,
Boden-Dm 0,135 m
Rethymnon, Archäologisches Museum
Unversehrtes Gefäß mit flachem Boden, weitem Körperumfang, hohem Hals mit Wulst am Ansatz und horizontalem Mündungsrand. Der schwarze Dekor ist nicht farbecht und ist in verschieden breite Zonen mit stilisiertem Blattmotiv, Wellen- und Zickzacklinien unterteilt.
Es wird angenommen, daß der Typus des hohen Alabastrons eine minoische, jedoch stark von ägyptischen Vorbildern beeinflußte Form ist.

154   Stamniskos
SM III B 1 (Beginn des 13. Jhs. v. Chr.)
Ton
Aus Agii Apostoli (Kammergrab), Amari
H 0,13 m, Mündungs-Dm 0,096 m,
Boden-Dm 0,073 m
Rethymnon, Archäologisches Museum
Unversehrtes Gefäß mit flachem Boden, konisch-kugeligem Körper, zylindrischem Hals und zwei Bogenhenkeln. Der schwarzbraune Dekor konzentriert sich auf die Schulter und besteht aus dem Motiv der „mykenischen Blüte" und Nebenmotiven (Bögen und Winkelgruppen).

155   Pyxis mit Tülle
SM III B1 (Beginn des 13. Jhs. v. Chr.)
Ton
Aus Agii Apostoli (Kammergrab), Amari
H 0,125 m, Mündungs-Dm 0,116 m,
Boden-Dm 0,11 m
Rethymnon, Archäologisches Museum
Schönes Beispiel dieser Gattung in sehr gutem Erhaltungszustand mit flachem Boden, zylindrischem Deckel, zwei Bogenhenkeln und röhrenförmiger Tülle. Der Hauptdekor entfaltet sich auf dem Gefäßdeckel und ist in Bildfelder, die mit Winkelgruppen verziert sind, gegliedert.

156 Saugnäpfchen
SM III A (14. Jh. v. Chr.)
Ton
Aus Stavromenos (Kammergrab), Rethymnon
H (mit Henkel) 0,16 m, max. Dm 0,12 m, Mündungs-Dm 0,078 m
Rethymnon, Archäologisches Museum
Ergänzungen an einem kleinen Teil der Lippe und der Tülle. Kugelig-doppelkonischer Körper, flacher Boden, zylindrischer Hals mit Wulst am Ansatz, röhrenförmige Tülle und Korbhenkel mit plastischem Ring an dem einen Ansatz. Die Oberseite des Henkels ist mit Vertiefungen versehen, die zur Verzierung mit Glaspaste ausgefüllt sind. Der rotbraune Firnisdekor entfaltet sich vor allem auf dem oberen Teil des Körpers und besteht aus einem Blattband.
Dieser Gefäßtypus tritt in der letzten Periode der späten Bronzezeit auf.

157 Tüllenbecher
SM III B (13. Jh. v. Chr.)
Ton
Aus Armeni (Kammergrab 206), Rethymnon
H 0,068 m, Mündungs-Dm 0,104 m
Rethymnon, Archäologisches Museum
Unversehrtes Gefäß mit zylindrischem Körper, ausladendem Mündungsrand, flachem Boden, senkrechtem Bandhenkel und einer Tülle, die durch einen Steg mit der Lippe verbunden ist. Der schwarze, teilweise verblaßte Dekor besteht aus Netzwerk, das die Oberfläche des Gefäßes bedeckt.
Gefäße von diesem Typus wurden Kleinkindern ins Grab mitgegeben und gehörten vielleicht auch im Leben zur Ausstattung.

158 Kylix
SM III A2 (Ende des 14. Jhs. v. Chr.)
Ton
Aus Pigi (Kammergrab), Rethymnon
H 0,198 m, Mündungs-Dm 0,208 m, Boden-Dm 0,097 m
Rethymnon, Archäologisches Museum
An Körper und Henkel zusammengesetzt und ergänzt. Besonders große Kylix mit konischer, weiter Schale, zwei Bandhenkeln und hohem, am Ansatz dünnen Fuß auf Standplatte. Der rotbraune, in zwei übereinanderliegende Zonen gegliederte Dekor füllt die ganze Außenfläche des Körpers und besteht aus Gruppen kurviger Linien. Innen ist die Schale gänzlich mit Firnis überzogen.

159 Schnabeltasse
SM III A2 (Ende des 14. Jhs. v. Chr.)
Ton
Aus Maroulas (Kammergrab), Rethymnon
H 0,051 m, Mündungs-Dm 0,113 m, Boden-Dm 0,04 m
Rethymnon, Archäologisches Museum
Sehr gut erhaltenes Gefäß mit weiter Mündung, eckigem Umriß, flachem Boden, Bandhenkel und schnabelförmigem Ausguß. Firnis rotbraun. Der Hautpdekor entfaltet sich in der Henkelzone und besteht aus hängenden konzentrischen Halbkreisen mit stilisierten Papyrusblüten in den Zwischenräumen. Der Gefäßboden ist mit einer Spirale verziert.

160 Becher
SM III A (14. Jh. v. Chr.)
Ton
Aus Armeni (Kammergrab 10), Rethymnon
H 0,067 m, Mündungs-Dm 0,09,
Boden-Dm 0,032 m
Rethymnon, Archäologisches Museum
Sorgfältig gearbeitetes und gut erhaltenes Gefäß mit halbkugeligem Körper, niedrigem Fuß, weiter Mündung und Bandhenkel. Der schwarzbraune Deckel beschränkt sich auf ein Zickzackband mit gegenständigen Bögen in den Winkeln des Bandes.

161 Einhenkeliger Becher
SM III A (14. Jh. v. Chr.)
Ton
Aus Armeni (Kammergrab 98), Rethymnon
H 0,061 m, Mündungs-Dm 0,106 - 0,113 m,
Boden-D 0,055 m
Rethymnon, Archäologisches Museum
Unversehrtes Gebrauchgefäß mit kleinen Stoßspuren. Niedriger halbkugeliger Körper mit senkrechtem Bandhenkel und niedrigem, konischen Fuß auf breitem Boden. Der Dekor besteht aus rotbraunem Firnis, der in kleinen Rinnsalen über die ganze Innen- und Außenfläche des Gefäßes herabgeflossen ist.

162 Kännchen mit weiter Mündung
SM III A2/B (Ende des 14. Jh. v. Chr.)
Ton
Aus Agii Apostoli (Kammergrab), Amari
H 0,107 m, Boden-Dm 0,047 m,
max. Dm 0,112 m
Rethymnon, Archäologisches Museum
Unversehrtes, grob gearbeitetes Kännchen mit flachem Boden, doppelkonischem Körper, rinnenförmiger, aufwärts geneigter Tülle und senkrechtem Bandhenkel. Der wenig sorgfältig ausgeführte Dekor beschränkt sich auf sichelförmige Motive, die vom Halsansatz herabhängen.

163 Kleine Kanne
SM III A (14. Jh. v. Chr.)
Ton
Aus Stavromenos (Kammergrab),
Rethymnon
H 0,07 m, max. Dm 0,058 m
Rethymnon, Archäologisches Museum
Kleines, fein gearbeitetes Gefäß mit gedrungenem, kugeligen Körper, schnabelförmigem Ausguß und einem senkrechten Henkel. Ein stilisierter, braunrot gefirnißter Blattkranz verziert die Schulterzone.
Dieses Gefäß wurde als Grabbeigabe in einer Larnax gefunden.

164 Kompositgefäß
SM III A (14. Jh. v. Chr.)
Ton
Aus Armeni (Kammergrab 188), Rethymnon
H (mit Henkel) 0,075 m, max. Dm 0,05 m
Rethymnon, Archäologisches Museum
Unversehrtes Gefäß, das aus einem Kännchen und einer geschlossenen Lekythos mit einem röhrenförmigen Verbindungsstück in Bauchhöhe besteht. Ein überrandständiger Bandhenkel verbindet die beiden Gefäße.
Die unhandliche Form und die Tatsache, daß solche Kompositgefäße häufig in Gräbern gefunden werden, führen zu dem Schluß, daß sie Kultgefäße sind.

165 Askos
SM III B (13. Jh. v. Chr.)
Ton
Aus Armeni (Kammergrab 110), Rethymnon
H 0,07 m, max. Dm 0,079 m
Rethymnon, Archäologisches Museeum
Kleines, vollständig erhaltenes Gefäß mit flachem Boden, zylindrischem Körper, Bogenhenkel, der auf der gewölbten Schulter ansetzt und ausladender Lippe. Der schwarzbraune Dekor konzentriert sich auf die Schulterzone, die in zwei halbkreisförmige Felder unterteilt ist: schraffierte Fische verzieren das eine und Halbkreise das andere Feld. Über die verbleibende Fläche sind Füllornamente verstreut.
Diese Gefäßform ist eine Schöpfung der minoischen Kultur und kommt in alle ihren Perioden vor.

166 Ringförmiges Gefäß
SM III B (13. Jh. v. Chr.)
Ton
Aus Armeni (Kammergrab 49), Rethymnon
H 0,065 m, max. Dm 0,107 m
Rethymnon, Archäologisches Museum
Unversehrtes, eigentümliches Gefäß, dessen Körper die Form eines Ringes von quadratischem Querschnitt hat. Zylindrischer Ausguß. Der Bogenhenkel setzt an zwei gegenüberliegenden Stellen der inneren Gefäßwandung an und überbrückt den Zwischenraum. Der schwarze, glänzende Dekor besteht aus Streifen, gestaffelten Winkeln und senkrechten Wellenlinien.
Gefäße dieser Form finden sich oft als Grabbeigaben und sind in der Periode SM III ziemlich verbreitet, vor allem in der mittleren und späten Phase. Der unhandliche Ausguß und das kleine Fassungsvermögen des Gefäßes sprechen für seine Bestimmung als Weihölbehälter.

167 Räuchergefäß
SM III B (13. Jh. v. Chr.)
Ton
Aus Armeni (Kammergrab), Rethymnon
Körper-H 0,05 m, Boden-Dm 0,117 m, Deckel-H 0,115 m
Rethymnon, Archäologisches Museum
Unversehrtes Gefäß aus zwei Teilen: a) dem Behälter für die Feuerung mit zylindrischem Körper und senkrechtem Henkel auf Standplatte und b) dem ebenfalls zylindrischen Deckel mit bogenförmiger Öffnung und konischem oberen Abschluß, der in einer ringförmigen Einfassung um ein Loch in der Mitte endet. Vier längliche Öffnungen sind in dem konischen Teil symmetrisch angeordnet. Der schwarzbraune Dekor besteht auf dem Räuchergefäß aus einer Wellenlinie, auf dem konischen Teil des Deckels aus parallelen Streifen und auf dem zylindrischen aus stilisierten gabelförmigen Blüten.
Die Fundorte solcher Gefäße, ihre unzweckmäßige Form und die Tatsache, daß die meisten keine Brandspuren aufweisen, sprechen dafür, daß es sich um Kultgeräte handelt.

168 Kalathos
SM III B (13. Jh. v. Chr.)
Ton
Aus Armeni (Kammergrab 65), Rethymnon
H (mit Henkel) 0,155 m,
Mündungs-Dm 0,14 m
Rethymnon, Archäologisches Museum
Eigenartiges Gefäß mit weiter Mündung, zusammengesetzt und an der Lippe ergänzt. Es besteht aus einem zylindrischen Körper mit doppeltem Bogenhenkel und trichterförmigem Becher, der an der Lippe angebracht ist. Der braune Dekor ist nicht farbecht. Er ist in metopenartige Bildfelder unterteilt, die mit Gruppen von Zickzacklinien, Schachbrettmuster, Netzwerk und konzentrischen Halbkreisen mit Schrägstrichen gefüllt sind.

169 Lekanis
SM III B (13. Jh. v. Chr.)
Ton
Aus Armeni (Kammergrab 24), Rethymnon
H 0,07 m, Mündungs-Dm 0,19 m,
Boden-DM 0,115 m
Rethymnon, Archäologisches Museum
Unversehrtes Gefäß mit weiter Mündung, flachem Boden, konischem Körper und zwei Löchern zum Befestigen eines Teiles unterhalb der Lippe. Eine rotbraun gefirnißte Kette aus schraffiertem Rauten läuft um den Körper; Strichgruppen verzieren die Lippe.
Die Lekane aus Ton sind Metallgefäßen nachgebildet und traten im beginnenden 14. Jh. v. Chr. auf.

170 Larnax
SM III B (Beginn des 13. Jhs. v. Chr.)
Ton
Aus Armeni (Kammergrab), Rethymnon
Sarkophag-H 0,72 m, Deckel-H 0,22 m, L 1,05 m, B 0,38-0,40 m
Rethymnon, Archäologisches Museum
Kistenförmiger, sehr gut erhaltener Tonsarkophag auf vier Füßen mit sattelförmigem Deckel. Er besteht aus braungelbem Ton mit Überzug in gleicher Farbe und braunem Firnis. Eine schlangenförmige Linie umläuft die beiden Lang- und Schmalseiten. Alle vier Seiten sind mit verschieden hohen, alternierend gereihten Papyrusblüten geschmückt. Gruppen horizontaler Wellenlinien rahmen diese Darstellung ein.
Das Motiv der Papyrusblüte, das schon in der ägyptischen Ikonographie vorkommt, wird von den minoischen Künstlern häufig zur Verzierung von Gegenständen angewandt, die mit dem Kult- oder Bestattungswesen zusammenhängen.

171 Larnax
SM III B (13. Jh. v. Chr.)
Ton
Aus Armeni (Kammergrab 24), Rethymnon
H 0,65 m, L 0,96 m, B 0,34 m
Rethymnon, Archäologisches Museum
Kistenförmiger Tonsarkophag mit vier Füßen. Der Deckel fehlt. Braungelber Ton mit Einschlüssen, Überzug von gleicher Farbe, braunrosa Firnis. Die Langseiten sind durch Gruppen von Wellenlinien in je zwei ungleiche Bildfelder gegliedert, die mit laufenden Spiralen verziert sind. Auf der einen Schmalseite sind gegenständige Kulthörner abgebildet. Jedes Hörnerpaar trägt in der Mitte eine Doppelaxt. Die Hauptdarstellung befindet sich jedoch auf der anderen Schmalseite: eine stilisierte weibliche Gestalt vom Typus der Göttin mit erhobenen Händen steht auf einer Fläche mit Schachbrettmuster. Linienornamente verzieren ihren fußlangen Rock. Ihren Händen entspringen Spiralen und Bögen.
Hingewiesen sei auf den Idoltypus in der gleichen Haltung (vgl. Kat.-Nr. 142). Bemerkenswert ist die Verbindung der göttlichen Gestalt mit dem Schachbrettmuster, das vielleicht eine architektonische Anlage wiedergeben soll, wie einige Forscher meinen.

172 Grabstele
SM III A-B (14.-13. Jh. v. Chr.)
Kalkstein
Aus Armeni (Kammergrab), Rethymnon
H 0,78 m, B 0,29 m
Rethymnon, Archäologisches Museum
Aus zwei Bruchstücken zusammengesetztes Grabmal. Der untere Teil ist nicht fertig bearbeitet, weil er zur Befestigung der Stele im Boden eingelassen war. Die ursprünglich sichtbare, geglättete Oberfläche ist mit einem einfachen Schachbrettmuster aus flachen senk- und waagerechten Linien verziert, die in den Stein gemeißelt sind.
Aus derselben Nekropole stammt eine entsprechende Stele, die denselben, allerdings sehr viel sorgfältiger ausgeführten Dekor trägt.

173 Larnax
SM III B (13. Jh. v. Chr.)
Ton
Aus Armeni (Kammergrab 55), Rethymnon
Sarkophag H 0,58 m, Deckel-H. 0,17 m,
L 0,91 - 0,94 m, B 0,38 - 0,40 m
Rethymnon, Archäologisches Museum
Kistenförmiger Tonsarkophag mit vier Füßen und sattelförmigem Deckel. Ton und Überzug rotbraun, Dekor orange bis schwarz. Beide Langseiten des Deckels sind mit alternierenden konzentrischen Bögen bedeckt. Die eine Langseite des Sarkophages ist mit drei stilisierten Oktopoden verziert, die andere mit Kulthörnern. In der Mitte eines jeden Hörnerpaares steht eine Doppelaxt. Über diesen heiligen Symbolen sind gestielte Spiralen gereiht. Die Schmalseiten sind mit je einer Papyrus- oder „minoischen" Blüte bemalt. Gerahmt werden die Darstellungen mit senkrechten Wellenbändern und Halbkreisen. Durch die Löcher im Deckel und oberen Teil des Sarkophags wurden Stricke gezogen, die beide Teile miteinander verbanden. Dagegen sollte durch die Löcher im Boden wohl die Flüssigkeit entweichen, die bei der Verwesung entstand.
Dieses eindrucksvolle Exemplar ist besonders reich verziert. Bemerkenswert ist, daß hier Ornamente aus den verschiedenen Themenkreisen zusammen auftreten.

174 Dreifußgefäß
SM III B 2 (Ende des 13. Jhs. v. Chr.)
Ton
Aus Armeni (Kammergrab 46), Rethymnon
H (mit Deckel) 0,33 m, max. Dm 0,295 m
Rethymnon, Archäologisches Museum
Kompositgefäß, an Hals und Körper beschädigt. Es besteht a) aus einem kugeligen Körper mit drei niedrigen Beinen, hohem, senkrechten Hals und vier Henkeln, zwei bogenförmigen und zwei senkrechten, und b) aus einem zylindrischen Deckel mit einem Korbhenkel. Der Hauptdekor aus braunrosa Firnis entfaltet sich auf den vier Flächen zwischen den Henkeln und umfaßt konzentrische Halbkreise, teilweise mit Schraffuren und Mittelpunkt, gestaffelte Zickzacklinien und konzentrische Bögen. Gestaffelte Winkel, Punkte und übereinanderliegende Bögen dienen als Nebenmotive. Es gibt nur eine begrenzte Anzahl von Exemplaren dieses Typus, die aus Stätten der kretisch-mykenischen Welt stammen; die meisten datieren vom Ende der Periode SH/SM III.

175 Alabastronförmiges Gefäß
SM III A 1 (1. Hälfte des 14. Jhs. v. Chr.)
Ton
Aus Armeni (Kammergrab 38), Rethymnon
H 0,15 m, max. Dm 0,16 m
Rethymnon, Archäologisches Museum
Ziemlich stark bestoßenes, sonst unversehrtes Gefäß mit kugelig-doppelkonischem Körper, flachem Boden, weitem Hals, ausladendem Mündungsrand und drei Bogenhenkeln auf der Schulter.
In braunrosa Firnis ist in den Zwischenräumen der Henkel je eine Lilie mit gewundenem Stengel gemalt.

176 Bügelkanne
SM III A 1 (14. Jh. v. Chr.)
Ton
Aus Armeni (Kammergrab 137), Rethymnon
H 0,10 m, max. Dm 0,08 m
Rethymnon, Archäologisches Museum
An vielen Stellen bestoßenes und abgenutztes Gefäß mit birnenförmigem Körper und schlankem, konischen Fuß. Der Hauptdekor entfaltet sich auf der Schulter, ist in zwei Bildfelder unterteilt und besteht a) aus unterschiedlich verzierten Dreiecken auf beiden Seiten des Ausgusses und b) aus einem stilisierten Blattband in dem zweiten halbkreisförmigen Bildfeld.

177 Dreihenkelige Amphora mit Deckel
SM III A 1 (14. Jh. v. Chr.)
Ton
Aus Armeni (Kammergrab 39), Rethymnon
H 0,20 m, max. Dm 0,16 m, Boden-Dm 0,07 m
Rethymnon, Archäologisches Museum
Grob gearbeitete, stellenweise bestoßene Amphora mit birnenförmigem Körper, Standplatte und drei Bogenhenkeln auf der Schulter. Der konische Deckel hat einen Knauf. Die Schulterzone des Gefäßes ist mit einer laufenden Spirale und der Bauch mit Bändern verziert.
Die Gefäße dieses Typus wurden zu Aufbewahrung oder Transport von Flüssigkeiten verwandt.

178 Messer
SM III A-B (14.-13. Jh. v. Chr.)
Bronze
Aus Armeni (Kammergrab 127), Rethymnon
L 0,243 m, max. B 0,024 m
Rethymnon, Archäologisches Museum
Korrodiert. Allgemein üblicher Gebrauchsmessertypus. Dreieckige Klinge mit geradem Rücken und scharfer Schneide. Viereckige Angel mit schwach aufgebogenem Rand und zwei Nieten zur Befestigung der hölzernen Griffschalen.

179 Hackmesser
SM III A-B (14. bis 13. Jh. v. Chr.)
Bronze
Aus Armeni (Kammergrab 115), Rethymnon
L 0,20 m, max. B 0,056 m
Rethymnon, Archäologisches Museum
Vollständig erhalten, korrodiert. Trapezförmige Klinge mit geradem Rücken und geschweifter Angel mit zwei Nieten und einem Loch zur Befestigung des hölzernen Griffes.
Dieser Typus taucht im minoischen Bereich in der Periode SM III A auf und zeigt den Einfluß ägyptischer Vorbilder. Es wird angenommen, daß Geräte dieser Form je nach ihrem Gewicht verschiedenen Zwecken dienten: die kleineren als Rasiermesser und die größeren zum Zerteilen von Fleisch.

180 Bügelkanne
SM III A (14. Jh. v. Chr.)
Ton
Aus Armeni (Kammergrab 144), Rethymnon
H 0,17 m, max. Dm 0,108 m
Rethymnon, Archäologisches Museum
Unversehrtes Gefäß, nur die Oberfläche ist stellenweise beschädigt. Es hat einen kugeligen Körper auf hohem Fuß mit konkaver Standfläche. Der schwarze Dekor ist nicht farbecht und besteht aus umlaufenden Bändern auf dem Körper und verschieden verzierten Dreiecken auf der Schulter.
Gefäße dieses Typus wurden zum Transport von ätherischen Ölen verwandt.

1 Seal
LM IB (mid-15th c. BC)
Clay.
Kastelli, Kissamos.
D 0.032, th 0.0063-0.018 m.
Chania, Archaeological Museum.
Circular shape, showing strong traces of fire. It was probably used to seal a document, a view borne out by the cord impressions on the back. The front carries the impression of a signet ring with an ovoid bezel: it depicts a group of buildings symmetrically arranged in a rocky coastal landscape; the centre is dominated by a large rock und the sea below is schematically rendered. The group of houses is surrounded by a wall with two gates; the gates are of wood and lintel is decorated with two opposed half-rosettes. The buildings, wich are up to three stories high, are crowned with horns of consecration. A lordly male figure is shown standing on the centrel building, holding a sceptre in his outstreched hand; he is distinguished by his profuse head of hair und Minoan loincloth.
This is particularly important find; it is interpreted as depicting a city, palace or shrine and the epiphany of a deity or appearance of a ruler. It is worthy of note, firstly because of the presence together of elements from both the Minoan und Mycenean worlds, and secondly, for its contribution to our better knowledge of the architecture of these two civilizations.

2 Sealing
LM IB (mid-15th c. BC)
Clay.
Town of Chania.
L 0.023, w 0.014 m.
Chania, Archaeological Museum.
Impression of the bezel of a signet ring; complete. Marks of thread on the sides and back reveal the way it was fixed to the object it sealed. It shows a goddess seated on a bench or a stepped background; she is dressed in the typical Minoan style and nurses an animal with horns.
The representation of the "Lady of the Beasts", one of the forms in wich'the Minoan female goddess manifested herself, was a favourite theme in Minoan minor art.

3 Sealing
LM IB (mid-15th c. BC)
Clay.
Town of Chania.
H 0.013, w 0,017.
Chania, Archaeological Museum.
Prismatic sealing with the impression of an amygdaloid sealstone; vertical perforation. It depicts a symmetrical plant design of a magical nature, known as a "lion's mask".
The category of so called magic seal stones seems to have developed during the MM III period; a similar example is known from Palaikastro.

4 Head of a warrior
LM III A-B (14th-13th c. BC)
Ivory.
Phylaki Apokoronou (tholes tomb).
H 0.06, max w 0.04, max th 0.012 m.
Chania, Archaeological Museum
Relief figure of a warrior in profile facing right, with the features cursorily rendered: a broad forehead, almond-shaped eyes, spiral-shaped ears, thin, slightly smiling lips and hair arranged in two planes. He wears a boars' tusk helmet, the characteristic Mycenean headgear, with two opposed rows of boars' tusks und a button-shaped terminal. The back of the plaque is flat and has two pegs to attach it, probably, to a wood surface. Similar examples come from the Greek mainland and Crete.

5 Sphinx
LM III A-B (14th-13th c. BC)
Ivory.
Phylaki (tholos tomb), Apokoronos.
H 0.07, w 0.0435 m.
Chania, Archaeological Museum.
Rectangular plaque with an engraved sphinx. It is shown upright and in profile. On the head with its long nose, almond eye and fleshy lips is a diadem with a crest. The body is heavy and sturdy, and the variegated wing is extended backwards: its neck is adorned with a necklace.
The sphinx, the mythical creature of the East with a lion's body, woman's head and gryphon's wings, was a favourite subject with the Mycenean craftsmen, in contrast to the Minoans, who made only limited use of it.

6 Figure-of-eight shield.
LM IIIA-B (14th-13th c. BC)
Ivory. Phylaki (tholos tomb), Apokoronos.
L 0.76, w 0.045, pres th 0.026 m.
Chania, Archaeological Museum.
Complete; body and edges chipped. It has a wide border and a relief band traverses the body, dividing it into two planes; the upper has six groups of three little circles each, to receive ornamental inlays of another material. Two deep holes in the surface served to fasten it with nails as an appliqué to some wooden luxury object.
The figure-of-eight shield, a characteristic Minoan religious symbol, was a popular ornamental motif found in the minor arts, wall-paintings and vase painting. The architectural construction of the tomb in which it was found, together with the rest of the finds, suggests Mycenean influence in this particular place.

7 Two figure-of-eight shields
LM III A-B (14th-13th c. BC)
Ivory. Phylaki (tholos tomb), Apokoronos.
L 0.028-0.029, w 0.017-0.019,
th 0.011-0.013 m.
Chania, Archaeological Museum.
Small complete shields; chipped in places. The fronts were polished and plain; in their lower surfaces there is a deep hole for nailing then to a wooden object.

8 Inscribed tablet
LM IB (mid-15th c. BC)
Clay.
Kastelli, Chania.
H. 0.11. w. 0.082 m.
Chania, Archaeological Museum.
Tablet of page-form type, mended from two fragments. The Linear A text, written in horizontal rows, concerns the recording of agricultural products and domestic animals; this is deduced from the following ideograms that accompany corresponding metrograms: wheat (wheat-type-plants), wine, figs, female sheep. There are five small holes at the upper edge of the document.
This tablet, made of reddish raw clay, was preserved like other similar ones when it was baked by the fire that destroyes the building it was in. The Minoan settlement at Kastelli is the only one so far apart from Knosos to have yielded examples of both systems of writing.

9 Inscribed tablet
LM III A-B (14th-13th c. BC)
Clay.
Knosos. H 0.028, l 0.14 m.
Herakleion, Archaeological Museum.
Leaf-shaped tablet, joined from three fragments. Strong traces of fire on the surface. It bears a text of incised syllabograms and ideograms in Linear-B writing. It mentions a special purple (po-pu-re-ja) garment (pu-ka-ta-ri-ja) that was probably intended for mourners.

A similar mention is found in Homer ("φάρος πορφύρεον": H 991), which shows the Greekness of the Mycenaean script.

10 Jug
MM IA (end of 3rd mill. BC)
Clay.
Phaistos.
Pres h 0.165, max d 0.145 m.
Herakleion, Archaeological Museum.
A striking vase, representative of the Barbotine ware; the spout is missing. Spherical-biconical body, flat base, vertical handle, narrow neck with two barbotine projections on either side and a serrated rim. It is covered with a brown-black to reddish slip, unevenly coloured due to the firing. Bands of fugitive white paint ring the lower half of the body. The barbotine decoration is confined to the upper half, enhanced by white spots and series of successive arcs. This style, wich became especially popular in about 2000 BC, is frequently found in Central Crete, unlike to the eastern and western parts of the island, where it is rare. A large number of examples come from Phaistos, wich was probably an important centre of its production.

11 Cup
MM II A (19th c. BC)
Clay.
Chalara, Phaistos.
H 0.062, d 0.091-0.097 m.
Herakleion, Archaeological Museum.
Carinated cup of Kamares ware, exceptionally well made and preserved. It has a vertical ribbon handle and a rim folded to form one main spout and many smaller ones. Brown-black slip inside and out. The added polychrome decoration comprises bands, a zone of pendent or standing arches and pairs of opposed spirals with a common stem.
These vases in the Kamares style, known as "eggshell ware" because of the thinness of their walls, constitute a separate category.

12 Jug
MM IIA (19 th c. BC)
Clay.
Phaistos.
H 0.17, max d 0.14 m.
Herakleion, Archaeological Museum.
A fine vase, typical of the Kamares style. It has an oval body wiht flat base, wide low neck with a spout and three vertical handles imitating metal originals. An uneven slip, black-brown to reddish, covers the whole body, and there is a large white rosette on both sides. With the Kamares ware, which was above all a palatial style, Minoan pottery attained a high level of perfection. A notable feature of this ware is the variety of polychrome motifs and the way the are applied to the ornate, dynamic shapes of the vases.

13 Jug
MM III (16th c. BC)
Clay.
Phaistos.
H 0.14, max. d 0.083 m.
Herakleion, Archaeological Museum.
Complete example of the Floral style; coarse fabric. Conical body, flat base, low neck with high spout. Two horizontal handles on the belly and a vertical one growing out of the rim; two plastic knobs on each side of the spout. Brown-red vertical reed-like plants are arrayed on the body of the vase.

14 Cup
LM I (end of 16th c. BC)
Clay.
Royal Road, Knosos.
H 0.068, d rim 0.101, d base 0.03 m.
Herakleion, Archaeological Museum.
Carefully made; typical of the Floral style. It has a conical body with slightly curving sides and a flat base. Brown-red lifelike reed plants cover the outside; painted overall inside.
In subject matter the Floral style was very much influenced by fresco decoration; this can be seen in some of the vases at Knosos.

15 Alabastron with lid
LM IB (end of 16th c. BC)
Clay.
Kastelli, Chania
H 0,185-0.190, max d 0.181, d rim 0.119, h lid 0.057, d body 0.153.
Chania, Archaeological Museum.
Complete; spherical-ovoid body, flat base, low cylindrical neck, four horizontal ribbon handles. A system of orange lines rings the lower part of the body; the upper is divided into two zones that are decorated with running spirals and free irises. The lid is conical with a flat button knob and horizontal cylindrical handle. Linear decoration.
The vase is a representative example of the local workshop. The finding of carbonised olives inside it shows it was used for storage.

16 Gablet
LM II (2nd half of 15th c. BC)
Clay.
Knosos, Unexplored Mansion.
H 0.113, d rim 0.132, d base 0.06 m.
Heraklion, Archaeological Museum.
Ephyrean goblet mended and restored. Deep body with everted rim, low foot, discoid base and two vertical ribbon handles. The brown-black decoration on both sides of the goblet consists of a trefoil eye palmette with a double outline; concentric arcs are used as fill ornaments. The bottom is painted overall.
This style, of Helladic origin, is characteristic of the LH II B phase; it is distinguished by the simplicity of its decoration, wich is limited to an isolated plant or marine motif.

17 Necklace
LM IIIA-B (14th-13th c. BC)
Sard.
Cemetery of Armeni, Rethymno.
Dm 0.003-0.025 m.
Rethymno, Archaeological Museum.
It consists of 49 beads: the five central ones are elliptical and prismatic and the rest spherical, of different sizes. Semiprecious sard was very popular in the Creto-Mycenean world, as is evident from its frequent use for beads and seal stones. Large amounts of it, chiefly in the form of raw material, were imported from the East.

18 Necklace
LM IIIA-B (14th-13th c. BC)
Glass paste.
Cemetery of Armeni, Rethymno.
L 0.027, w 0.01 m.
Rethymno, Archaeological Museum.
It consists of 17 beads in the form of oblong plaques; three vertically disposed relief spirals with an eye decorate the front of each.
Glass paste, an artifical substance used in Mesopotamia from the 4th mill. BC, was know in Crete from the 16th c. BC on. The beads, grey-white or blue in colour, were made in a mould.

19 Necklace
LM III A-B (14th-13th c. BC)
Rock crystal.
Cemetery of Armeni, Rethymno.
D 0.005-0.015 m.
Rethymno, Archaeological Museum.
It consists of 19 different-sized beads of spherical, cylindrical and oval shapes. Rock crystal, a mineral known from the Middle Minoan period, was widely used for making jewellery and also vases.

20 Necklace
LM IIIA-B (14th-13th c. BC)
Faience.
Cemetery of Armeni, Rethymno.
L 0.016 m.
Rethymno, Archaeological Museum.
The necklace consists of 20 beads: 12 biconical and 8 shaped like a wheat grain.
Faience, an artificial substance, like glass paste, was known in Mesopotamia as early as the 5th mill. BC. In Crete it was used for making beads and vases from the 1st half of the 3rd mill. BC.

21 Pyxis with lid
LM IIIA (14th c. BC)
Clay.
Vigla Stavromenou (chamber tomb), Rethymno.
H with lid 0.091, d rim 0.085, d base 0.093 m.
Rethymno, Archaeological Museum.
Complete. Flat base, cylindrical body with four holes on the shoulder and a lid of the same shape with a central hole. The lustrous black-painted decoration consists of parallel lines and stylized papyrus motifs on the body and concentric circles on the lid.
Cylindrical and oval pyxides, common as grave goods, appear in Crete from the Early Minoan period und Cycladic influence. These vessels were most probably used as containers for personal objects of adornment, a view that is styrengthened by the presence of holes through wich string was threaded for the better attachment of the lid.

22 Bracelet
LM IIIA-B (14th-13th c. BC)
Bronze.
Armeni (chamber tomb 140), Rethymno.
D 0.053-0.055 m.
Rethymno, Archaeological Museum.
Well-preserved bracelet. It is made of heavy wire tapering at the ends, wich are curled into a spiral around each other. In this way the diameter of the bracelet can be made larger or smaller.

23 Bracelet
LM IIIA-B (14th-13th c. BC)
Bronze.
Armeni (chamber tomb 140), Rethymno.
D 0.071 m.
Rethymno, Archaeological Museum.
Complete, made of heavy wire tapering at the ends, wich are twisted in a spiral around each other.

24 Barcelet
LM III A-B (14th-13th c. BC)
Bronze.
Armeni (chamber tomb 124), Rethymno.
D. 0.08 m.
Rethymno, Archaeological Museum.
Common type of onament made from a hollow bar bent in a circle with the free ends overlapping and triangular teminations.

25 Ring
LM IIIA-B (14th-13th c. BC)
Bronze.
Armeni (chamber tomb 86), Rethymno.
D 0.145 m.
Rethymno, Archaeological Museum.
Spiral ring made of wire twisted round to form three contiguous circles; one end is free and the other fixes to the spiral.

26 Ring
LM IIIA-B (14th-13th c. BC)
Bronze.
Armeni (chamber tomb 108), Rethymno.
D 0.019 m.
Rethymno, Archaeological Museum.
Complete; personal ornament. It is made from a strip of sheet metal bent into a circle so that the ends overlap.

27 Tweezers
LM IIIA-B (14th-13th c. BC)
Bronze.
Armeni (chamber tomb 100), Rethymno.
L 0.08 m.
Rethymno, Archaeological Museum.
Cosmetic instrument that made its first appearance in the Aegean in the 3rd millennium BC and has remained unchanged until our day. It is made from a bronze strip bent in the middle to form an open loop; the ends of the arms are bent inwards. There is an incised line along the edge.

28 Mirror
LM II (15th c. BC)
Bronze.
Knosos, Zapher Papouras cemetery.
D 0.12 m.
Herakleion, Archaeological Museum.
Complete disk of a mirror with two holes near the circumference to attach the handle, which was of organic material (wood or bone). Polishing scratches are visible on the smooth surface.
This type of mirror, which gave a satisfactory reflection, was the result of Egyptian influence and it remained unchanged throughout the Late Bronze Age.

29 Pin
LM IIIA-B (14th-13th c. BC)
Bronze.
Armeni (chamber tomb 67), Rethymno.
L 0.135 m.
Rethymno, Archaeological Museum.
Hook-shaped pin; mended. Long thin shaft, square in section; one end is pointed and the other bent round in a hook.
Small personal ornament; the shape was known in the Aegean from the 3rd millennium BC. It was probably used to fasten a woman's hair and not a garment.

30 Cylinder seal
LM IIIA-B (14th-13th c. BC)
Faience.
Armeni (chamber tomb 108), Rethymno.
H 0.019, d 0.010 m.
Rethymno, Archaeological Museum.
The engraved representation on the surface of the cylinder is confined to two animal figures placed side by side: a stylized bird with a long tail, linear feathers and legs and a probable wild goat in the same style.
Cylinder seals had their origin in southern Mesopotamia, where they were first used in about the middle of the fourth millennium BC.

31 Seal stone
LM IIIA-B (14th-13th c. BC)
Steatite.
Armeni (chamber tomb 104), Rethymno.
D 0.018 m.
Rethymno, Archaeological Museum.
Lentoid, with slight damage to both faces. The half-finished decoration is of interest: it depicts consecutive circular lines which probably framed an animal's limb.

32 Cylinder seal
LM IIIA-B (14th-13th c. BC)
Chlorite.
Armeni (chamber tomb 80), Rethymno.
H 0.015, d 0.010 m.
Rethymno, Archaeological Museum.
Complete. Two deep vertical lines divide the surface into two unequal fields with similar decoration: a diagonal incision flanked above and below by a small, eyed circle.

33 Seal stone
LM IIIA-B (14th-13th c. BC)
Rock crystal.
Armeni (chamber tomb 85), Rethymno.
D 0.0195 x 0.210 m.
Rethymno, Archaeological Museum.
Lentoid seal; slightly damaged on both faces. The field is decorated with intersecting vertical and horizontal bands; the spaces thus formed are filled with consecutive lines.

34 Seal stone
LM IIIA-B (14th-13th c. BC)
Rock crystal.
Armeni (chamber tomb 108), Rethymno.
D 0.015 m.
Rethymno, Archaeological Museum.
Letoid. The edge of the surface is slightly chipped. The main face is decorated with pairs of vertical and horizontal lines cutting each other; the net motif is used as a fill.

35 Seal stone
LM IIIA-B) (14th-13th c. BC)
Rock crystal.
Armeni (chamber tomb 79), Rethymno.
D 0.013 x 0.015 m.
Rethymno, Archaeological Museum.
Complete; amygdaloid. Perforated vertically. The face is decorated with simple linear designs: two crossed bands divide the usable space into four triangles: two are hatched and the other two filled with succisive angles.

36 Seal stone
LM IIIA-B (14th-13th c. BC)
Chlorite.
Armeni (chamber tomb 115), Rethymno.
D 0.017 m.
Rethymno, Archaeological Museum.
Complete; lentoid. A broad band cuts the field diagonally; oblique lines run from its centre to the edge, forming hatched triangles.

37 Seal stone
LM IIIA-B (14th-13th c. BC)
Chlorite.
Armeni (chamber tomb 138), Rethymno.
D 0.019 m.
Rethymno, Archaeological Museum.
Lentoid with slightly chipped edge. Perforated horizontally. The field is completely filled with a bird shown frontally. The presence should be noted of both Minoan and Mycenean stylistic elements, observable in the schematic manner of depicting the figure and in the precise rendering of detail (eyes, feathers), respectively. The line below the bird's legs probably indicates the ground. The filling motif is a crescent with a dot in the centre.

38 Seal stone
LM IIIA-B (14th-13th c. BC).
Green stone.
Armeni (chamber tomb 24), Rethymno.
D 0.016.
Rethymno, Archaeological Museum.
Complete; lentoid. It depicts a favourite Minoan theme: a galloping bull. The animal, compressed into the shape of the seal, has its head turned sharply backwards so that its horns cut the firm line of the body. The frontal head of a second bull is used as a fill ornament in the empty space above the body of the first.

39 Seal stone
LM III A-B (14th-13th c. BC)
Serpentine.
Armeni (chamber tomb 114), Rethymno.
D 0.014 m.
Rethymno, Archaeological Museum.
Complete, lentoid. Linear decoration consisting of a double rhomboid motif: four dots decorate the perimeter and there is one in the centre.

40 Seal stone
LM IIIA-B (14th-13th c. BC)
Rock crystal.
Armeni (chamber tomb 123), Rethymno.
D 0.013 x 0.019 m.
Rethymno, Archaeological Museum.
Complete, letoid. Horizontally perforated. It depicts a stylized tree with a thick trunk, asymmetrical projecting branches and linear leaves; two lunate motifs are visible to the right of the tree.
The individual representation of a tree occurs preeminently in Minoan seal engraving and is directly connected with religion; on Mycenean seals, by contrast, it was used as a fill ornament.

41 Seal stone
LM IIIA-B (14th-13th c. BC)
Carnelian.
Armeni (chamber tomb 115), Rethymno.
Pres. 1 0.015, w 0.014 m.
Rethymno, Archaeological Museum.
Very flattened cylinder; part of one end missing. It depicts a wild goat in profile with a sturdy body, large twisted horns and a beard. A shrub with lanceolate leaves fills the empty space in front of it.

42 Seal stone
LM IIIA-B (14th-13th c. BC)
Chlorite.
Armeni (chamber tomb 83), Rethymno.
L 0.023, w 0.011, th 0.007 m.
Rethymno, Archaeological Museum.
Four-sided, slightly narrowing on one side. Perforated lengthwise. All four sides were used for the sealing surface: they are covered with parallel dots encircled by small complete or incomplete circles.

43 Seal stone
LM IIIA-B (14th-13th c. BC)
Haematite.
Armeni (chamber tomb 115), Rethymno.
D 0.016 m.
Rethymno, Archaeological Museum.
Fine complete example of a lentoid seal stone. Perforated horizontally. It depicts a galloping bull with its head turned sharply backwards. It is remarkable for the detailed rendering of the features.

44 Two-handled jar
Neolithic/EM I transition (beginning of 3rd mill. BC)
Clay.
Elenes, Amari.
H 0.156, max d 0.158, d rim 0.138 m.
Rethymno, Archaeoligical Museum.
Utility vessel; restored with plaster. It has a conical body, flat base. wide cylindrical neck and two vertical handles on the shoulder.

45 Cup
EM I (1st half of 3rd mill. BC)
Clay.
Elenes, Amari.
H 0.148 m.
Rethymno, Archaeological Museum.
High-footed cup, restored; a representative example of the Pyrgos style. Deep conical body with a triangular perforated lug und a high, hollow foot; a plastic ring at the junction. Burnished decoration; incised lines encircle the foot, the incisions being filled with brown paint.
This style, whose name is taken from the eponymous site in the province of Heraklion, is

characterized by the marked survival of Sub-Neolithic elements.

46 Deep bowl
Neolithic/EM I transition (beginning of 3rd mill. BC)
Clay.
Elenes, Amari.
H 0.114, d rim 0.147 m.
Rethymno, Archaeological Museum.
Mended and restored. Deep body with vertical walls, slightly concave, and a convex bottom; four lugs on the carination, two of them perforated. The surface is carefully smoothed and covered with a brown-black slip. The decoration, by burnishing, is limited to groups of three vertical parallel lines from the lugs to the rim.

47 Ladle
Neolithic/EM I transition (beginning of 3rd mill. BC)
Clay.
Elenes, Amari.
Pres 0.08 m.
Rethymno, Archaeological Museum.
Small handmade implement; handle restored. It has an oval body with traces of burning on the surface.
Similar examples come from Knosos and Mochlos.

48 Cup
EM II B (2nd half of 3rd mill. BC)
Clay.
Cave of Platyvola.
H 0.078, d rim 0.083, d base 0.048 m.
Chania, Archaeological Museum.
Vasiliki style; mended and restored. Hemispherical body with low conical foot. Brown-red and brown-black spots cover the whole surface.
This decoration, typical of the Vasiliki style, was achieved by deliberately uneven firing.

49 Basin
LM I/II (mid-3rd mill. BC)
Clay.
Cave of Platyvola.
H 0.08, d rim 0.207 m.
Chania, Archaeological Museum.
A household vessel, mended from many fragments. It has a wide body with a horizontal handle in the middle and a curved base with three projections.

50 Jug
MM I (beginning of 2nd mill. BC)
Clay.
Apodoulou, Amari.
H 0.16, max d 0.16 m.
Rethymno, Archaeological Museum
Mended and restored. Ovoid body with flat base, vertical cylindrical neck and beaked spout. The decoration, confined to the belly and shoulder zones, consists of excrescences formed when the clay was still soft and making a lattice pattern. This singular decoration is a variation of the Barbotine ware, known as the Barnacle ware.

51 Jug
MM II (19th - 18th c. BC)
Clay.
Monastiraki, Amari.
H 0.30, d base 0.08 m.
Rethymno, Archaeological Museum.
Beaked jug; mended, with two button knobs on the neck. Brown-yellow clay wuth traces of fire; black paint. Decorated with rough dots in white fugitive paint.

52 Jug
MM II (19th - 18th c. BC)
Clay.
Monastiraki, Amari.
H 0.126, d rim 0.078, d base 0.06 m.
Rethymno, Archaeological Museum.
Bridge-spouted vase; mended, with two horizontal handles. Brown-grey clay, brown-red paint.

53 Jug
MM II (19th - 18th c. BC)
Clay.
Monastiraki, Amari.
H 0.15, d base 0.072 m.
Rethymno, Archaeological Museum.
Mended and restored; traces of fire on the surface. Brown-orange clay, trefoil mouth and vertical handle.
This shape is also known as a "milk jug" to pottery experts.

54 Jug
MM II (19th - 18th c. BC)
Clay.
Monastiraki, Amari.
H 0.14, d base 0.04 m.
Rethymno, Archaeological Museum.
Body and spout restored. Brown-grey clay; rough surface with traces of fire.

55 Jug
MM II (19th - 18th c. BC)
Clay.
Monastiraki, Amari.
H 0.09, d base 0.049 m.
Rethymno, Archaeological Museum.
One handled jug, slightly restored. Pale orange clay; rough surface with sporadic leaf impressions.

56 Cup
MM II (19th - 18th c. BC)
Clay.
Monastiraki, Amari.
H 0.04, d rim 0.067 m.
Rethymno, Archaeological Museum.
Complete cup from a triple "kernos"; the other two ar missing. Brown-pink clay with a rough surface, on which finger and leaf impressions are visible.

57 Cup
MM II (19th - 18th c. BC)
Clay.
Monastiraki, Amari.
H 0.005, d rim 0.075, d base 0.032 m.
Rethymno, Archaeological Museum.
Carinated cup; mended and restored. Good quality clay; black fugitive paint outside and in. The plase where this vase was found has produced evidence of administrative organization and religious happenings.

58 Cup
MM II (19th - 18th c. BC)
Clay.
Apodoulou, Amari. H 0.042,
d rim 0.065-0.069, d base 0.03 m.
Rethymno, Archaeological Museum.
Small cup; mended; roughly made. It has a conical body and flat base.

59 Cup
MM II (19th - 18th c. BC)
Clay.
Apodoulou, Amari.
H 0.078, d rim 0.076-0.082, d base 0.04 m.
Rethymno, Archaeological Museum.
Household vessel; mended. Deep oval body with a spout on the rim and two button knobs set opposite each other. The decoration is limited to brown-red chevrons.

60 Kernos ("salt cellar")
MM II (19th - 18 th c. BC)
Clay.
Monastiraki, Amari.
H 0.026, total d 0.125 m.
Rethymno, Archaeological Museum.
Mended and restored; brown-yellow clay. It consists of two conical cups joined at one sides, with a rough surface and traces of fire on the interior.
This shape is also refered to as a "salt cellar" in the literatur.

61 Seals
MM II (19th - 18th c. BC)
Clay.
Monastiraki, Amari.
L 0.03-0.09, w 0.038-012, th 0.014-0.03 m.
Rethymno, Archaeological Museum.
Four seals of irregular form, made with brown or orange clay. Cord impressions from the sealing of some object are visible on the back. The front of each of them bears from 4 to 11 seal impressions, chiefly with linear subjects: octagonal or S-shaped motifs and a crooked cross, framed by fill ornaments.
The finding of two archives of seals in the archive room and storerooms of the house group indicates the existence of a strictly organized system of administration and control.

62 Loom weight
MM II (19th - 18th c. BC)
Clay.
Monastiraki, Amari.
L 0.075, d hole 0.01 m.
Rethymno, Archaeological Museum.
Cylindrical loom weight of unlevigated brown clay. It has a vertical perforation and traces of burning on the surface.

63 Lid with handle
MM II (19th - 18th c. BC)
Clay. Monastiraki, Amari.
H with handle 0.06, d 0.15 m.
Rethymno, Archaeological Museum.
Mended; pale orange clay, brown-pink paint. The surface has traces of a lustrous slip. Plain bands decorate the body and handle.

64 Miniature teapot
MM II (19th - 18th c. BC)
Clay.
Apodoulou, Amari.
H 0.025, max d 0.047, d rim 0.034 m.
Rethymno, Archaeological Museum.
Small vase; restored. It has a biconical body with two diametrically opposed knobs, a flat base and high cylindrical spout.
Similar examples of this shape coming from Phaistos have been described as lamps.

65 "Grater"
MM II (19th - 18th c. BC)
Clay.
Monastiraki, Amari. H 0.075, max 1 0.15 m.
Rethymno, Archaeological Museum.
Bowl with two horizontal handles on the rim and on the inside a raised area with incisions. About a third of the vessel is preserved, giving a clear picture of its shape. Light grey clay and traces of black paint on the inside.
This is an excellent example of a utility vessel, wich has stayes unchanged until the present day. A similar vessel comes from the ancient Palace of Phaistos.

66 Pithos
MM II (19th - 18th c. BC)
Clay.
Monastiraki, Amari.
H 0.315, d rim 0.145, d base 0.11 m.
Rethymno, Archaeological Museum.
Two-handled pithos; mended, with two button knobs. Brown-grey clay, black paint. It is decorated with bands on the lower part of the body and the neck, and with pendant arches on the shoulder.

67 Tripod pot
MM II (19th - 18th c. BC)
Clay.
Monastiraki, Amari.
H 0.32 m, d rim 0.17 m, d base 0.13 m.
Rethymno, Archaeological Museum.
Cooking vessel; mended and restored. Brown-red clay; rough surface.

68 Pithoid vase
MM II (19th - 18th c. BC)
Clay.
Monastiraki, Amari.
H 0.18, d rim 012, d base 0,08 m.
Rethymno, Archaeological Museum.
Complete; small handleless vase with a pithos shape. Pale orange clay; rough surface with leaf ipressions.

69 Amphora
MM II (19th - 18th c. BC)
Clay.
Monastiraki, Amari.
H 0.32, d rim 0.097, d base 0.10 m.
Rethymno, Archaeological Museum.
Complete. Brown-yellog clay; it was covered overall with brown-black paint, of which traces have survived on the rim and inside the neck.

70 Lamp
MM II (19th - 18th c. BC)
Clay.
Monastiraki, Amari.
Pres h 0.08, outside d 0.313 m.
Rethymno, Archaeological Museum.
Brown-yellog clay; lustrous slip in the surface, and strong traces of fire inside the burner bowl.

71 Pithos
MM II (19th - 18th c. BC)
Clay.
Monastiraki, Amari.
H 0.44, d rim 0.025, d base 0.135 m.
Rethymno, Archaeological Museum.
Restored pithos with spout and four handles: two horizontal and two vertical. Brown-yellow clay with traces of fire; rough surface.

72 Pithos
MM II (19th - 18th c. BC)
Clay.
Monastiraki, Amari.
H 0.69, max d 0.50, d rim 0.39 m.
Rethymno, Archaeological Museum.
Mended from many fragments. Brown-yellow clay; brown paint. Ovoid shape, with four vertical handles on the neck. Decorated with chevrons inside and out.

73 Lamp
LM I (16th c. BC)
Serpentine.
Unknown provenance.
H 0.045, max d 0.12 m.
Rethymno, Archaeological Museum.
Stone lamp with incomplete handle and chipping on the perimeter. It has a flat raised base, conical body with an elliptical depression for the oil, an integral horizontal handle and a channelled nozzle.
This type, a copy of MM clay originals, is found from the MMI to the LM I period.

74 Jug
LM IB (end of 16th c. BC)
Clay. Town of Chania.
H 0.137, d rim 0.117-0.122, d base 0.051 m.
Chania, Archaeological Museum.
Vase mended; carelessly made. It has a conical body, discoid base, wid low neck, semicylindrical spout and a vertical handle whose termination recalls metal originals. The body and neck are encircled by bands; running spirals with helical stems decorate the shoulder.

75 Spouted cup
LM IB (end of 16th c. BC)
Clay.
Kastelli, Chania.
H 0.082, max d 0.098 m.
Chania, Archaeological Museum.
Complete; slight surface damage. Flattened spherical body with wide neck and cylindrical spout; a vertical handle and two oblong knobs on the shoulder. The main decorated zone has brown-pink pendent and running spirals.

76 Hydria
LM II (15th c. BC)
Bronze.
Koufi, Rethymno.
H 0.48, d rim 0.15, max d 0.38, d base 0.163 m.
Rethymno, Archaeological Museum.
Shoulder damaged. Piriform body consisting of three horizontal bronze sheets joines by rivets. It has two handles: one vertical, joining the rim and shoulder, and the other horizontal on the lower part of the body. Flat discoid base. Bronze hydriae appear in Minoan Crete during the 2nd half of the 16th c. BC.

77 Jug
LM IIIA (14th c. BC)
Clay.
Unknown provenance. H 0.28, max d 0.185 m.
Rethymno, Archaeological Museum.
Slender vase, well made and preserved, imitating a metal original. Conical-piriform body, a nearly discoid base, tubular neck, beaked spout and vertical ribbon handle with an impressed print where the handle joins the shoulder. The bright orange painted decoration is limited to simple band around the vase and a row of sigma-shaped motifs on the shoulder.

78 Two-handled collar-jar
LM III A (14th c. BC)
Clay.
Armeni (chamber tomb 95), Rethymno.
H 0.133, d rim 0.09, d base 0.42 m.
Rethymno, Archaeological Museum.
Complete; high foot, piriform body, discoid base, wide neck and two ribbon handles. The principal decoration, unevenly painted, is limited to a concentric arc in the shoulder.
These small jars had a wide distribution in the Eastern Mediterranean during the 14th and 13th centuries BC.

79 Alabastron vase
LM IIIA (14th c. BC)
Clay.
Armeni (chamber tomb 35), Rethymno.
H 0.15, max d 0.17.
Rethymno, Archaeological Museum.
Alabastron; surface chipped and abraided. Flattened spherical body, cylindrical neck with a plastic band at the junction and a flat rim; two loop handles and two button knobs on the shoulder. Groups of brown bands encircle the body. The shoulder is decorated with an zone af stylized scallops; dots, alternating triangles and opposed arcs are used as fill ornaments.

80 Juglet
LM IIIA (14th c. BC)
Clay.
Armeni (chamber tomb 89), Rethymno.
H 0.65, max d 0.67 m.
Rethymno, Archaeological Museum.
Complete monochrome juglet. Spherical body with near ring-base, a beaked spout and a ribbon handle.

81 Three-handled alabastron
LM III A (14th c. BS)
Clay.
Armeni (chamber tomb 78), Rethymno.
H 0.153, d rim 0.088, d base 0.112 m.
Rethymno, Archaeological Museum.
Complete vase, abraided in places. Cylindrical body with flat base, vertical neck, broad rim and three loop handles.
Brown-red papyrus flowers are arrayed on the shoulder; the spaces between the handles are decorated with concentric semicircles.

82 Two-handled collar-jar
LM IIIA 1 (beginning of 14th c. BC)
Clay.
Armeni (chamber tomb 94), Rethymno.
H 0.103, max d 0.11, d rim 0.082 m.
Rethymno, Archaeological Museum.
Small vase, well preserved. Spherical-conical body with flat base and wide neck. The "metallic" lustre of the black paint that covers it overall is striking.

83 Alabastron
LM IIIA (14th c. BC)
Clay.
Armeni (chamber tomb 67), Rethymno.
H 0.10, d rim 0.093, d base 0.15 m.
Rethymno, Archaeological Museum.
Complete; rim slightly restored; vertical walls and three loop handles. The principal zone of decoration on the shoulder has a stylized foliate band.
Squat and cylindrical alabastra, considered to be Minoan in origin, and probably of distant Egyptian descent, were numerous in the LM III period and served as containers for aromatic substances.

84 Kylix
LM IIIA 2/B (end of 14th c. BC)
Clay.
Stavromenos, Rethymno.
H with handles 0.20, d rim 0.174,
d base 0.094 m.
Rethymno, Archaeological Museum.
Mended; high-footet kylix with a deep conical body, wide curved base and two high vertical handles. In the zone between the handles forked Minoan flowers are drawn in brown-red paint; consecutive bands decorate the stem and base; the interior is painted overall.

85 Stirrup jar
LM IIIA 2 (end of 14th c. BC)
Clay.
Armeni (chamber tomb 29) Rethymno.
H 0.17, max d 0.163, d base 0.062 m.
Rethymno, Archaeological Museum.
A slender vase, in good condition. Piriform body with ring-base and two ribbon handles. The principal decoration is on the shoulder and divided into two semicircles: a) variegated triangels on each side of the spout, and b) an array of forked "Minoan" flowers.

86 One-handled mug
LM IIIA 2/B 1 (end of 14th c. BC)
Clay.
Chamber tomb at Ayii Apostoli, Amari.
H 0.078, d rim 0.105-0.115, d base 0.057 m.
Rethymno, Archaeological Museum.
Cup painted overall, excellently preserved.

Noteworthy is the presence of features of two periods, wich sets it in the transitional phase: the ribbon handle, conical foot and angular outline are earlier features, wihile the deep belly and vertical rim are later.

87   Shallow bowl
LM III B (13th c. BC)
Clay.
Chamber tomb at Ayii Apostoli, Amari.
H 0.055, d rim 0.164, d base 0.045 m.
Rethymno, Archaeological Museum.
Complete vase, painted overall, with flat base, conical body and two horizontal handles. This shape, functional in character, is a frequent find in settlements and graves as early as the LM IA period.

88   Juglet
LM IIIB (13th c. BC)
Clay.
Armeni (chamber tomb 140), Rethymno.
H 0.64, max d 0.067 m.
Rethymno, Archaeological Museum.
Charming vase, slightly restored. Flattened spherical body, small flat base, high semicylindrical spout and vertical handle. The principal decoration consists of guilloches on the shoulder.

89   Juglet
LM IIIA (14th c. BC)
Clay.
Armeni (chamber tomb 98), Rethymno.
H 0.64. max d 0.067 m.
Rethymno, Archaeological Museum.
Finely crafted monochrome vase in good condition. Flattened spherical body with cylindrical neck, beaked spout and a vertical handle.

90   Cup
LM IIIB (13th c. BC)
Clay.
Chamber tomb at Ayii Apostoli. Amari.
H 0.06, d rim 0.10, d base 0.37 m.
Rethymno, Archaeological Museum.
Very well preserved vase with flat base, hemisperical body and vertical handle. The lustrous black-painted decoration on the upper part of the body is limited to sporadic pendant stems; painted overall on the inside.

91   Short-stemmed kylix
LM IIIB (13th c. BC)
Clay.
Town of Chania (chamber tomb 1).
H 0.11, d rim 0.125, d base 0.065 m.
Chania, Archaeological Museum.
Fine example of the Chania (Cydonia) workshop; mended and restored. Conical body, slightly carinated, with two vertical handles; it has a low conical foot with a wide base.
The principal decoration, with orange paint in the handle zone, is limited to two single papyrus flowers on each side. Spiral band on the bottom.

92   Stirrup jar
LM IIIB (13th c. BC)
Clay.
Armeni (chamber tomb 139), Rethymno.
H 0.12, max d 0.156 m.
Rethymno, Archaeological Museum.
Complete; spout slightly restored. It has a conical body, ring-base and vertical spout. The principal decoration, on the shoulder, is divided into two semicircles: a) an array of bird's heads, and b) variegated triangles.
The bird array, a favourite Minoan subject, appears in art, from the MM III period on, in fresco decoration.

93   Tripod vessel
LM IIIB (13th c. BC)
Clay.
Armeni (chamber tomb 148), Rethymno.
H 0.204, max d 0.192, d rim 0.082 m.
Rethymno, Archaeological Museum.
Complete, surface damaged. Spherical body, flat base with three legs, four handles on the shoulder (two vertical und two loop) and a wide cylindircal neck. The principal brown-red decoration consists of a) double or single spirals in the spaces between the handles; b) alternating spiraloid stems on the lower part of the body.

94   Three-handled amphoriskos
LM IIIA 2 (end of 14th c. BC)
Clay.
Armeni (chamber tomb 67), Rethymno.
H 0.16, max d 0.145, d rim 0.097 m
Rethymno, Archaeological Museum.
Complete, slightly chipped. Piriform body, cylindrical neck, ring-base, loop handles. The principal decoration in fugitive black paint on the shoulder is divided into panels containing opposed arcs.

95   Cup
LM IIIA 2/B (end of 14th c. BC)
Clay.
Chamber tomb at Ayii Apostoli, Amari.
H 0.04, d rim 0.106 m.
Rethymno, Archaeological Museum.
This conical cup is complete and undecorated. It occurs in Crete from the EM period, and is always utility in character.

96   Small jug
LM III B (beginning of 13th c. BC)
Clay.
Armeni (chamber tomb 100), Rethymno.
H 0.055, max d 0.059 m.
Rethymno, Archaeological Museum.
A charming little vase with a flattened spherical body, ring-base, wide mouth and vertical handle. The shoulder is decorated with a brown-black broken braid. It was used for an infant's toy or as a container for aromatic substances.

97   Amphorbid krater
LM IIIB (13th c. BC)
Clay.
Town of Rethymno (chamber tomb).
H 0.45, d rim 0.38, max d 0.34 m.
Rethymno, Archaeological Museum.
A fine krater; rim restored. Piriform body, conical base, tall cylindrical neck with flat rim and two vertical ribbon handles. The body is decorated on either face with a brown-orange stylized octopus with curling tentacles.
This particular vase is a preeminently Minoan creation inasmuch as both the shape and decorative subject developed in Crete and subsequently spread troughout the Aegean area.

98   Knife
LM IIIA-B (14th – 13th c. BC)
Bronze.
Armeni (chamber tomb 16), Rethymno.
L 0.18, max w 0.017 m.
Rethymno, Archaeological Museum.
Single-edged knife; the integral handle is damaged. Long triangular blade with straight back and rounded point; hilt with two rivets for attaching the wooden handle, part of which has survived. A fragment of fabric in which the knife was wrapped is preserved on one surface of the blade.

99 Knife
LM IIIA-B (4th - 13th c. BC)
Bronze.
Armeni (chamber tomb 25), Rethymno.
L 0.195 .
Rethymno, Archaeological Museum.
Complete single-edged knife. It has a triangular blade with straight back and square butt wich has two holes and a rivet for attaching the organic hilt.
This is a type of functional knife that had a wide distribution in the Late Helladic period. It spread to Crete from the mainland in about the middle of the 14th c. BC (LM III).

100 Knife
LM III A-B (14th - 13th c. BC)
Bronze.
Armeni (chamber tomb 95), Rethymno.
L 0.128, max w 0.035.
Rethymno, Archaeological Museum.
Leaf-shaped two-edged blade with damage to the point and sheet-metal hilt; two rivets for attaching the wooden handle are preserved. The function of these tools is a basic problem for researchers; they are also often interpreted as examples of an early type of "razor".

101 Knife
LM IIIA-B (14th - 13th c. BC)
Bronze.
Armeni (chamber tomb 71), Rethymno.
L 0.142, max w 0.014 m.
Rethymno, Archaeological Museum.
Small single-blades knife, with damage to the sheet-metal handle; the two rivets for attaching the wooden handel are preserved. The blade is triangular with a straight back and slightly rounded point.

102 Knife-axe
LM III A-B (14th - 13th c. BC)
Bronze.
Armeni (chamber tomb 55), Rethymno.
L 0.215, max. w 0.07 m.
Rethymno, Archaeological Museum.
Complete, utility implement; edge slightly damaged. Trapeziform blade with concave back und curved butt with a rivet and two holes for attaching the wooden haft. There are three successive incised.
Lines along the back of the blade. This type of tool was in use troughout the LM III period, after which it disappears completely.

103 Razor
LM IIIA-B (14th - 13th c. BC)
Bronze.
Armeni (chamber tomb 127), Rethymno.
L 0.155, max w 0.035 m.
Rethymno, Archaeological Museum.
Complete; oxidised surface. An almost trapezoidal blade with slightly concave back und curved butt in wich two rivets are preserved to attach the wooden handle.
The function of objects of this type, with all their variations, is a basic problem for researches (cf Cat. no. 179). Nevertheless, we think that the short length of this particular specimen suggests that it had a cosmetic function.

104 Axe
LM II (15th c. BC)
Bronze.
Unknown provenance.
L 0.185, max. w 0.063 m.
Rethymno, Archaeological Museum.
Double-axe; cutting edges damaged; it has a circular hole for the wooden haft. This type of tool was developed and distributed troughout the Aegean during the Bronze Age. Apart from its functional character, it was the Minoan religious symbol par exeellence. It is divided into two types, according to whether the shafthole is oval or circular.

105 Saw
LM IIIA-B (14th - 13th c. BC)
Bronze.
Armeni (chamber tomb 115), Rethymno.
L 0.42, max w 0.055 m.
Rethymno, Archaeological Museum.
Complete woodworking tool. Long triangular blade with straight back with three holes for attaching the wooden handle, and a serrated cutting edge.
This type of saw was purely Cretan in origin and occurs in two variations: with or without holes. Examples have also been found on the Greek mainland.

106 Spearhead
LM IIIA-B (14th - 13th c. BC)
Bronze.
Armeni (chamber tomb 35), Rethymno.
L 0.255 m.
Rethymno, Archaeological Museum.
Complete, flame-shaped. The octagonal socket has two holes for attachment to the wooden shaft, of which fragments are preserved inside the socket. The spearhead has a prominent central rib.

107 Spearhead
LM IIIA-B (14th - 13th c. BC)
Bronze.
Armeni (chamber tomb 43), Rethymno.
L 0.283 m.
Rethymno, Archaeological Museum.
Part of the conical socket is missing. It has a flat reinforcing ring around the orifice and two holes for attaching it to the wooden shaft. The flame-shaped spearhead has a broad rib.

108 Short sword
LM IIIA-B (14th - 13th c. BC)
Bronze.
Armeni (chamber tomb 35), Rethymno.
L 0.375, w shoulder 0.062 m.
Rethymno, Archaeological Museum.
Sword, mended from two fragments. Its has an integral T-handle with a crescentic pommel, a flange as far as the beginning of the blade and five rivets for the attachment of an organic handle. The shoulders ar rounded, and the blade flat and linguiform.
Most examples of this type are dated to the first half of the 14th c. BC.

109 Knife
LM IIIA-B (14th - 13th c. BC)
Bronze.
Armeni (chamber tomb 115), Rethymno.
L 0.345 m.
Rethymno, Archaeological Museum.
Complete single-edged knife. It has an integral T-shaped hilt with a crescent-shaped pommel, four rivets and a continuous flange to support the wooden haft, part of wich has survived. The blade is triangular with a straight back and rounded point. Two successive incised lines traverse both surfaces of the blade close to the back.
The flanged handle appeared at the end of LM II and characterizes the weapons of the last phase of the Late Bronze Age.

110 Ingot
LM I-II (16th - 15th c. BC)
Bronze.
Tylisos. L 0.345, w 0.25, th 0.06 m.
Heraklion, Archaeological Museum.
Rectangular in shape with slightly concave sides. On the one smooth surface, beside each corner, is an irregular hollow; there is an incised X on one corner.
Ingots were probably the usual form in which pure copper, a raw material and thus a stable medium of exanche, was transported. A large

number com from sites on Crete and limited number fom Mycenae.

111   Stirrup jar
LM IIIB (13th c. BC)
Clay.
Armeni (chamber tomb 8), Rethymno.
H 0.132, max d 0.11, d base 0.047 m.
Rethymno, Archaeological Museum.
Fine example form the Chania (Cydonia) workshop (cf Cat. no 115), wich is distinguished for the fineness of its workmanship and decoration. It has a spherical body with a discoid base. Three four-leafed rosettes with dots between the petals and a multiple wavy stem cover the body of the vase.

112   Stirrup jar
LM III B 1 (beginning of 13th c. BC)
Clay.
Armeni (chamber tomb 132), Rethymno.
H 0.122, max d 0.138 m.
Rethymno, Archaeological Museum.
Carefully made: representative of the Chania (Cydonia) workshop. It has a conical body wiht a ring-base. Black lustrous bands of equal width ring the body; forked Minoan flowers decorate the shoulder.
The finding of the stirrup jar at Armeni, in conjunction with its function as a vessel for transporting precious liquids, points to an extensive export trade for the products of the Cydonian workshop.

113   Stirrup jar
LM IIIA (14th c. BC)
Clay.
Armeni (chamber tomb 79), Rethymno.
H 0.20, max d 0.154 m.
Retyhmno, Archaeological Museum.
Slim vessel; surface chipped and abraided. It has a piriform body with high conical base. A brown-red stylized combined purpura covers the belly; symmetrical variegated triangles decorate the shoulder.

114   Stirrup jar
LM IIIB (13th c. BC)
Clay.
Armeni (chamber tomb 143), Rethymno.
H 0.077, max d 0.123, d base 0.045 m.
Rethymno, Archaeological Museum.
Small jar, well preserved. Sturdy conical body with ring-base. The shoulder is decorated with a) two forked "Minoan flowers" on either side of the true mouth and one with a spiral stem on the other half; b) a chain of rhombs with a central dot around the circumference bordered by a wavy line.

115   Askos
LM III A 2/B (end of 14 th c. BC)
Clay.
Armeni (chamber tomb 108), Rethymno.
H 0.08, max d 0.095 m.
Rethymno, Archaeological Museum.
Mended and restored with plaster on the base. Flattened spherical body, loop handles and vertical cylindrical mouth. The brown-orange decoration is limited to parallel bands on the body and concentric circles on the shoulder. This vase is a representative example of the Postpalatial pottery workshop of Chania (Cydonia). The finding of these products at sites on Crete, the Greek mainland and Cyprus is an indication of the importance of the export trade of this region during the Creto-Mycenean period.

116   Goblet
LM II (2nd half of 15th c. BC)
Clay.
Knosos, Unexplored Mansion.
H 0.96, d rim 0.111, d base 0.53 m.
Herakleion, Archaeological Museum.
Small Ephyrean goblet (cf Cat. no. 16) mended and restored. Hemispherical body with oblique rim, low cylindrical foot, wide circular base and two ribbon handles. Each side is decorated with a cross with successive chevrons in the spaces between its arms. Painted overall inside. The shape and decoration follow closely the Mycenean models.

117   Alabastroid lekythos
LM IIIA 1 (beginning of 14th c. BC)
Clay.
Armeni (chamber tomb 206), Rethymno.
H 0.123, max d 0.15, d rim 0.061 m.
Rethymno, Archaeological Museum.
Complete handleless vase slightly chipped. Spherical-conical body, flat base and chous-like rim. Brown stippled decoration probably made with a brush covers the exterior.
This decoration, thought by some to imitate an ostrich egg and by other fresco decoration, first appears in the LM IB period.

118   Three-handled amphoriskos
LM IIIA 2 (2nd half of 14th c. BC)
Clay.
Armeni (chamber tomb 198), Rethymno.
H 0.174, max d 0.141 m.
Rethymno, Archaeological Museum.
Fine example of an imported Mycenean amphoriskos. Complete; slight chipping. Conical-piriform body, ring base, wide cylindrical neck and three loop handles on the shoulder. Lustrous brown bands encircle the body, and groups of vertical lines decorate the handle zone.

119   "Calyx" vase
MM III/LM I (mid 16th c. BC)
Serpentine.
Town of Chania.
H 0.097, max d 0.155 m.
Chania, Archaeological Museum.
Made of grey-white stone; restored. It has a conical body, flat base and cylindrical usable space. Six vertical leaves in relief with a double channel in their centres decorate the outside. A large number of vases of this type is known from all over Crete. Their use is hard to define; some of them were probably vessels for keeping rouge or perfumes in.

120   Stirrup jar
LM III B (13 th c. BC)
Clay.
Angeliana (chamber tomb), Mylopotamos.
H 0.32, max d 0.23 m.
Rethymno, Archaeological Museum.
Large vessel, coarse fabric, well preserved. Spherical-ovoid shape with a conical foot and flat base. An uneven slip, black to red, covers the whole surface. The added white decoration includes serpentine bands on the body and successive wavy lines on the shoulder.
Stirrup jars of this type were used in the export trade to transport wine or aromatic oils.

121   Ox figurine
MM II (19th–18th c. BC)
Clay.
Vrysinas, Rethymno; peak sanctuary.
Pres h 0.145, max l 0.215 m.
Rethymno, Archaeological Museum.
Mended. It has a solid body with hollowed lower suface, integral cylindrical legs, triangular head and tail turned back. The stylized treatment of certain morphological details is interesting: shallow holes and incisions indicate the features of the head, the hooves and the tuft of the tail.

122 Ox figurine
MM II (19th-18th c. BC)
Clay.
Vrysinas, Rethymno; peak sanctuary.
Pres h 0.08 m, max l 0.14 m.
Rethymno, Archaeological Museum.
Incomplete zoomorphic figurine with traces of brown-red paint. Solid cylindrical body on four integral legs. Vestigial rendering of the details of the head. Genital organs clearly shown.

123 Ox figurine
MM II (19th-18th c. BC)
Clay.
Vrysinas, Rethymno; peak sanctuary.
Pres h 0.12, l 0.18 m.
Rethymno, Archaeological Museum.
Mended zoomorphic figurine with traces of brown paint. The long cylindrical body is supported on four conical legs. The features of the triangular head are shown by means of holes and incision; the ears and horns are rendered plastically. The tail is bent back and lies along the animal's back.

124 Bird figurine
MM II (19th-18th c. BC)
Clay.
Vrysinas, Rethymno; peak sanctuary.
H 0.028, l 0.07 m.
Rethymno, Archaeological Museum.
Solid handmade figurine; chipped. It depicts a bird in the round with slender body and long narrow wings; the raised neck ends in a small head with an open beak and two holes for eyes.
Birds were a popular subject in Minoan iconography, and were widely used in religious contexts (dedication to a divinity), for functional objekts (as a plaything) and for decoration.

125 Female figurine
MM II (19th-18th c. BC)
Clay.
Vrysinas, Rethymno, peak sanctuary.
Pres h 0.094 m.
Rethymno, Archaeological Museum.
Standing female figurine, preserved to the waist. She is shown naked with the arms bent and joined to the body. Conical projections indicate the breasts and a vertical groove the anatomy of the back. She wears a variegated polos on her head; the features of the face are shown schematically. An interesting feature is the necklace she wears, with pendant disks to indicate beads.

126 Female figurine
MM II (19th-18th c. BC)
Clay.
Vrysinas, Rethymno; peak sanctuary.
H 0.09 m.
Rethymno, Archaeological Museum.
Handmade; incomplete. It shows a naked female figure frontally. She wears a polos on her head and a girdle round her waist. Plastic additions indicate the eyes, ears, and breasts, and incisions the nostrils and mouth.

127 Female figurine
MM II (19th-18th c. BC)
Clay.
Vrysinas, Rethymno, peak sanctuary.
Pres h 0.086 m.
Rethymno, Archaeological Museum.
Handmade, carelessly modelled. She is shown bare to the waist; the lower part with the skirt is missing. The preserved arm is against the body; conical projections denote the breasts. The indication of the features is vestigial; a polos adorns the head.

128 Female figurine
MM II (19th-18th c. BC)
Clay.
Vrysinas, Rethymno; peak sanctuary.
Pres h 0.10 m.
Rethymno, Archaeological Museum.
Mended; preserved down to the waist. Upright naked female figure with flattened body and conical projections for breasts. The head is raised and has a triangular nose and discoid eyes, plastic ears and an unusual spiraloid polos.

129 Female figurine
MM II (19th-18th c. BC)
Clay.
Vrysinas, Rethymno; peak sanctuary.
Pres h 0.098 m.
Rethymno, Archaeological Museum.
Fragmentarily preserved; badly chipped. Long naked body with plastically rendered breasts; the full-length skirt and the arms are missing; the hands are attached to the body. There is a low polos on the head; the features are shown schematically.

130 Male figurine
MM II (19th-18th c. BC)
Clay.
Vrysinas, Rethymno; peak sanctuary.
H 0.125 m.
Rethymno, Archaeological Museum.
Standing male figurine, painted overall. He is shown naked on an integral square base with his head raised and arms bent toward the body. The facial features and sex organs are shown vestigially.
The position of the arms, which are bent against his chest, first appears in the EM period on figurines identified as worshippers.

131 Male figurine
MM II (19th-18th c. BC)
Clay.
Vrysinas, Rethymno; peak sanctuary.
H 0.14 m.
Rethymno, Archaeological Museum.
Frontal stance; fragmentarily preserved. It is shown naked, elongated discoid projections denote the eyes, nose and sex of the figure. The hair is shown by transverse lines and plaits.

132 Female figurine
MM II (19th-18th c. BC)
Clay.
Vrysinas, Rethymno, peak sanctuary.
Pres h 0.11 m.
Rethymno, Archaeological Museum.
Female figure; frontal stance; traces of black paint overall. She is shown naked to the waist, and a full-length skirt covers the lower part of the body. The arms are against the breast, probably pressing the breasts, a position known from the figurine-rhyton from Mochlos. An almost discoid polos adorns the head; the features are coarsely rendered.

133 Mal figurine heads
MM II (19th-18th c. BC)
Clay.
Vrysinas, Rethymno; peak sanctuary.
H 0.032-0.045 m.
Rethymno, Archaeological Museum.
Two figurine heads with "discoid" projections to denote the eyes and a long one for the nose: worth noting are holes in the vestigial ears. The hair is represented by a zone of transverse incised lines and plaits.

134 Male figurine
MM II (19th-18th c. BC)
Clay.
Vrysinas, Rethymno, peak sanctuary.
Pres h 0.102 m.
Rethymno, Archaeological Museum.
Handmade. It has "discoid" eyes, an open

mouth, long nose, plastic ears and long braided hair. The arms are against the chest. A Minoan loincloth, from wich hangs a dagger, covers the lumbar region.
A similar warrior figure is known from the Petsophas peak sanctuary.

135 Model of an offering table
MM II (19th-18th c. BC)
Serpentine.
Vrysinas, Rethymno; peak sanctuary.
H 0.068 m.
Rethymno, Archaeological Museum.
Rectangular offering table of grey stone; half of it preserved. Linear A signs are incised on the perimeter of the upper surface.
Similar Linear A inscriptions on other sacred stone utensils are interpreted as names or salutations by the female divinity.

136 Ritual basin
MM III (17th c. BC)
Clay.
Cave of Mameloukos, Perivolia.
H 0.08, d rim 0.20 m.
Chania, Archaeological Museum.
Mended; open conical body with flat base. Seven tiny overlapping imitations of conical cups are attached to the inside wall below the rim.
Their presence identifies the vase as a kernos, a ritual vessel, appropriate for the offering of fruit.

137 Axe
LM I (beginning of 15th c. BC)
Bronze.
Malia, House E.
L 0.19, max w 0.067 m.
Heraklion, Archaeological Museum.
Complete double-axe, with curved edges and an oval shafthole. The casting channels formed during its manufacture are visible on the narrow sides.
This particular variation (see Cat. no. 104) with the oval shafthole was prevalent on the Greek mainland and is considered to be a preeminently Mycenean type.

138 Basin
LM IIIB (13th c. BC)
Clay.
Armeni (chamber tomb 24), Rethymno.
H with handle 0.13, d rim 0.16, d base 0.09 m
Rethymno, Archaeological Museum.
Open vase, well-preserved. It has a deep conical body with a flat base, double handle and a cup integral with the rim. Successive bands of equal width encircle the body; the cup and rim are painted overall (cf Cat. no. 139).

139 Basin
LM IIIB (13th c. BC)
Clay.
Armeni (chamber tomb), Rethymno.
H (with handles) 0.105, d base 0.11 m.
Rethymno, Archaeological Museum.
Open vessel; complete, slightly chipped. Conical body, flat base, double loop handle and chous-shaped cup integral with the rim. The brown-red decoration is limited to bands and concentric circles.
Basins of this type are considered to be a kind of kernos, a vase intended for burial rites.

140 Two-handled alabastron
LM IIIB (13th c. BC)
Clay.
Armeni (chamber tomb 119), Rethymno.
H 0,068, d rim 0.073, d base 0.033 m.
Rethymno, Archaeological Museum.
Complete small alabaster with biconical body, flat base and wide mouth. Brown hatched double-axes are arrayed in the handle zone. This Minoan religious symbol first appeared as a decorative motif an pottery during the MM III to LM IA transition period.

141 Ring vase
LM IIIA2 (2nd half of 14th c. BC)
Clay.
Armeni (chamber tomb 206), Rethymno.
H 0.053, max d 0.075 m.
Rethymno, Archaeological Museum.
Complete; perfume container. The body forms a ring, oval in section, with a loop handle spanning the inside circumference, and a sloping cylindrical mouth. A brown-pink stylized foliate band decorates the body.

142 Figurine of a goddess
LM III B (13th c. BC)
Clay.
Kannia, Gortyna.
Pres h 0.338, d base 0.17 m.
Herakleion, Archaeological Museum.
Figurine on wheels of the goddess type with raised hands. The head and most of the upper extremities are missing. She is depicted bare to the waist; the lower part is covered with a schematically rendered skirt. The effort to render the body plastically is characteristic: little appliqué cones mimic breasts, and vertical grooves on the chest and back denote the anatomical details of the body.
Known from Mesopotamian iconography, this type of figurine was imported into Crete during the MM I/II period and became popular in the late phase of the Bronze Age. The position of the hands is interpreted as a gesture of welcome, farewell or blessing to the worshippers.

143 Double ritual vase
LM III A 2 (second half of 14th c. BC)
Clay.
Town of Chania (chamber tomb 11).
Max h 0.205, d strainer spout 0.117,
d closed spout 0.122 m.
Chania, Archaeological Museum.
Peculiar vessel from the Cydonia workshop; extremely well made and preserved. It consists of two piriform jugs with flat bases, joined a) at the level of the belly by a tube reinforced on either side, and b) at their mouths by a high ribbon handle. Striking are the neck of the closed vessel, on which has been stuck a stylized bird in the act of drinking. Another bird with variegated plumage and tufted tail is depicted on the body of the strainer jug in a landscape with papyrus plants. The second vase is decorated only with papyrus plants variously arranged.
The exceptionally meticulous decoration of the vase and the repetition of the bird subject, which was one of the manifestations of the divinity, suggest it had a ritual function; this view is strengthened by its non-functional shape.

144 Incense burner
LM IIIB (13th c. BC)
Clay.
Armeni (chamber tomb 94), Rethymno.
H body 0.065, d base 0.13, h cover 0.135 m.
Rethymno, Archaeological Museum.
Complete, roughly made. It consists of a cylindrical body, in which the substance was burnt, with a vertical handle and flat base, and a cover, which is cylindrical below and conical in section above, in wich there are four consecutive rows of holes, and a perforated top.
The main decorative zone is confined to the cylindrical part of the cover; it is divided into panels in which there are vertical wavy lines and concentric semicircles, eyed or hatched, disposed vertically and antithetically.

145 Incense burner
LM IIIB (13th c. BC)
Clay.
Armeni (chamber tomb 25), Rethymno.
H body 0.06, d base 0.115, h cover 0.112 m.
Rethymno, Archaeological Museum.
Ceremonial vessel; mended. It consists of a) the base with a central cylindrical body and vertical handle, and b) the cover, also cylindrical with an arched opening, conical upper part and apertures to let the smoke escape. A zone of stylized scallops, bounded by continous arcs, decorated the body of the cover.

146 Aphoriskos
LM IIIA 2 (end of 14th c. BC)
Clay.
Armeni (chamber tomb 167), Rethymno.
H 0.191, d rim 0.12, d base 0.065 m.
Rethymno, Archaeological Museum.
Fine example of an amphoriskos imitating a Mycenean model. It has a piriform body, flat base, wide cylindrical neck with a border and three ribbon handles. Variegated feathery decoration in black semi-fugitive paint fills the spaces between the handles.

147 Stirrup jar
LM IIIB (13th c. BC)
Clay.
Armeni (chamber tomb 140), Rethymno.
H 0.133, max d 0.182 m.
Rethymno, Archaeological Museum.
Complete vase; typical product of a Post-Palatial Chania (Cydonia) workshop. Conical body with ring-base. Two stylized octopi, one on each side, cover the body, the shoulder is decorated with variegated triangles on either side of the spout, and with hatched rhombs; opposed arcs are used as fill onaments.

148 Hydria
LM IIIB (13th c. BC)
Clay.
Piyi (chamber tomb), Rethymno.
H 0.185, max d 0.15, d base 0.058 m.
Rethymno, Archaeological Museum.
Complete; flat base, biconical shape, mouth with spout, one vertical handle and two loop handles. The pink painted decoration on the shoulder zone consists of vertical chevrons. The hydria shape in clay made a simultaneous appearence on Crete and the Greek mainland during the LM IIIB 1 period.

149 Stirrup jar
LM III B (13th c. BC)
Clay.
Armeni (chamber tomb 149), Rethymno.
H 0.15, max d 0.145 m.
Rethymno, Archaeological Museum.
Carefully made; surface chipped. It has a spherical body with an almost ring-base. The metallic lustre of the black paint used to draw an octopus on each face of the vase is striking.

150 Flask
LM IIIA (14th c. BC)
Clay.
Armeni (chamber tomb 13), Rethymno.
H 0.225, max d 0.165 m.
Rethymno, Archaeological Museum.
Complete flask with badly worn surface. Lentoid biconvex body, tubular mouth and two vertical handles. Brown-orange concentric circles of unequal cover both sides of the body.-
This is rare type of vase; it held aromatic oils or wine and was offered as a gift to important persons.

151 Three-handled alabastron
LM IIIA 2/B 1 (end of 14th c. BC)
Clay.
Armeni (chamber tomb 74), Rethymno.
H 0.10, max d 0.141, d base 0.121 m.
Rethymno, Archaeological Museum.
Complete; sporadic chipping, Cylindrical body with flat base, three loop handles on the shoulder and a short neck with wide mouth. Arrays of double-line spirals decorate the shoulder and belly.

152 Four-handled collar-jar
LM IIIB (13th c. BC)
Clay.
Armeni (chamber tomb 138), Rethymno.
H 0.157, max d 0.181, d rim 0.119 m.
Rethymno, Archaeological Museum.
Mended and restored with plaster. Spherical body with flat base, wide neck with plastic ring at the junction, and vertical handles. The zone between the handles is filled with alternate arcs containing successive zigzag lines.

153 Tall alabastron
LM IIIA (14th c. BC)
Clay.
Armeni (chamber tomb), Rethymno.
H 0.22, d rim 0.13, d base 0.135 m.
Rethymno, Archaeological Museum.
Complete vase with flat base and wide body, tall neck with reliefband and its base and flat rim. The decoration with fugitive black paint is divided into parallel bands of unequal width with a stylized foliate motif, wavy lines and zigzag bands.
The tall alabaster is considered to be a Minoan shape, strongly influenced by Egyptian models.

154 Collar-jar with lid
LM IIIB 1 (beginning of 13th c. BC)
Clay.
Chamber tomb at Ayii Apostoli, Amari.
H 0.13, d rim 0.096, d base 0.073 m.
Rethymno, Archaeological Museum.
Complete vase with flat base, conical-spherical body, cylindrical neck and two loop handles. The brown-black painted decoration is concentrated on the shoulder and consists of a "Mycenean flower" and filling ornaments (arcs and chevrons).

155 Pyxis with spout
LM III B 1 (Beginning of 13th c. BC)
Clay.
Chamber tomb at Ayii Apostoli, Amari.
H 0.125, d rim 0.116, d base 0.11 m.
Rethymno, Archaeological Museum.
Fine example of a pyxis, excellent state of preservation. Flat base, cylindrical body, two loop handles and tubular spout. The principal band of decoration, on the body of the vase, is divided into panels with alternating chevrons.

156 Feeding bottle
LM IIIA (14th c. BC)
Clay.
Stavromenos (chamber tomb), Rethymno.
H with handle 0.16, max d. 0.12, d rim 0.078 m.
Rethymno, Archaeological Museum.
Part of the rim and spout restored. Spherical-biconical body, flat base, cylindrical neck with a plastic band where it meets the body, tubular spout and basket handle with a conical knob at one end. Upper side of the handle decorated with hollows filled with glass paste. Red-brown decor on the upper part of the body in form of a foliate band.
This type appears in the last period of the Late Bronze Age.

157 Cup
LM III B (13th c. BC)
Clay.
Armeni (chamber tomb 206), Rethymno.
H 0.068, d rim 0.104 m.
Rethymno, Archaeological Museum.
Complete cup with cylindrical body, everted rim, flat base, vertical ribbon handle and bridge spout. The surface is covered with a fugitive black net pattern. Vessels of this type accompanied the burials of infants and were probably used in their care.

158 Kylix
LM IIIA 2 (end of the 14th c. BC)
Clay.
Piyi (chamber tomb), Rethymno.
H 0.198, d rim 0.208, d base 0.097 m.
Rethymno, Archaeological Museum.
Body and handles mended and restored. This is a particularly large vase with a wide conical body, tall slender foot, flat base and two ribbon handles. Groups of brown-red curved bands arranged in two consecutive zones cover the exterior of the body; painted overall inside.

159 Cup
LM IIIA 2 (end of 14th c. BC)
Clay.
Maroulas (chamber tomb), Rethymno.
H 0.051, d rim 0.113, d base 0.04 m.
Rethymno, Archaeological Museum.
Open vase, very well preserved. The body has an angular profile, flat base, ribbon handle and beaked spout. The principal decoration, in reddish brown paint, is on the handle zone and includes pendant concentric semicircles with stylized papyrus motifs in the interspaces; the bottom is decorated with a spiral.

160 Cup
LM III A (14th c. BC)
Clay.
Armeni (chamber tomb 10), Rethymno.
H 0.067, d rim 0.09, d base 0.032 m.
Rethymno, Archaeological Museum.
Well made vase in good condition. Hemispherical body with small base, wide mouth and ribbon handle. The brown-black decoration is limited to a zigzag band, with opposed arcs in the triangular spaces formed by the zigzag.

161 One-handled cup
LM III A (14th c. BC)
Clay.
Armeni (chamber tomb 98), Rethymno.
H 0.061, d rim 0.106-0.113, d base 0.55 m.
Rethymno, Archaeological Museum.
Utility vessel, complete; slight chipping. Shallow hemispherical body, low foot with broad conical base and a vertical ribbon handle. The cup is painted with brown-red splatter inside and out.

162 Wide-mouth juglet
LM III A 2/B 1 (end of 14th c. BC)
Clay.
Chamber tomb at Ayii Apostoli, Amari.
H 0.107, d base 0.047, max d 0.119 m.
Rethymno, Archaeological Museum.
Complete juglet, roughly made. Flat base, biconical body, grooved raised spout, vertical ribbon handle. Careless decoration confined to Minoan motifs pendant from the base of the neck.

163 Juglet
LM III A (14th c. BC)
Clay.
Stavromenos (chamber tomb), Rethymno.
H 0.07, max d 0.058 m.
Rethymno, Archaeological Museum.
Small finely crafted vase, with flattened spherical body, beaked spout and vertical handle. A brown-red stylized foliate garland decorates the shoulder.
This vase was found inside a larnax as a grave offering.

164 Double vase
LM III A (4th c. BC)
Clay.
Armeni (chamber tomb 188), Rethymno.
H with handle 0.075, max d 0.05 m.
Rethymno, Archaeological Museum.
Complete vase. It consists of a jug joined at the belly by a small tube to a closed lekythos. A high ribbon handle unites the two vases.
The non-functional shape and its frequent occurrency in graves suggest that these vessels had a ceremonial religious character.

165 Askos
LM III B (13th c. BC)
Clay.
Armeni (chamber tomb 110), Rethymno.
H 0.07, max d 0.079 m.
Rethymno, Archaeological Museum.
Complete small vase with flat base, cylindrical body, loop handle springing from a curved shoulder, and oblique mouth. The brown-black painted decoration is concentrated on the shoulder zone which is divided into two semicircles: the first is decorated with fish outlines and the second with semicircles. The empty space is occupied with filling ornament.
This shape was the creation of the Minoan civilization and occurs in every period.

166 Ring vase
LM III B (13th c. BC)
Clay.
Armeni (chamber tomb 49), Rethymno.
H 0.065, max d 0.107 m.
Rethymno, Archaeological Museum.
Complete; an odd vase with a circular body of square section, a cylindrical mouth and loop handle spanning the inner periphery of the ring-body. The lustrous black-painted decoration consists of bands, chevrons and vertical wavy lines.
This shape, common as a grave good, has a wide distribution in the LH III period, especially in its middle and late phases. The mouth, which is difficult to use, and its small capacity have suggested that it served as a perfume flask.

167 Incense burner
LM III B (13th c. BC)
Clay.
Armeni (chamber tomb), Rethymno.
H body 0.05, d base 0.117, h cover 0.115 m.
Rethymno, Archaeological Museum.
Complete, consisting of two parts: a) the burner, with a cylindrical body, flat base projecting at the perimeter and vertical handle; b) the cover, also cylindrical, with an apsidal opening and conical section terminating in a shaft with a hole; four elongated holes are arranged symmetrically on the conical section. The brown-black painted decoration consists of a wavy line on the burner, parallel lines on the conical section of the cover and stylized forked flowers on the cylindrical part.
The findspots of these objects, the non-functional shape and the fact that there are no traces of burning on most of them emphasize their ceremonial character.

168 Kalathos
LM III B (13th c. BC)
Clay.
Armeni (chamber tomb 65), Rethymno.
H with handle 0.155, d rim 0.14 m.
Rethymno, Archaeological Museum.

Distinctive open vessel; mended and restored at the rim. It has a cylindrical body with a double loop handle and jug-shaped cup integral with the rim. The brown fugitive decoration is divided into panels, within which are successive zigzag bands, chequerboards, lattice motives and concentric semicircles with diagonals.

169 Basin
LM III B (13th c. BC)
Clay.
Armeni (chamber tomb 24), Rethymno.
H 0.07, s rim 0.19, d base 0.115 m.
Rethymno, Archaeological Museum.
Complete; wide vase with flat base, conical body and two suspension holes below the rim. A chain of brown-red painted hatched rhombs circles the body; groups of oblique lines decorate the rim.
The shape of the clay basins was taken over from metal originals, and goes back to the beginning of the 14th c. BC.

170 Larnax
LM III B (beginning of 13th c. BC)
Clay.
Armeni (chamber tomb), Rethymno.
H body 0.72, h lid 0.22, l 1.05, w 0.38-0.40 m.
Rethymno, Archaeological Museum.
Box-shaped larnax, very well preserved. It is supported by four integral feet and has a double pitched lid. Brown-yellow clay with slip of the same colour and brown paint. A serpentine band runs round the four sides of the lid. The four sides of the chest are decorated with papyrus flowers different height, which alternate in orderly fashion. Groups of horizontal wavy lines flank the representations. The papyrus subject, knows from Egyptian iconography, was often employed by Minoan craftsmen for decorating religious or funerary objects.

171 Larnax
LM III B (13th c. BC)
Clay.
Armeni (chamber tomb 24), Rethymno.
H 0.65, l 0.96, w 0.34 m.
Rethymno, Archaeological Museum.
Larnax in the shape of a box, wiht four integral feet; the lid is missing. Brown-yellow clay with inclusions, a slip of the same colour, and brown-pink paint. A group of vertical wavy lines divides each long side into two unequal panels decorated with linked running spirals. One of the ends has counterpoised horns of consecration with a double-axe sprouting from the middle of each one. The principal scene is depicted on the other end of the larnax: a stylized female figure of the goddess type with raised hands is depicted upright on a chequerboard ground. Linear motifs decorate the full-length skirt, and spirals and arcs grow from her hands. For the posture of the goddess, refer to the corresponding type of figurine (see Cat. no. 142). Note also the association of the figure of a divinity with the chequerboard motif, which according to some archaeologists denotes an architectural structure.

172 Grave stele
LM III A-B (14th-13th c. BC)
Limestone.
Armeni (chamber tomb), Rethymno.
H 0.78, w 0.29 m.
Rethymno, Archaeological Museum.
Oblong marker, joined from two fragments. The lower part is unworked for insertion into the ground to support the stele. The smoothed visible surface is carelessly decorated: shallow horizontal incised lines are intersected by vertical ones, forming a chequerboard pattern. The same decoration, but very carefully executed, covers the whole surface of a similar stele from the same cemetery.

173 Larnax
LM III B (13th c. BC)
Clay.
Armeni (chamber tomb 55), Rethymno.
H body 0.58, h lid 0.17, l 0.91-0.94, w 0.38-0.40 m.
Rethymno, Archaeological Museum.
Box-shaped, with four integral feet and a double pitched lid. Brown-red clay, slip of the same colour, uneven orange to black paint. Successive concentric arcs cover both sides of the lid. One of the long sides of the body is decorated with three stylized octopoi; on the other is a representation of horns of consecration from the middle of which sprout double-axes, while spirals with stalks are arrayed above the sacred symbols. Each end has a papyrus and a Minoan flower respectively. Vertical wavy bands and semicircles frame the central representations. The holes in the lid and upper part of the body served to attach the lid; holes in the bottom were to drain the fluids from the decomposing corpse. This an impressive example of a larnax, distinguished for the variety of its decoration and the presence together of all the groups of subjects.

174 Tripod vessel
LM III B 2 (end of 13th c. BC)
Clay.
Armeni (chamber tomb 46), Rethymno.
H with lid 0.33, max d 0.295 m.
Rethymno, Archaeological Museum.
Composite form of a vessel; body and neck damaged. It consists of a) a spherical body supported on three low legs, with a high vertical neck and four handles (two loop and two vertical) on the shoulder zone; and b) a cylindrical lid with a basket handle. The principal decoration in the four spaces between the handles consists of brown-pink concentric semicircles, hatched or eyed, consecutive zigzag bands and concentric arcs. The fill ornaments are chevrons, dots and consecutive arcs.
The number of examples of this type coming from sites in the Creto-Mycenean world are few; for the most part they date to the end of the LH/LM III period.

175 Alabastron vase
LM III A 1 (1st half of 14th c. BC)
Clay.
Armeni (chamber tomb 38), Rethymno.
H 0.15 m, max d 0.16 m.
Rethymno, Archaeological Museum.
Complete; very chipped. Spherical-conical body, flat base, wide neck and rim, and three loop handles on the shoulder. The space between each of the handles is decorated with a brown-pink lily with a helical stem.

176 Stirrup jar
LM III A (14th c. BC)
Clay.
Armeni (chamber tomb 137), Rethymno.
H 0.10 , max d 0.08 m.
Rethymno, Archaeological Museum.
Vase with much surface chipping and abrasion. Piriform body with narrow conical base. The principal decoration, on the shoulder, is divided into two fields: a) variegated triangles on either side of the spout, and b) a foliate band in the other semicircular section.

177 Three-handled amphora with lid
LM III A (14th c. BC)
Clay.
Armeni (chamber tomb 39), Rethymno.
H 0.20, max d 0.16 m, d base 0.07 m.
Rethymno, Archaeological Museum.
Coarsely made amphora; chipped. It has a piriform body, discoid base, three loop handles on the shoulder and a conical lid with button

knob. A running spiral decorates the shoulder and bands encircle the body.
Vases of this type were used for the storage and transport of liquids.

178 Knife
LM III A-B (14th - 13th c. BC)
Bronze.
Armeni (chamber tomb 127), Rethymno.
L 0.243, max w 0.024 m.
Rethymno, Archaeological Museum.
Common type of utility knife; corroded. Triangular blade with straight back and sharp edge. Squared butt with low flange and two rivets for the wooden handle.

179 Knife-axe
LM III A-B (14th - 13th c. BC)
Bronze.
Armeni (chamber tomb 115), Rethymno.
L 0.20, max w 0.056 m.
Rethymno, Archaeological Museum.
Complete, oxidised. Trapezoidal blade with straight back and curved butt with two preserved rivets and a hole for attaching the wooden handle.
This shape makes it appearance in the Minoan world in LM IA inspired by Egyptian models. It has been suggested that perhaps they had different functions according to their weight: the smallest as razors for shaving and the largest as cleavers for jointing meat.

180 Stirrup jar
LM III A (14th c. BC)
Clay.
Armeni (chamber tomb 144), Rethymno.
H 0.17, max d 0.108 m.
Rethymno, Archaeological Museum.
Complete; surface abraided. It has a spherical body with a tall conical foot and hollow base. Fugitive black-painted bands encircle the body, and variegated triangles the shoulder.
Vases of this type were used to transport olive oil.

1 Empreinte de sceau
MR I B (milieu du 15e s. av. J.C)
Argile. Kastelli Kissamou.
Diam. 0.032 m, épaisseur, 0,0063-0,018 m.
La Canée, Musée archéologique.
De forme ronde, fortes traces de feu. Ce sceau a sans doute été utilisé pour sceller un écrit, ce que confirment les empreintes de ficelle sur la face arrière. La face prineipale porte la représentation d'une bague sceau, au chaton ovale: dans un paysage de côte rocheuse on voit un groupe de bâtiments disposés symétriqments au centre domine un grand rocher, la mer est schématisée à l'arrière. Le groupe de bâtiments est entouré par un mur percé de deux portes; les portes sont en bois, a linteau orné de demirosaces opposées. Les bâtiments, qui ont jusqu'à trois étages, sont couronnés de cornes de consécration. Une figure masculine impériale est représentée debout sur le bâtiment central, tenant un sceptre dans sa main tendue, on remarque sa riche chevelure et sa ceinture minoenne.
Cette trouvaille est tout à fait importante : elle est interprétée comme représentant une ville, un palais ou un sanctuaire, avec l'apparition d'une divinité ou la représentation d'une chef. On doit noter d'une part la coexistance d'éléments des mondes minoens et mycéniens, et d'autre part son apport dans la connaissance de l'architecture de ces cultures.

2 Empreinte de sceau
MR I R (milieu du 15e. av. J.C.)
Argile. La Canée.
Long. 0,023 m, larg. 0,014 m.
La Canée, Musée archéologique.
Empreinte du chaton ovoïde d'une bague sceau, entièrement conservée : les traces de ficelle sur les côtés et derrière révèlent la manière dont elle était fixée à l'objet scellé. Le sceau représente un déesse assise sur un banc ou un piédestal à degrés. Elle est vêtue à la minoenne, et nourrit un animal cornu.
La représentation de la "Potnia théron", une des formes sous lesquelles apparait la divinité féminine minoenne, était un motif aimé des arts mineurs.

3 Empreinte de sceau
MR IB (milieu du 15e. av. J.C)
Argile. La Canée.
Haut. 0,013 m, larg. 0,017 m.
La Canée, Musée archéologique..
Prisme portant l'empreinte d'un sceau en amande. Trou selon l'axe vertical. Représentation d'un végétal symétrique, de caractère magique, connu sous le nom de "masque de lion". Ce que l'on apelle les sceaux magiques paraissent se développer durant le MM III. Un exemple analogue à celui-ci a été trouvé à Palaiocastro.

4 Tête de guerrier
MR III A-B (14e-13e s. av. J.C.)
Ivoire. Phylaki Apokoronou (tome è tholos).
Haut. 0,06 m, larg. max. 0,04 m, épaisseur max, 0,012 m.
La Canée, Musée archéologique.
Relief représentant un guerrier de profil tourné vers la gauche, aux caractéristiques suivantes : front large, yeux en amande, oreilles ovales, lèvres fines au léger sourire, chevelure disposée sur deux plans. Il porte un casque typiquement mycénien, fait de deux rangées opposées de défenses de sanglier, au faîte en forme de bouton. La face arrière de la plaque d'ivoire est plate et présente deux chevilles parallèles servant à l'ajuster, sans doute sur un morceau de bois.
Des exemples analogues viennent de Grèce continentale et de Crète.

5 Sphynx
MR III A-B (14e-13e s. av. J.C.)
Ivoire. Phylaki Apokoronou (tombe à tholos).
Haut. 0,07 m, larg. 0,043 m.
La Canée, Musée archéologique.
Plaquette rectangulaire, portant la représentation gravée d'un sphynx debout de profil. La tête au nez ablong, à l'oeil en amande et à la lèvre charnue porte une couronne à gland. Le corps est lourd, le buste vigoureux, et les ailes élaborées sont allongées vers l'arrière. Un collier orne son cou.
Le sphynx, animal mythique d'Anatolie, au corps de lion, à la tête de femme, et aux ailes de griffon, était un motif aimé des artistes mycèniens, par contre les minoens l'utilisaient beaucoup moins.

6 Bouclier en forme de huit
MR III A-B (14e-13e s. av. J.C.)
Ivoire. Phylaki Apokoronou (tombe à tholos).
Haut. 0,076 m, larg. 0,045 m, épaisseur cons. 0,026 m.
La Canée, Musée archéologique.
Entier, abîmé et ébréché. Un large rebord l'entoure, et une bande en relief sépare le corps en deux champs : le haut porte six groupes de trois cercles, qui recevaient des incrustations d'autre matière. Deux trous profonds sur la face arrière servaient à le fixer en application sur un riche support en bois.
Le bouclier en forme de huit, symbole religieux mycénien par excellence, est devenu un motif ornemental aimé, rencontré dans les arts mineurs, la fresque et la peinture sur vases. La structure architecturale du tombeau où ce bouclier a été trouvé, en liaison avec les autres trouvailles qui y ont été faites, plaide pour une influence mycénienne sur ce site précis.

7 Deux boucliers en forme de huit
MR III A-B (14e-13e s. av. J.C.)
Ivoire. Phylaki Apokoronou (tombe à tholos).
Long. 0,028-0,029 m, larg. 0,017-0,019 m, épaisseur 0,011-0,02 m.
La Canée, Musée archéologique.
Petits boucliers entiers, écaillés par endroits. La face principale est polie et sans ornement; la face arrière porte un trou profond, où se logeait un clou pour les fixer sur le support de bois.

8 Tablette
MR IB (milieu du 15e. s. av. J.)
Argile. Kastelli
Haut. 0,11 m, larg. 0,082 m.
La Canée, Musée archéologique.
Tablette rectangulaire, recollée de deux fragments. Le texte en linéaire A, disposé en lignes horizontales, énumère des produits agricoles et des animaux domestiques, comme l'on peut le conclure d'après les idéogrammes suivants, qui accompagnent chaque signe exprimant une mesure : blé (céréale), vin, figues, brebis. Cinq petites trous sont conservés sur la partie supérieure de l'inscription.
Cette tablette, faite d'argile rougeâtre crue, a été conservée, comme d'autres, par la cuisson qu'elle a subi dans l'incendie qui a détruit le bâtiment dans lequel elle se trouvait. L'installation minoenne à Kastelli est la seule jusqu'à présent, si l'on excepte Cnossos qui nous ait donné des exemples des deux systèmes d'écriture.

9 Tablette
MR III A-B (14e-13e s. av. J.C.)
Argile. Cnossos.
Haut 0,028 m, long. 0,14 m
Heraklio, Musée archéologique.
Tablette recollée d'après trois fragments. Fortes traces de feu à la surface. Elle porte un texte gravé en écriture syllabique et idéogrammes du linéaire B. II s'agit d'un vêtement (pu-ka-ta-ri-ja) poupre (po-pu-re-ja), sans doute destiné aux pleureuses.
On trouve unse référence analogue chez Homère ("phoros porohyreon" H 881), ce qui montre le caractère hellénique de l'écriture minoenne.

10 Cruche
MM I A (fin du 3e mill. av. J.C.)
Argile. Phaestos.
Haut. cons 0,165 m, diam. max. 0,145 m.
Héraklio, Musée archéologique.
Beau vase, représentatif du stylo barbotino, il manque le bec. Panse sphérico-biconique, base plate, anse verticale col étroit portant deux excroissances en barbotine et lèvre dentelée. La peinture est irrégulière à cause de la cuisson, du brun noir au rougeâtre; elle recouvre tout le vase. Des bandes blanches effacées parcourent le bas de la panse. Le décor de barbotine est sur la moitié supérieure, enrichi de mouchetures blanches et d'arcs imbriqués.
Ce genre de vases, qui devient particulièrement populaire au 2e millénaire av. J.C., est localisé surtout en Crète centrale, par contre on le rencontre isolément dans l'est et l'ouest de l'île. Un grand nombre de ces vases viennent de Phaestos, où, selon toute probabilité, il existait un grand centre de production.

11 Coupe
Argile, Halara, Phaestos
Haut 0,062 m diam. max. 0,091-0,097 m.
Héraklio, Musée archéologique.
Coupe carénée du style de Camarès, excellente fabrication et conservation. Elle possède une anse verticale en ruban et sa lèvre dessine un bec par un pli, ainsi que d'autres plus petits. Le vase est recouvert intérieurement et extérieurement de peinture brun rouge. Le décor polychrome comprend: des bandes, une zone d'arcs pendants et dressés, et un couple de spirales opposées, à la tige commune.
Ces vases du style de Camarès, connus, sous le nom de "coquille d'oeuf" à cause de la finesse des parois, forment une catégorie à part.

12 Cruche
MM II A (19e s. av. J.C.)
Argile. Phaestos.
Haut 0,17 m, diam. max. 0,14 m.
Héraklio, Musée archéologique.
Beau vase, représentatif du style polychrome de Camarès. Panse ovoïde, base plate, col large et bas se terminant par un bec et trois anses verticales qui imitent les modèles métalliques. Une peinture allant du brun noir au rougeâtre couvre le vase sur les deux faces, qui portent chacune une grande rosace blanche.
Dans le monde minoen, la civilisation du palais par excellence, la céramique minoenne atteint la perfection. On doit noter la variété des décors polychromes et leur accord avec le formes travaillées et dynamiques des vases.

13 Cruche
MM III (16e s. av. J.C.)
Agile. Phaestos.
Haut 0,14 m, diam, max. 0,083 m.
Héraklio, Musée archéologique.
Entier. "Style floral", de fabrication grossière. Panse conique, base plate et col bas à bec dressé. Deux anses horizontales sur la panse et une troisième verticale qui part de la lèvre. De chaque côté du bec, deux excroissances plastiques. Un décor végétal de roseaux se déploie sur la panse du vase.

14 Coupe
MR I (fin du 16e s. av. J.C.)
Argile. Cnossos, Route Royale.
Haut 0,068 m, diam à la levre 0,101 m, diam. base 0,03 m.
Héraklio, Musée archéologique.
Vase de farbrication soignée, caractéristique du "style floral". Panse conique, parois légèrement convexes, base plate. Un motif végétal de roseau, de couleur brun rouge, couvre toute la surface extérieure. L'intérieur est entièrement peint.
Les motifs du style végétal sont fortement influencés par les fresques, comme le montrent certains vase de Cnossos.

15 Alabastre à courvercle
MR I B (fin du 16e s. av. J.C.)
Argile. Kastelli Hanion.
Haut. 0,185-0,190 m, diam, max. 0,181 m, diam. à la lèvre 0,119 m. Haut du courvercle 0,057 m, diam. du couvercle 0,153 m.
La Canée, Musée archéologique.
Entier, panse sphérico-ovoïde, base plate, col bas et cylindrique, quatre anses en ruban horizontales. Des groupes de lignes de peinture orange parcourent le bas de la panse; le haut est divisé en deux zones, décorées de spirales continues et de lis stylisés. Le couvercle de forme commune a une poignée plate en forme de bouton, et une anse horizontale cylindrique. Décor de lignes.
Ce vase est un exemple représentatif de l'atelier local. La découverte d'olives carbonisées à l'intérieur confirme son caractère de récipient destiné à conserver des denrées.

16 Kylix
MR II (2e moitié du 15e s. av. J.C.)
Argile Cnossos, Maison inexplorée.
Haut. 0,113 m, diam à la lèvre 0,132 m, diam. base 0,06 m.
Héraklio, Musée archéologique.

Kylix éphyréenne, recollée et restaurée. Panse profonde en entonnoir, lèvre recourbée vers l'extérieur, pied bas, base discoïde et deux anses verticales en ruban. Le décor, de peinture brun noir, se déploie sur les deux faces du vase, il comporte un fleuron trilobé au centre marqué d'un point, au double encadrement; des arcs concentriques sont utilisés en motif complémentaire. Le fond est entièrement peint.
Ce type de vases, de provenance helladique, caractérise la phase HR II B; il se distingue par la simplicité et la pureté du décor, qui se limite à un motif végétal ou marin isolé.

17 Collier
MR III A-B (14e-13e s. av. J.C.)
Sardoine. Nécropole d'Arménoi Réthymnes.
Diam 0,003-0,025 m Réthymno, Musée archéologique..
Composé de 49 perles : les 5 du milieu sont des prismes ellipsoïdes, et les autres sont sphériques, de taille différente.
La sardoine, pierre semi-précieuse, était très appréciée dans le monde créto-mycénien, comme en témoigne son usage très fréquent pour la fabrication des perles et des sceaux. Elle était importée d'Anatolie, en grande quantité, sous forme de matière première.

18 Collier
MR III A-B (14e-13e s. av. J.C.)
Pâte de verre.
Nécropole d'Arménoi Réthymnes.
Long 0,027 m, larg 0,01 m.
Réthymno, Musée archéologique.
Il est fait de 17 perles en forme de plaquette allongée; trois spirales en relief à point central disposée verticalement ornent chacune d'entre elles.
La pâte de verre, matière artificielle en usage en Mésopotamie depuis le 4e millénaire av. J.C., a été connue en Crète durant le 16e s. av. J.C.. Les perles, blanc gris ou bleues, étaient coulées dans un moule en pierre.

19 Collier
MR III A-B (14e-13e s. av. J.C.)
Cristal de roche.
Nécropole d'Arménoi, Réthymnes.
Diam. 0,005-0,018 m.
Réthymno, Musée archéologique.
Le collier comporte 19 perles sphériques, cylindriques et ovoïdes, de taille différente.
Le cristal de roche, minéral connu depuis le Minoen moyen, était tres souvent utilisé pour le confection de bijoux mais aussi de vases.

20   Collier
MR III A-B (14e-13e s. av. J.C.)
Faience. Nécropole d'Arménoi Réthymnes.
Long 0,016 m.
Réthymno, Musée archéologique.
Ce collier est fait de 20 perles, dont 12 biconiques et 8 en forme de grain de blé.
La faience, matière artificielle comme la pâte de verre, était déjà connue en Mésopotamie au 5e millénaire av. J.C.; en Crète, elle est utilisée pour la confection de perles et de vases à partir de la première moitié du 3e millénaire av. J.C.

21   Pyxide à couvercle
MR III A (14e s. av. J.C.)
Argile. Vigla Stavroménou, nome de Réthymne (tombe (l) chambre).
Haut. (avec couvercle) 0,091 m, diam à la lèvre 0,085 m, diam. base 0,093 m.
Réthymno, Musée archéologique.
Entier. Base plate, panse cylindique portant quatre trous à l'épaule et couvercle de même forme à trou central. Le décor noir brillant est fait sur la panse de lignes parallèles et de motifs en fleur de papyrus stylisés, et sur le couvercle de cercles concentriques.
Les pyxides cylindriques et ovoïdes, offrandes funéraires habituelles, apparaissent en Crète au MA, après l'influence cycladique. Il est très probable que ces ustensiles étaient utilisés pour ranger des objets personnels de toilette, ce que confirme l'existence de trous par lesquels passait un cordon assurant un meilleure tenue du couvercles.

22   Bracelet
MR III A-B (14-13e s. av. J.C.)
Bronze. Arménoi, nome de Réthymne (tombe à chambre 140).
Diam. 0,053,-0,055 m.
Réthymno, Musée archéologique.
Bracelet trés bien conservé. Il est fait d'un épais fil de métal qui s'amincit aux extrémités, lesquelles sont enroulées en spirale l'une autour de l'autre. Cette technique rend possible les variations du diamètre du bracelet.

23   Bracelet
MR III A-B (14e-13e. s. av. J.C.)
Bronze. Arménoi, nome de Réthymne (tombe à chambre 140).
Diam 0,071 m.
Réthymno, Musée archéologique.
Entier, formé d'un épais fil de métal qui devient très fin aux entrémités; elles sont enroulées l'une autour de l'autre en spirale.
Cette variante de ce type de bracelet provient de Mésomotamie, et s'étend vers l'Europe occidentale à partir du début du 3e millénaire av. J. C.

24   Bracelet
MR III A-B (14e-13e s. av. J.C.)
Bronze. Arménoi, nome de Réthymne (tombe à chambre 124).
Diam. 0,08 m.
Réthymno, Musée archéologique..
Type commun de bijou fait d'une barre cylindrique recourbée, de manière à former un cercle dont les extrémités se rejoignent librement. Les pointes sont triangulaires.

25   Bague
MR III A-B (14e-13e s. av. J.C.)
Bague faite d'un fil de bronze enroulé trois fois en spirale. L'une des extrémités est libre, l'autre soudée à la spirale.

26   Bague
MR III A-B (14e-13e s. av. J.C.)
Bronze Arménoi, nome de Réthymne (tombe à chambre 108).
Diam. 0,019.
Réthymno, Musée archéologique.
Entiére. Elle est formée d'un ruban arrondi jusqu'à ce que les deux extrémités se recouvrent librement.

27   Pince à épiler
MR III A-B (14e-13e s. av. J.C.)
Bronze. Arménoi, nome de Réthymne (tombe à chambre 100)
Long. 0.08 m.
Réthmno, Musée archéologique..
Ustensile de toilette, qui apparaît en Egée au 3e millénaire av. J. C., et reste inchangé jusqu'à nos jours. Fait d'une lame de bronze, courbée au milieu de sa longueur, affectant la forme d'un anneau ouvert. L'extremité des branches est recourbée vers l'intérieur. Une incision parcourt le bord de la lame.

28   Miroir
MR II (15e s. av. J.C.)
Bronze. Cnossos, nécropole Zaphéo Papouras.
Diam 0,12 m.
Héaklio, Musée archéologique.
Miroir circulaire intact, portant deux trous près du bord pour fixer le manche, qui était en matière organique (bois ou os). Sur la face lisse, on distingue les traces laissées par le polissage. Ce type de miroir, qui donnait une surface réfléchissante satisfaisante, est dû à une influence égyptienne et demeure inchangé pendant toute la dernière période de l'âge du bronze.

29   Agrafe
MR III A-B (14e-13e s. av. J.C.)
Bronze. Arménoi, nome de Réthymne (tombe à chambre 67).
Long. 0,135 m.
Réthymno, Musée archéologique.
Agrafe en forme de hameçon, soudée. Tige mince, oblongue, de section carrée. L'une de ses extrémités se termine en pointe, alors que l'autre est courbe, affectant la forme d'un hameçon en ruban.
Petit ustensile de toilette, dont la forme est connue en Egée depuis le 3e millénaire av. J.C. Il était sans doute utilisé pour maintenir les coiffures des femmes, et non pour les vêtements.

30   Cylindre-sceau
MR III A-B (14e-13e s. av. J.C)
Faience. Arménoi, nome de Réthymne (tombe à chambre 108).
Haut. 0,019 m, diam. 0,010 m.
Réthymno, Musée archéologique..
La représentation incisée sur la surface cylindrique est celle de deux formes animales affrontées. Un oiseau stylisé au corps allongé, les ailes et les pattes figurées par des lignes, et sans doute une chèvre sauvage rendue.
Les sceaux cylindriques sont originaires du sud de la Mésopotamie, où ils ont été utilisés pour la première fois au milieu du 4e millénaire av. J.C.

31   Sceau
MR III A-B (14e-13e s. av. J.C.)
Stéatite. Arménoi, nome de Réthymne (tombe à chambre 104).
Diam. 0,018 m.
Réthymno, Musée archéologique.
Lenticulaire, légèrement abîmé sur les deux faces. Son décor inachevé est intéressant : des lignes courbes alternées entourant ce qui est sans doute une patte d'animal.

32   Cylindre-sceau
MR III A-B (14e-13e s. av. J.C.)
Chlorite. Arménoi, nome de Réthymne (tombe à chambre 89).
Haut. 0,015 m, diam. 0,010 m.
Réthymno, Musée archéologique.
Entier. Deux profondes lignes verticales parta-

gent la surface du cylindre en deux parties inégales au même décor : incision en diagonale encadrée en haut et en bas d'un rond au centre marqué d'un point.

33   Sceau
MR III A-B (14e-13e s. av. J.C.)
Christal de roche. Arménoi, nome de Réthymne (tombe à chambre 85).
Diam 0,0195-0,0210 m.
Réthymno, Musée archéologique.
Sceau lenticulaire, petites ébréchures sur les deux faces. Il est décoré de bandes entrecroisées, horizontales et verticales. Les intervalles ainsi délimités sont remplis par des zébrures.

34   Sceau
MR III A-B (14e-13e s. av. J.C.)
Cristal de roche. Arménoi, nome de Réthymne (tombe à chambre 108).
Diam. 0,015 m.
Réthymno, Musée archéologique.
Lenticulaire. Légèrment ébréché sur le pourtour. La face principale porte des paires de lignes verticales et horizontales qui s'entrecroisent. Le motif du filet est utilisé en remplissage.

35   Sceau
MR III A-B (14e-13e s. av. J.C.)
Christal de roche. Arménoi, nome de Réthymne (tombe à chambre 79).
Diam. 0,013 x 0,010 m.
Réthymno, Musée archéologique.
Entier, en forme d'amande. Trou selon l'axe vertical. Dessin linéaire simple, deux bandes en croix divisent le sceau en quatre triangles : deux portent des dessins, et les deux autres sont remplis de chevrons imbriqués.

36   Sceau
MR III A-B (14e-13e s. av. J.C.)
Chlorite. Arménoi, nome de Réthymne (tombe à chambre 115)
Diam. 0,017 m.
Réthymno, Musée archéologique.
Entier, lenticulaire. Une large bande incisée coupe la surface en diagonale. De son centre partent des lignes obliques qui forment des triangles.

37   Sceau
MR III A-B (14e-13e s. av. J.C.)
Chlorite. Arménoi, nome de Réthymne (tombe à chambre 138).

Diam. 0,019 m.
Réthymno, Musée archéologique.
Lenticulaire, petite ébréchure sur le pourtour. Trou selon l'axe horizontal. La surface du sceau est entièrement couverte par la représentation d'un oiseau de face. Il faut noter la coexistence d'éléments stylistiques minoens et mycéniens en parallèle dans la manière schématique de représenter la forme, et l'exactitude du dessin dans le rendu des détails (yeux, plumage). La ligne sous les pattes de l'oiseau représente sans doute le sol. Un "ménisque", un point en son centre, est utilisé comme motif complémentaire.

38   Sceau
MR III A-B (14e-13e s. av. J.C.)
Pierre verdâtre. Arménoi, nome de Réthymne (tombe à chambre 24).
Diam. 0,016. Réthymno, Musée archéologique.
Entier, lenticulaire. Il porte un des motifs minoens préférés, un taureau au galop. L'animal, aplati à cause de la forme de la pierre, tourne la tête en arrière si vigoureusement que ses cornes coupent son corps robuste. La tête d'un deuxième taureau, de face, est utilisée comme ornement complémentaire au-dessus du corps du premier.

39   Sceau
MR III A-B (14e-13e s. av. J.C.)
Ophite. Arménoi, nome de Rétyhmne (tombe à chambre 114).
Diam. 0,014 m.
Réthymno, Musée archéologique.
Entier, lenticulaire. Décor linéaire sur la face principale : motif de double losange, quatre points aux extrémités, un au centre.

40   Sceau
MR III A-B (14e-13e s. av. J.C.)
Cristal de roche. Arménoi, nome de Réthymne (tombe à chambre 123).
Diam. 0,013-0,012.
Réthymno, Musée archéologique.
Entier, lenticulaire. Trou suivant l'axe horizontal. Représente un arbre stylisé au tronc large, dont partent asymétriquement les branches et les feuilles figurées par des lignes; deux motifs en demi-lune se distinguent à droite de l'arbre.
La représation indépendante d'un arbre se rencontre par excellence dans la glyptique minoenne, en liaison immédiate avec la religion. Au contraire, elle est utilisée comme motif complémentaire dans la glyptique mycénienne.

41   Sceau
MR III A-B (14e-13e s. av. J.C.)
Cornaline. Arménoi, nome de Réthymne (tombe à chambre 115).
Long. cons. 0.015 m, larg. 0,014 m.
Réthymno, Musée archéologique.
Sûrement cylindre aplati. Il manque un morceau à l'une des extrémités. Représente une chèvre sauvage de profil, le corps robuste, grandes cornes hélicoïdales et barbiche. Un motif végétal, rameau aux feuilles lancéolées emplit l'espace vide devant l'animal.

42   Sceau
MR III A-B (14e-13e s. av. J.C.)
Chlorite. Arménoi, nome de Réthymne (tombe à chambre 83).
Long. 0,023 m., larg. 0,011 m, épaiss. 0,007 m.
Réthymno, Musée archéologique.
A quatre faces, légèrement convergentes à une extrémité. Trou parallèle à la longueur. Les quatre faces servaient de sceau : elles sont couvertes de points disposés parallélement, entourés de cercles ou de demi-cercles.

43   Sceau
MR III A-B (14e-13e s. av. J.C.)
Hématite. Arménoi Réthymnes (tombe à chambre 115).
Diam 0,016 m.
Réthymno, Musée archéologique.
Bel exemple de sceau lenticulaire intact. Trou selon l'axe vertical. La face principale porte la représentation d'un taureau au galop; sa tête est fortement tournée en arrière. Ce sceau se distingue par le rendu plein de détails des caractéristiques du taureau.

44   Cruche à deux anses
Transition Néolithique / MA I (début du 3e millénaire av. J.C.)
Argile. Elénès Amariou.
Haut. 0,156 m, diam. max. 0,158 m, diam. à la lèvre 0,138 m.
Réthymno, Musée archéologique.
Vase d'usage commun, restauré au plâtre. Panse conique, base plate, col large cylindrique, et deux anses verticales sur l'épaule.

45   Coupe
MA I (1re moitié du 3e millénaire av. J.C.)
Coupe à haut pied, restaurée, exemple représentatif du style du Pygros. La panse profonde, conique, porte une excroissance triangulaire perforée et repose sur un pied haut, creux. An-

neau en relief à l'articulation. Décor brillant, des lignes incisées parcourent le pied, remplies de peinture brune.
Ce style, dont le nom vient du site du nom d'Héraklio, est caractérisé par la forte survivance d'éléments subnéolithiques.

46 Skyphos
Transition Néolithique / MA I (début du 3e millénaire av. J.C.)
Argile. Elénès Amariou.
Haut. 0,114 m, diam à la lèvre 0.147 m.
Réthymno. Musée archéologique.
Recollé et restauré. Panse profonde, parois verticales, légèrement renflées, fond convexe. Quatre excroissances sur la partie convexe, dont deux sont perforées. La surface est soigneusement lissée et couverte d'un enduit brun noir. Le décor, de vernis, se borne à des groupes de trois lignes verticales parallèles, allant des excroissances à la lèvre.

47 Cuillère
Transition Néolithique / MA I (début du 3e millénaire av. J.C.)
Argile. Elénès Amariou.
Long. cons. 0.08 m.
Réthymno, Musée archéologique.
Petit ustensible de cuisine fait main, manche restauré. Ellipsoide, traces de feu.
Des exemples semblables à celui-ci viennent de Cnossos et de Mochlo.

48 Coupe
MA II B (2e moitié du 3e mill. av. J.C.)
Argile. Grotte de Platyvola.
Haut. 0,078 m, diam, lèvre 0,083 m. diam. base 0,048 m.
La Canée, Musée archéologique.
Coupe du style "vasiliki", recollée et restaurée. Vasque hémisphérique, pied bas conique. Des mouchetures de peinture brun rouge et brun noir couvrent tout le vase.
Ce décor, caractéristique du style "vassiliki", se rencontrait accompagné d'une cuisson délibérément inégale.

49 Bassine
MA I/II (milieu du 3e mill. av. J.C.)
Argile. Grotte de Platyvola.
Haut. 0,08 m, diam. à la lèvre 0,207 m.
La Canée, Musée archéologique.
Ustensile d'usage domestique, recollé d'après de nombreux fragments. Vasque large, une anse horizontale au milieu, base courbe à trois petites excroissances.

50 Cruche
MM I (début du 2e millénaire av. J.C.)
Argile. Apodolou Amariou.
Haut. 0,16 m, diam. max. 0,15 m.
Réthymno, Musée archéologique.
Vase recollé et restauré. Panse oviforme, base plate, anse cylindrique verticale et bec rostriforme. Le décor, limité à la zone de la panse et de l'épaule, se compose d'un motif de filet saillant, formé lorsque la terre était encore humide.
Ce décor particulier constitue une variante du style barbotine ware connue comme barnaikle ware.

51 Cruche
MM II (19e-18e. s. av. J.C.)
Argile. Monastiraki Amariou.
Haut. 0,30 m, diam. base 0,08 m.
Réthymno, Musée archéologique.
Cruche à bec rostriforme recollée, deux excroissances en bouton sur le col. Argile brun jaune, traces de feu et peinture noire, Ornée de gros points de couleur blanche presque effacée.

52 Cruche
MM II (19e-18e. s. av. J.C.)
Argile. Monastiraki Amariou.
Haut. 0,126 m, diam. à la lèvre 0,078 m, diam base 0,06 m.
Réthymno, Musée archéologique.
Cruche à bec ponté recollée, deux anses horizontales. Argile brun gris, peinture brun rouge.

53 Cruche
MM II (19e-18e. s. av. J.C.)
Argile. Monastiraki Amariou.
Haut 0,15 m, diam. base 0,072 m.
Réthymno, Musée archéologique.
Recollée, restaurée, traces de feu à la surface. Argile brun orange. Embouchure trilobée, une anse verticale.
Cette forme est appelée par les chercheurs "pot à lait".

54 Cruche
MM II (19e-18e. s. av. J.C.)
Argile Monastiraki Amariou.
Haut. 0,14 m, diam. base 0,04 m.
Réthymno, Musée archéologique.
Panse et bec restaurés. Argile brun gris; surface brute, traces de feu.

55 Cruche
MM II (19e-18e s. av. J.C.)
Argile. Monastiraki Amariou. Haut 0,09 m, diam base 0,049 m.
Réthymno, Musée archéologique.
Cruche à anse, légèrement restaurée. Argile orange clair; surface brute, quelques empreintes de feuilles.

56 Coupe
MM II (19e-18e s. av. J.C.)
Argile. Monastiraki Amariou.
Haut. 0,04 m, diam. à la lèvre 0,067 m.
Réthymno, Musée archéologique.
Coupe entière provenant d'un triple kernos, les deux autres coupes ont disparu. Argile brun rose, surface brute, où l'on remarque des empreintes de doigts et de feuilles.

57 Coupe
MM II (19e-18e s. av. J.C.)
Argile. Monastiraki Amariou.
Haut 0,05 m, diam à la lèvre 0,075 m, diam. base 0,032 m.
Réthymno, Musée archéologique.
Coupe carénée restaurée et recollée, faite d'une argile de bonne qualité. Une peinture noire effacée couvre l'intérieur et l'extérieur.
L'endroit de la trouvaille donne des éléments sur l'organisation administrative et les manifestations religieuses.

58 Coupe
MM II (19e-18e. s. av. J.C.)
Argile. Apodoulo Amariou.
Haut. 0,042 m, diam à la lèvre 0,065-0,069 m, diam. base 0,03 m.
Réthymno, Musée archéologique.
Petite coupe recollée, de fabrication grossière. Vasque conique et base plate.

59 Coupe
MM II (19e-18e. s. av. J.C.)
Argile. Apodoulo Amariou.
Haut 0,078 m, diam. à la lèvre 0,076-0,002, diam. base 0,04 m.
Réthymno, Musée archéologique.
Ustensile ménager recollé. Vasque profonde ellipsoide, bec sur la lèvre et deux protubérances en bouton diamétralement opposées. Le décor se limite à des chevrons brun rouge.

60 Kernos ("salière")
MM II (19e-18e s. av. J.C.)
Argile. Monastiraki Amariou.
Haut 0,026 m, diam. tot. 0,125 m.
Réthymno, Musée archéologique.
Vase recollé et restauré, en argile brun jaune. Il est fait de deux coupes coniques réunies d'un côté. à la surface brute, portant des traces de feu à l'intérieur.
Cette forme est connue sous le nom de "salière" dans la bibliographie.

61 Empreintes de sceau
MM II (19e-18e s. av. J.C.)
Argile. Monastriraki Amariou.
Long. 0,03-0,09 m, larg 0,038-0,12 m, épaisseur 0,014-0,03 m.
Réthymno, Musée archéologique.
Quatre empreintes de sceaux de forme irrégulière, en argile brune ou orange. Sur la face arrière est visible l'empreinte de la ficelle fermant l'objet scellé. Chaque face pricipale porte de 4 à 11 empreintes de sceau, surtout des motifs géométriques : des 8 ou des sigmoides et une croix aux branches recourbées entourés de motifs de remplissage.
La découverte de deux empreintes de sceaux d'archives dans la salle du même nom, et dans les magasins du groupe de bâtiments, nous font penser l'existense d'un système rigoureux d'organisation admistrative et de contrôle.

62 Peson
MM II (19e-18e s. av. J.C)
Argile. Monastiraki Amariou.
Long. 0,075 m, diam. du trou 0,01 m.
Réthymno, Musée archéologique.
Peson cylindrique d'argile brune impure. Trou selon d'axe vertical et traces de feu à la surface.

63 Couvercle à anse
MM II (19e-18e s. av. J.C.)
Argile. Monastiraki Amariou.
Haut. avec l'anse 0,06 m, diam. base 0,15 m.
Réthymno, Musée archéologique.
Recollé. Argile orange clair, peinture brun rose. Des traces d'un vernis brillant subsistent. De simples bandes ornent le couvercle et l'anse.

64 Théière miniature
MM II (19e-18e. s. av. J.C.)
Argile. Apodoulo Amariou.
Haut. 0,026 m, diam. max. 0,047 m, diam. à la lèvre 0,034 m.
Réthymno, Musée archéologique.
Petit vase restauré. Panse biconique, deux excroissances diamétralement opposées, base plate et bec surélevé cylindrique.
Des exemples de cette forme, que l'on considère comme des lampes, proviennent de Phaestos.

65 "Râpe"
MM II (19e-18e s. av. J.C.)
Argile. Monastiraki Amariou.
Haut. 0,075 m, long. max. 0,015 m.
Réthymno, Musée archéologique.
Flacon ayant deux anses horizontales sur la lèvre et à l'intérieur une protubéance portant des entailles. Un tiers du vase environ est conservé, ce qui nous donne une idée sûre de sa forme. Argile gris clair, traces de peinture noire à l'intérieur.
Remarquable exemple d'ustensile qui reste inchangé jusqu'à nos jours. Un objet analogue provient de l'ancien palais de Phaestos.

66 Pithos
MM II (19e-18e. s. av. J.C.)
Argile. Monastiraki Amariou.
haut 0,315 m, diam. à la lèvre
Réthymno, Musée archéologique.
Pithos à deux anses recollé, portant deux excroissances en bouton. Argile brun gris, peinture noire. Il est orné de bandes au bas de la panse et sur le col, et d'arcs pendants sur l'épaule.

67 Marmite à trois pieds
MM II (19e-18e s. av. J.C.)
Argile. Monastrikari Amariou.
Haut. 0, m, diam à la lèvre 0,0 m.
Réthymno, Musée archéologique.
Ustensile de cuisine recollé et restauré. Argile brun rouge; surface bute.

68 Vase en forme de pithos
MM II (19e-18e s. av. J.C.)
Argile. Monastiraki Amariou.
Haut. 0,18 m, diam. à la lèvre 0,12 m, diam. base 0,08 m,
Réthymno, Musée archéologique.
Petit vase sans anse, entier, en forme de pithos. Argile orange clair. Surface brute, empreintes de feuilles.

69 Amphore
MM II (19e-18e s. av. J.C.)
Argile. Monastiraki Amariou.
Haut. 0,33 m, diam. à la lèvre 0,7 m, diam. base 0,10 m.
Réthymno, Musée archéologique.
Entière. Argile brun jaune, une peinture brun noir la couvrant entièrement, dont des traces subsistent sur la lèvre et à l'intérieur du col.

70 Lampe
MM II (19e-18e s. av. J.C.)
Argile. Monastiraki Amariou.
Haut. cons. 0,08 m, diam. ext. 0,318 m.
Recollé et restauré. Le pied manque. Argile brun jaune, surface enduite de vernis brillant, fortes traces de feu dans la cavité ad'hoc.

71 Pithos
MM II (19e-18e s. av. J.C.)
Argile. Monastiraki Amariou.
Haut. 0,44 m, diam. à la lèvre 0,25 m, diam. base 0,135 m.
Réthymno, Musée archéologique.
Pithos recollé, à bec et quatre anses (deux horizontales et deux verticales). Argile brun jaune, traces de feu, surface brute.

72 Pithos
MM II (19e-18e s. av. J.C.)
Argile Monastiraki Amariou.
Haut. 0,69 m, diam. max. 0,50 m, diam. à la lèvre 0,39 m.
Réthymno, Musée archéologique.
Recollé de multiples fragments. Argile brun jaune, peinture brune. Panse ovoïde, quatre anses verticales sur le col. Décoré de chevrons, à l'intérieur comme à l'extérieur.

73 Lampe
MR I (16e s. av. J.C.)
Ophite. Provenance inconnue.
Haut. 0,045 m, diam. max. 0,12 m.
Réthymno, Musée archéologique.
Lampe en pierre à l'anse incomplète. Petites ébréchures sur les bords. Base plate, haute, corps conique. La cavité qui contenait l'huile est ovoïde, anse horizontale dans le prolongement, et bec cannelé.
Ce type, imitation des modèles en argile du MMM, se rencontre du MM I MR I.

74 Cruche
MR I B (fin du 16e s. av. J.C.)
Argile. La Canée.
Haut. 0,137 m, diam. à la lèvre 0,117-0,122 m, diam. base 0,051 m.

La Canée, Musée archéologique.
Vase recollé, de fabrication négligée. Panse conique, base discoïde, col large et bas, bec demi-cylindrique, anse verticale dont l'extrémité rappelle les modèles métalliques. Des bandes parcourent la panse et le col; des spirales continues à tige hélicoïdale ornent l'épaule.

75 Coupe à bec
MR I B (fin du 16e s. av. J.C.)
Argile. Kastelli Chanion.
Haut. 0,082 m, diam. max. 0,098 m.
La Canée, Musée archéologique.
Coupe entière, légèrement écaillée. Panse en sphère aplatie, col large et bec cylindrique; anse verticale et deux protubérances allongées sur l'épaule. La zone du décor principal, de couleur brun rose, comprend des spirales continues et pendantes.

76 Hydrie
MR II (15e s. av. J.C.)
Bronze. Kouti, nome de Réthymne.
Haut 0,48 m, diam à la lèvre 0,15, diam. base 0,163 m.
Réthymno, Musée archéologique.
Hydrie abîmée à l'épaule. Panse piriforme, faites de trois lames horizontales rénuies par des rivets. Deux anses : une verticale, du bord à l'épaule, une horizontale sur la moitié inférieure de la panse. Base plate, discoïde:
Les hydries de bronze apparaissent dans le monde crétomycénien durant la deuxième moitié du 16e. s. av. J.C.

77 Cruche
MR III a (14e s. av. J.C.)
Argile. Provenance inconnue.
Haut 0,28 m, diam. max. 0,185 m.
Réthymno, Musée archéologique.
Vase élancé, bonne fabrication et bon état de conservation; la forme imite celle des récipients métalliques. Panse conique-piriforme, base presque discoïde, col tubulaire, bec rostriforme et anse verticale en ruban, portant des traces de compression là où elle est rattachée à l'épaule.
Le décor, de peinture orange vif, se limite à de simples bandes qui parcourent la surface du vase, et une série de sigmoïdes sur l'épaule.

78 Petite cruche à deux anses
MR III A (14e s. av. J.C.)
Argile. Arménoi, nome de Réthymne (tombe à chambre 95).
Haut. 0,133 m, diam. à la lèvre 0,09 m, diam. base 0,042 m.
Réthymno, Musée archéologique.
Entier, au fond haut, panse piriforme, base discoïde, col large et deux anses en ruban. Le décor principal de peintures différentes, se borne à des arcs concentriques dans la zone de l'épaule.
Les petites cruches de ce type sont très largement répandues dans la Méditerranée orientale aux 14e et 13e s. av. J.C.

79 Vase en forme d'alabastre
MR III A (14e s. av. J.C.)
Argile. Arménoi Réthymnes (tombe à chambre 35).
Haut. 0,15 m, diam. max. 0,17 m.
Réthymno, Musée archéologique.
Alabastre abîmé, à la surface endommagée. Panse sphérique aplatie, col cylindrique portant un anneau en relief à l'articulation et lèvre plate. Deux anses courbes et deux excroissances en bouton sur l'épaule. Des groupes de bandes de couleur brune parcourent la panse. L'épaule est ornée d'une zone de coquillages stylisés. Des points, des triangles en série et des arcs opposés sont les motifs de remplissage.

80 Cruche à bec
MR III A (14e s. av. J.C.)
Argile. Arménoi Réthymnes (tombe à chambre 89).
Haut. 0,064 m, diam. max. 0.067 m.
Réthymno, Musée archéologique.
Cruche entière monochrome. Panse en sphère, base presque en anneau, bec rostriforme et anse en ruban.

81 Alabastre à trois anses
MR III A (14e s. av. J.C.)
Argile. Arménoi, nome de Réthymne (tombe à chambre 78).
Haut. 0,153 m, diam à la lèvre 0,088 m, diam. base 0,112 m.
Réthymno, Musée archéologique.
Vase entier, détérioré par endroits. Panse cylindrique, bas plate, col vertical, large anneau et trois anses en arc.
Des fleurs de papyrus, de couleur marron, sont disposées en ligne sur la panse. Entre les anses, des demi-cercles.

82 Stamnisque à deux anses
MR III A1 (début du 14e s. av. J.C.)
Argile. Arménoi Réthymnis (tombe à chambre 94).
Haut 0,103 m, diam. max. 0,11 m, diam. à la lèvre 0,082 m.
Réthymno, Musée archéologique.
Petit vase bien conservé. Panses sphérico-conique, base plate et col large. L'aspect de poli "métallique" de la peinture noire qui le recouvre est ipressionnant.

83 Alabastre
MR III A (14e s. av. J.C.)
Argile. Arménoi, nome de Réthymne (tombe à chambre 67).
Haut 0,10 m, diam à la lèvre 0,093 m, diam base 0,15 m.
Réthymno, Musée archéologique.
Entier, une petite partie de la lèvre est refaite, parois droites, trois anses courbes. Le principal décor est sur l'épaule du vase, où l'on voit une zone de feuilles stylisées. Les alabatres piriformes et cylindriques, que l'on considère comme minoens, avec une probable lointaine origine égyptienne, abondent au MR III, utilisés comme vases à parfum.

84 Kylix
MR III A2/B (fin du 14e s. av. J.C.)
Argile. Stavroménos, nome de Réthymne.
Haut. (avec les anses) 0,020 m, diam. à la lèvre 0,174 m, diam. base 0,94 m.
Réthymno, Musée archéologique.
Kylix recollée au pied haut, vasque conique profonde, base large convexe, deux anses verticales surélevées. Entre les anses sont dessinées des fleurs minoennes bifides. Bandes parallèles ornant le corps et la base, intérieur entièrement peint.

85 Vase à étrier
MR III A2 (fin du 14e s. av. J.C.)
Argile. Arménoi Réthymnes (tombe à chambre 20).
Haut. 0,17 m, diam. max. 0,163 m, diam. base 0,062 m.
Réthymno, Musée archéologique.
Vase élancé, bien conservé. Panse piriforme, base en anneau, deux anses en ruban. La principale zone décorée est sur l'épaule, composée de deux demi-cercles : a) triangles élaborés de chaque côté du bec b) une rangée de fleurs "minoennes" bifides.

86 Tasse
MR III A2/b1 (fin du 14e s. av. J.C.)
Argile. Tombe à chambre d'Aghii Apostoli, nome de Amari
Haut. 0,078 m, diam. à la lèvre 0,105-0,115 m, diam. base 0,057 m.
Réthymno, Musée archéologique.
Tasse entièrement peinte, très bien conservée. On doit noter la coexistence d'éléments de deux périodes, qui la placent dans une phase de transition : l'anse en ruban, la base conique et la ligne anguleuse de la vasque sont des éléments précoces, au contraire de la profondeur de la vasque et de la lévre verticale.

87 Skyphos bas
MR III B (13e s. av. J.C.)
Argile. Aghii Apostoli, nome de Amari (tombe à chambre).
Haut. 0,055 m, diam. à la lèvre 0,164 m, diam. base 0,045 m.
Réthymno, Musée archéologique.
Vase entier, entièrement peint, base plate, panse conique, deux anses horizontales. Cette forme, d'usage courant, se trouve souvent dans les habitations et dans les tombes depuis la période MR III A.

88 Cruche à bec
MR III B (13e s. av. J.C.)
Argile. Arménoi Réthymnes (tombe à chambre 140).
Haut. 0,64 m, diam. max 0,067 m.
Réthymno, Musée archéologique.
Charmant vase, légèrement restauré. Panse en sphère aplatie, petite base plate, bec dressé demi-cylindirque, anse verticale. Le décor principal s'étend sur l'épaule, c'est un motif de tentacules.

89 Cruche à bec
MR III A (14e s. av. J.C.)
Argile. Arménoi Réthymnes (tombe à chambre 98).
Haut. 0,064 m, diam. max. 0,067 m.
Rétyhmno, Musée archéologique.
Vase monochrome délicat, en bon état de conservation. Panse en sphère aplatie, col cylindrique, bec rostriforme et anse verticale.

90 Coupe
MR III A-B (14e-13e. s. av. J.C.)
Argile. Aghii Apostoli, nome de Amari (tombe à chambre).
Haut. 0,06 m, diam. à la lèvre 0,10 m, diam. base 0,037 m.
Réthymno, Musée archéologique.
Vase très bien conservé, à base plate, vasque hémisphérique et anse verticale. Le décor, noir brillant, se dèveloppe sur le haut de la vasque, et se borne à des tiges en spirale pendant de la lèvre. Intérieur entièrement peint.

91 Kylix à pied bas
MR III B (13e s. av. J.C.)
Argile. La Canée (tombe à chambre 1).
Haut. 0,11 m, diam à la lèvre 0,125 m, diam. base 0,065 m.
La Canée, Musée archéologique.
Bel exemple de la production de l'atelier de la Canée (Kydonia). Recollée et restaurée. Panse conique, légèrement anguleuse, deux anses verticales; elle se tient sur un pied conique bas à base large.
Le décor principal de peinture orange est limité à la zone des anses : deux fleurs de papyrus isolées sur chaque face. Une bande en spirale orne le fond.

92 Vase à étrier
MR III B (13e s. av. J.C.)
Argile. Arménoi Réthymnes (tombe à chambre 139).
Haut. 0,12 m, diam. max. 0,156 m.
Réthymno, Musée archéologique.
Entier, le bec est restauré. Panse conique, base en anneau, bec dressé. Le décor principal se trouve sur l'épaule, partagé en deux demi-cercles: a) des têtes d'oisseau en ligne, b) des triangles élaborés.
La représentation d'oiseaux, motif aimé des minoens, apparaît dans l'art au MM III, sur des fresques.

93 Vase á trois pieds
MR III B (13e s. av. J.C.)
Argile. Arménoi Réthymnes (tombe à chambre 148).
Haut. 0,204 m, diam. max. 0,192 m, diam. à la lèvre 0,082 m.
Réthymno, Musée archéologique.
Entier, surface endommagée. Panse sphérique, base plate à trois pieds, quatre anses sur l'épaule (deux verticales et deux courbes), col cylindrique large. Le décor principal, de peinture brun rouge, se compose a) de spirales simples ou doubles entre les anses b) de tiges spiroidales alternées au bas de la panse.

94 Amphorisque à trois anses.
MR III A2 (fin du 14e s. av. J.C.)
Argile. Arménoi, nome de Réthymne (tombe à chambre 67).
Haut. 0,16 m, diam. mx. 0,145 m, diam. à la lèvre 0,097.
Réthyno, Musée archéologique.
Entier, petites ébréchures. Panse piriforme, col cylindrique, base en anneau, anses courbes. Le principal décor, de peintures brun rose à moitié effacée, se trouve sur l'épaule. Ce sont des métopes où des lignes en arc sont disposées de façon opposée.

95 Gobelet
MR III A2/B (fin du 14e s. av. J.C.)
Argile. Aghii Apostoli, nome de Amari (tombe à chambre).
Haut. 0,04 m, diam. à la lèvre 0,106 m.
Réthymno, Musée archéologique.
Gobelet conique sans anse, entier, sans décor. On le rencontre en Crète depuis le MA, toujours, d'un caractére utilitaire.

96 Cruche
MR III B (début du 13e s. av. J.C.)
Argile. Arménoi Réthymnes (tombe à chambre 100).
Haut. 0,055 m, diam. max. 0,059 m.
Réthymno, Musée archéologique.
Charmant petit vase; panse en sphère aplatie, base en anneau, embouchure large, et anse verticale. La zone de l'épaule est décorée d'un motif de tentacule coupé, de couleur brun noir. C'était soit un jouet d'enfant, soit un vase à parfum.

97 Cratère amphoroide
MR III B (13e s. av. J.C.)
Réthymno (tombe à chambre).
Haut. 0,45 m, diam. à la lèvre 0,38 m, diam. max. 0,34 m.
Réthymnom, Musée archéologique.
Cratère impressionnant, recollé à la lèvre. Panse piriforme, base conique, col haut cylindrique à lèvre. Panse piriforme, base conique, col haut cylindrque à lèvre plate, deux anses verticales. Le décor, de peinture marron orgnge, se déploie sur la panse du vase et consiste, sur chaque face, en un poulpe stylisé aux tentacules serpentiformes.
Ce vase constitue un exemple par excellence de l'art minoen, puisque la forme aussi bien que le motif décoratif ont été concus en Crète, pour être ensuite répandus dans le monde égéen.

98 Couteau
MR III A-B (14e-13e s. av. J.C.)
Bronze. Arménoi, nome de Réthymne (tombe à chambre 15).
Long. 0,18 m, larg. max. 0,017 m
Réthymo, Musée archéologique.
Couteau à un seul tranchant, poignée d'un seul tenant ébréchée. Lame triangulaire allongée, au dos droit et à la pointe arrondie; talon comportant deux rivets pour fixer le manche en bois dont une partie est conservée. Un fragment de tissu, dont devait être entouré le couteau, est conservé sur une face de la lame.

99 Couteau
MR III A-B (14e-13e s. av. J.C.)
Bronze. Arménoi, nome de Réthymne (tombe à chambre 25).
Long. 0,195 m.
Réthymno, Musée archéologique.
Couteau entier à un seul tranchant. Lame triangulaire au dos droit, talon carré où l'on voit deux trous et un rivet servant à fixer le manche de matière organique.
Il s'agit d'un type de couteau commun, largement répandu à l'HR. Il se propage en Crète, depuis la Grèce continentale, vers le milieu du 14e. s. av. J.C. (MR III).

100 Couteau
MR III A-B (14e-13e s. av. J.C.)
Bronze. Arménoi, nome de Réthymne (tombe à chambre 95).
Long. 0,128 m.
Réthymno, Musée archéologique.
Lame en forme de feuille à double tranchant, la pointe et la partie formant le manche sont ébréchées. Deux rivets pour la fixation du manche en bois.
L'usage de ces outils pose un problème de base aux chercheurs, qui les considèrent finalement comme un type précoce de rasoir.

101 Couteau
MR III A-B (14e-13e s. av. J.C.)
Bronze. Arménoi, nome de Réthymne (tombe à chambre 71).
Long 0,142 m, larg. max. 0,014 m.
Réthymno, Musée archéologique.
Petit couteau à un seul tranchant, la partie formant le manche est détérioré. Les deux rivets servant à fixer le manche en bois sont conservés. La lame est triangulaire, le dos droit, et la pointe est légèrement arrondie.

102 Couteau à hacher
MR III A-B (14e-13e s. av. J.C.)
Bronze. Arménoi, nome de Réhymne (tombe à chambre 55).
Long 0,215 m, larg. max. 0,07 m.
Réthymno, Musée archéologique.
Outil entier, tranchant un peu ébréché. Lame trapézoidale au dos concave. Rivet et deux trous pour fixer le manche en bois. Trois incisions parallèles parcourent le dos de la lame. Ce type d'outil est utilisé durant tout le MR III. Il disparaît entièrement par la suite (voir n. du cat.)

103 Rasoir
MR III A-B (14e-13e s. av. J.C.)
Bronze. Arménoi, nome de Réthymne (tombe à chambre 127).
Long. 0,155 m, larg. max. 0,035 m.
Réthymno, Musée archéologique.
Entier, surface oxydée. Lame presque en trapèze au dos légèrement concave et au talon courbe où sont conservés deux rivets pour la fixation du manche en bois.
L'usage des instruments dece genre, leurs variantes, posent un problème de base aux chercheurs (cf. n° 100 du cat.). La petite taille de cet exemple précis, pourtant, nous conduit à le considérer comme un ustensile de toilette.

104 Hache
MR III Bronze. Provenance inconnue.
Long. 0,185m, larg. max. 0,063 m.
Réthymno, Musée archéologique.
Double hache aux tranchants ébréchés, trou rond pour l'emmanchement.
Ce type d'instrument a été inventé et façonné en Egée à l'âge du Bronze. Hormis son caractère utilitaire, c'est le symbole sacré minoen par excellence. On distingue deux types, selon la forme du trou d'emmanchement, ovale ou rond.

105 Scie
MR III A-B (14e-13e s. av. J.C.)
Bronze. Arménoi, nome de Réthymne (tombe à chambre 115).
Long. 0,42, larg. max. 0,055 m.
Réthymno, Musée archéologique.
Outil de charpentier entier. Lame allongée, triangulaire, au dos droit. Trois trous pour la fixation du manche en bois, tranchant à dents. Talon carré et bout arrondi.
Ce type de scie est de provenance crétoise évidente; on rencontre deux variantes, avec ou sans trous. Des exemples ont été trouvés aussi en Grèce continentale.

106 Pointe de lance
MR III A-B (14e-13e s. av. J.C.)
Bronze. Arménoi, nome de Réthymne (tombe à chambre 35).
Long. 0.255 m.
Réthymno, Musée archéologique.
Entière, en forme de flamme. La douille, de section octogonale, porte deux trous pour fixer la hampe en bois dont des fragments sont conservés à l'intérieur. Une forte nervure centrale parcourt la pointe.

107 Pointe de lance
MR III A-B (14e-13e s. av. J.C.)
Bronze. Arménoi, nome de Réthymne (tombe à chambre 43).
Long. 0,283 m.
Réthymno, Musée archéologique.
Il manque un morceau de la douille. Un anneau plat de renforcement a été forgé près de l'ouverture. Deux trous servent à la fixation de la hampe de bois. Une large nervure parcourt la pointe en forme de flamme.

108 Epée courte
MR III A-B (14e-13e s. av. J.C.)
Bronze. Arménoi, nome de Réthymne (tombe à chambre 35).
Long. 0,375 m, larg. des épaules 0,062 m.
Réthymno, Musée archéologique.
Epée en deux morceaux (recollée). Manche dans le prolongement en forme de T, au pommeau en croissant, bordure jusqu'au départ de la lame; cinq rivets pour fixer le manche en matière organique. Les épaules sont arrondies, et la lame plate, linguiforme. La majorité des exemples de ce type est datée de la première moitié du 14e. s. av. J.C.

109 Couteau
MR III A-B (14e.-13e. s. av. J.C.)
Bronze. Arménoi, nome de Réthymne (tombe à chambre 115)
Larg. 0,345 m.
Réthymno, Musée archéologique.
Couteau entier à un tranchant. Manche dans le prolongement, en T, au pommeau en croissant, quatre rivets et bordure continue servant à fixer le manche en bois, en partie conservé. Lame triangulaire au dos droit et à la pointe arrondie. Deux incisions parallèles parcourent la lame près du dos, sur les deux faces. Le manche à bordure apparaît à la fin du MR II, et caractérise les armes de la dernière phase de l'âge du Bronze récent.

110 Lingot
MR II (16e-15e s. av. J.C.)
Bronze. Tylissos.
Long. 0,345 m, larg. 0,25 m, épaisseur 0,06 m.
Héraklio, Musée archéologique.
De forme rectangulaire, aux côtés légèrement bombés. Sur une face et près des coins, un renflement irrégulier; une incision en X est conservée à l'un des angles.
Le lingot a constitué, selon toute probabilité, la forme habituelle du transport du bronze pur, comme matière première, puis un instrument stable des transactions commerciales. Nombre d'entre eux viennent de sites crétois, quelques-uns seulement ont été trouvés à Mycènes.

111 Vase à étrier.
MR III B 13e s. av. J.C.
Argile. Arménoi Réthymnes (tombe à chambre 8).
Haut. 0,132 m, diam. max. 0,11 m, diam. base 0,047 m.
Réthymno, Musée archéologique.
Bel exemple de l'atelier de La Canée (Kydonia) (voir n. du cat.). On remarque la finesse de sa fabrication et de son décor. La panse est sphérique, la base discoïde. Trois rosaces à quatre lobes, portant des points entre les pétales, et une tige ondulée, couvrent la panse du vase.

112 Amphore à étrier
MR III B1 (début du 13e s. av. J.C.)
Argile. Arménoi Réthymnes (tombe à chambre 132).
Haut. 0,122 m, diam. max. 0,138 m.
Réthymno, Musée archéologique.
Vase fait avec soin, représentatif de l'atelier de La Canée (Kydonia). Panse conique, base en anneau. Des bandes de même épaisseur, de peinture noire brillante, entourent la panse; des fleurs minoennes bifides décorent la zone de l'épaule. La découverte de l'amphore dans la nécropole d'Arménoi, en liaison avec son utilisation pour transporter des liquides précieux, plaide en faveur d'un commerce d'exportation établi par l'atelier de Kydonia.

113 Vase à étrier
MR III A (14e s. av. J.C.)
Argile. Arménoi Réthymnes, (tombe à chambre 79).
Haut. 0,20 m, diam. max. 0,154 m.
Réthymno, Musée archéologique.
Vase élancé, à la surface endommagée. Corps piriforme, haute base conique. Un bivalve stylisé, de couleur brun rose, couvre, la panse du vase. Des triangles opposés élaborés décorent l'épaule.

114 Vase à étrier
MR III B (14 s. av. J.C.)
Argile. Arménoi Réthymnes, (tombe à chambre 143).
Haut 0,077 m, diam max. 0.123 m, diam base 0,045 m.
Réthymno, Musée archéologique.
Petite amphore en bon état de conservation. Panse robuste conique, base en anneau. L'épaule est ornée de a) deux "fleurs minoennes" bifides de chaque côté de la véritable embouchure, et d'une troisième, à la tige hèlicoïdale, sur l'autre moitié; b) une chaine de losanges portant un point au centre l'entoure, encadrée de lignes ondulées.

115 Askos
MR III A2/B (fin du 14e s. av. J.C.)
Argile. Arménoi, nome de Réthymne (tombe à chambre 108).
Haut. 0,08 m, diam. max. 0,095 m.
Réthymno, Musée archéologique.
Base recollée, restaurée avec du plâtre. Panse en sphère aplatie, anses courbes et embouchure cylindrique verticale. Le décor, brun orangé, se borne à des bandes parallèles sur la panse et des demi-cercles concentriques sur l'épaule. Ce vase est un exemple représentatif de l'atelier de céramique post-palatial de La Canée (nome de Kydonia). La découverte de ces productions sur des sites de Crète, de Grèce continentale et de Chypre, plaide pour l'importance du commerce d'exportation de cette région, à l'époque crétomycénienne.

116 Kylix
MR II (2e moité du 15e s. av. J.C.)
Argile. Cnossos, Maison inexplorée.
Haut. 0,096 m, diam à la lèvre 0,111 m, diam. base 0,053 m.
Héraklio, Musée archéologique.
Petite kylix de style éphyréen (voir n. du cat. 16). recollée et restaurée. Panse hémisphérique, lèvre coupèe en oblique, pied bas cylindrique, base large circulaire, deux anses en ruban. Une croix portant des chevrons imbriqués entre les branches orne chaque face. Intérieur entièrement peint.
La forme et le décor suivent fidèlement les modèles mycéniens.

117 Lécythe en forme d'alabastre
MR III A1 (début du 14e s. av. J.C.)
Argile. Arménoi, nome de Réthymne (tombe à chambre 206).
Haut. 0,123, diam. max. 0,15 m, diam. à la lèvre 0,061 m.
Réthymno, Musée archéologique.
Vase sans anse entier, petites ébréchures. Panse sphéricoconique, base plate et lèvre évasée. Un décor de mouchetures de peinture marron, appliqué sans doute avec l'extrémité du pinceau, couvre toute la surface entérieure du vase.
Ce motif, dont en pense qu'il imite l'oeuf d'autruche, ou selon d'autres un décor de fresque, apparaît en Crète durant le MR IB.

118 Amphorisque à trois anses
MR III A 2 (2e moitié du 14e s. av. J.C.)
Argile. Arménoi Réthymnes (tombe à chambre 198),
Haut. 0,174 m, diam. max. 0,11 m.
Réthymno, Musée archéologique.
Bel exemple d'amphorisque mycénien importé, entier, légèrement abîmé. Panse conicopiriforme, base en anneau, col large cylindrique, trois anses courbes sur l'épaule. Des bandes d'un brun brillant parcourent la panse tandis que des groupes de lignes verticales ornent la zone des anses.

119 "Calice"
MM III/ MR I (milieu du 16e s. av. J.C.)
Ophite. La Canée.
Haut. 0,097 m, diam. max. 0,155 m.
La Canée, Musée archéologique.
Vase restauré en pierre gris blanc. Base plate et vasque conique, cylindrique à l'intérieur. Six feuilles en relief disposées verticalement, portant chacune une double nervure, décorent l'extérieur.
Un grand nombre de vases de ce type sont connus dans toute la Crète. Leur usage est difficile à définir. Selon toute probabilité toutefois, certains servaient à conserver des fards ou des parfums.

120 Amphore à étrier
MR III B (13e s. av. J.C.)
Argile. Angèliana Myloptomaou (tombe à chambre).
Haut. 0,32 m, diam. max. 0,23 m.
Réthymno, Musée archéologique.
Grande amphore de fabrication grossière, bien conservée. Panse sphéico-ovoide, pied conique, base plate. Une peinture irrégulière, du

brun au rouge, couvre toute la surface. Le décor, de peinture blanche effacée, est fait d'un bande serpentiforme sur la panse, et de lignes ondulées parallèles sur l'épaule.
Les amphores de ce type étaient utilisées dans le commerce d'exportation, pour le transport du vin ou d'huiles parfumées.

121   Statuette de boeuf
MM II (19e-18e s. av. J.C.)
Argile. Vrysina Réthymnes, Iéro, Koryphes.
Haut. cons. 0,145 m, long. max. 0,215 m.
Réthymno, Musée archéologique.
Statuette recollées. Corps massif, la face inférieure porte un creux; pattes cylindriques, tête triangulaire et queue repliée. La stylisation de certains détails morphologiques est intéressante : des trous peu profonds et des entailles expriment les caractéristiques de la tête, des sabots et du pompon de la queue.

122   Statuette de boeuf
MM II (19e-18e s. av. J.C.)
Argile. Vrysina Réthymnes, Iéro Koryphes.
Haut. cons. 0,08 m, long. max. 0,14 m.
Réthymno, Musée archéologique.
Statuette zoomorphe incomplète, traces de peinture brun rouge. Corps cylindrique massif, se tenant sur quatre pattes. Caractéristiques de la tête esquissées. Les organes génitaux sont clairement représentés.

123   Statuette de boeuf
MM II (19e-18e s. av. J.C.)
Argile. Vrysina Réthymnes, Iéro Koryphes.
Haut. 0,12 m, long. 0,18 m.
Réthymno, Musée archéologique.
Statuette zoomorphe recollée, traces de peinture brune. Le corps cylindrique, allongé, repose sur quatre pattes coniques. Les caractéristiques de la tête, triangulaire, sont exprimées par des trous et des entailles. Le rendu des oreilles et des cornes est plastique. La queue est repliée sur le dos de l'animal.

124   Statuette d'oiseau
MM II (19e-18e s. av. J.C.)
Argile. Vrysina Réthymnes. Iéro Koryphes.
Haut. 0,028 m, long 0,07 m.
Réthymno, Musée archéologique.
Statuette massive faite à la main, écaillée. Elle représente un oiseau au corps mince et aux ailes étroites et allongées. Le cou, dressé, porte la petite tête au bec ouvert, deux trous figurent les yeux.

L'oiseau, motif aimé de l'iconographie minoenne, était souvent un objet religieux (il était dédié à une divinité), utile (jouet, ou décoratif).

125   Statuette de femme
MM II (19e-18e s. av. J.C.)
Argikle. Vrysina Réthymnes, Iéro Koryphes.
Haut. cons. 0,094 m.
Réthymno, Musée archéologique.
Représentation d'une femme debout, conservée jusqu'à la taille. Elle est nue, les bras pliés, croisés sur le tronc. Des protubérances coniques figurent les seins, et un sillon vertical sur la tête, la morphologie du dos alors que le rendu des traits du visage est stylisé. Il faut remarquer le collier de disques suspendus figurant des perles.

126   Statuette de femme
MM II (19e-18e s. av. J.C.)
Argile. Vrysina Réthymnes, Iéros Koryphes.
Haut. 0,09 m.
Réthymno, Musée archéologique.
Statuette faite à la main, incomplète. C'est une forme féminine en position frontale. Elle porte un polos sur la tête et une ceinture. Les yeux. les oreilles et la poitrine sont rendus par des excroissances, les narines et la bouche par des entailles.

127   Statuette de femme
MM II (19e-18e s. av. J.C.)
Argile. Vrysina Réthymno, Musée archéologique.
Statuette faite à la main, de fabrication tout à fait négligente. Forme féminine représentée nue jusqu'à la taille, la partie inférieure, qui portait un vêtement, manque. Le bras conservé est plaqué sur le tronc. La poitrine est représentée par des protubérances coniques. Les traits du visage sont esquissés, un polos orne la tête.

128   Statuette de femme
MM II (19e-18e s. av. J.C.)
Argile. Vrysina Réthmnes, Iéro Koryphes.
Haut. cons. 0,10 m.
Réthymno, Musée archéologique.
Statuette recollée, conservée jusqu'à la taille. Forme féminine droite, nue, au corps large, deux protubérances coniques forment la poitrine. La tête est levée, nez triangulaire, yeux ronds, oreilles "plastiques" et polos singulier en spirale.

129   Statuette de femme
MM II (19e-18e s. av. J.C.)
Argile. Vrysina Réthymnes, Iéro Koryphes.
Haut. cons. 0,098 m.
Réthymno, Musée archéologique.
Statuette fragmentée, très abîmée. Corps nu allongé, rendu "plastique" de la poitrine. Il manque le vêtement descendant jusqu'aux pieds et les bras, les mains sont collées au tronc. Polos bas sur la tête, les traits du visage sont esquissés.

130   Statuette d'homme
MM II (19e-18e s. av. J.C.)
Argile. Vrysina Réthymnes, Iéro Koryphes.
Haut. cons. 0,11 m.
Réthymno, Musée archéologique.
Figure masculine debout, entièrement peinte. Elle est nue, sur une base carrée. La tête est levée, les bras repliés sur le corps. Les traits du visage et le sexe sont esquissés.
Le position des bras sur la poitrine apparaît au MA, sur des statuettes indentifiées comme des adorateurs.

131   Statuette d'homme
MM II (18e-19e s. av. J.C.)
Argile. Vrysina Réthymnes, Iéro Koryphes.
Haut. 0,14 m.
Réthymno, Musée archéologique.
Statuette en position frontale, fragmentée. L'homme est nu, des protubérances rondes ou allongées figurent les yeux, le nez et le sexe. La chevelure est représentée par des lignes obliques et des entrelacs.

132   Statuette de femme
MM II (19e-18e s. av. J.C.)
Argile. Vrysina Réthymnes, Iéro Koryphes.
Haut. cons 0,11 m.
Réthymno, Musée archéologique.
Figure féminine en position frontale, traces de peinture noire sur toute la surface. Elle est nue jusqu'à la taille, un vêtement descendant jusqu'aux pieds couvrait le bas du corps. Les mains sont sur la poitrine, appuyant sans doute sur les seins, une posture connue d'après un rhyton-statuette chypriote. Un polos presque discoide orne la tête, grossièrement rendu.

133   Têtes de statuettes d'homme
MM II (19e-18e s. av. J.C.)
Argile. Vrysina Réthymnes, Iéro Koryphes.
Haut. 0,033-0,045 m.
Réthymno, Musée archéologique.

Deux têtes de statuettes, portant des excroissances "discoides" pour figurer les yeux, et une autre allongée pour le nez. Il faut noter la présence de trous sur les oreilles, esquissées. La chevelure est représentée par une zone d'entailles obliques et d'entrelacs.

134 Statuette d'homme
MM II (19e-18e s. av. J.C.)
Argile. Vrysina Réthymnes, Iéro Koryphes.
Haut. cons. 0,102 m.
Réthymno, Musée archéologique.
Statuette faite à la main. Yeux "discoides", bouche ouverte, nez allongé, oreilles "plastiques" et chevelure longue nattée. Les mains sont contre la poitrine. Une ceinture minoenne couvre les reins, un poignard y est glissé.
Une statuette de guerrier semblable est connue, provenant, du Iéro Koryphes de Petsopha.

135 Effigie de table à offrande
MM II (19e-18e s. av. J.C.)
Ophite. Vrysina Réthymnes, Iéro Koryphes.
Haut 0,060 m, long. cons. 0,07 m.
Réthymno, Musée archéologique.
Table à offrande carrée, en pierre grise, dont la moitié est conservée. Sur le poutour de la face supérieure sont gravés des signes en linéaire A. Des écrits analogues en linéaire A, sur d'autres instruments sacrés en pierre, sont interprétés comme des noms de la divinité féminine ou des dédicaces.

136 Petite bassine funéraire
MM III (17e-16e s. av. J.C.)
Argile. Grotte du Mameluk, Périvolia.
Haut. 0,08 m, diam à la lèvre, 0,20 m.
La Canée, Musée archéologique.
Vase recollé, panse conique évasée et base plate. Sept minuscules imitations de coupes coniques se recouvrant les unes les autres sont appliquées à l'intérieur, sous la lèvre.
Ces rajouts caractérisent cet objet comme un kernos, vase funéraire où l'on mettait des fruits en offrande.

137 Hache
MR I (début du 15e s. av. J.C.)
Bronze. Mallia,
Maison E. Long. 0,19 m., larg. max. 0,067 m.
Héraklio, Musée archéologique.
Double hache entière, tranchants convexes et trou d'emmanchement ovale. On distingue sur les côtés étroits les rainures laissées par le moule.

Cette variante du type (voir n. 104 du cat.) au trou d'emmanchement ovale, dominait dans le monds helladique, et on la considère comme mycènienne.

138 Bassine
MR III B (13e s. av. J.C.)
Argile. Arménoi, nome de Réthymne (tombe à chambre 24.)
Haut. (avec l'anse) 0,13 m, diam à la lèvre 0,16 m, diam. base 0,09 m.
Réthymno, Musée archéologique.
Vase évasé, bien conservé. Vasque profonde conique et base plate. Anse double et s'élargissant en entonnoir, lèvre dans le prolongement. Des bandes parallèles de même largeur couvrent la vasque. L'évasement et la lèvre sont entièrement peints. (Voir n. 139 du cat.)

139 Bassine
MR III B (13e s. av. J.C.)
Argile. Arsani, nome de Réthymne (tombe à chambre).
Haut. (avec l'anse) 0,106 m, diam base 0,11 m, Réthymno, Musée archéologique.
Ustensile évasé, entier, petites ébréchures. Profil conique, double anse courbe et vasque en forme d'entonnoir, lèvre dans le prolongement. Le décor, de peinture rouge, se borne à des bandes et des cercles concentriques.
Les vasques de ce type sont considérées comme une sorte de kernos, c'est à dire un vase réservé à des usages mortuaires.

140 Alabastre à deux anses.
MR III B (13e s. av. J.C.)
ARgile. Arménoi, Réthymnes (tombe à chambre 119).
Haut 0,68 m, diam. à la lèvre 0,073 m, diam. base 0,033 m.
Réthymno, Musée archéologique.
Petit alabastre entier, corps biconique, base plate et large embouchure. Le décor est fait de doubles haches, de couleur marron, disposées en ligne sur la zone des anses. Ce symbole minoen de caractère religieux apparaît en tant que motif ornemental sur les décors de vases pendant la transition du MM III au MR I A.

141 Vase-couronne
MR III A2 (2e moitié du 14e s. av. J.C.)
Argile. Arménoi Réthymnes (tombe à chambre 206).
Haut. 0.053 m, diam. max. 0,075 m.
Réthymno, Musée archéologique.

Vase à parfum entier. Son corps est en forme de couronne, de section ovale, une anse courbe rejoint la face stylisées, brun rose, orne la surface du corps.

142 Statuette de déesse
MR III B (13e s. av. J.C.)
Argile. Kannia Gorthyne.
Haut. cons. 0,339 m, diam. base 0,17 m.
Héraklio, Musée archéologique.
Statuette du type déesse aux mains levées. La tête manque, ainsi que la plus grande partie des membres supérieurs. Elle est nue jusqu'à la taille, et la partie inférieure du corps est couverte d'un vêtement stylisé. La tentative de rendu plastique du corps est caractéristique : des cônes appliqués figurent la poitrine, et des sillons verticaux sur le thorax et le dos montrent les détails anatomiques du tronc. Connue par l'iconographie mésopotamienne, ce type d'idole est importé en Crète durant le MM I-II, et devient commun durant la fin de l'âge du bronze. La position des mains est interprétée comme exprimant un accueil, un salut ou une bénédiction adressés aux adorateurs.

143 Vase funéraire double
MR III A2 (2e moitié du 14e s. av. J.C.)
Argile. La Canée (tombe à chambre 11).
Haut. max. 0,205 m, diam 0,117 m, diam. du vase fermé 0,122 m.
La Canée, Musée archéologique.
Vase de forme particulière, de l'atelier de Kydonia, excellente fabrication et conservation. Il est fait de deux cruches piriformes, à base plate, reliées a) à la hauteur de la panse par un tube renforcé de chaque côté, b) à l'embouchure par une anse surélevée en ruban. Le col du vase fermé est remarquable, qui a la forme d'un buste d'animal (lièvre), ainsi que le filtre du vase ouvert, où a été appliqué un oiseau stylisé en train de boire. Un autre oiseau au plumage travaillé et à la queue en pompon est représenté sur la panse de la cruche à filtre, parmi des papyrus. Le deuxième vase est décoré seulement de papyrus, disposés de façon variée.
Le décor remarquablement soigné du vase et la répétition du motif de l'oiseau, l'une des apparences que prend la divinité, plaident pour un usage funéraire, ce qui est confirmé par sa forme incommode.

144 Encensoir
MR III B (13e s. av. J.C.)
Argile. Arménoi, nome de Réthymne (tombe à chambre 94).
Haut. du corps 0,065 m, diam. base 0,013 m, haut. couvercle 0,185 m.
Réthymno, Musée archéologique
Entier, de fabrication grossière. Il se compose du corps cylindrique du foyer, anse verticale et base plate saillante, et du couvercle, cylindrique en bas et conique en haut où sont percés des trous sur quatre lignes parallèles, qui se termine par une tige percée. La principale zone décorée est la partie supérieure du couvercle, divisée en métopes où sont incisées des lignes ondulées verticales et demi-cercles concentriques au centre marqué par un point, ou dessinés selon une diposition antithétique verticalement.

145 Encensoir
MR III B (13e s. av. J.C.)
Argile. Arménoi Réthymnes (tombe à chambre 25).
Haut du corps 0,06 m, diam. base 0,115 m, haut. du couvercle 0,112 m.
Réthymno, Musée archéologique.
Objet de caractère religieux, recollé. Il est formé de : a) la base au corps central cylindrique, anse verticale; b) le couvercle, cylindrique aussi, ouverture cintrée, partie supérieure conique, portant des ouvertures pour laisser s'échapper la fumée. Une zone de coquillags stylisés, encadrés d'une série d'arcs, orne la partie cylindrique du couvercle.

146 Amphorisque
MR III A2 (fin 14e s. av. J.C.)
Argile. Arménoi, nome de Réthymne, (tombe à chambre 167).
Haut. 0,191 m, diam. à la lèvre 0,12 m, diam. base 0,065 m.
Réthymno, Musée archéologique.
Bel exemple d'amphorisque qui imite les modèles mycéniens. Panse piriforme, base plate, col large cylindrique à anneau et trois anses en ruban. Un décor varié de mouchetures, en peinture noire à moitié effacée, couvre les intervalles compris entre les anses.

147 Vase à étrier
MR III B (13e s. av. J.C.)
Argile. Arménoi Réthymnes (tombe à chambre 140).
Haut. 0,133 m, diam. max. 0,182 .
Réthymno, Musée archéologique.
Vase entier, exemple caractéristique de l'atelier postpalatial de la Canée (Kydonia). Panse conique, base en anneau. Deux poulpes stylisés, un sur chaque face, couvrent la panse. L'epaule est décorée de triangles élaborés de chaque côté du bec, ainsi que de dessins en forme de losanges. Des arcs en opposition sont utilisés comme motif de remplissage.

148 Hydrie
MR III B (13e s. av. J.C.)
Argile. Pighi, nome de Réthymne (tombe à chambre).
Haut. 0,185 m, diam. max. 0,15 m, diam. base 0.058 m.
Réthymno, Musée archéologique.
Entière. Base plate, panse biconique, embouchure évasée, une anse verticale et deux courbes. Le décor de peinture rose s'étend sur la région de l'épaule et est composé de croisillons verticaux. L'hydrie en argile apparaît en même temps en Crète et en Grèce continentale, durant le MR III B1.

149 Vase à étrier
MR III B (13e s. av. J.C.)
Argile. Arménoi Réthymnes (tombe à chambre 149).
Haut. 0,15 m, diam. max. 0,14 m.
Réthymno, Musée archéologique.
Vase de fabrication soignée, surface écaillée. Corps sphérique, base presque en anneau. Une peinture noire à l'éclat métallique, impressionnante, dessine un poulpe sur chaque face du vase.

150 Flasque
MR III A (14e s. av. J.C.)
Argile. Arménoi, nome de Réthymne (tombe à chambre 13).
Haut. 0,225 , diam. max. 0,165 m.
Réthymno, Musée archéologique.
Flasque entière, à la surface très abîmée. Panse lenticulaire, embouchure cylindrique, deux anses verticales. Des cercles concentriques d'épaisseur inégale, de couleur marron orange, couvrent les deux faces de la panse.
C'est un type de vase rare. Il contenait de l'huile parfumée ou du vin, et était offert à des personnages importants.

151 Alabastre à trois anses
MR III A 2/B 1 (fin du 14e s. av. J.C.)
Argile. Arménoi, nome de Réthymne.
Haut. 0,10 m, diam. max. 0,141 m, diam. base 0,121 m.
Réthymno, Musée archéologique.
Entier, légèrement détérioré. Panse cylindrique et base plate, poignées en forme d'arc sur l'épaule et col bas à l'embouchure large. Des spirales à double tige, disposées en rang ornent l'épaule et la panse du vase.

152 Cruche à quatre anses
MR III B (13e s. av. J.C.)
Argile. Arménoi, nome de Réthymne (tombe à chambre 138).
haut. 0,157 m, diam. max. 0,181 m, diam à la lèvre 0,119 m.
Réthymno, Musée archéologique.
Recollée et restaurée au plâtre. Panse sphérique, base plate, col large portant un anneau en relief à la base, anses verticales. Des lignes en arcs parallèles, à l'intérieur desquelles sont inscrites des lignes brisées, décorant l'espace compris entre les anses.

153 Alabastre haut
MR III A (14e s. av. J.C.)
Argile. Arménoi, nome de Réthymne (tombe à chambre).
Haut. 0,22 m, diam. à la lèvre 0,13 m, diam. base 0,135 m.
Réthymno, Musée archéologique.
Vase entier à la base plate, panse large, col haut à bande en relief à la base et lèvre plate. Le décor de peinture noire presque effacée est partagé en zones de largeur inégale portant un motif végétal stylisé, des lignes ondulées et des bandes brisées.
Le type haut d'alabastre est considéré comme une forme minoenne, mais sûrement influencée par des modèles égyptiens.

154 Stamnisque à couvercle
MR III B1 (début du 13e s. av. J.C.)
Argile. Aghii Apostoli, nome de Réthymne (tombe à chambre).
haut. 0,13 m, diam. à la lèvre 0,096 m, diam. base 0,073 m.
Réthymno, Musée archéologique.
Vase entier à base plate, panse conico-sphérique, col cylindrique, deux anses courbes. Le décor, marron noir, se cantonne sur l'épaule : c'est une "fleur mycénienne", et des motifs de remplissage (arcs et croisillons).

155 Pyxide à bec
MR III B1 (début du 13e s. av. J.C.)
Argile. Aghii Apostoli, nome de Amari (tombe à chambre).

Haut. 0,125 m, diam. à la lèvre 0,116 m, diam base 0,11 m.
Réthymno, Musée archéologique.
Bel exemple de pyxide en très bon état de conservation. Base plate, panse cylindrique, deux anses courbes et bec tubulaire.
La principale zone de décoration, sur la panse du vase, est constituée de métopes ornées de chevrons emboîtés.

156 Biberon
MR III A (14e s. av. J.C.)
Argile. Stavreménée, nome de Réthymne (tombe à chambre)
Haut. (avec l'anse) 0,16 m, diam. max. 0,12 m, diam à la lèvre 0.078 m.
Réthymno, Musée archéologique.
Une petite partie de la lèvre et du bec est refaite. Panse sphérique-biconique, base plate, col cylindrique portant un anneau en relief à la base, bec tubulaire et anse en panier portant une excroissance (cône replié en anneau) à l'une de ses attaches : son dos est orné de creux remplis de pâte de verre.
Le décor principal, rouge brillant, sur le haut de la panse, consiste en une zone de feuilles "foliate band".
Ce type de récipients apparaît à la dernière période de la fin de l'age du Bronze.

157 Coupe
MR III B (13e s. av. J.C.)
Argile. Arménoi Réthymnes (tombe à chambre 206).
Haut. 0,068 m, diam. à la lèvre 0,104 m.
Réthymno, Musée archéologique.
Coupe entière au corps cylindrique, embouchures évasée, base plate, anse en ruban verticale et bec ponté. Un motif de quadrillage, en peinture noire presque effacée, couvre le vase. Les ustensiles de ce type accompagnaient les sépultures d'enfant, sans doute étaient-ils justement utilisés dans les soins donnés à ces derniers.

158 Kylix
MR III A2 (fin 14e s. av. J.C.)
Argile. Pighi, nome de Réthymne (tombe à chambre).
Haut. 0,198 m, diam. à la lèvre 0,208 , diam. base 0,097 m.
Réthymno, Musée archéologique.
Panse et pied recollés et restaurés. Vase particulièrement grand, à la vasque large conique, au pied haut et fin, base plate, deux anses en ruban. Des groupes de bandes courbes, de couleur brun rouge, disposée en deux zones parallèles, recouvrent l'extérieur. Intérieur entièrement peint.

159 Coupe
MR III A2 (fin du 14e s. av. J.C.)
Argile. Maroulas, nome de Réthymne (tombe à chambre).
Haut. 0,051 m, diam à la lèvre 0,113 m, diam. base 0,04 m.
Réthymno, Musée archéologique.
Récipient évasé très bien conservé. Vasque de profil anguleux, base plate, anse en ruban et bec restriforme. Le décor principal, de peinture brun rouge, s'étend sur la zone de l'anse : des demi-cercles concentriques pendants, et des fleurs de papyrus dans les intervalles. Une spirale orne le fond.

160 Coupelle
MR III A (14e s. av. J.C.)
Argile. Arménoi Réthymnes (tombe à chambre 10).
Haut. 0,067 m, diam. à la lèvre 0,09 m, diam. base 0,032 m.
Réthymno, Musée archéologique
Objet de bonne fabrication et bien conservé. Panse hémisphérique, petite vase, lèvre en déversoir et anse en ruban. Le décor de peinture brun noir se limite à une bande brisée et des arcs opposés dans les triangles qu'elle forme.

161 Coupe à anse
MR III A (14e s. av. J.C.)
Argile, Arménoi Réthymnes, (tombe à chambre 98).
Haut. 0,061 m, diam. à la lèvre 0,106-0,113 m, diam base 0,55 m.
Réthymno, Musée archéologique.
Vase d'usage commun, entier, légèrement abîmé. Corps non peint hémisphérique, pied bas, base large conique, anse verticale en ruban. Des coulées de couleur brun rouge, couvrent la surface du vase à l'intérieur comme à l'extérieur.

162 Cruche à embouchure large
MR III A2 (fin du 14e s. av. J.C.)
Argile. Aghii Apostoli, nome de Amari (tombe à chambre).
Haut. 0.107 m, diam. base 0,047 m, diam. max. 0,112 m.
Réthymno, Musée archéologique.
Cruche entière, de fabrication grossière. Base plate, panse biconique, bec cannelé dressé, anse verticale en ruban. Décoration assez négligente qui se limite à des lunules pendant de la base du col.

163 Cruche à bec
MR III A (14e s. av. J.C.)
Argile. Stavroménos Réthymnes (tombe à chambre).
Haut. 0,047 m, diam. max. 0,058 m,
Réthymno, Musée archéologique.
Petit vase délicat, panse en sphère aplatie, bec rostriforme et anse verticale. Une couronne de feuilles stylisées, de couleur brun rouge, orne l'épaule.
Ce vase a été trouvé en offrande dans une urne funéraire.

164 Vase double
MR III A (14e s. av. J.C.)
Argile. Arménoi, nome de Réthymne (tombe (al chambre 188).
Haut. (avec l'anse) 2.075 m, diam max. 0.05 m.
Réthymno, Musée archéologique.
Vase entier. Il est composé d'une cruche réunie, par l'intermédiaire d'un petit tube à la hauteur de la panse, à un lécythe fermé. Une anse en ruban surélevée unit les deux vases. La forme non fonctionnelle, et le fait que ces vases soient souvent trouvés dans des tombes, nous conduisent à penser qu'ils étaient réservés à un usage du cérémonial religieux.

165 Askos
MR III B (13e s. av. J.C.)
Argile. Arménoi, nome de Réthymne (tombe à chambre 110).
Haut. 0,07 m, diam. 0,079 m.
Réthymno, Musée archéologique.
Petit vase entier à base plate, panse cylindrique, anse courbe prenant naissance à la courbure de l'épaule, et embouchure oblique. Le décor marron noir se concentre dans la région de l'épaule, en deux demi-cercles : le premier est orné de poissons peints, le second de demi-cercles. Des motifs complémentaires remplissent les vides. Cette forme est une création de la civilisation minoenne et se rencontre à toutes ses périodes.

166 Vase-couronne
MR III B (13e s. av. J.C.)
Argile. Arménoi, nome de Réthymne (tombe à chambre 49).
Haut. 0,065 m, diam max. 0,0107 m.

Réthymno, Musée archéologique.
Entier. Vase de forme particulière au corps en couronne de section carrée, embouchure cylindrique et anse courbe rejoignant la face interne de la couronne. Le décor noir brillant est formé de bandes, de lignes entrecroisées et de lignes ondulées verticales.
Cette forme offrande funéraire habituelle, est assez répandue au MR III, surtout dans sa phase médiane et finale. Son embouchure incommode et sa petite contenance nous conduisent à le caractériser comme le vase à parfum par excellence.

167   Encensoir
MR III B (13e s. av. J.C.)
Argile. Arménoi, nome de Réthymne (tombe à chambre).
Haut. corps 0,05 m, diam. base 0,0117 m, haut. du couvercle 0,115 m.
Réthmno, Musée archéologique.
Entier, en deux parties: a) le foyer, corps cylindrique, base plate saillante, anse verticale; b) le couvercle, cylindrique lui aussi, à ouverture cintrée, et une partie conique où quatre ouvertures oblongues sont symétriquement disposées, se terminant par une tige percée. Le décor, marron noir, se compose d'une ligne ondulée sur le foyer, de bandes parallèles sur la partie conique du couvercle, et de fleurs bifides stylisées sur la partie cylindrique.
Le lieu où ont été trouvés ces objets, leur forme non utilitaire, et le fait qu'on n'ait pas trouvé de trace de feu sur la plupart, en accentuent le caractère funéraire.

168   Kalathos
MR III B (13e s. J.C.)
Argile. Arménoi Réthymnes (tombe à chambre 65).
Haut. (avec l'anse) 0,155 m, diam. à la lèvre 0,14 m,
Réthymno, Musée archéologique.
Récipient évasé de forme pariculière, recollé et restauré au bord. Corps cylindrique à double anse en arc, terminé par un évasement, lèvre dans le prolongement. Le décor de peinture marron effacée, se trouve sur des métopes, où l'on voit des lignes brisées successives, un damier, un motif de filet et des demi-cercles concentriques portant des diagonales.

169   Bassine
MR III B (13e s. J.C.)
Argile. Arménoi, nome de Réthymne (tombe à chambre 24).
Haut. 0,07 m, diam. à la lèvre 0,19 m, diam. base 0,115 m.
Réthymno, Musée archéologique.
Récipient large entier à base plate, panse conique, deux trous de suspension sous la lèvre. Une chaîne de losanges brun rouge parcourt la panse, des groupes de lignes obliques ornent la lèvre.
les bassines en argile résultent d'un emprunt à des récipients en métal, attesté au début du 14e s. av. J.C.

170   Larnax
MR III B (début du 13e s. av. J.C.)
Argile. Arménoi Réthymnes (tombe à chambre).
Haut 0,72, haut. du couvercle 0,22 m, long. 1,05 m, lar. 0,38-0,40 m.
Réthymno, Musée archéologique
Larnax en forme de coffre, très bien conservé. Il a un couvercle à double pente, et quatre pieds. Argile brun jaune, enduit uniforme et peinture marron. Une bande serpentiforme parcourt les quatre côtés du couvercle. Les quatre faces du coffre sont décorées de fleurs de papyrus alternées de hauteur différente. Des groupes de lignes ondulées horizontales les encadrent.
Le motif de fleur de papyrus, connu dans l'iconographie égyptienne, est souvent utilisé par les artistes minoens dans la décoration d'objets ayant trait à la religion ou aux funérailles.

171   Larnax
MR IIIB (13e s. av. J.C.)
Argile. Arménoi Réthymnes (tombe à chambre 24).
Haut. 0,65 m. long. 0,96 m, larg. 0,34 m.
Réthymno, Musée archéologique.
Larnax en forme de coffre, à quatre pieds. Le couvercle manque. Argile brun jaune à impuretés, enduit de couleur régulière et peinture brun rose. Un groupe de lignes ondulées verticales divise chaque côté large en deux métopes décorées de spirales continues, reliées entre elles. L'un des côtés étroits porte des cornes sacrés opposées, du milieu desquels partent des doubles haches. La scène principale du larnax se trouve sur l'autre côté étroit: une forme féminine stylisée, du type de la déesse aux bras levés, est représentée debout sur un champ de damier. Des motifs géométriques décorent son vêtement, qui descend jusqu'aux pieds, des spirales et des arcs partent de ses mains.
La position de la déesse renvoie au type correspondant de statuette (vori n. du cat.). Il faut souligner le lien entre la figure de la déesse et le motif du damier, qui selon quelques chercheurs exprime une structure architecturale.

172   Stèle funéraire
MR III A-B (14e-13e s. av. J.C.)
Calcaire. Arménoi Réthymnes (tombe à chambre).
Haut. 0,78 m, larg. 0,29 m.
Réthymno, Musée archéologique.
Allongé, recollé d'après deux fragments. La partie inferieure n'est pas travaillée, puisqu'elle était destinée à être plantée dans le sol. La partie visible, polle, porte un décor exquissé, des lignes horizontales incisées superficiellement sont coupées par des verticales, dessinant un motif en damier. Le même décor, mais très travaillé, couvre toute la surface d'une stèle semblable, provenant de la même nécropole.

173   Larnax
MR III B (13e s. av. J.C.)
Argile. Arménoi Réthymnes (tombe à chambre 55).
Haut cons. 0,58 m, haut. du couvercle 0,17 m, long. 0,91-0,94 m, larg. 0,38-0,40 m.
Réthymno, Musée archéologique.
En forme de coffre, à quatre pieds et couvercle à deux pentes. Argile brun rouge, enduit de couleur régulière et peinture changeante, de l'orange au noir. Des arcs concentriques alternés couvrent les deux côtés larges du couvercle. Le larnax lui-même est décoré de trois poulpes stylisés sur l'un des côtes larges; l'autre porte des cornes sacrées du milieu desquelles partent des haches doubles, et des spirales à tige se trouvent au-dessus des symboles sacrés. Sur les côtés étroits, une fleur de papyrus et une fleur minoenne se répondent. Des bandes ondulées verticales et des demi-cercles encadrent les représentations centrales. Les trous sur le couvercle et en haut du coffre servaient à assembler les deux parties. Ceux qui se trouvent sur le fond étaient destinés à l'écoulement des liquides provenant de la décomposition du corps.
Larnax impressionnant, qui se distingue par la variété de son décor où coexistent toutes sortes de motifs.

174   Vase tripode
MR III B2 (fin 13e s. av. J.C.)
Argile. Arménoi, nome de Réthymne (tombe à chambre 46).
Haut. (avec le couvercle) 0,37 m, diam. max. 0,295 m.
Réthymno, Musée archéologique.

Forme composite. Détériorations sur le col et la panse. Il est formé de a) corps cylindrique reposant sur trois pieds bas, haut col vertical, quatre anses (deux courbes, deux verticales) sur l'épaule; b) couvercle cylindrique, anse en panier. Le décor principal, brun rose, s'étend entre les quatre anses. demi-cercles concentriques ou au centre marqué d'un point, lignes brisées parallèles et arcs de cercles concentriques. Les ornements complémentaires sont des croisillons, des points et des lignes courbes parallèles.
Les exemples de ce type sont rares dans les sites crétomycéniens, on les date d'ordinaire de la fin du HR / MR III.

175 Vase en forme d'alabastre
MR III A1 (1e moitié du 14e s. av. J.C.)
Argile. Arménoi Réthymnes (tombe à chambre 38).
Haut. 0,15 m, diam. max. 0,16 m.
Réthymno, Musée archéologique.
Vase entier, assez abîmé. Panse sphérico-biconique, base plate, col large à rebord, trois anses courbes sur l'épaule. Un lis, de couleur brun rose, à la tige hélicoïdale, orne chaque intervalle entre les anses.

176 Amphorisque à étrier
MR III A (14e s. av. J.C.)
Argile. Arménoi Réthymnes (tombe à chambre 137).
Haut. 0,10 m, diam. max. 0,08 m.
Réthymno, Musée archéologique.
Vase à la surface très endommagée. Panse piriforme, base étroite conique. Le décor principal, sur l'épaule, se divise en deux champs: a) triangles élaborés de chaque côté du bec, b) bande de feuilles sur l'autre moitié de la zone.

177 Amphore à trois anses avec couvercle
MR III A (14e s. av. J.C.)
Argile. Arménoi Réthymnes (tombe à chambre 39).
Haut. 0.20 m, diam. max. m, diam. base m.
Réthymno, Musée archéologique.
Amphore de fabrication grossière, abîmée. Panse piriforme, base discoide, trois anses courbes sur l'épaule et un couvercle conique, avec un poignée en bouton. Une spirale continue orne l'épaule, et des bandes décorent la panse.
Les vase de ce type étaient utilisés pour la conservation et le transport des liquides.

178 Couteau
MR III A.B (14e-13e s. av. J.C.)
Bronze. Arménoi, nome de Réthymne (tombe à chambre 127).
Long. 0,243 m, larg. max. 0,024 m.
Réthymno, Musée archéologique.
Type commun de couteau, oxydé. Lame triangulaire au dos droit et tranchant pointu. Talon carré à la bordure basse, deux rivets servant à fixer le manche en bois.

179 Couteau à hacher
MR III A-B (14e-13e s. av. J.C.)
Bronze. Arménoi, nome de Réthymne (tombe à chambre 115).
Long. 0,20 m, larg. max. 0,056 m.
Réthymno, Musée archéologique.
Entier, oxydé. Lame trapézoïdale au dos droit et au talon courbe, où sont conservés deux clous et une mortaise servant à fixer le manche en bois.
Cette forme est observée dans le monde minoen à la période MR III A, inspirée de modèles égyptiens. On a soutenu que l'on peut distinguer plusieurs usages - peut être d'après le poids: rasoir pour les petits, et couteau à découper la viande pour les grands.

180 Vase à étrier
MR III A (14e s. av. J.C.)
Argile. Arménoi Réthymnes (tombe à chambre 144).
Haut. 0,17 m, diam. max. 0,108 m.
Réthymno, Musée archéologique.
Entier, surface écaillée par endroits. Panse sphérique, pied haut conique et base concave. Des bandes de peinture noire effacée parcourent la panse, et des triangles élaborés décorant l'épaule.
Les vases de ce type étaient utilisées pour transporter des huiles essentielles.